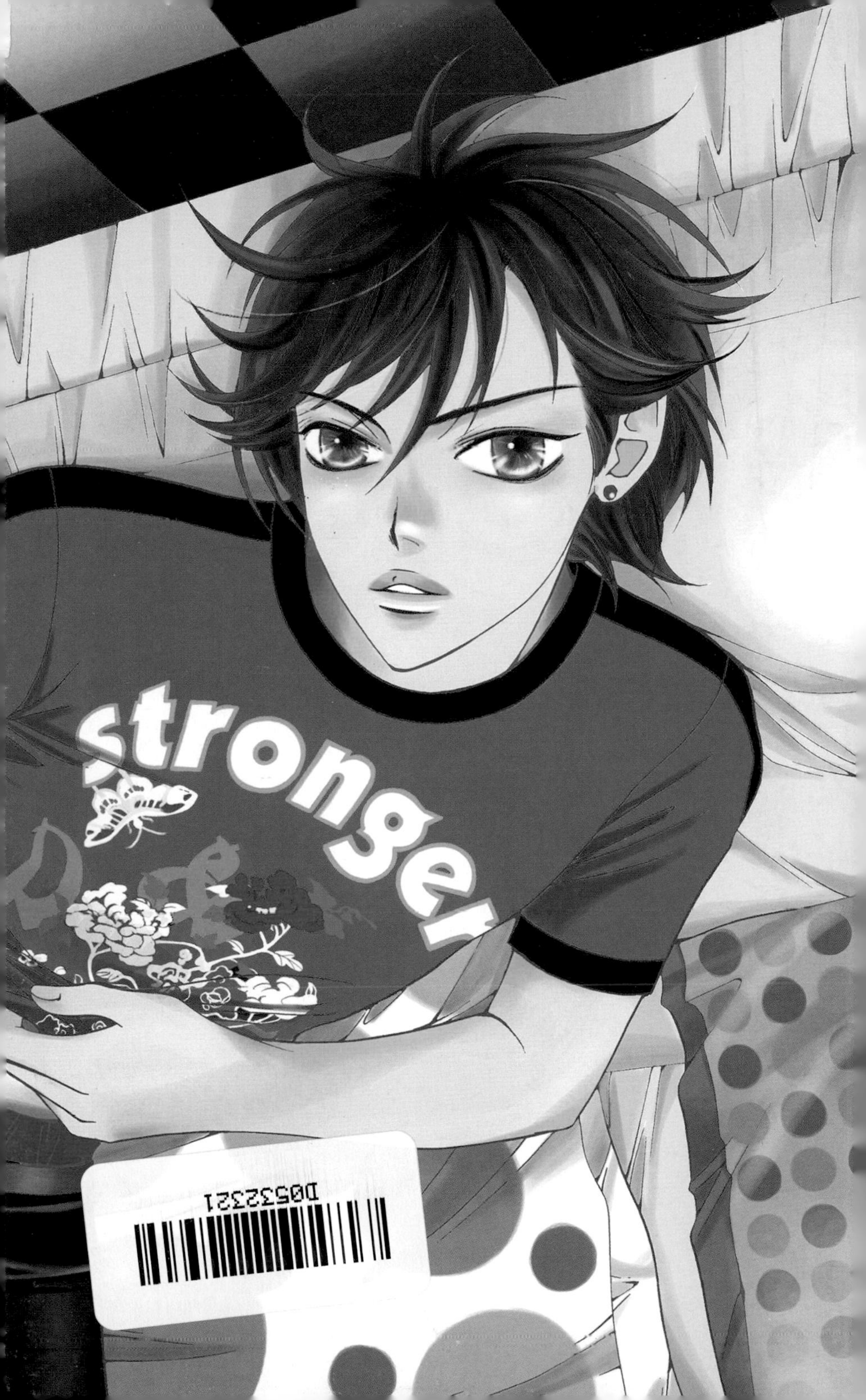
stronger

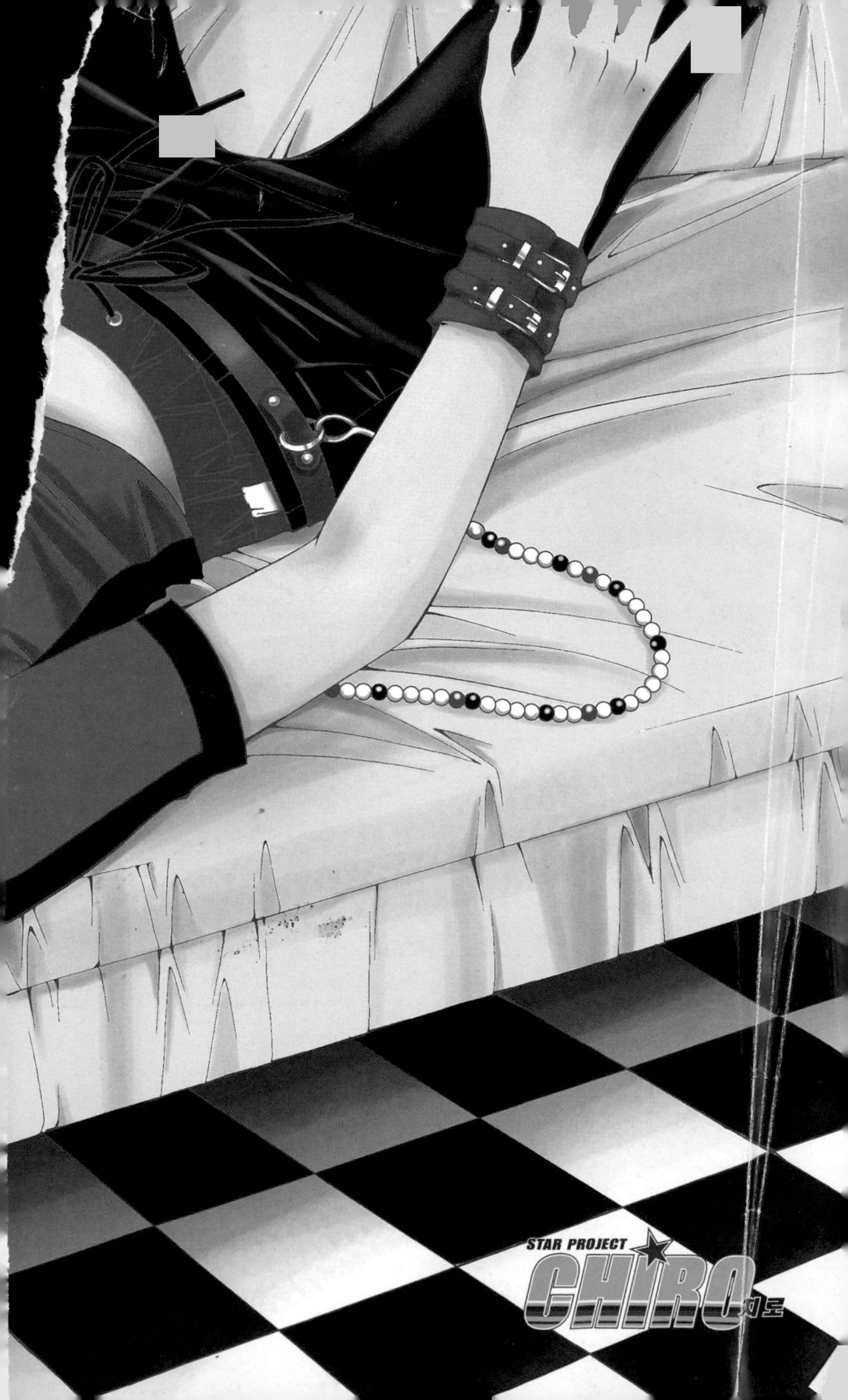
STAR PROJECT
CHIRO
치로

STAR PROJECT ★ CHIRO 지로

2

BAEK HYE-KYOUNG

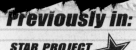

Previously in:

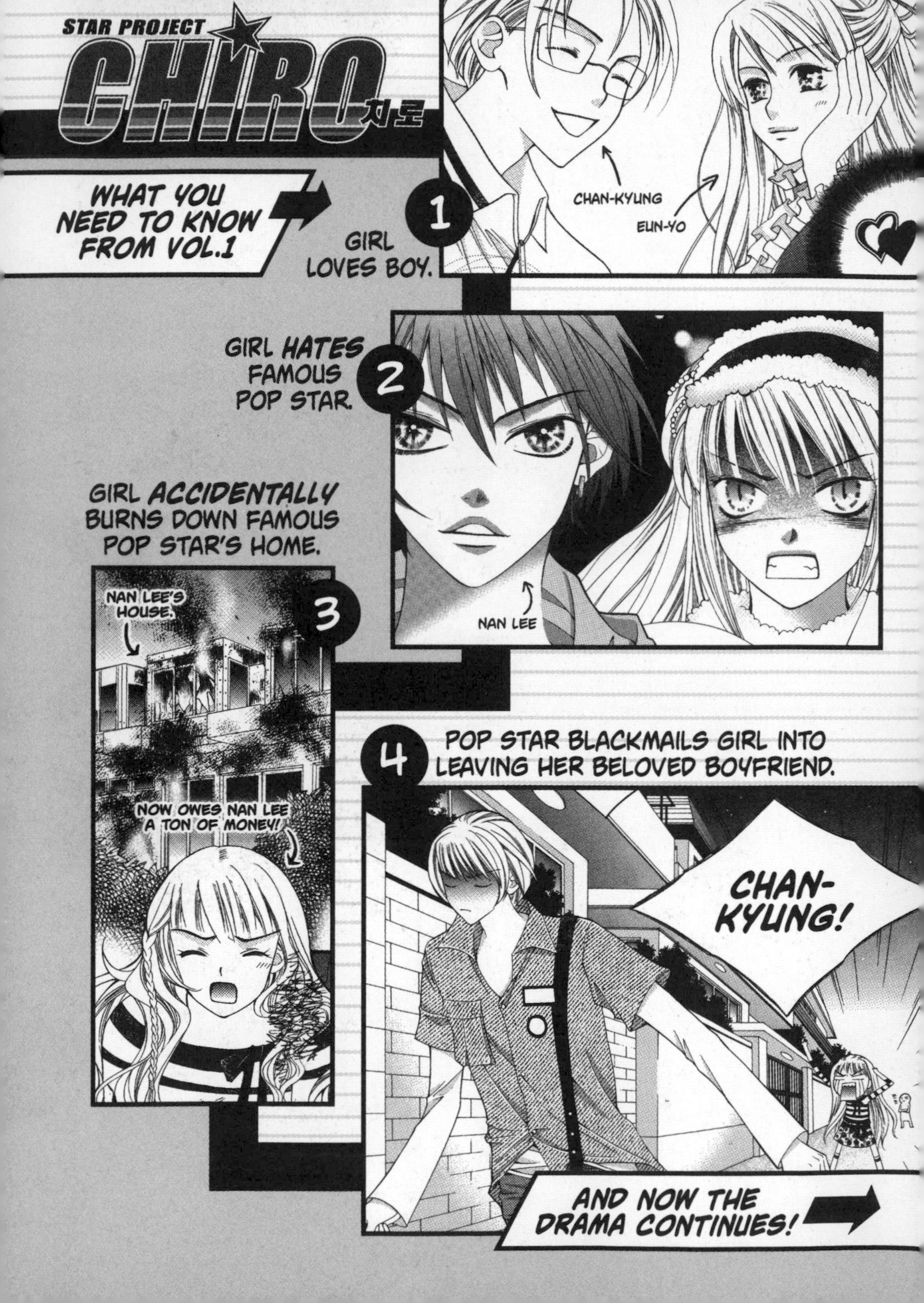

STAR PROJECT
CHIRO 치로
WHAT YOU NEED TO KNOW FROM VOL.1
1
GIRL LOVES BOY.
CHAN-KYUNG
EUN-YO
2
GIRL HATES FAMOUS POP STAR.
NAN LEE
GIRL ACCIDENTALLY BURNS DOWN FAMOUS POP STAR'S HOME.
3
NAN LEE'S HOUSE.
NOW OWES NAN LEE A TON OF MONEY!
4
POP STAR BLACKMAILS GIRL INTO LEAVING HER BELOVED BOYFRIEND.
CHAN-KYUNG!
AND NOW THE DRAMA CONTINUES!

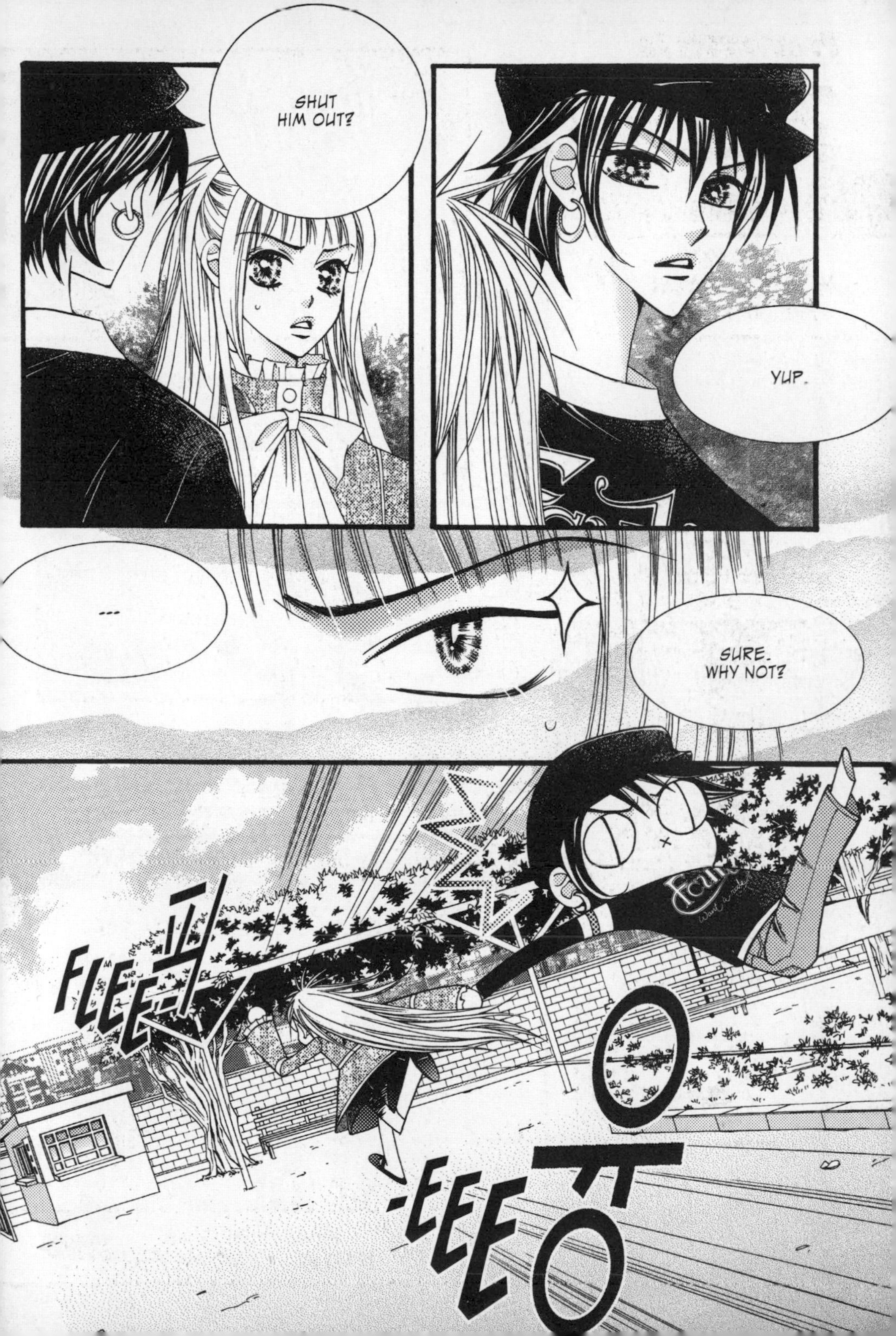
SHUT HIM OUT?
YUP.
...
SURE. WHY NOT?

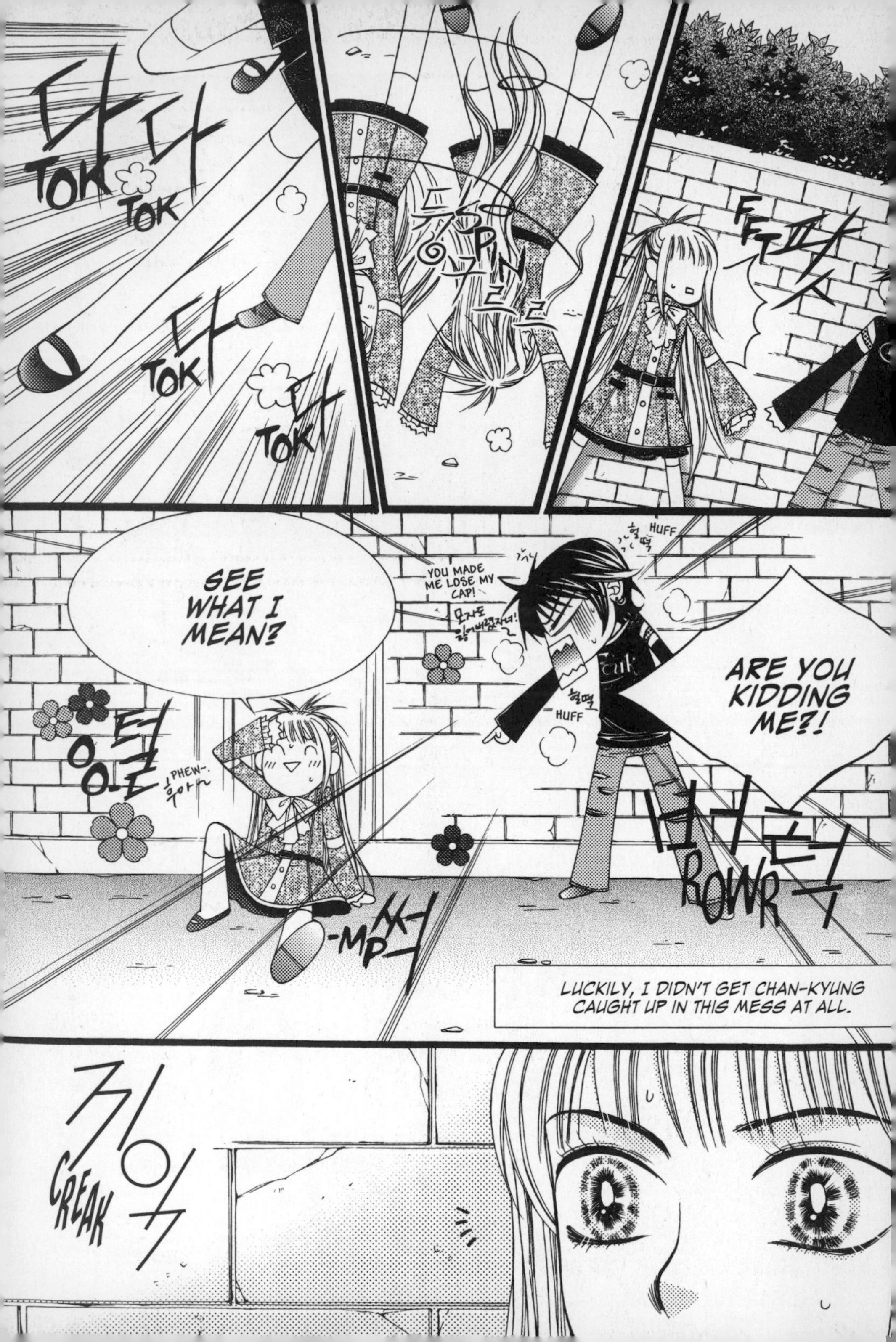
TOK
TOK
TOK
TOK
SPIN
FFT
HUFF
YOU MADE ME LOSE MY CAP!
HUFF
ARE YOU KIDDING ME?!
SEE WHAT I MEAN?
PHEW~
-MP
ROWR
LUCKILY, I DIDN'T GET CHAN-KYUNG CAUGHT UP IN THIS MESS AT ALL.
CREAK

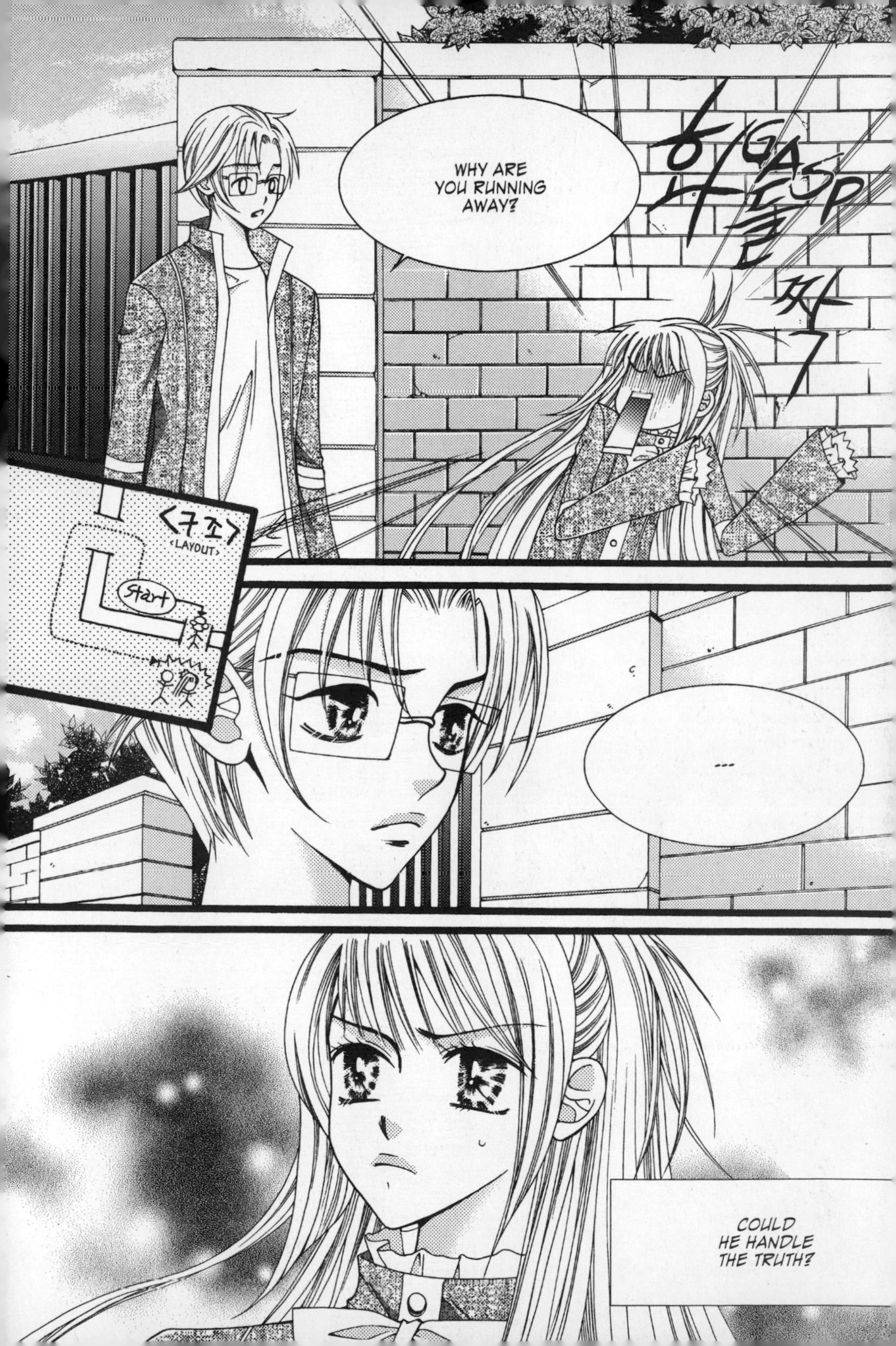
WHY ARE YOU RUNNING AWAY?
GASP
...
COULD HE HANDLE THE TRUTH?

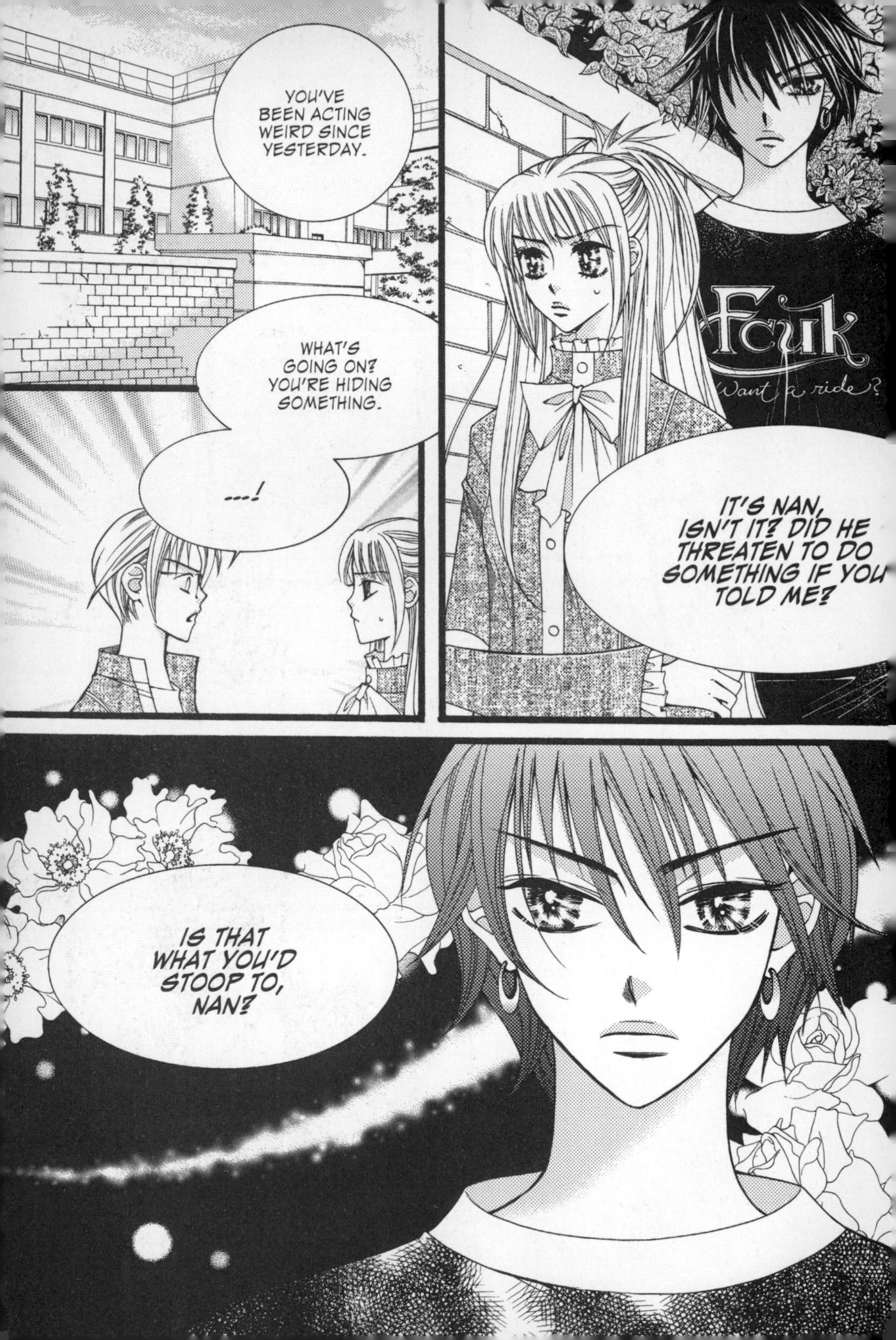
YOU'VE BEEN ACTING WEIRD SINCE YESTERDAY.
WHAT'S GOING ON? YOU'RE HIDING SOMETHING.
...!
Fcuk
Want a ride?
IT'S NAN, ISN'T IT? DID HE THREATEN TO DO SOMETHING IF YOU TOLD ME?
IS THAT WHAT YOU'D STOOP TO, NAN?

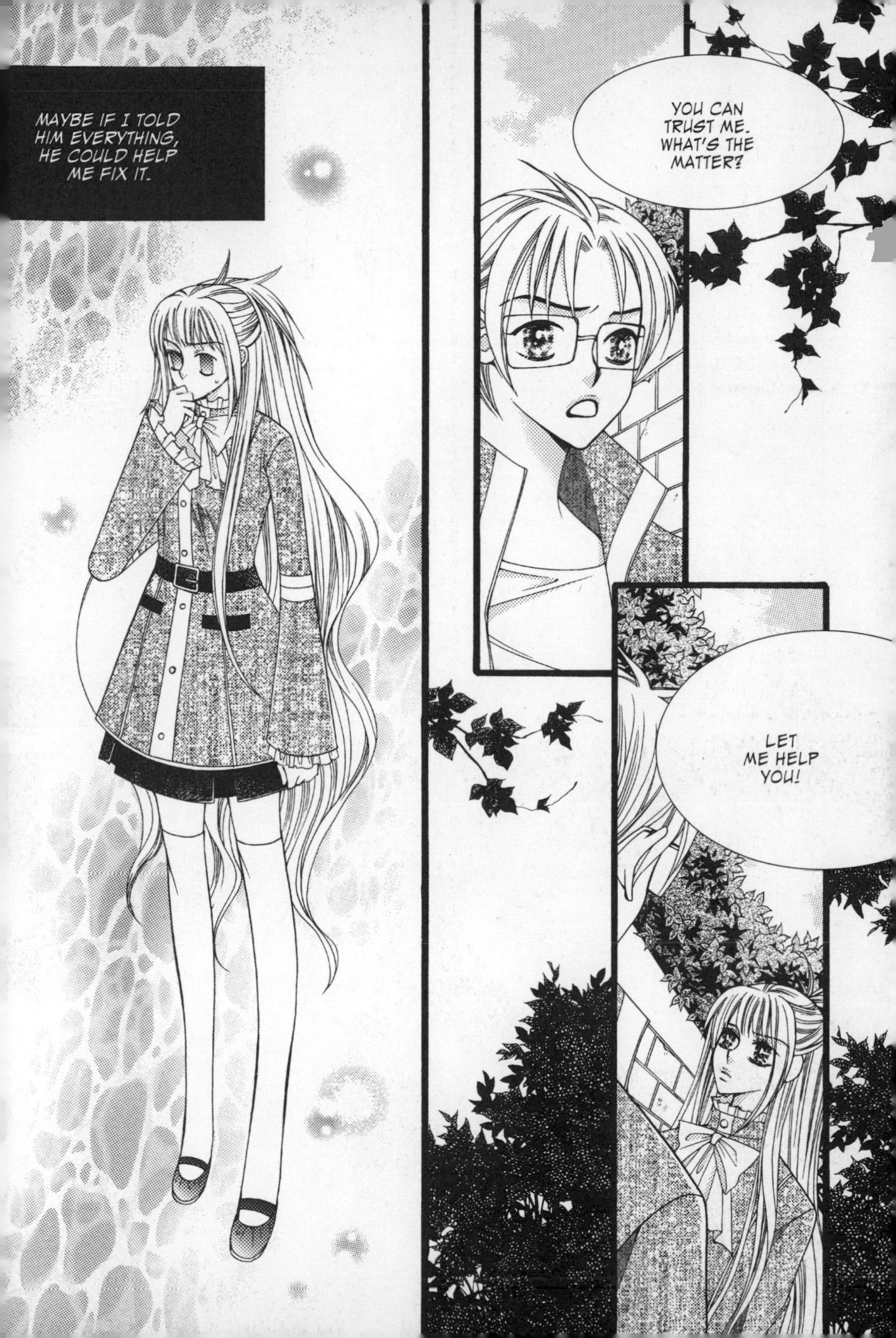
MAYBE IF I TOLD HIM EVERYTHING, HE COULD HELP ME FIX IT.
YOU CAN TRUST ME. WHAT'S THE MATTER?
LET ME HELP YOU!

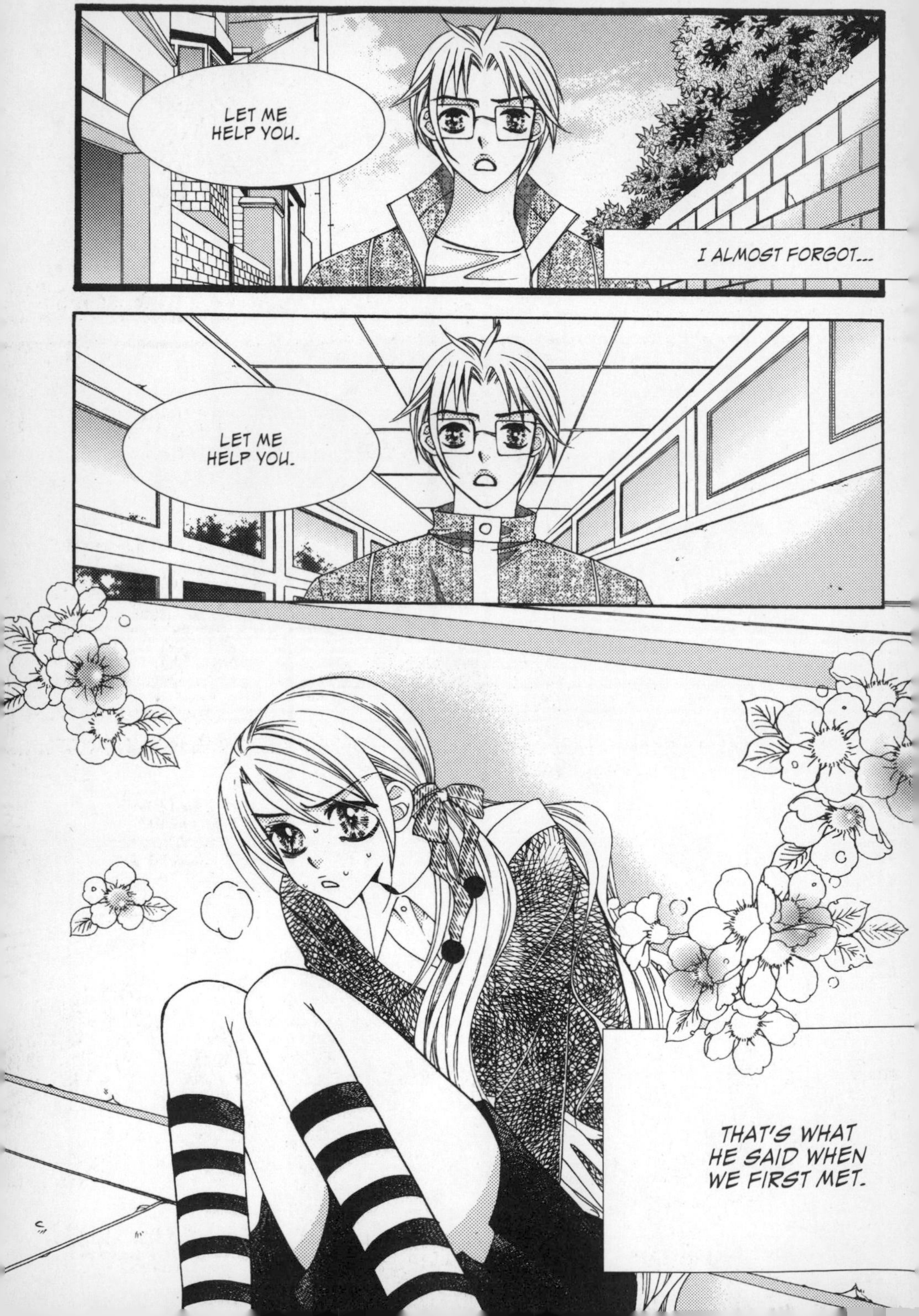
LET ME HELP YOU.
I ALMOST FORGOT...
LET ME HELP YOU.
THAT'S WHAT HE SAID WHEN WE FIRST MET.

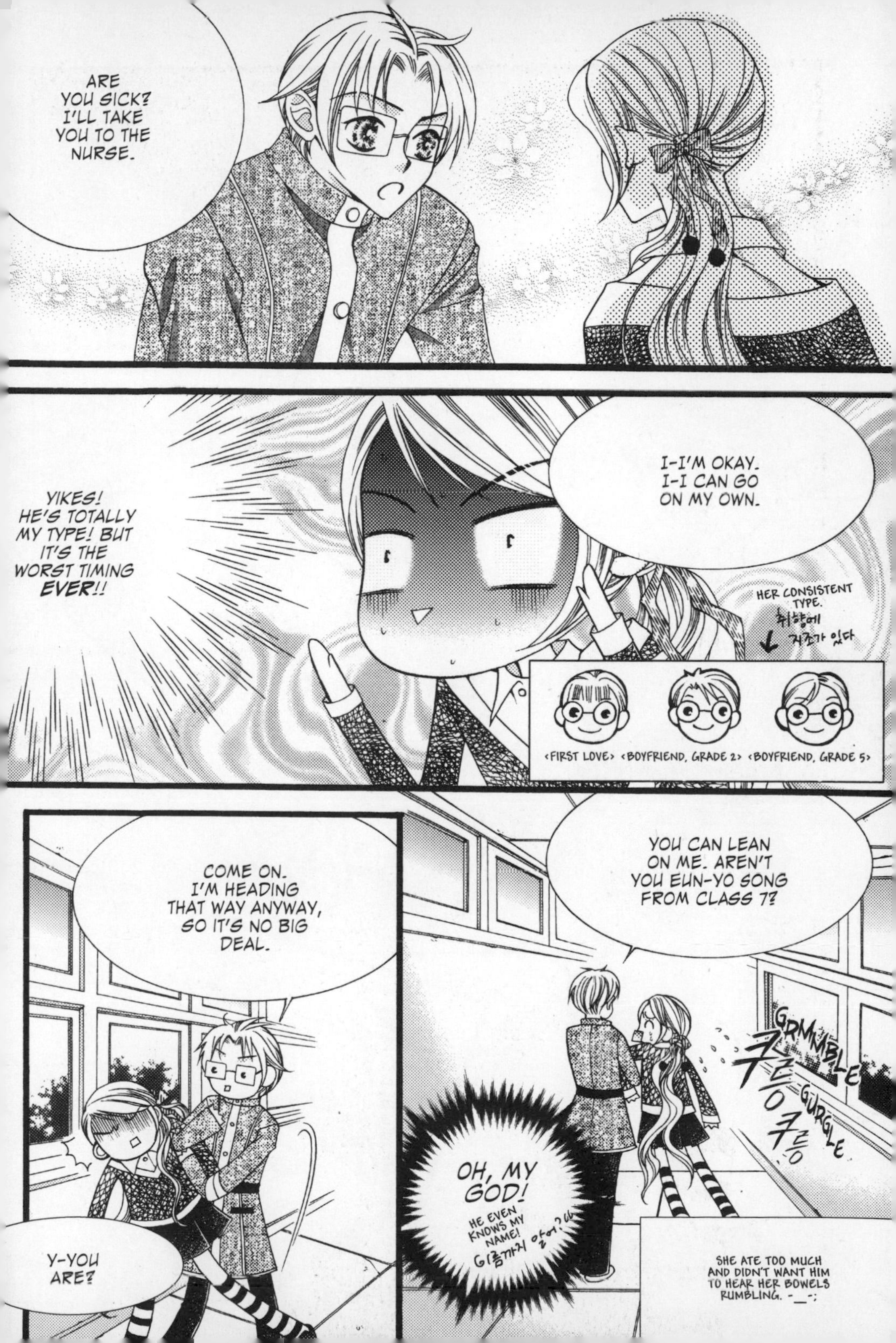

ARE YOU SICK? I'LL TAKE YOU TO THE NURSE.
YIKES! HE'S TOTALLY MY TYPE! BUT IT'S THE WORST TIMING EVER!!
I-I'M OKAY. I-I CAN GO ON MY OWN.
HER CONSISTENT TYPE.
취향에 지조가 있다
<FIRST LOVE> <BOYFRIEND, GRADE 2> <BOYFRIEND, GRADE 5>
COME ON. I'M HEADING THAT WAY ANYWAY, SO IT'S NO BIG DEAL.
Y-YOU ARE?
YOU CAN LEAN ON ME. AREN'T YOU EUN-YO SONG FROM CLASS 7?
GRMMBLE
GURGLE
OH, MY GOD!
HE EVEN KNOWS MY NAME!
이름까지 알어?
SHE ATE TOO MUCH AND DIDN'T WANT HIM TO HEAR HER BOWELS RUMBLING. -_-;

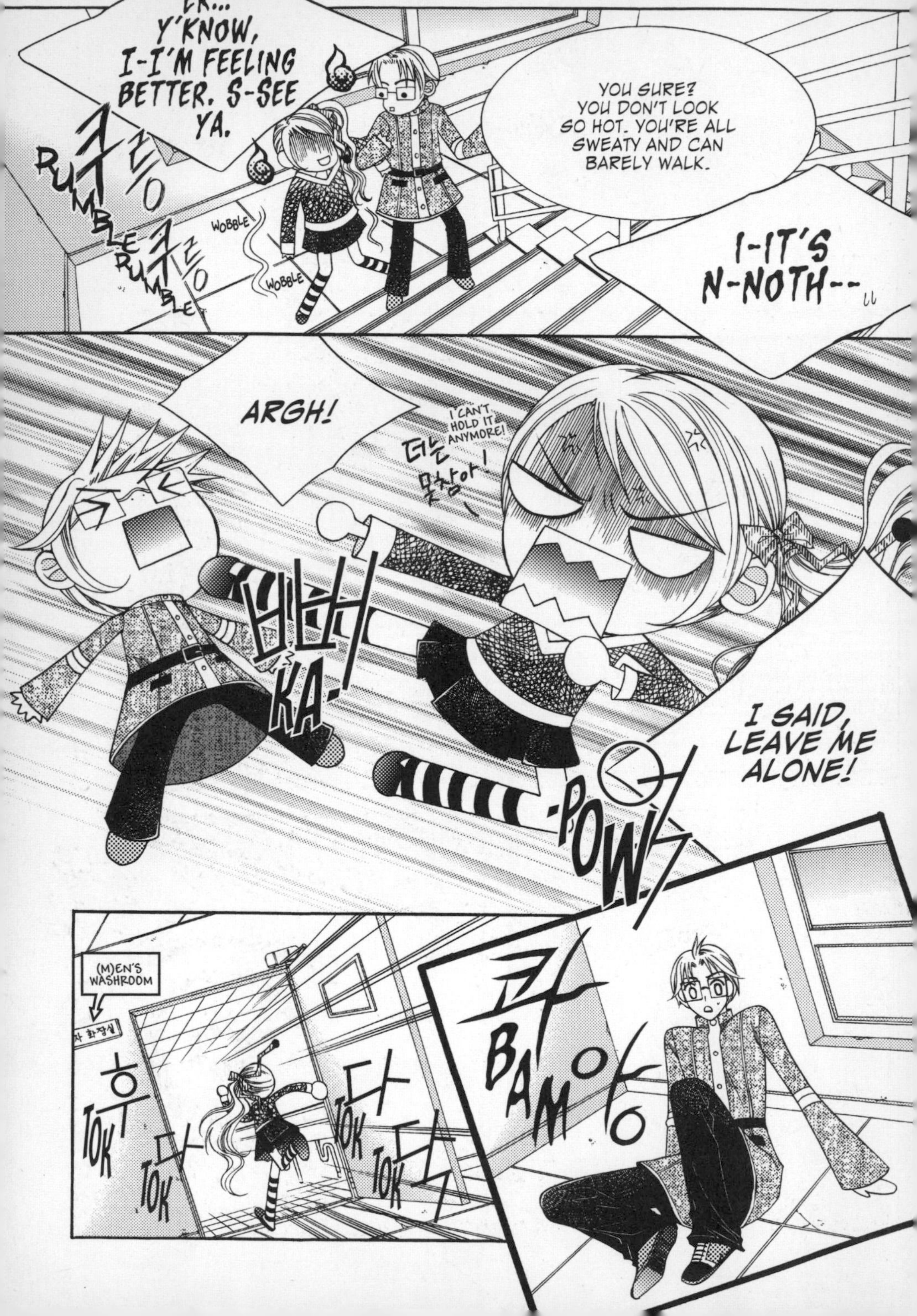
ER... Y'KNOW, I-I'M FEELING BETTER. S-SEE YA.
RUMBLE RUMBLE
WOBBLE
WOBBLE
YOU SURE? YOU DON'T LOOK SO HOT. YOU'RE ALL SWEATY AND CAN BARELY WALK.
I-IT'S N-NOTH--
ARGH!
I CAN'T HOLD IT ANYMORE!
KA-
-POW
I SAID, LEAVE ME ALONE!
(M)EN'S WASHROOM
TOK
TOK
TOK
TOK
BAM

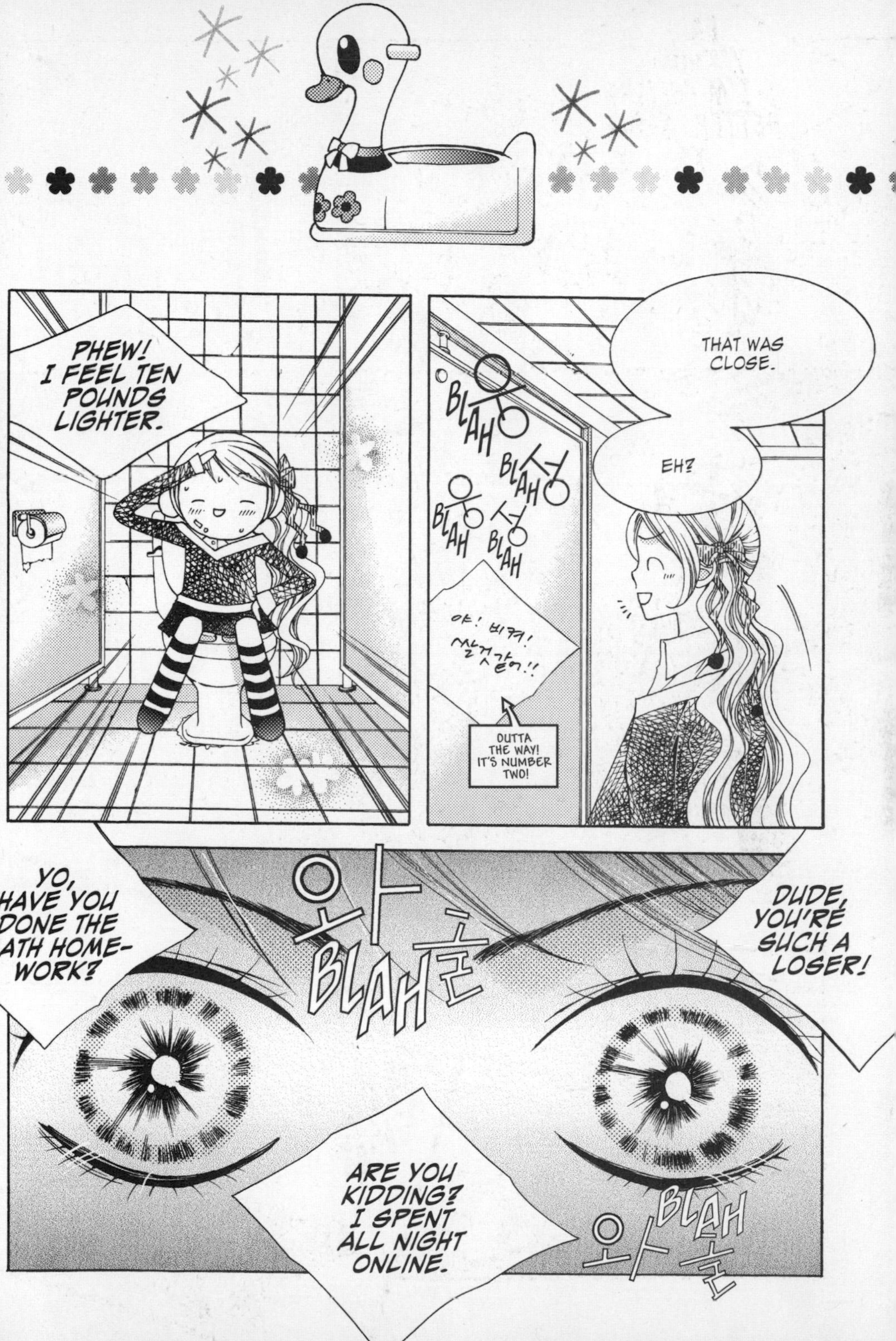
PHEW! I FEEL TEN POUNDS LIGHTER.
BLAH BLAH BLAH BLAH
야! 비켜! 쌀것같아!!
OUTTA THE WAY! IT'S NUMBER TWO!
THAT WAS CLOSE.
EH?
YO, HAVE YOU DONE THE MATH HOME-WORK?
BLAH
DUDE, YOU'RE SUCH A LOSER!
ARE YOU KIDDING? I SPENT ALL NIGHT ONLINE.
BLAH

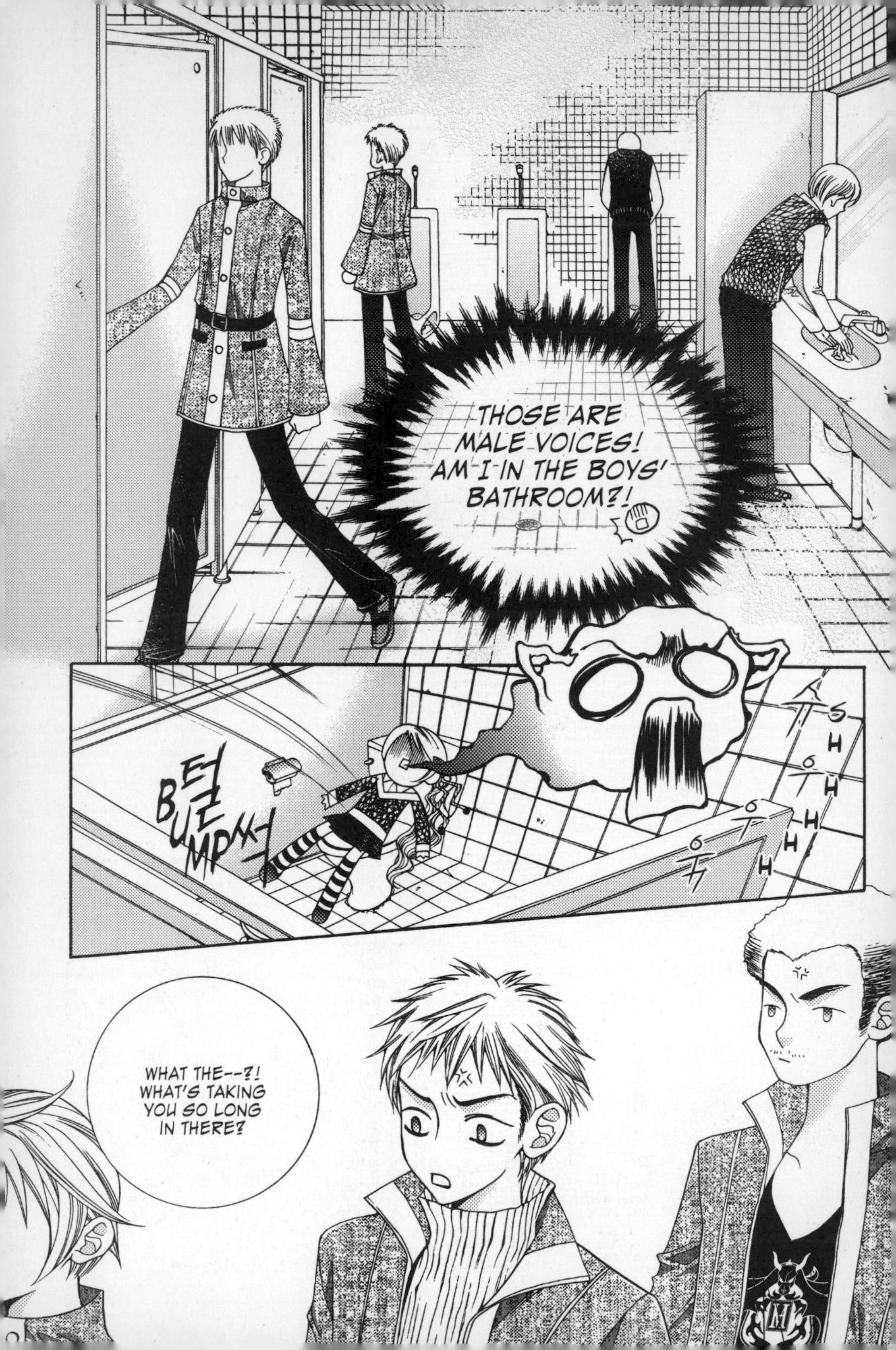
THOSE ARE MALE VOICES! AM I IN THE BOYS' BATHROOM?!
BUMP
WHAT THE--?! WHAT'S TAKING YOU SO LONG IN THERE?

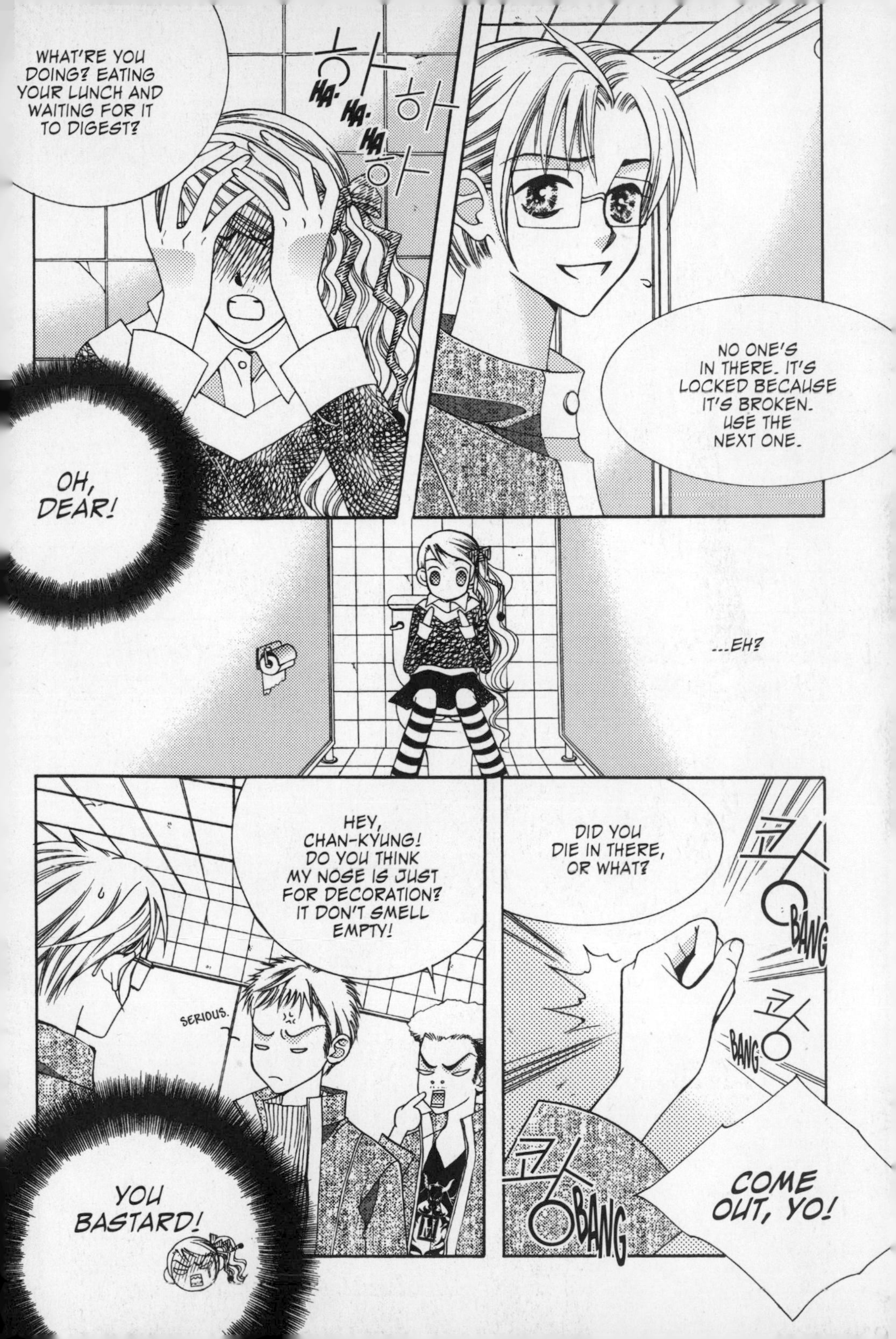
WHAT'RE YOU DOING? EATING YOUR LUNCH AND WAITING FOR IT TO DIGEST?
HA. HA. HA.
OH, DEAR!
NO ONE'S IN THERE. IT'S LOCKED BECAUSE IT'S BROKEN. USE THE NEXT ONE.
...EH?
HEY, CHAN-KYUNG! DO YOU THINK MY NOSE IS JUST FOR DECORATION? IT DON'T SMELL EMPTY!
SERIOUS.
YOU BASTARD!
DID YOU DIE IN THERE, OR WHAT?
BANG
BANG
BANG
COME OUT, YO!

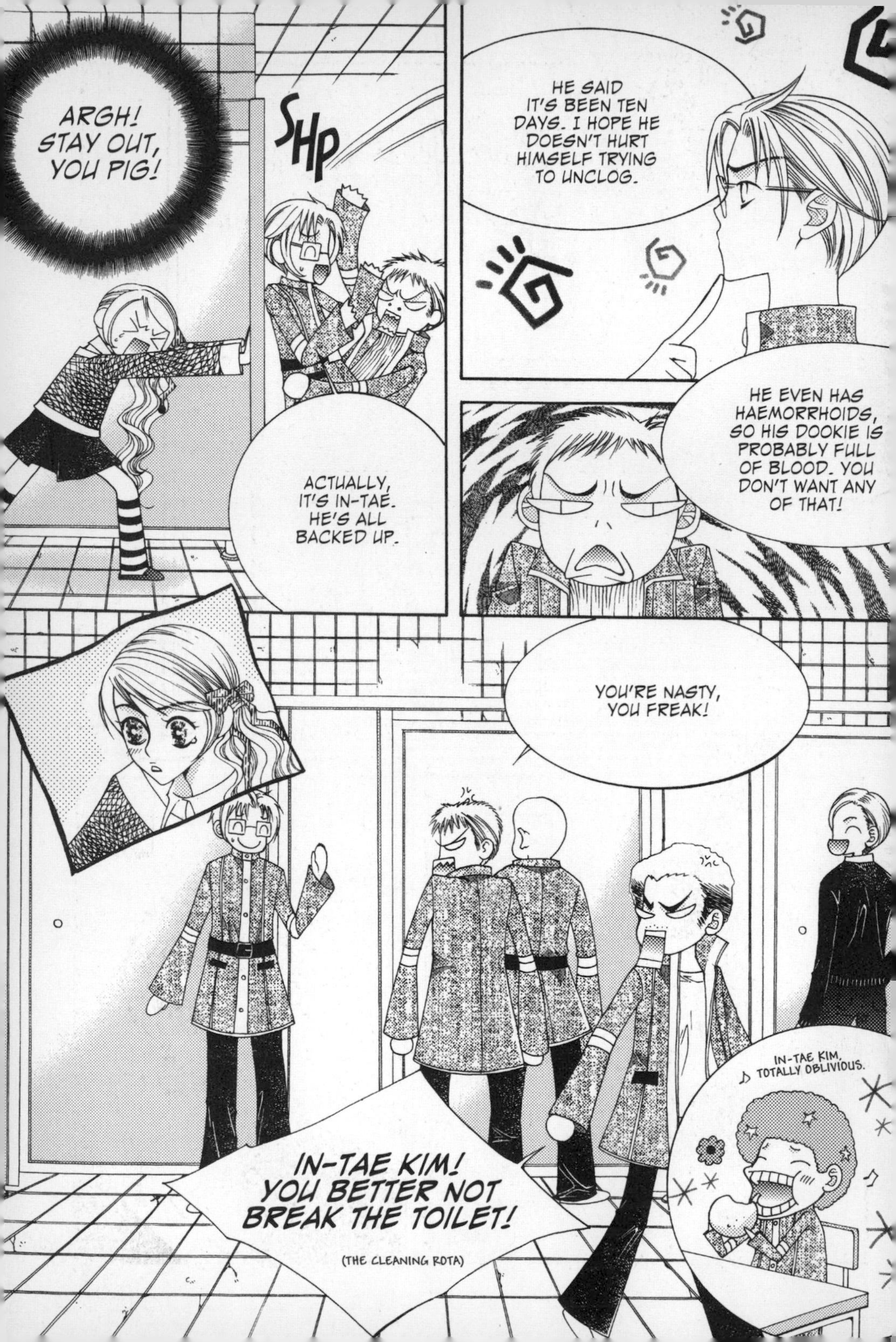
ARGH! STAY OUT, YOU PIG!
SHP
ACTUALLY, IT'S IN-TAE. HE'S ALL BACKED UP.
HE SAID IT'S BEEN TEN DAYS. I HOPE HE DOESN'T HURT HIMSELF TRYING TO UNCLOG.
HE EVEN HAS HAEMORRHOIDS, SO HIS DOOKIE IS PROBABLY FULL OF BLOOD. YOU DON'T WANT ANY OF THAT!
YOU'RE NASTY, YOU FREAK!
IN-TAE KIM! YOU BETTER NOT BREAK THE TOILET!
(THE CLEANING ROTA)
IN-TAE KIM, TOTALLY OBLIVIOUS.

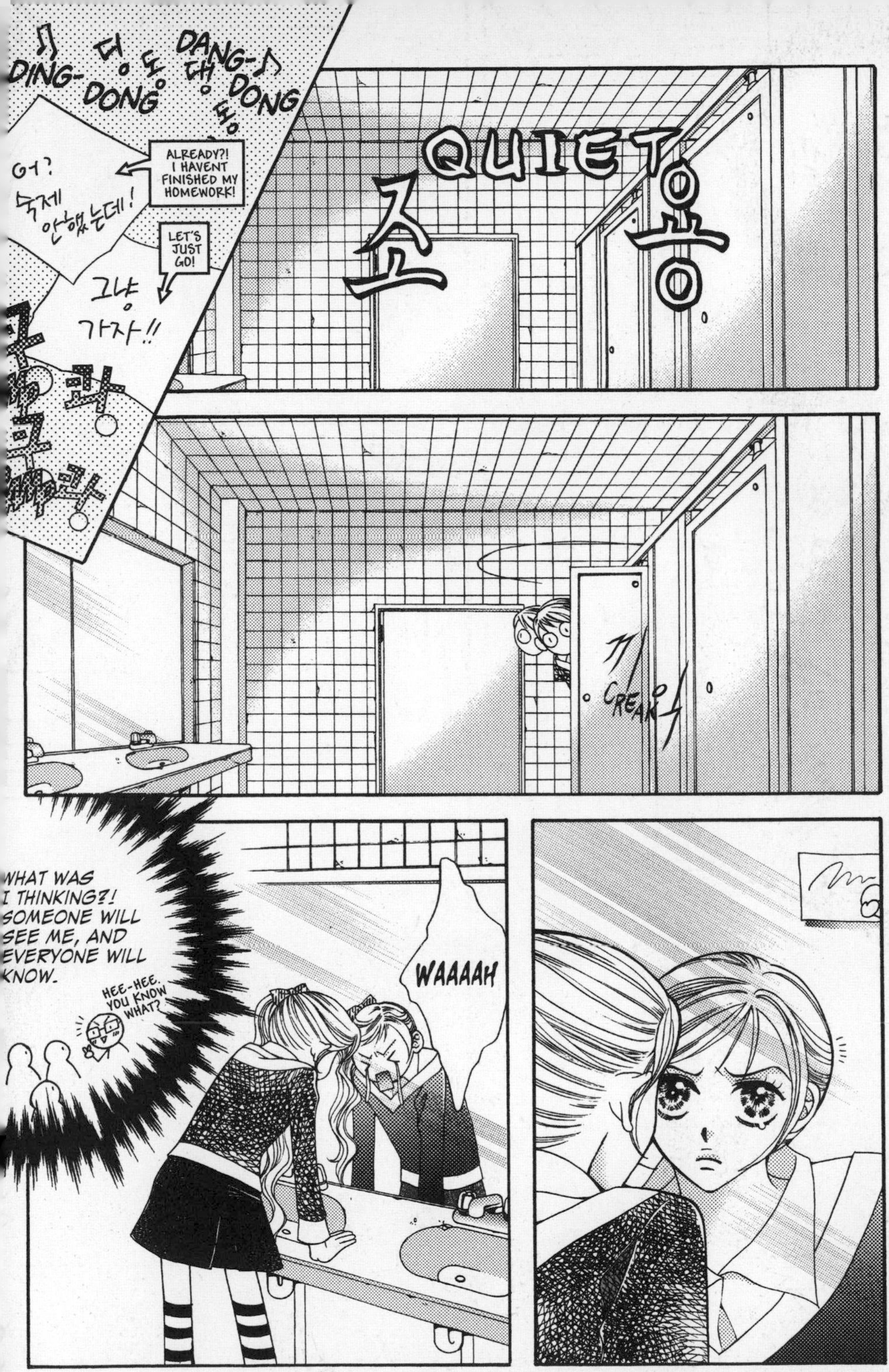
♫ 딩 동 댕 동 ♪
DING-DONG DANG-DONG
어? 숙제 안했는데!
ALREADY?! I HAVENT FINISHED MY HOMEWORK!
그냥 가자!!
LET'S JUST GO!
조용
QUIET
끼익
CREAK
WHAT WAS I THINKING?! SOMEONE WILL SEE ME, AND EVERYONE WILL KNOW.
HEE-HEE. YOU KNOW WHAT?
WAAAAH

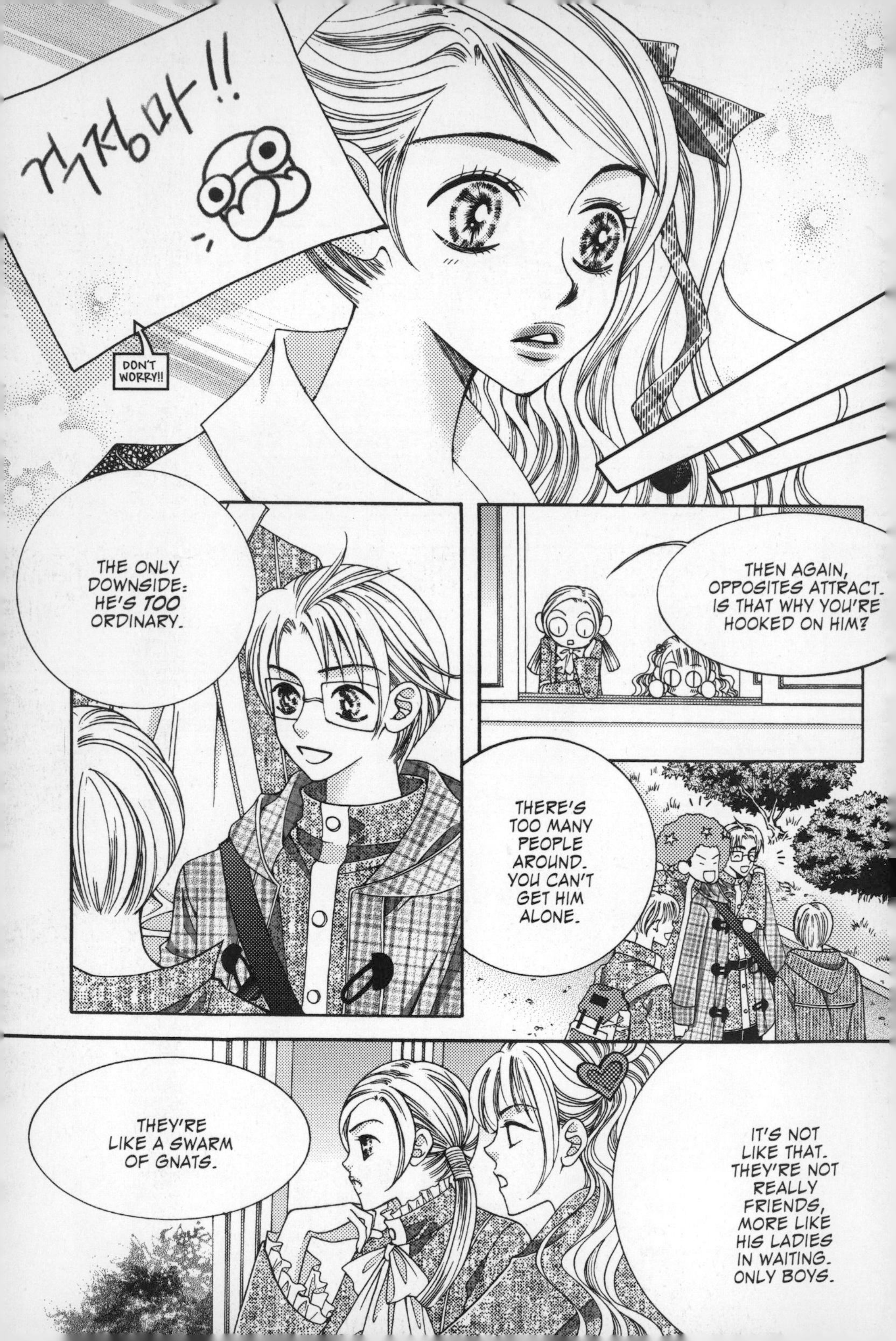
걱정마!!
DON'T WORRY!!
THE ONLY DOWNSIDE: HE'S *TOO* ORDINARY.
THEN AGAIN, OPPOSITES ATTRACT. IS THAT WHY YOU'RE HOOKED ON HIM?
THERE'S TOO MANY PEOPLE AROUND. YOU CAN'T GET HIM ALONE.
THEY'RE LIKE A SWARM OF GNATS.
IT'S NOT LIKE THAT. THEY'RE NOT REALLY FRIENDS, MORE LIKE HIS LADIES IN WAITING. ONLY BOYS.

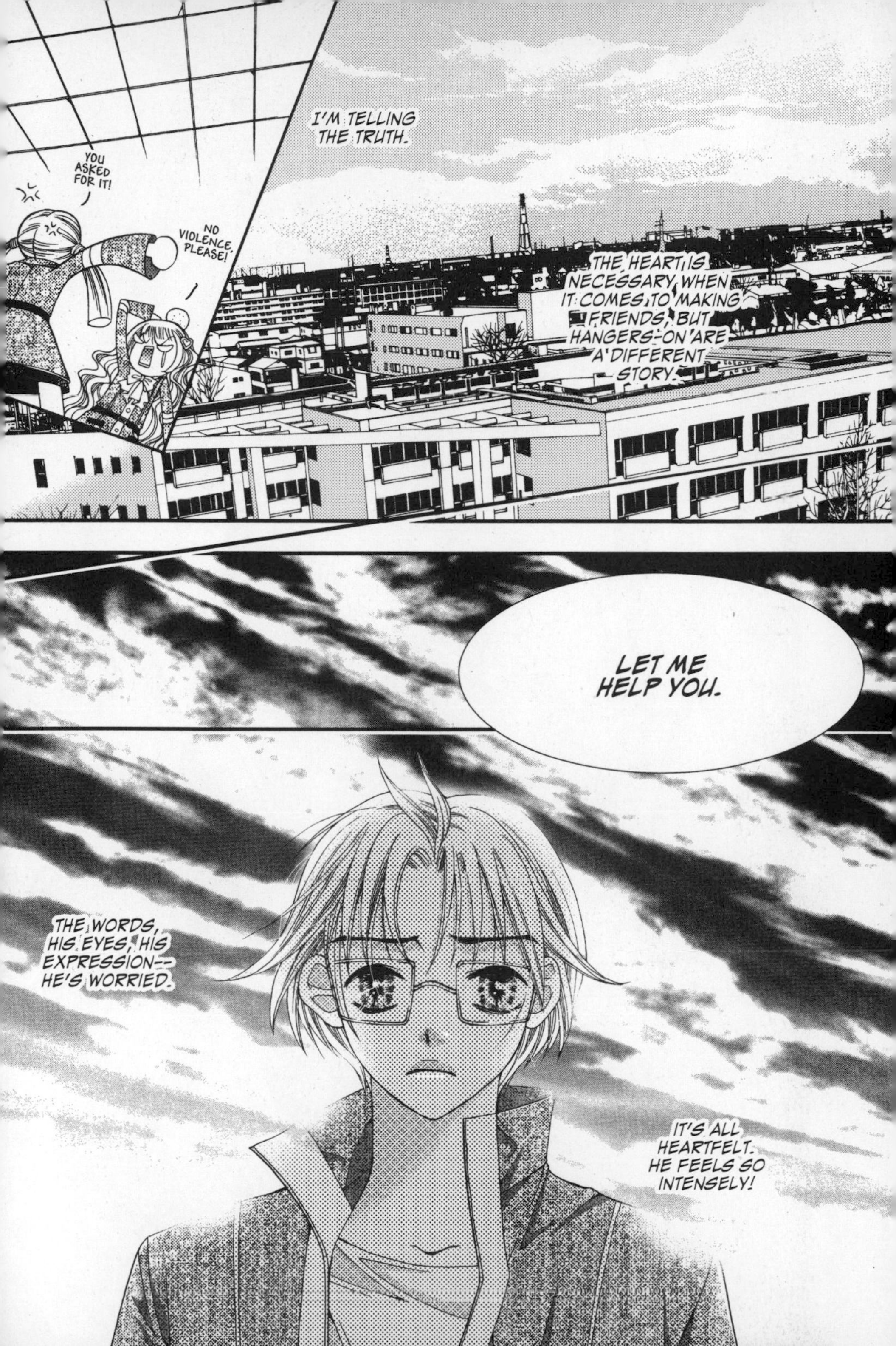
I'M TELLING THE TRUTH.
THE HEART IS NECESSARY WHEN IT COMES TO MAKING FRIENDS, BUT HANGERS-ON ARE A DIFFERENT STORY.
YOU ASKED FOR IT!
NO VIOLENCE, PLEASE!
LET ME HELP YOU.
IT'S ALL HEARTFELT. HE FEELS SO INTENSELY!
THE WORDS, HIS EYES, HIS EXPRESSION-- HE'S WORRIED.

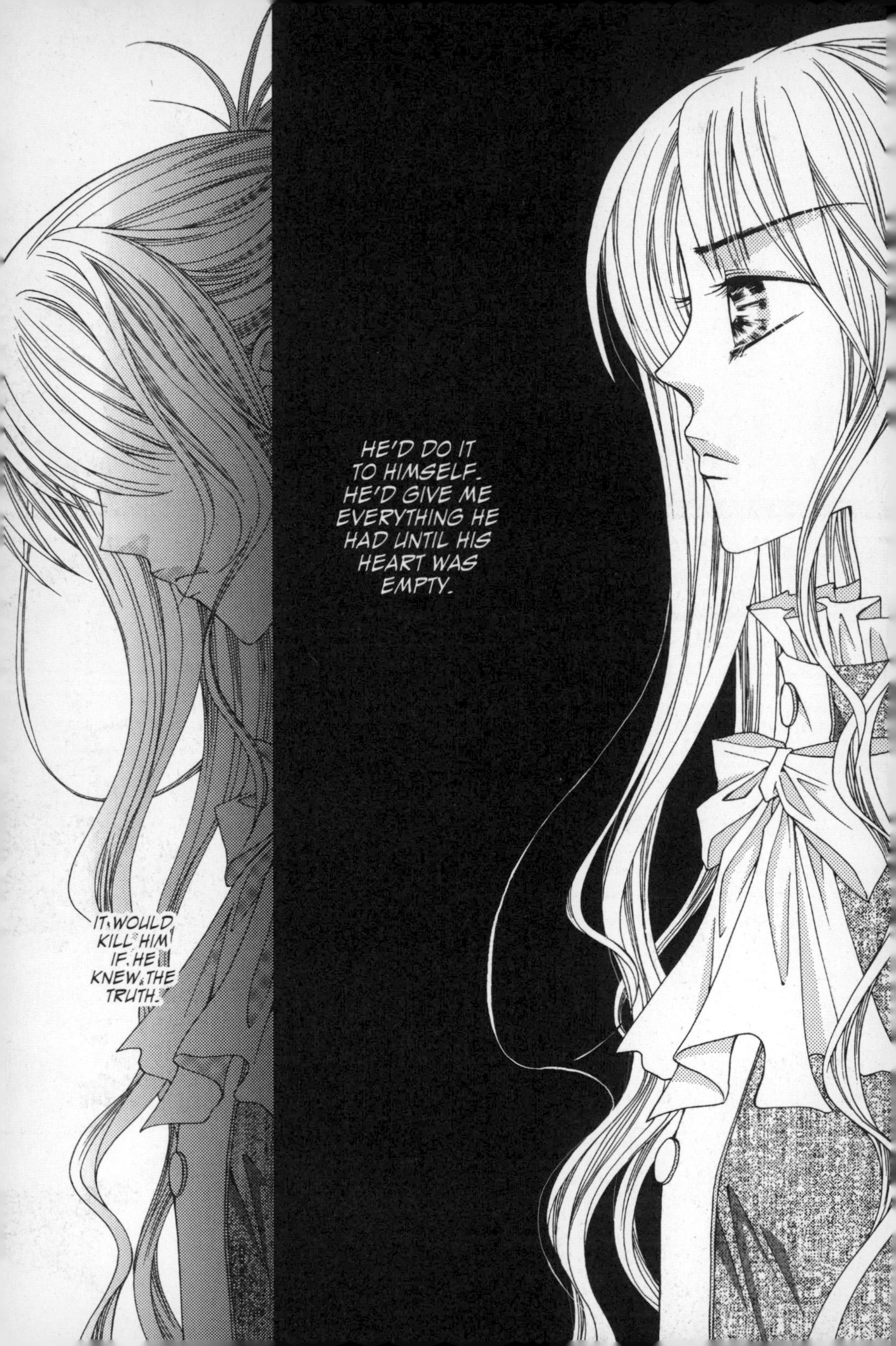
HE'D DO IT TO HIMSELF. HE'D GIVE ME EVERYTHING HE HAD UNTIL HIS HEART WAS EMPTY.
IT WOULD KILL HIM IF HE KNEW THE TRUTH.

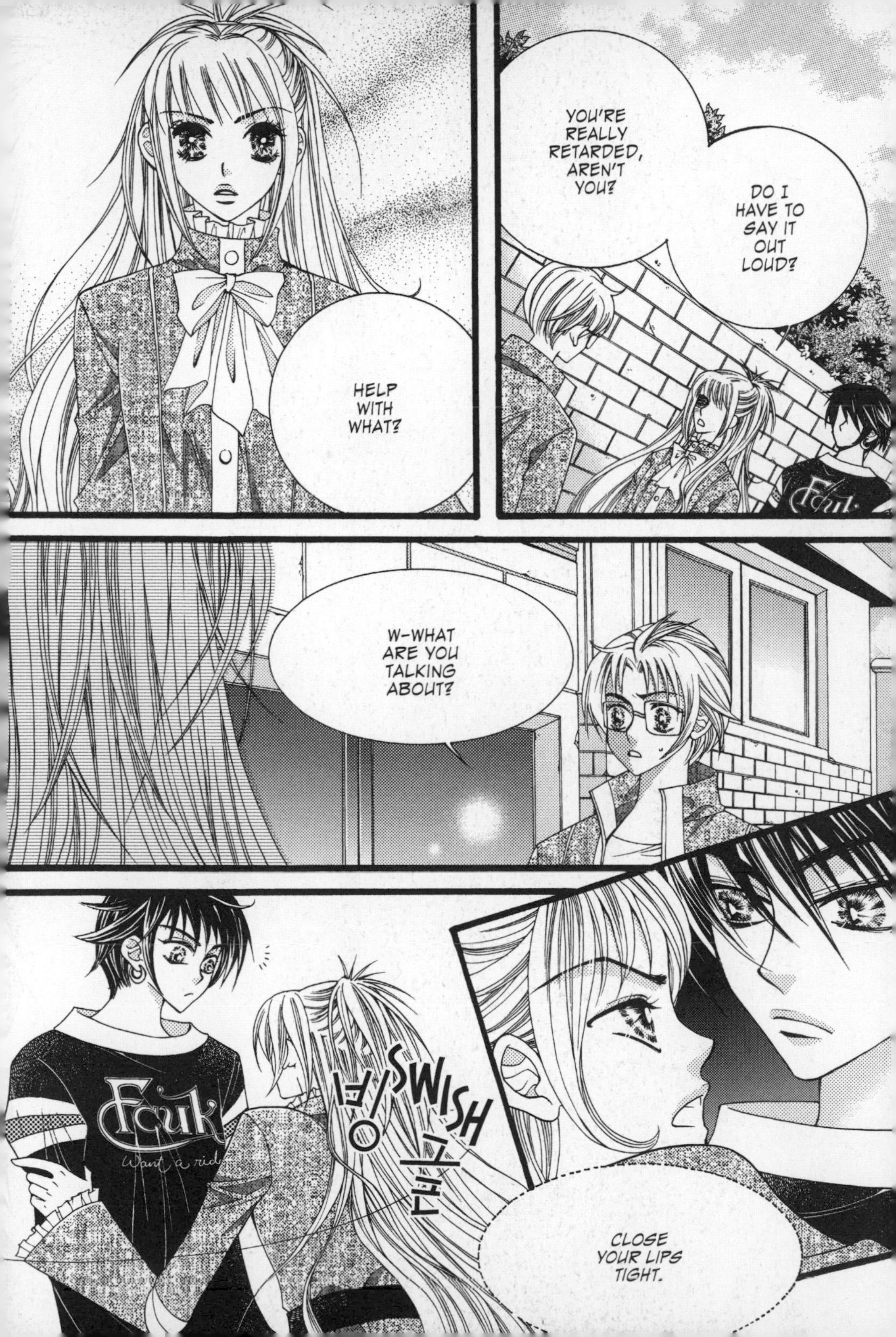
HELP WITH WHAT?
YOU'RE REALLY RETARDED, AREN'T YOU?
DO I HAVE TO SAY IT OUT LOUD?
W-WHAT ARE YOU TALKING ABOUT?
SWISH
CLOSE YOUR LIPS TIGHT.

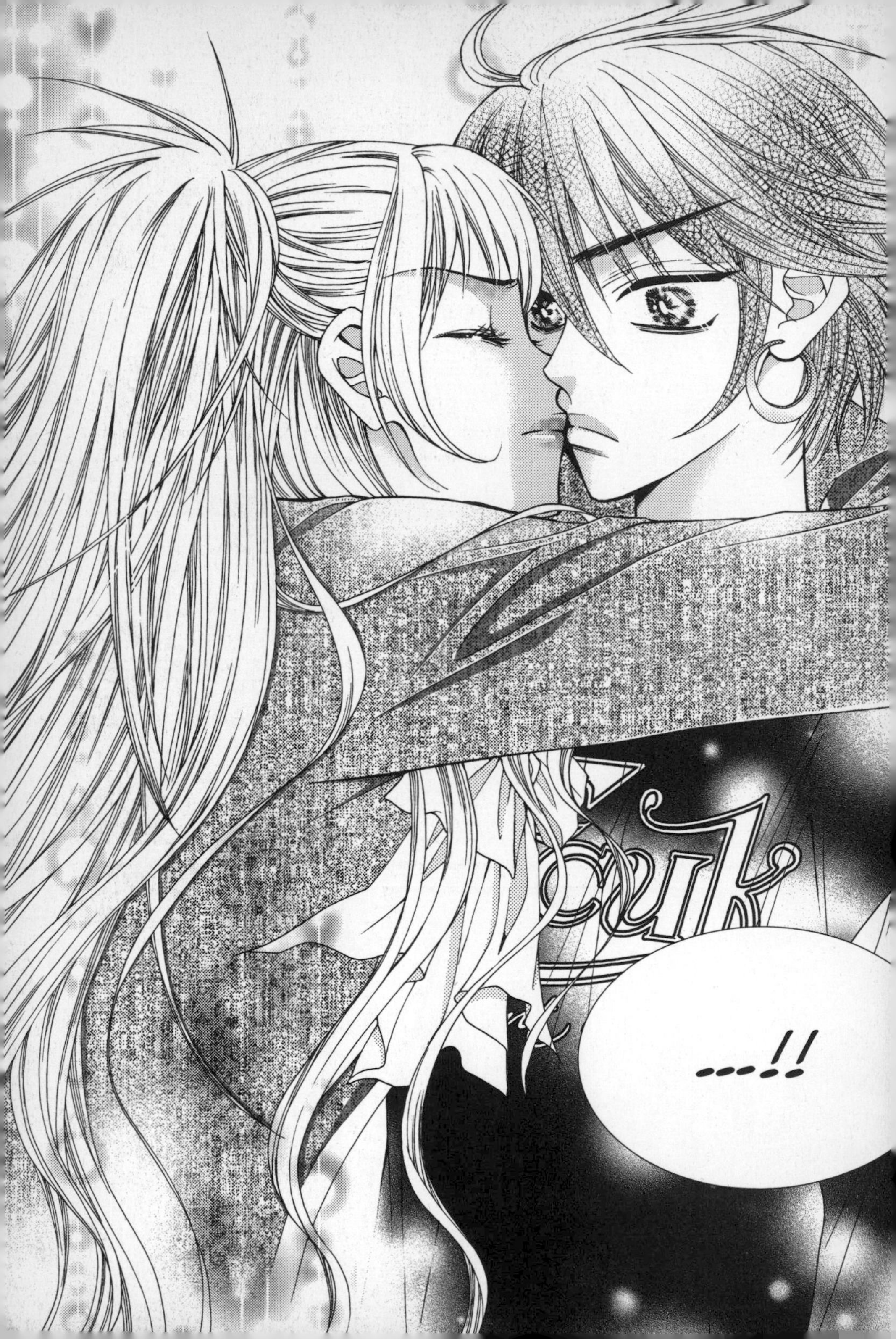

...!!

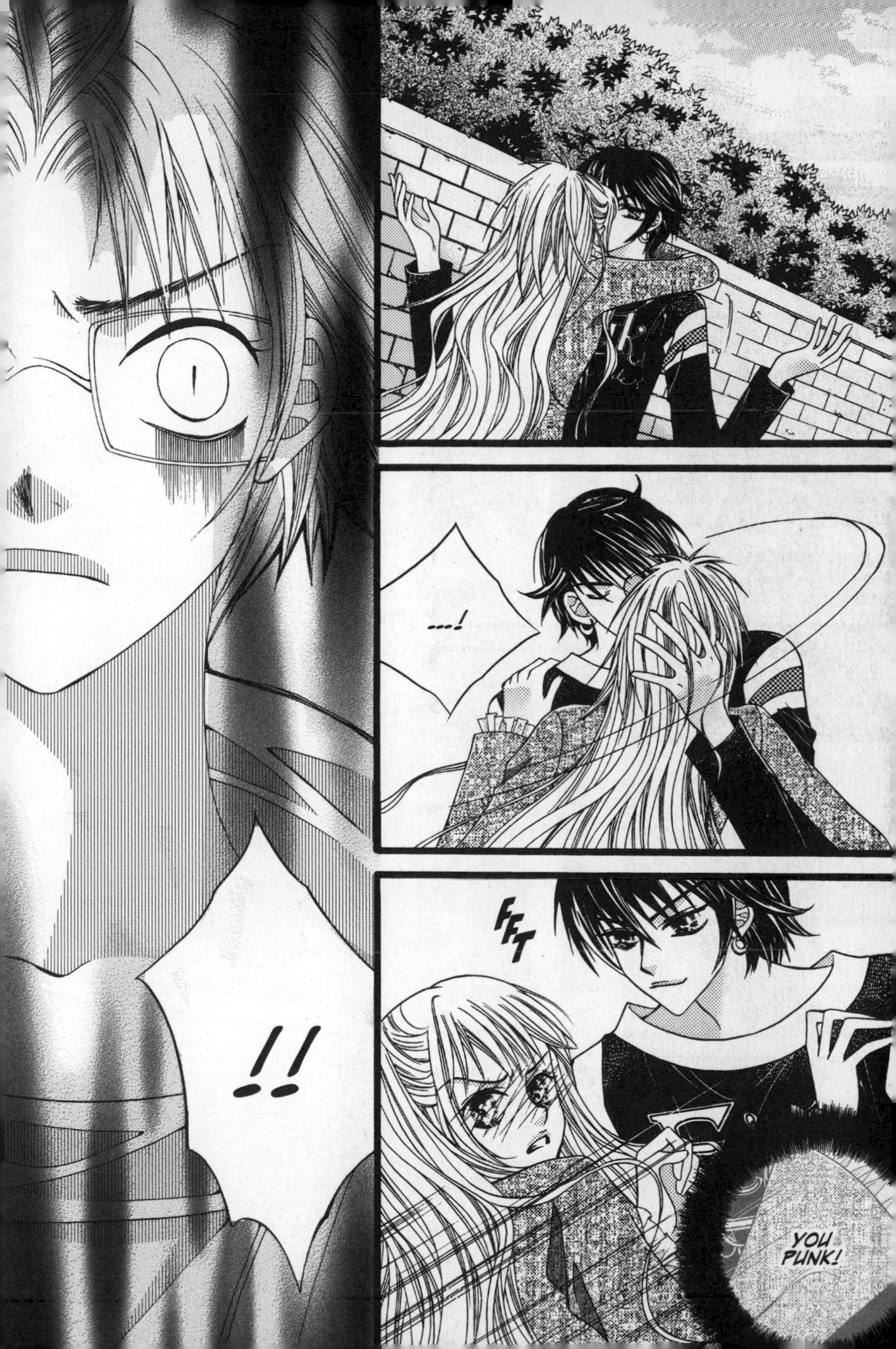
...!
!!
FFT
YOU PUNK!

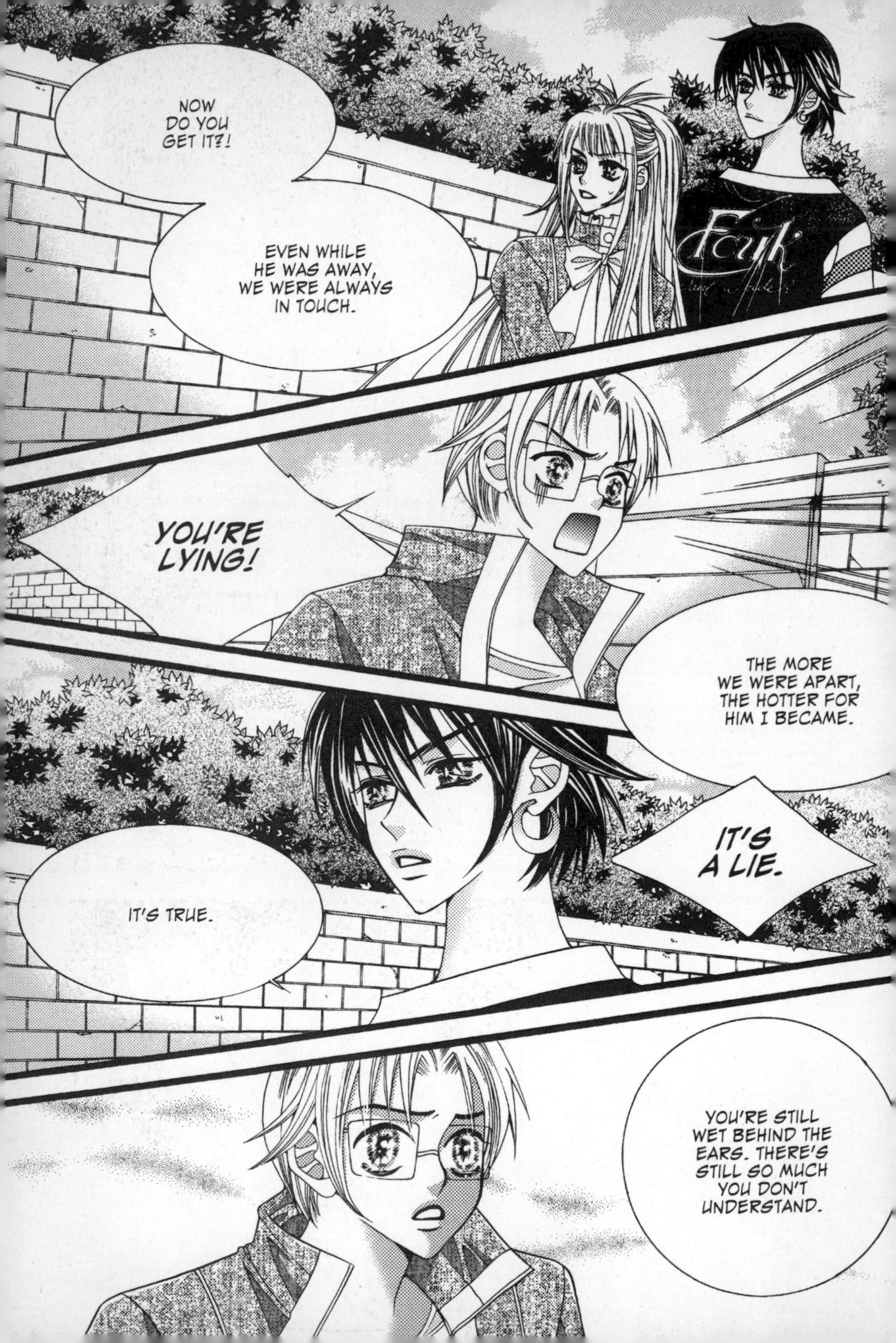
NOW DO YOU GET IT?!
EVEN WHILE HE WAS AWAY, WE WERE ALWAYS IN TOUCH.
YOU'RE LYING!
THE MORE WE WERE APART, THE HOTTER FOR HIM I BECAME.
IT'S A LIE.
IT'S TRUE.
YOU'RE STILL WET BEHIND THE EARS. THERE'S STILL SO MUCH YOU DON'T UNDERSTAND.

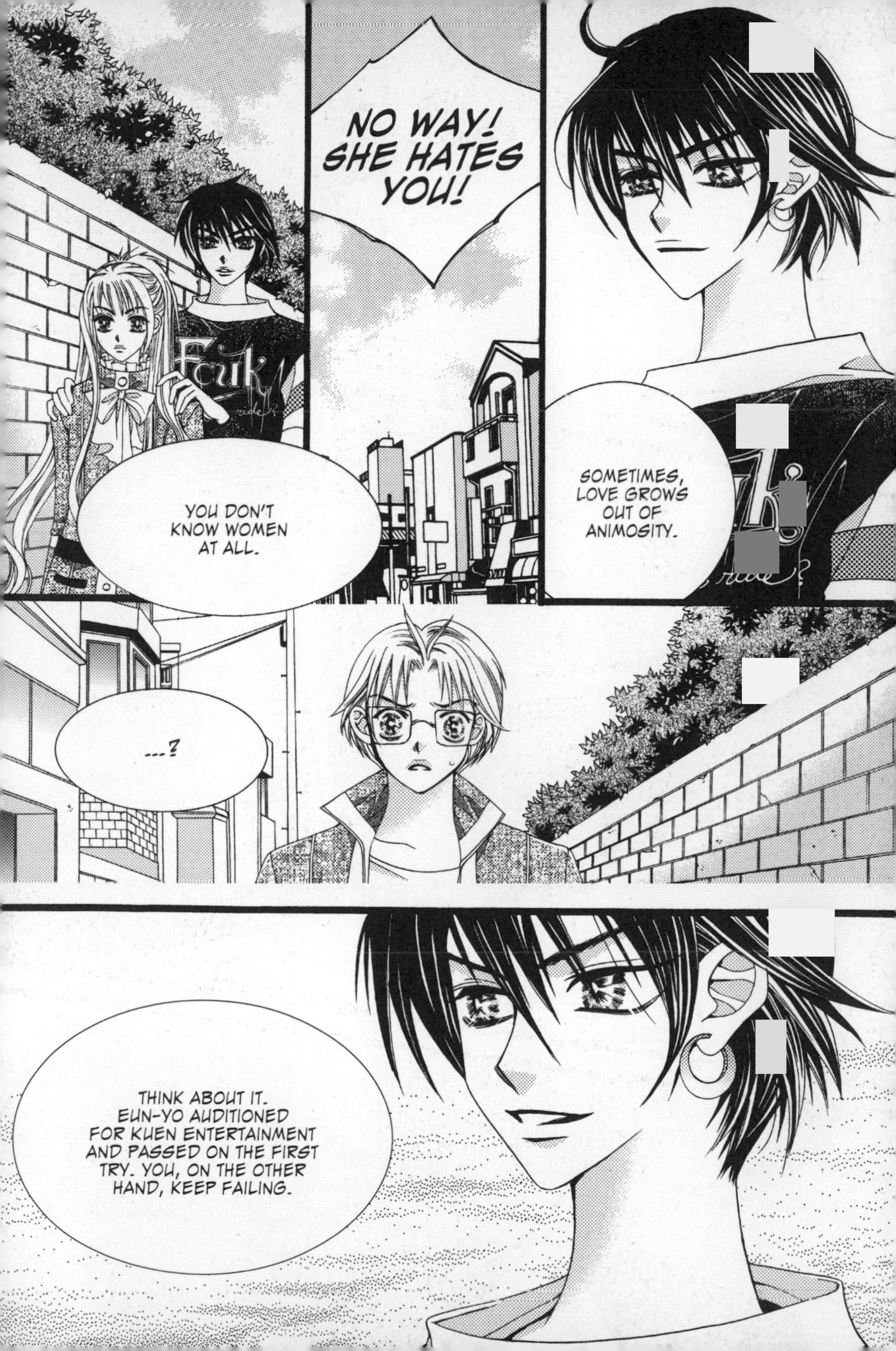
YOU DON'T KNOW WOMEN AT ALL.
NO WAY! SHE HATES YOU!
SOMETIMES, LOVE GROWS OUT OF ANIMOSITY.
...?
THINK ABOUT IT. EUN-YO AUDITIONED FOR KUEN ENTERTAINMENT AND PASSED ON THE FIRST TRY. YOU, ON THE OTHER HAND, KEEP FAILING.

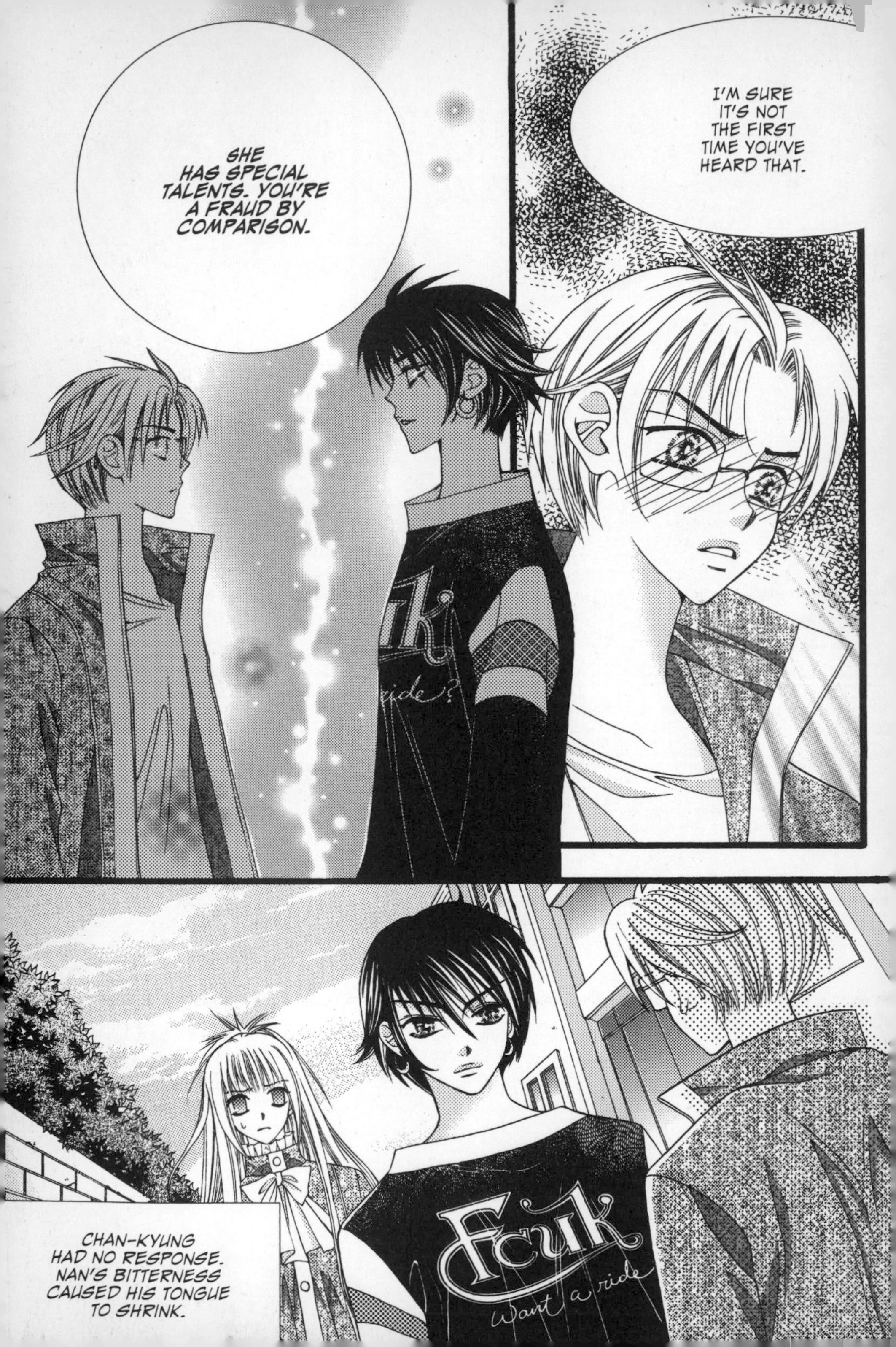
I'M SURE IT'S NOT THE FIRST TIME YOU'VE HEARD THAT.
SHE HAS SPECIAL TALENTS. YOU'RE A FRAUD BY COMPARISON.
Fcuk
Want a ride
CHAN-KYUNG HAD NO RESPONSE. NAN'S BITTERNESS CAUSED HIS TONGUE TO SHRINK.

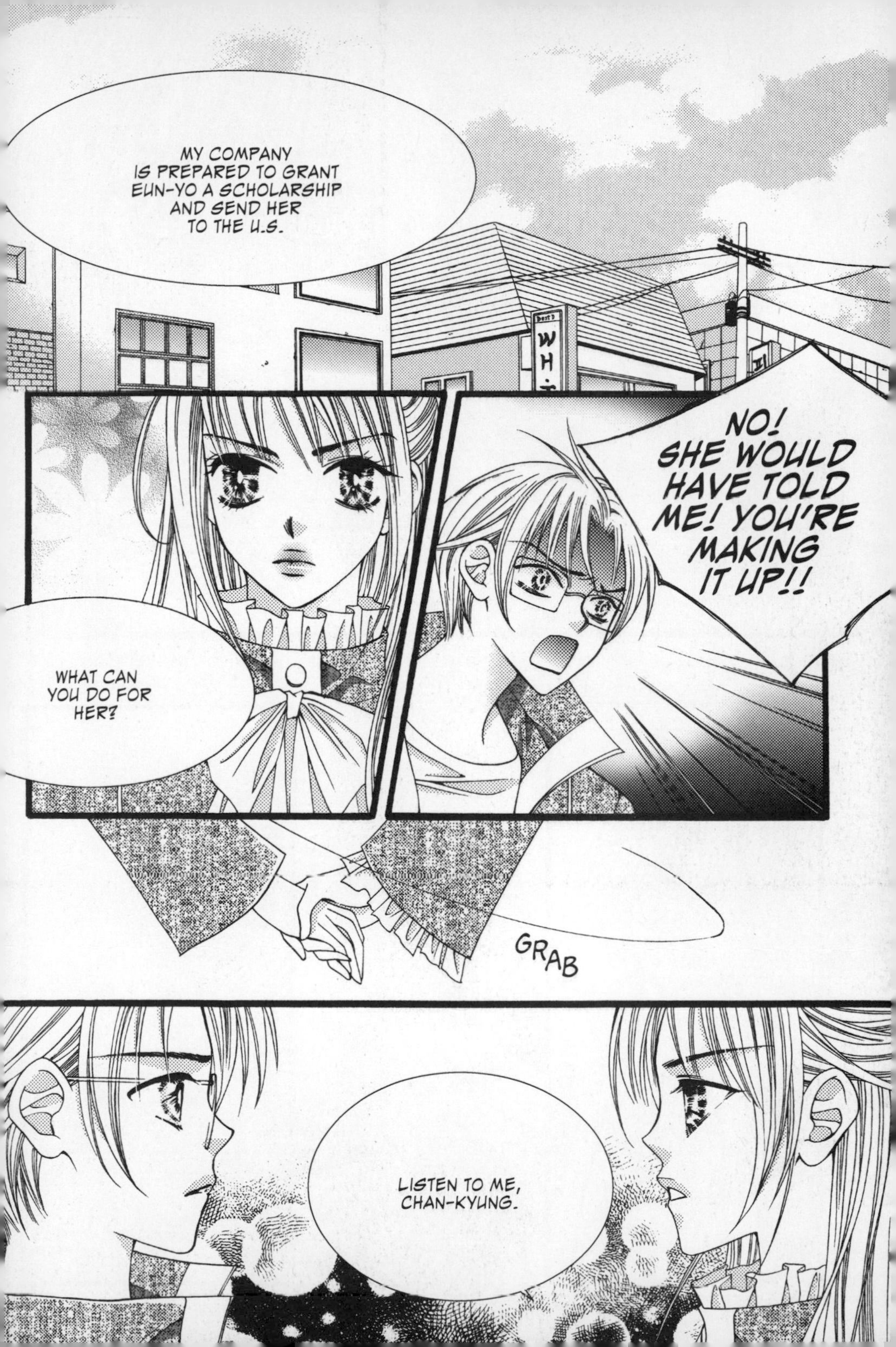

MY COMPANY IS PREPARED TO GRANT EUN-YO A SCHOLARSHIP AND SEND HER TO THE U.S.
WHAT CAN YOU DO FOR HER?
NO! SHE WOULD HAVE TOLD ME! YOU'RE MAKING IT UP!!
GRAB
LISTEN TO ME, CHAN-KYUNG.

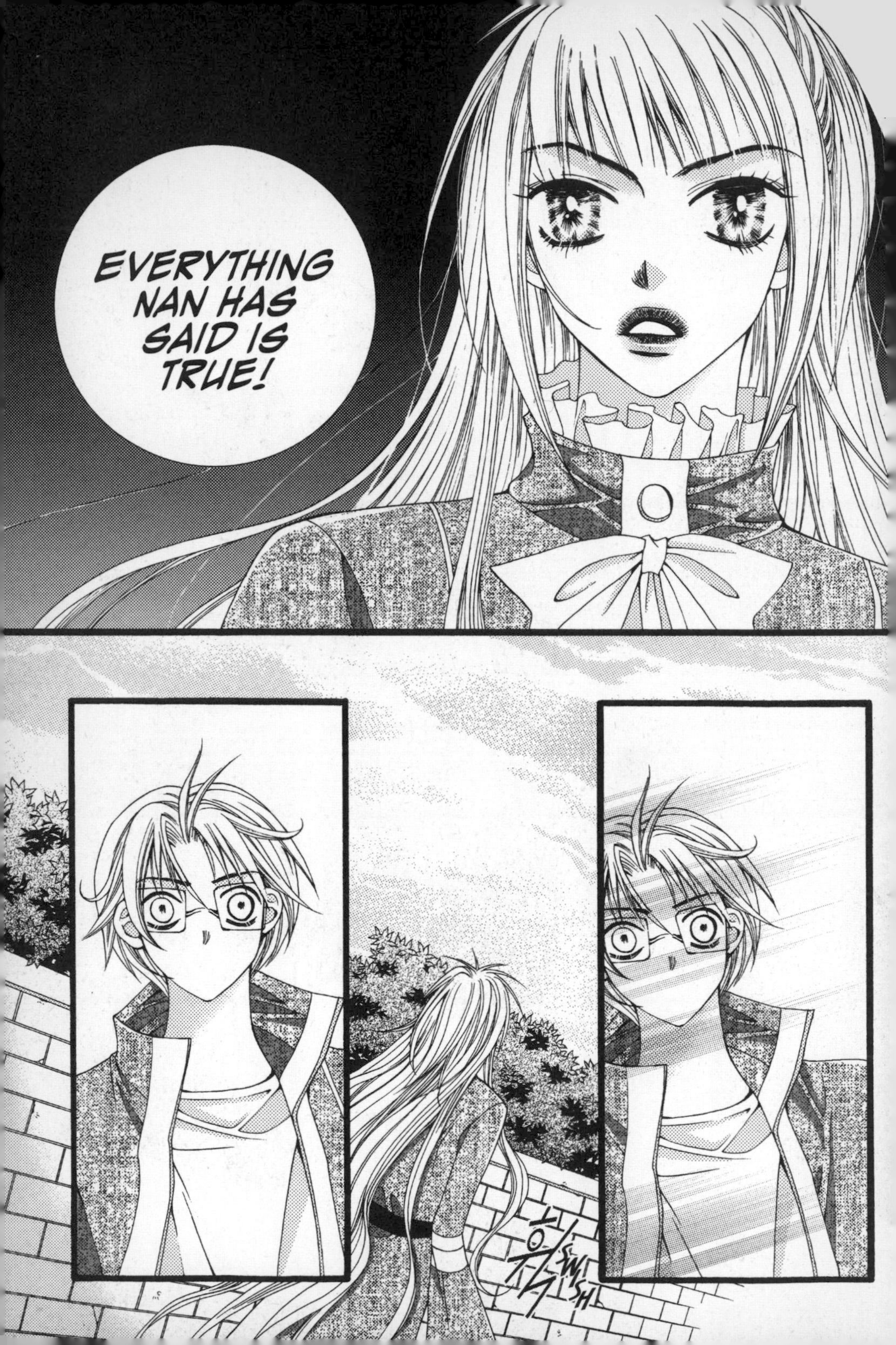
EVERYTHING NAN HAS SAID IS TRUE!
SWISH

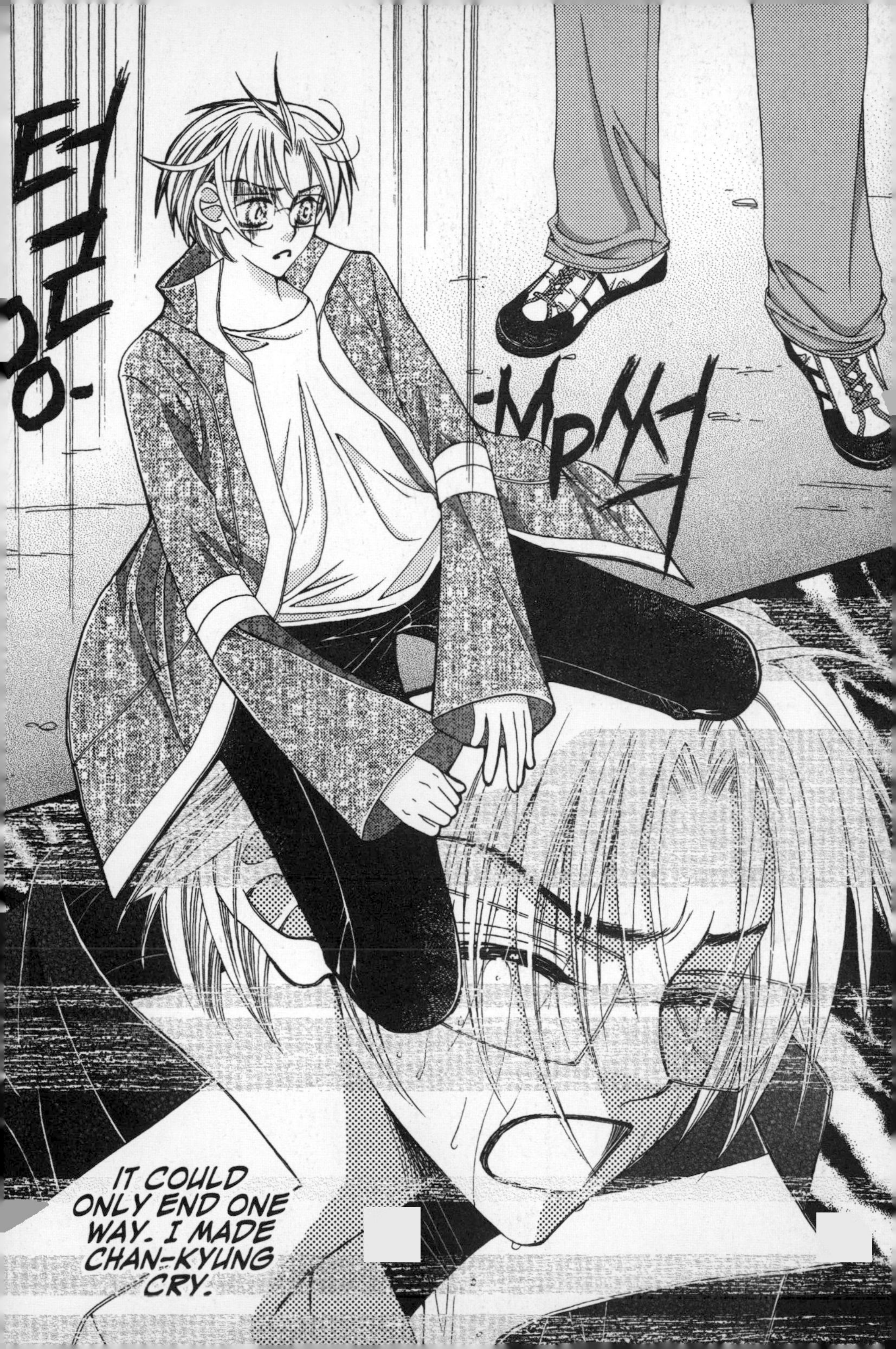
IT COULD ONLY END ONE WAY. I MADE CHAN-KYUNG CRY.

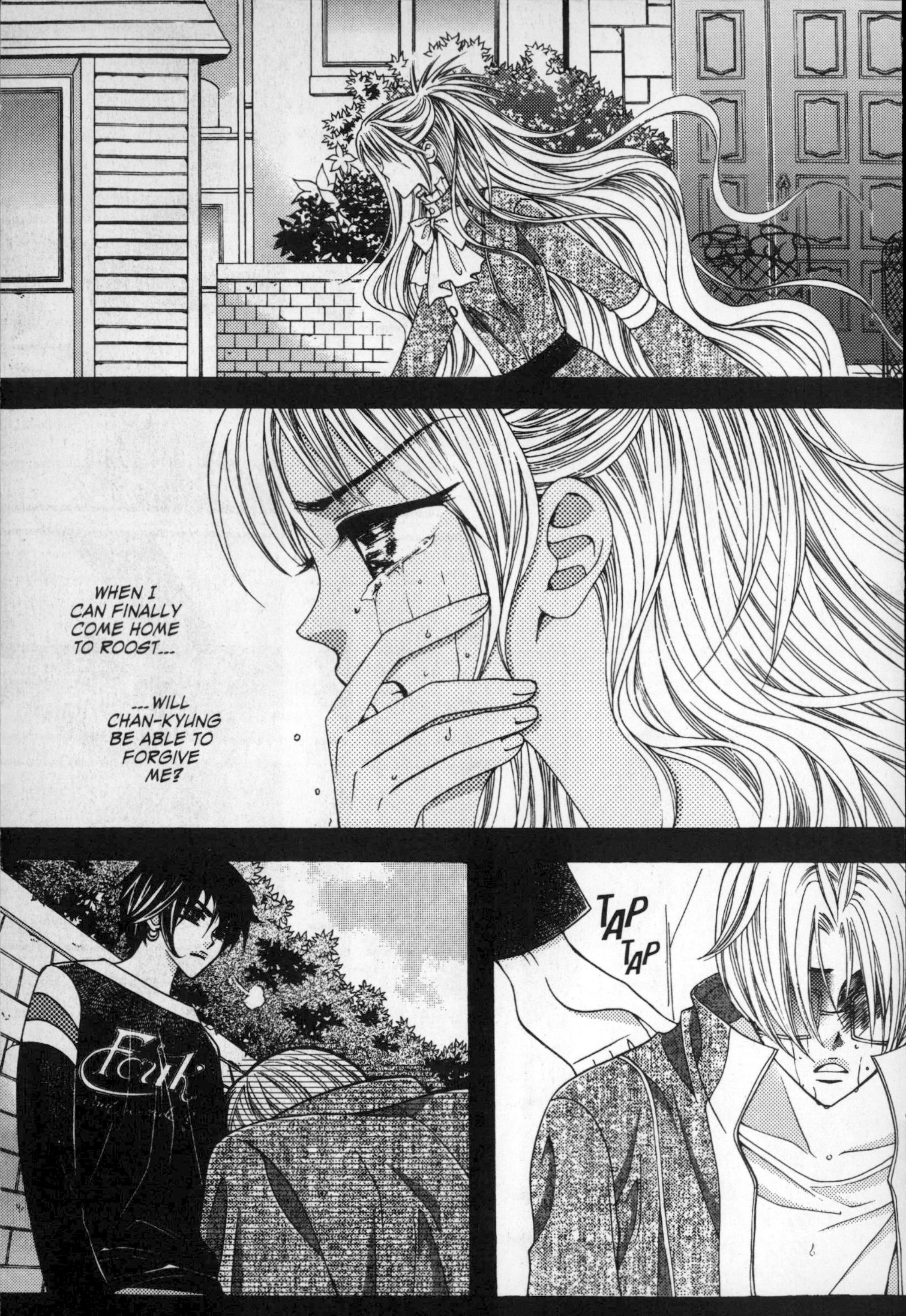

WHEN I CAN FINALLY COME HOME TO ROOST...
...WILL CHAN-KYUNG BE ABLE TO FORGIVE ME?
TAP TAP

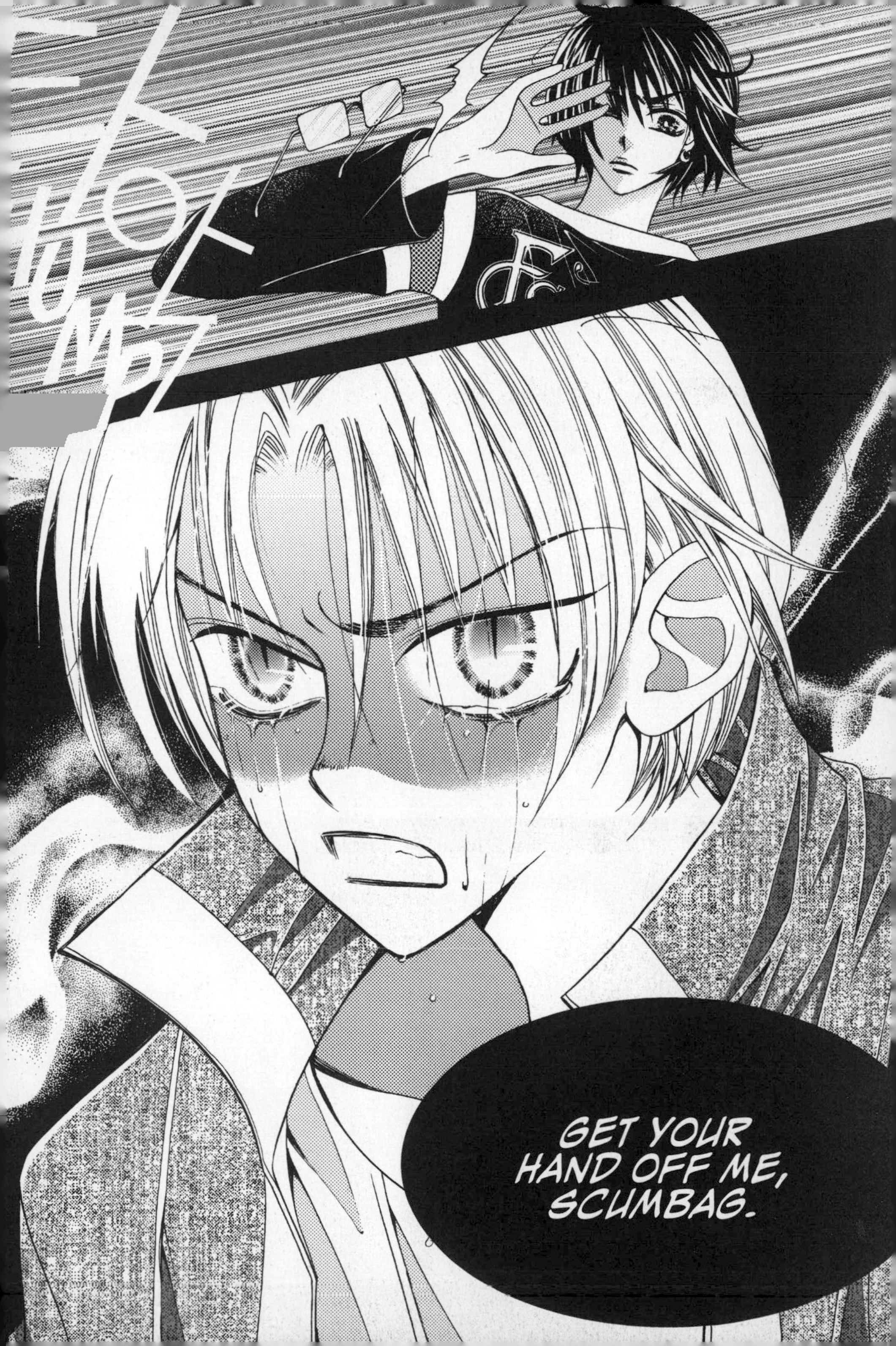
THUMP!
GET YOUR HAND OFF ME, SCUMBAG.

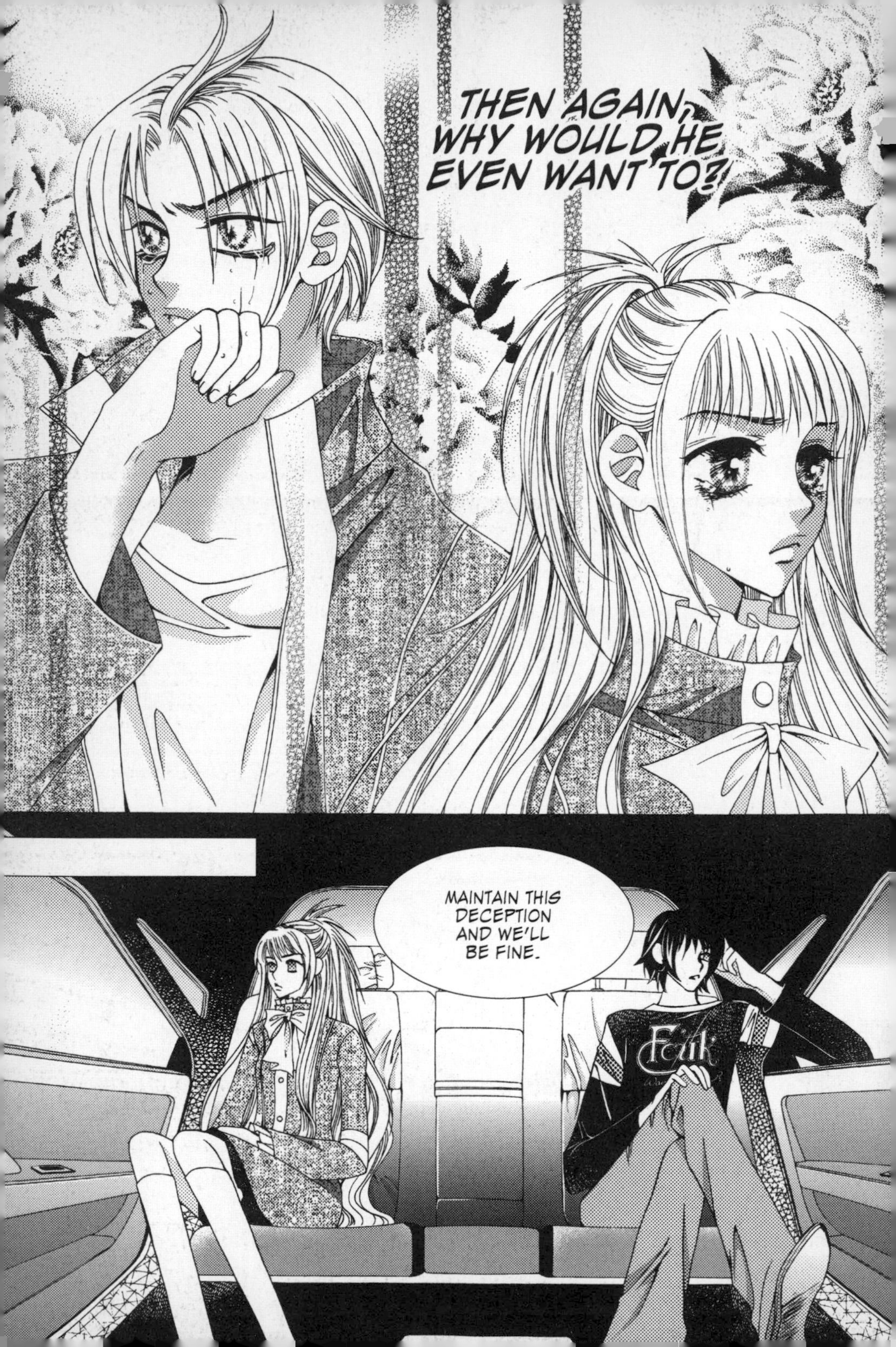
THEN AGAIN, WHY WOULD HE EVEN WANT TO?
MAINTAIN THIS DECEPTION AND WE'LL BE FINE.

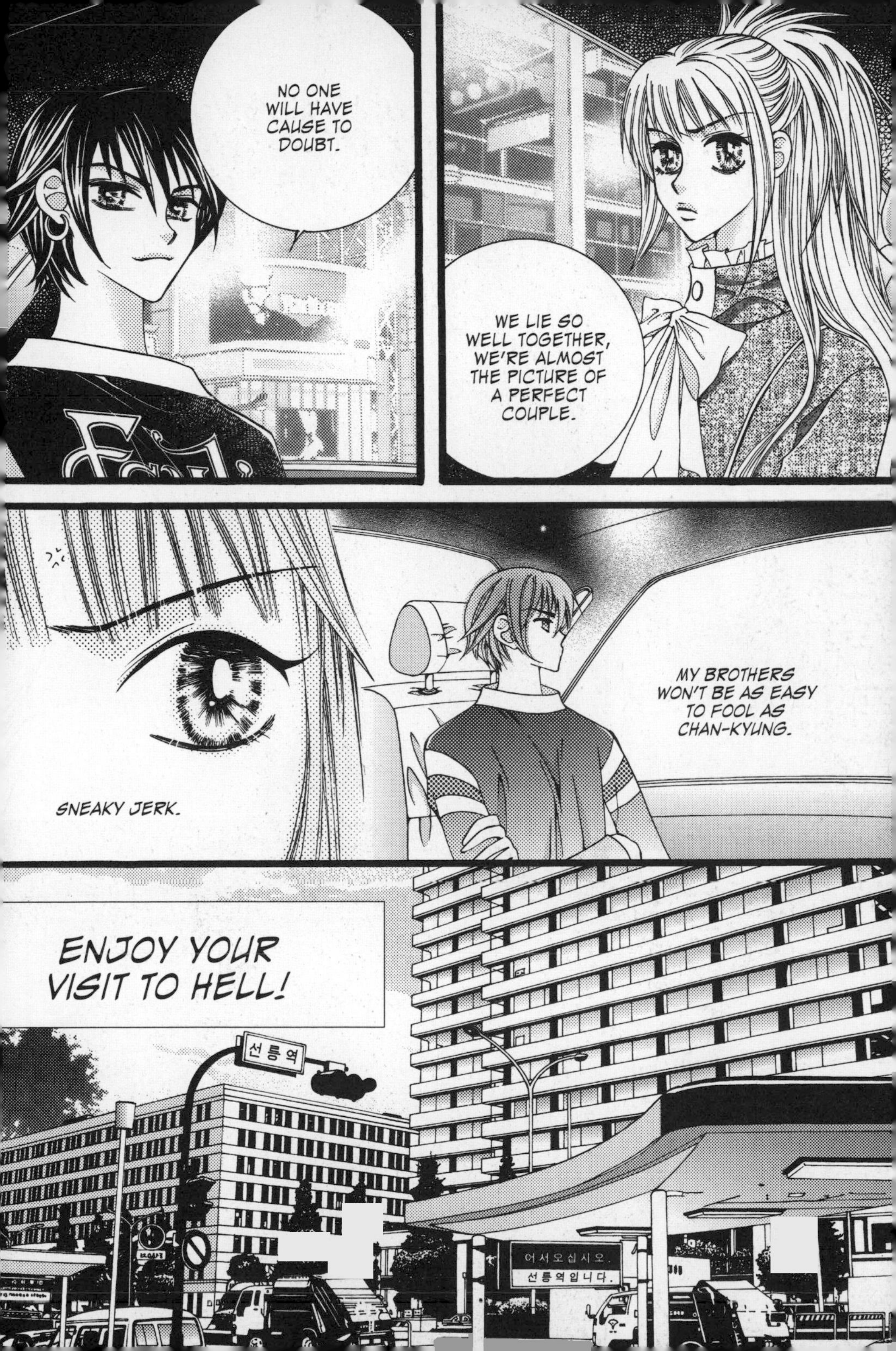
NO ONE WILL HAVE CAUSE TO DOUBT.
WE LIE SO WELL TOGETHER, WE'RE ALMOST THE PICTURE OF A PERFECT COUPLE.
SNEAKY JERK.
MY BROTHERS WON'T BE AS EASY TO FOOL AS CHAN-KYUNG.
ENJOY YOUR VISIT TO HELL!
선릉역
어서오십시오.
선릉역입니다.

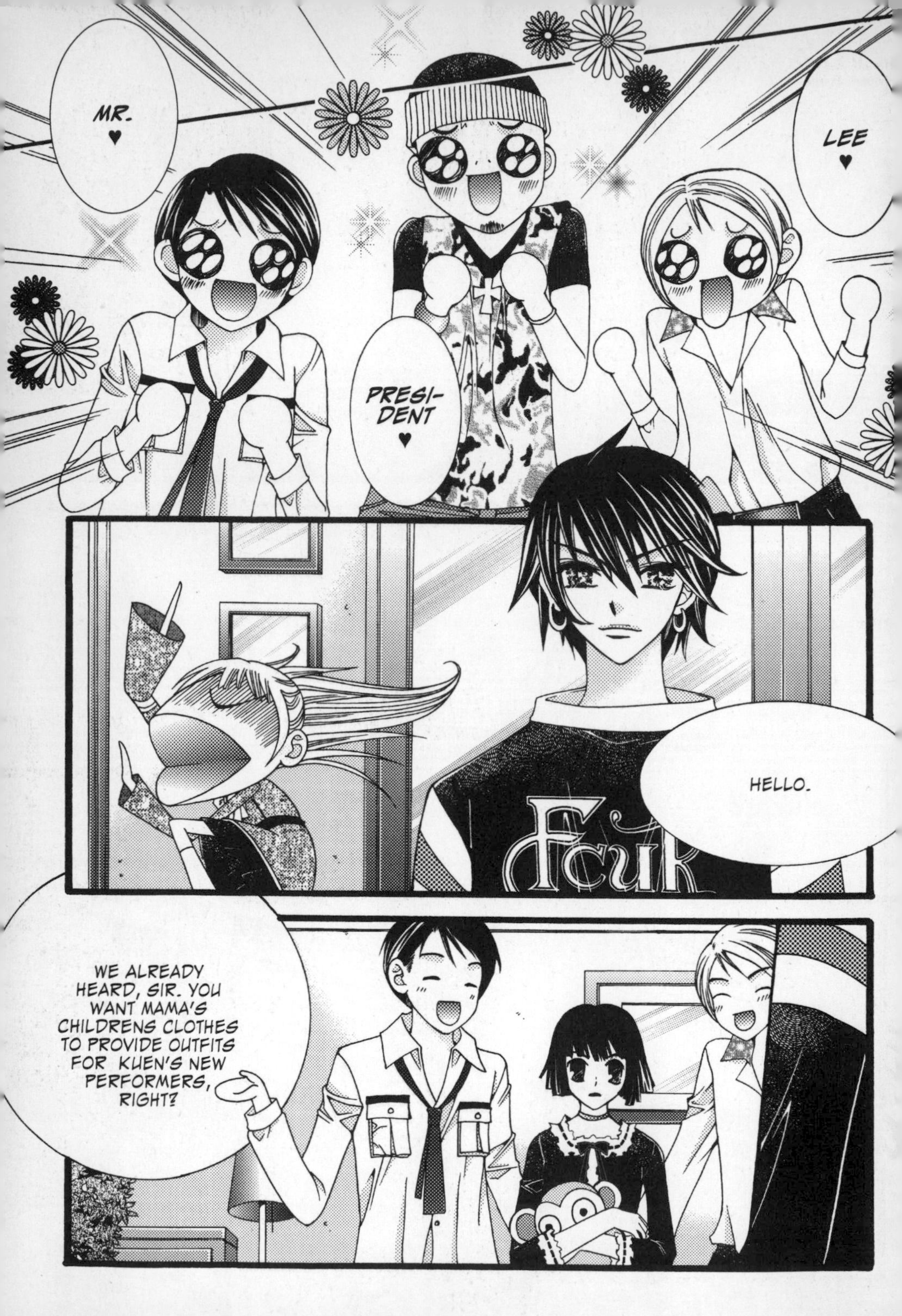
MR. ♥
PRESI-DENT ♥
LEE ♥
HELLO.
FCUK
WE ALREADY HEARD, SIR. YOU WANT MAMA'S CHILDRENS CLOTHES TO PROVIDE OUTFITS FOR KUEN'S NEW PERFORMERS, RIGHT?

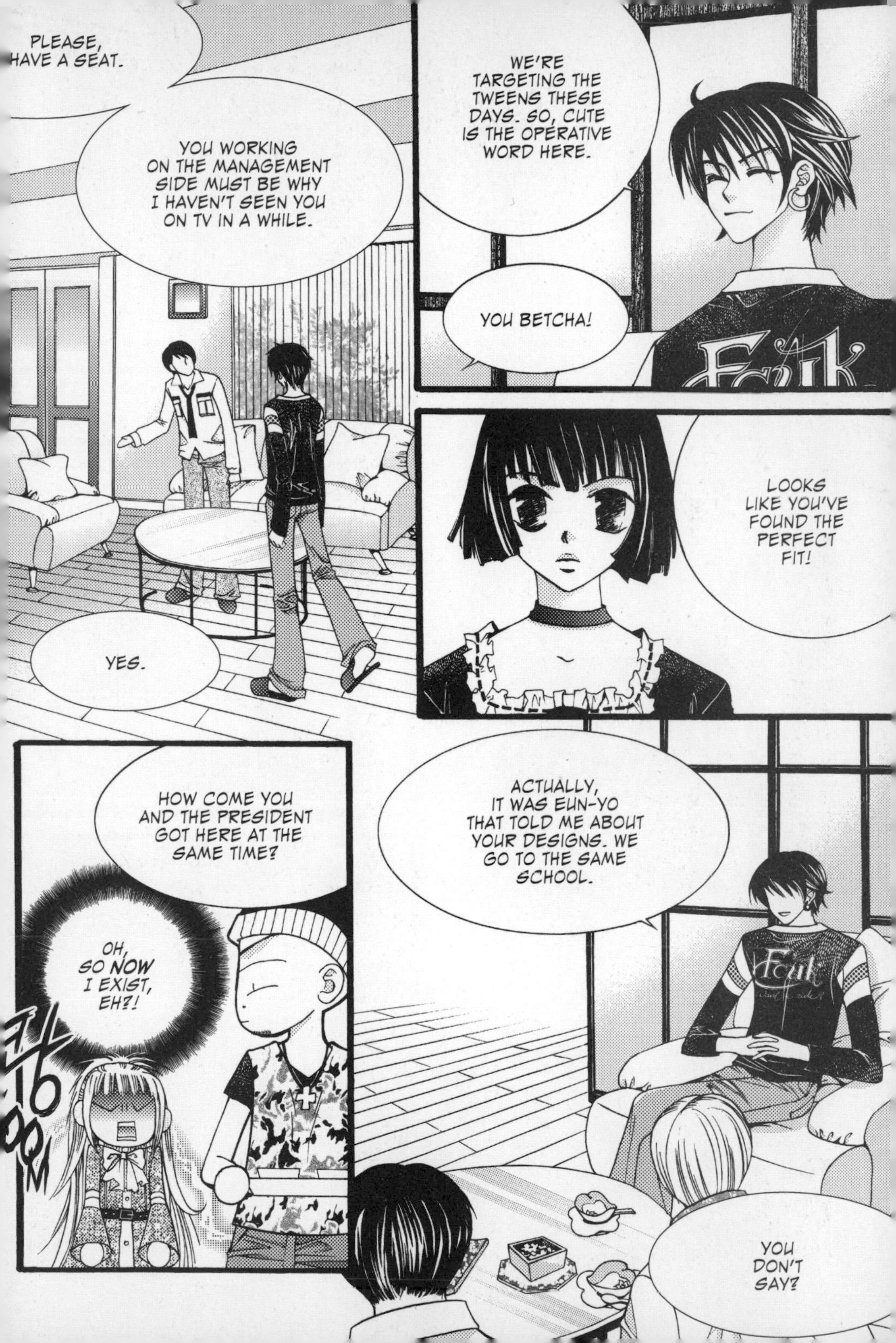
PLEASE, HAVE A SEAT.
YOU WORKING ON THE MANAGEMENT SIDE MUST BE WHY I HAVEN'T SEEN YOU ON TV IN A WHILE.
YES.
WE'RE TARGETING THE TWEENS THESE DAYS. SO, CUTE IS THE OPERATIVE WORD HERE.
YOU BETCHA!
LOOKS LIKE YOU'VE FOUND THE PERFECT FIT!
HOW COME YOU AND THE PRESIDENT GOT HERE AT THE SAME TIME?
OH, SO **NOW** I EXIST, EH?!
ACTUALLY, IT WAS EUN-YO THAT TOLD ME ABOUT YOUR DESIGNS. WE GO TO THE SAME SCHOOL.
YOU DON'T SAY?

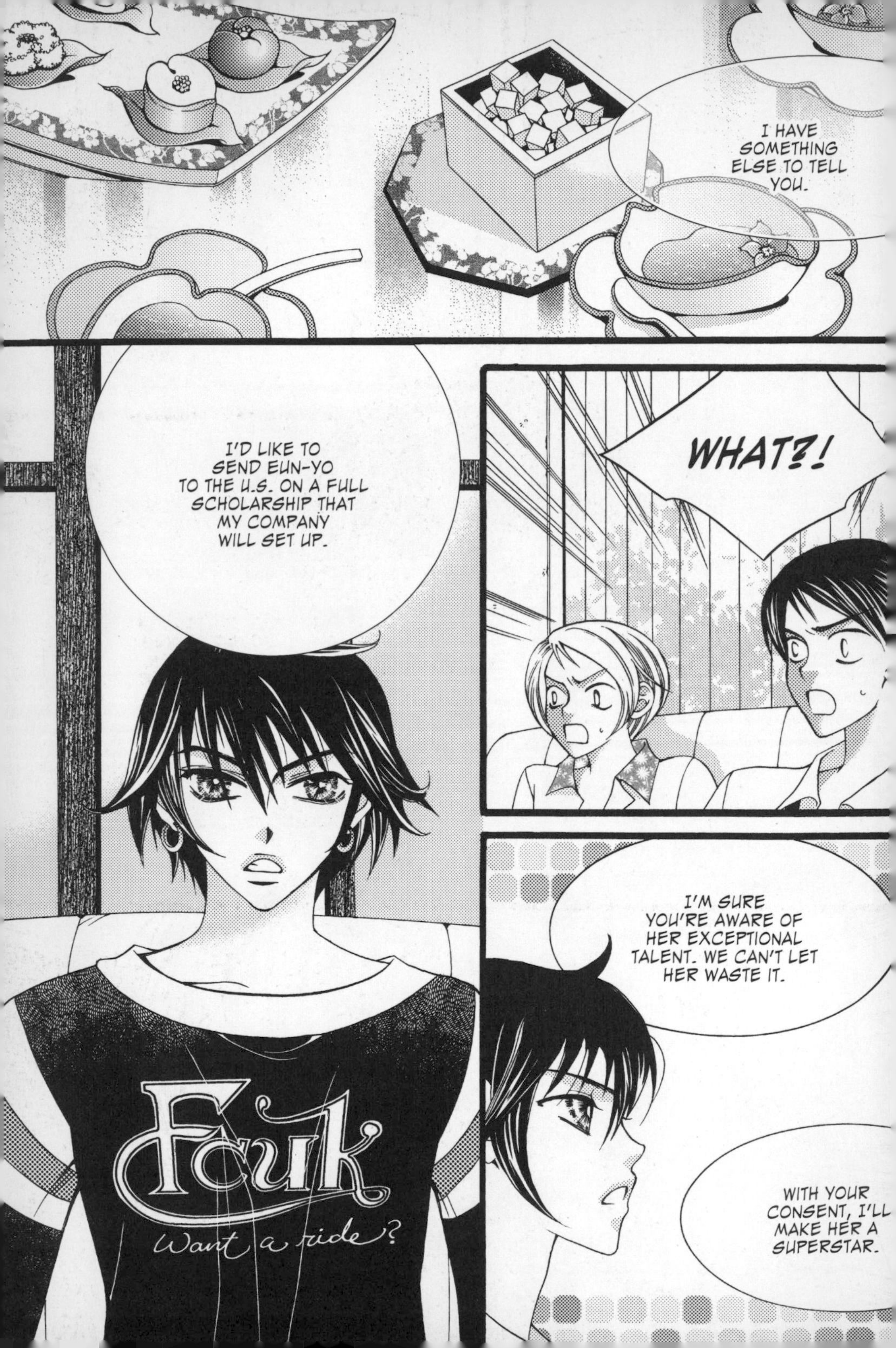
I HAVE SOMETHING ELSE TO TELL YOU.
I'D LIKE TO SEND EUN-YO TO THE U.S. ON A FULL SCHOLARSHIP THAT MY COMPANY WILL SET UP.
WHAT?!
I'M SURE YOU'RE AWARE OF HER EXCEPTIONAL TALENT. WE CAN'T LET HER WASTE IT.
WITH YOUR CONSENT, I'LL MAKE HER A SUPERSTAR.
Fcuk
Want a ride?

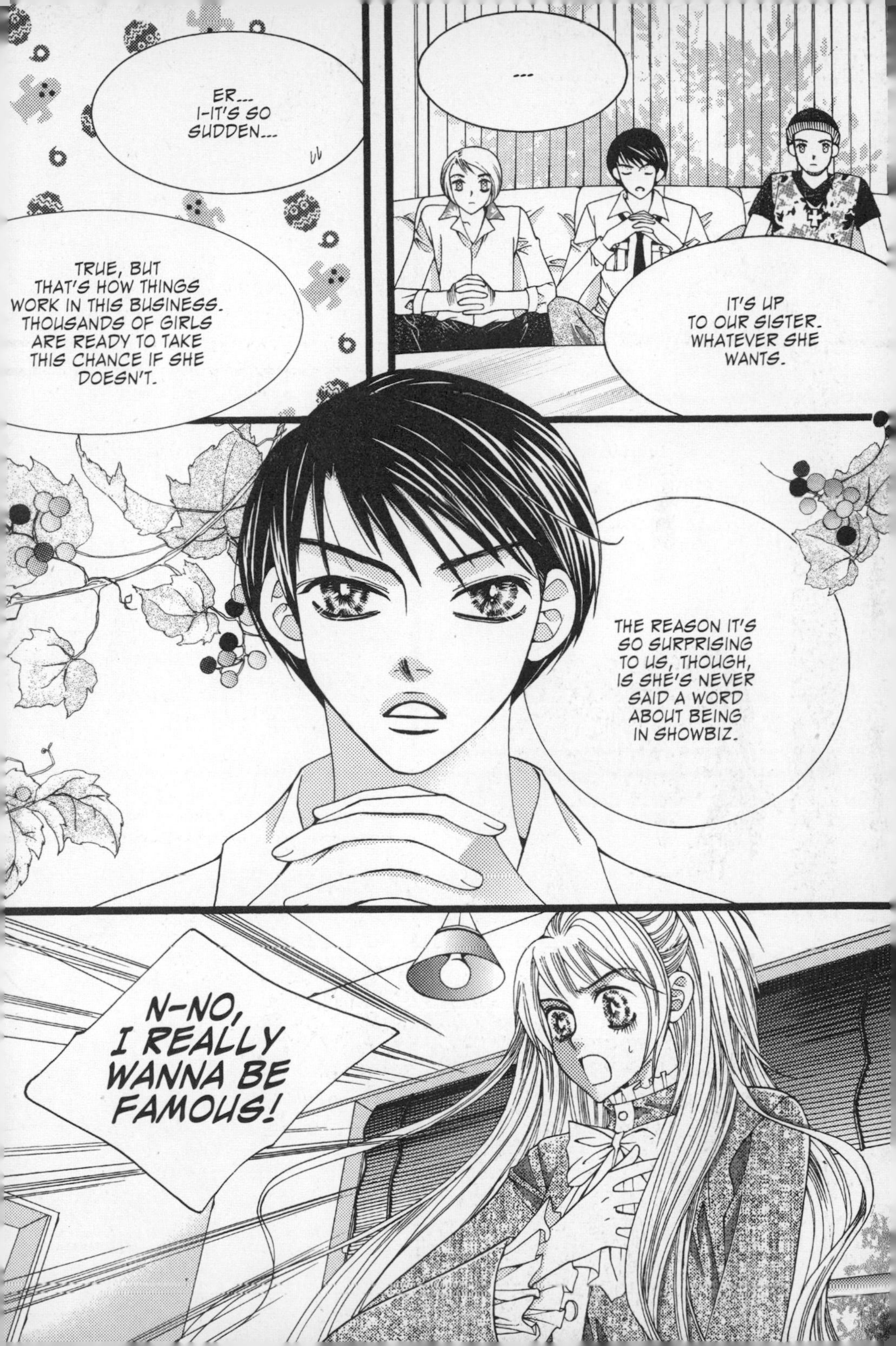
...
ER... I-IT'S SO SUDDEN...
TRUE, BUT THAT'S HOW THINGS WORK IN THIS BUSINESS. THOUSANDS OF GIRLS ARE READY TO TAKE THIS CHANCE IF SHE DOESN'T.
IT'S UP TO OUR SISTER. WHATEVER SHE WANTS.
THE REASON IT'S SO SURPRISING TO US, THOUGH, IS SHE'S NEVER SAID A WORD ABOUT BEING IN SHOWBIZ.
N-NO, I REALLY WANNA BE FAMOUS!

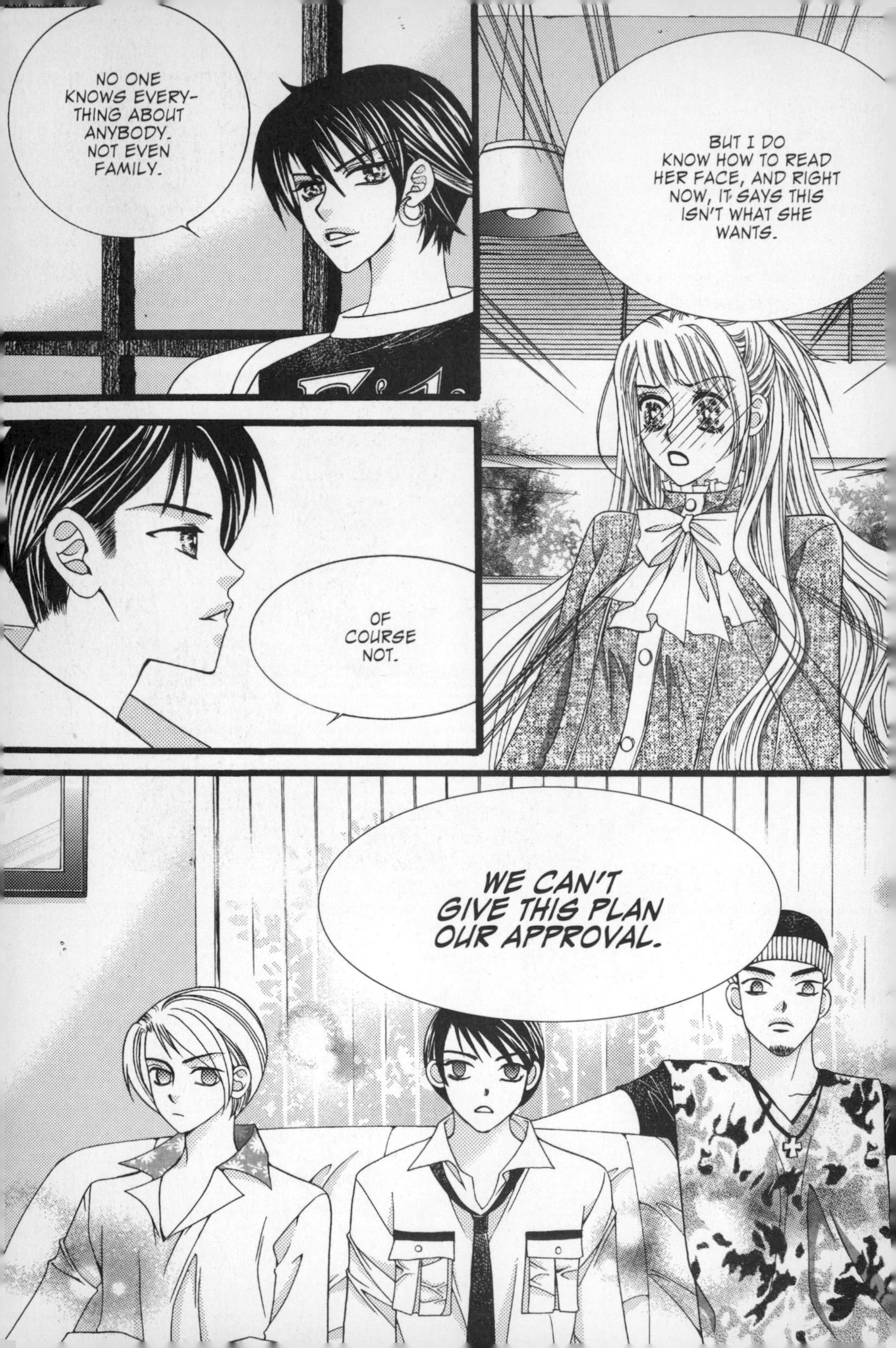
NO ONE KNOWS EVERY-THING ABOUT ANYBODY. NOT EVEN FAMILY.
BUT I DO KNOW HOW TO READ HER FACE, AND RIGHT NOW, IT SAYS THIS ISN'T WHAT SHE WANTS.
OF COURSE NOT.
WE CAN'T GIVE THIS PLAN OUR APPROVAL.

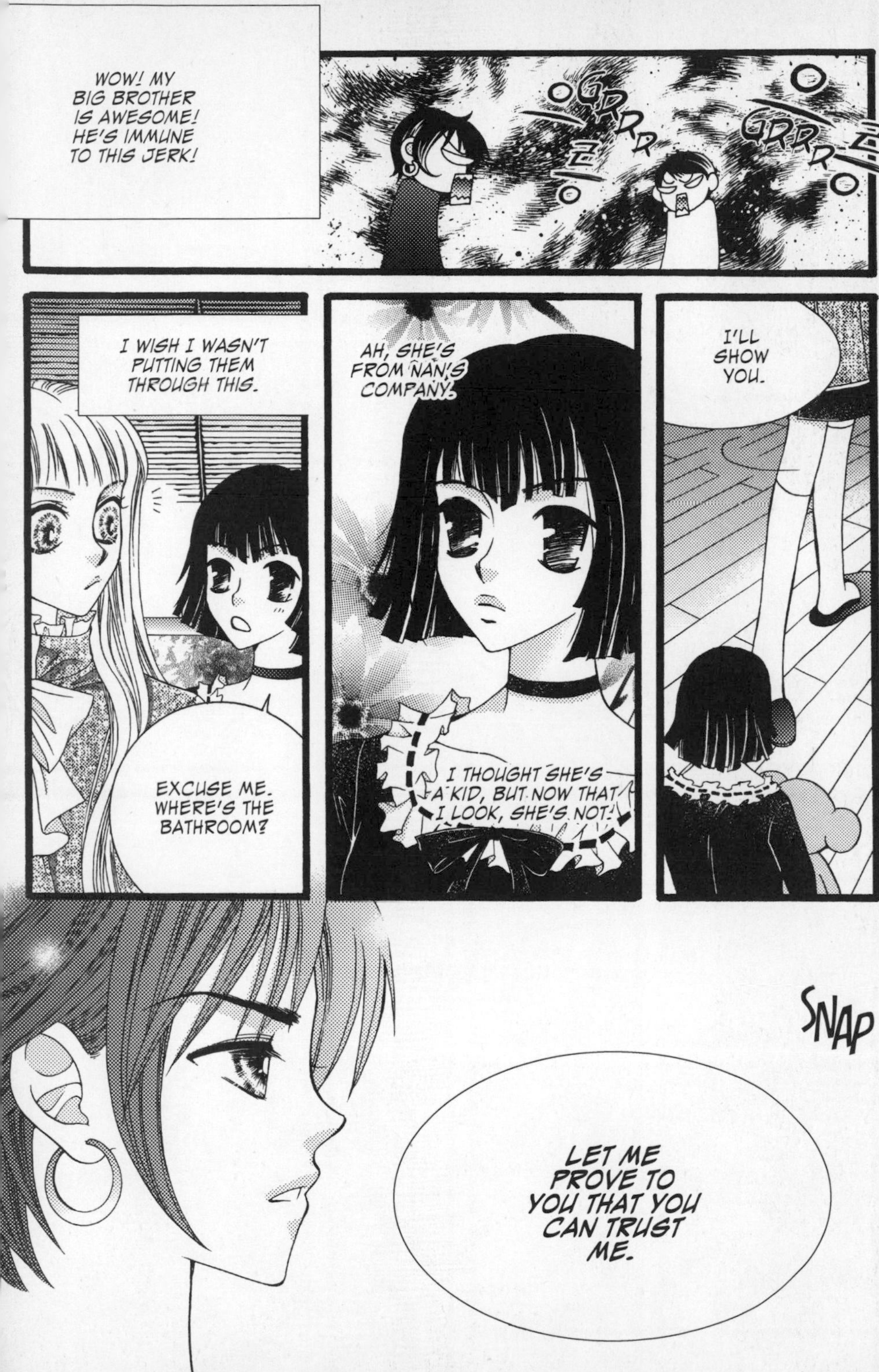
WOW! MY BIG BROTHER IS AWESOME! HE'S IMMUNE TO THIS JERK!
GRRRR
GRRRR
I WISH I WASN'T PUTTING THEM THROUGH THIS.
EXCUSE ME. WHERE'S THE BATHROOM?
AH, SHE'S FROM NAN'S COMPANY.
I THOUGHT SHE'S A KID, BUT NOW THAT I LOOK, SHE'S NOT!
I'LL SHOW YOU.
SNAP
LET ME PROVE TO YOU THAT YOU CAN TRUST ME.

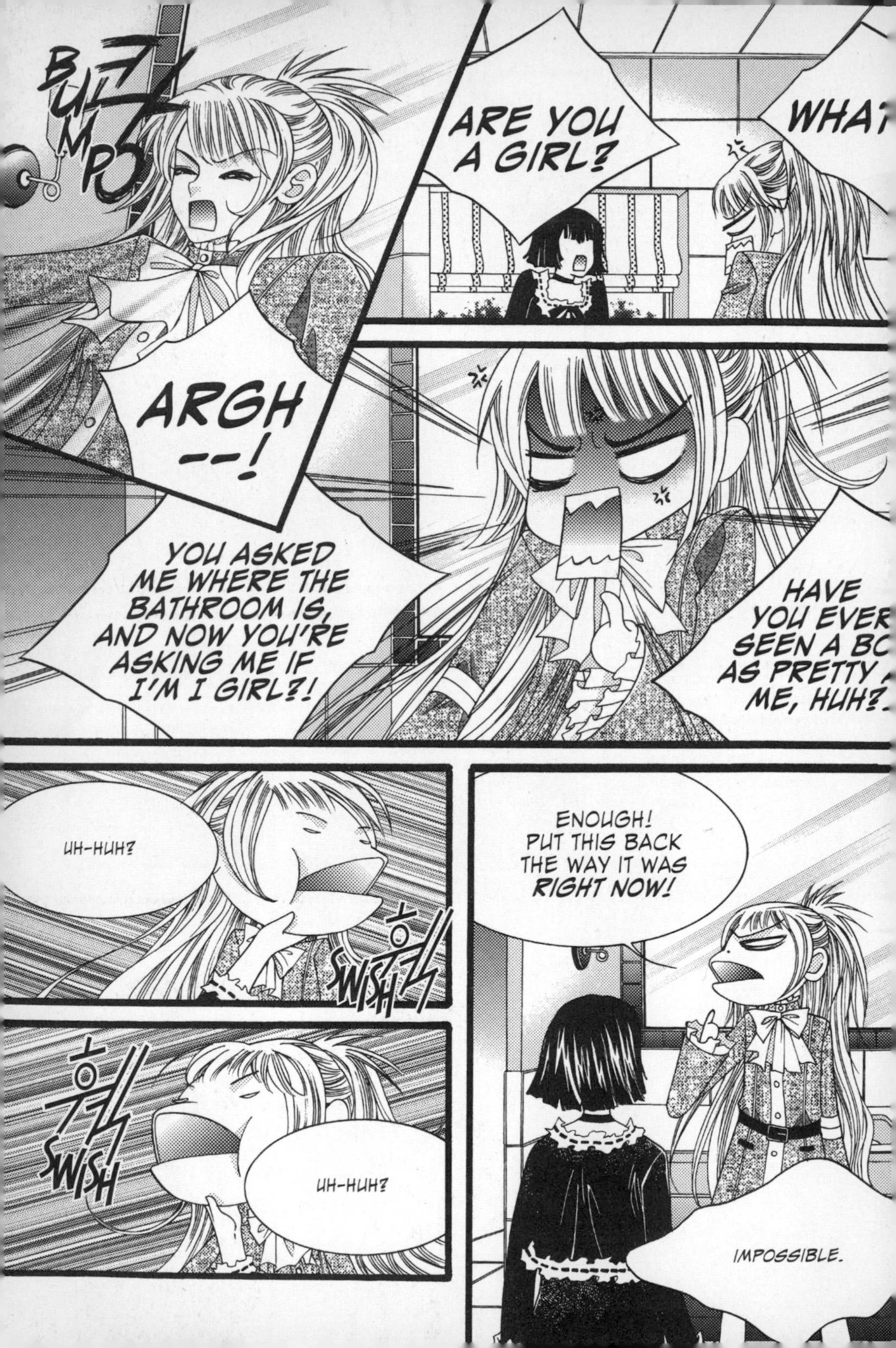
BUMP
ARGH --!
ARE YOU A GIRL?
WHAT
YOU ASKED ME WHERE THE BATHROOM IS, AND NOW YOU'RE ASKING ME IF I'M I GIRL?!
HAVE YOU EVER SEEN A BO AS PRETTY A ME, HUH?!
UH-HUH?
SWISH
SWISH
UH-HUH?
ENOUGH! PUT THIS BACK THE WAY IT WAS RIGHT NOW!
IMPOSSIBLE.

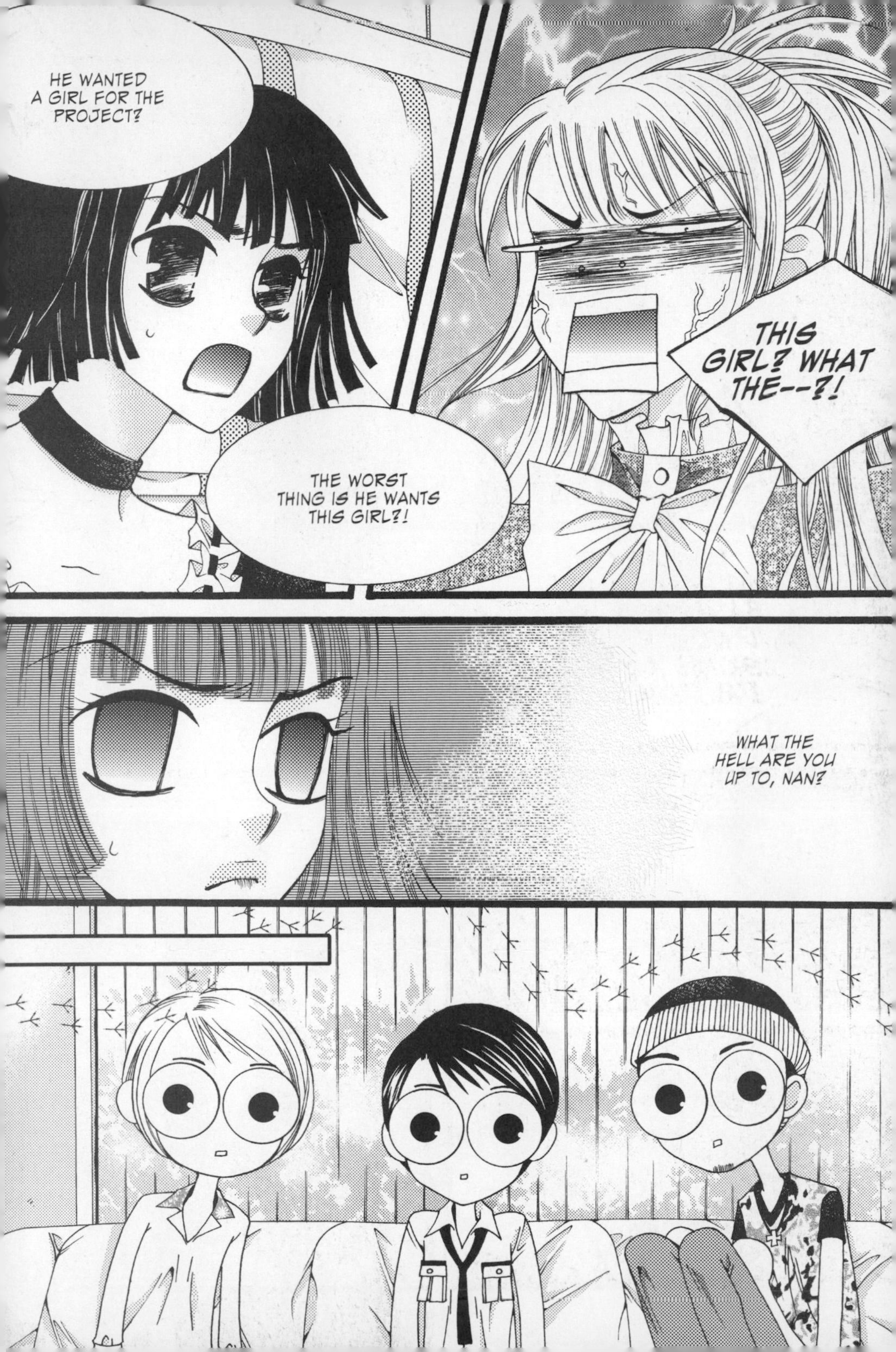
HE WANTED A GIRL FOR THE PROJECT?
THIS GIRL? WHAT THE--?!
THE WORST THING IS HE WANTS THIS GIRL?!
WHAT THE HELL ARE YOU UP TO, NAN?

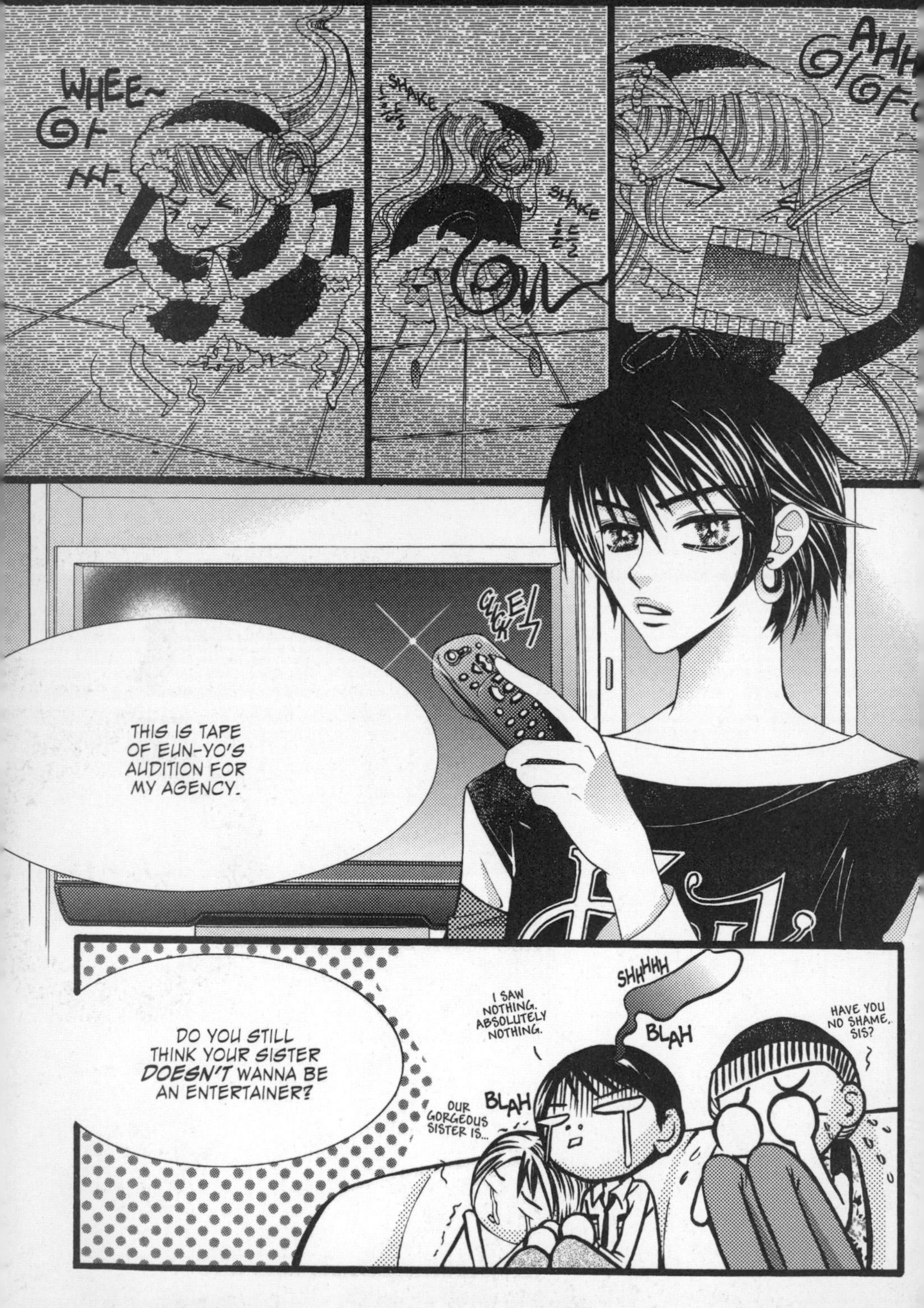
WHEE~
SHAKE
SHAKE
THIS IS TAPE OF EUN-YO'S AUDITION FOR MY AGENCY.
DO YOU STILL THINK YOUR SISTER *DOESN'T* WANNA BE AN ENTERTAINER?
I SAW NOTHING. ABSOLUTELY NOTHING.
SHHHHH
BLAH
HAVE YOU NO SHAME, SIS?
BLAH
OUR GORGEOUS SISTER IS...

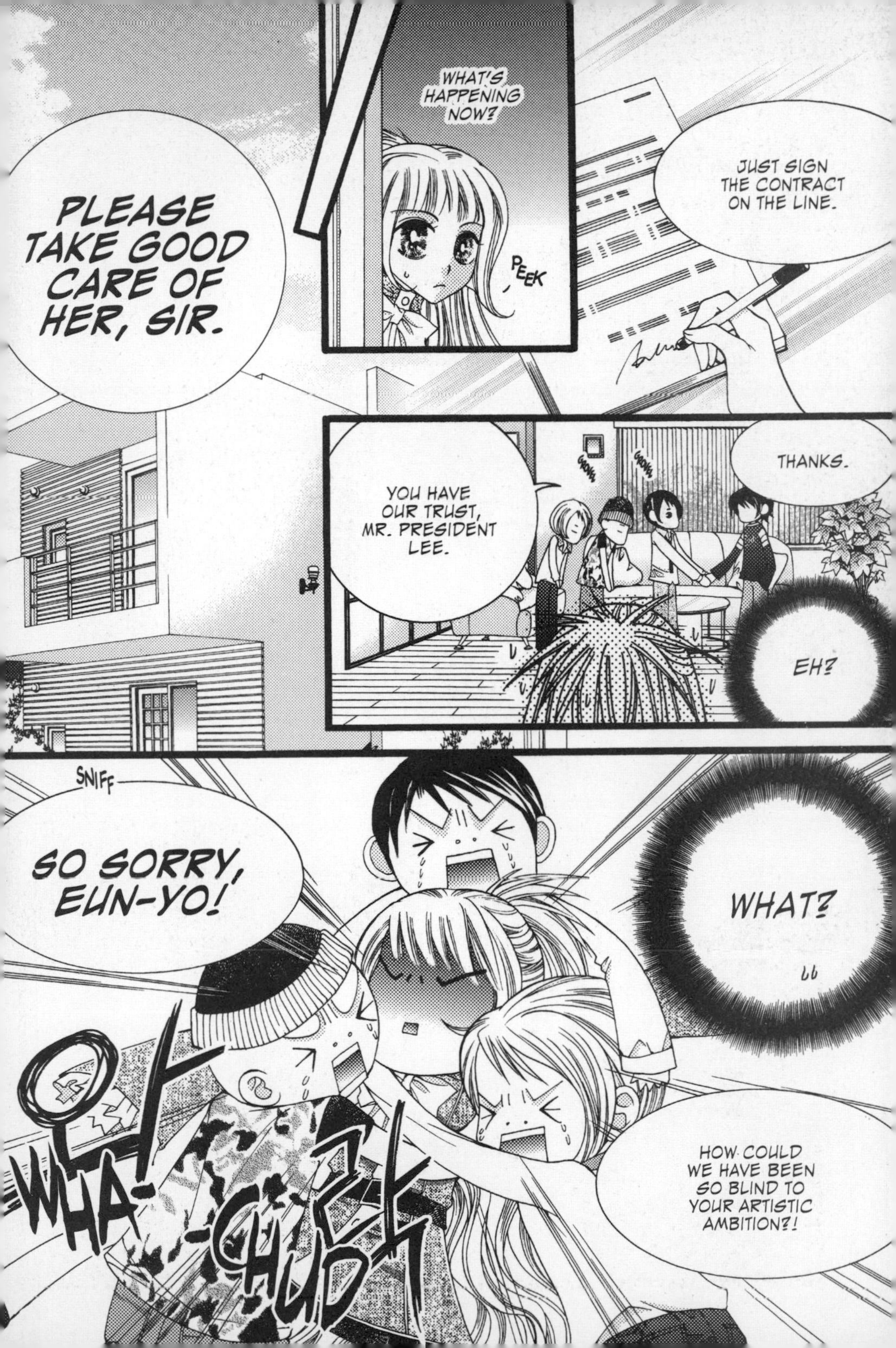
PLEASE TAKE GOOD CARE OF HER, SIR.
WHAT'S HAPPENING NOW?
PEEK
JUST SIGN THE CONTRACT ON THE LINE.
YOU HAVE OUR TRUST, MR. PRESIDENT LEE.
THANKS.
EH?
SNIFF
SO SORRY, EUN-YO!
WHAT?
HOW COULD WE HAVE BEEN SO BLIND TO YOUR ARTISTIC AMBITION?!
WHA-
CHUD

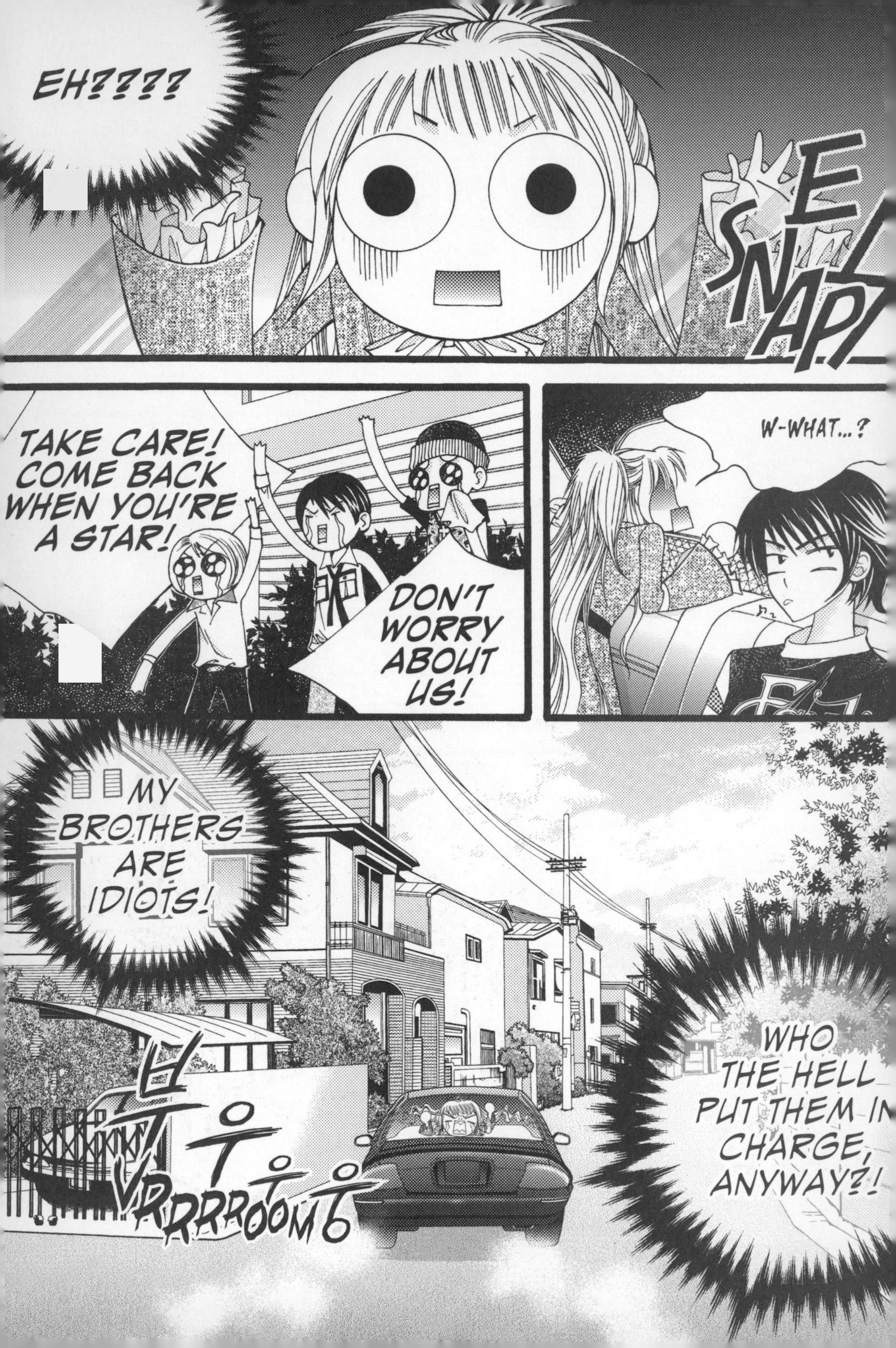
EH????
SNAP!
TAKE CARE! COME BACK WHEN YOU'RE A STAR!
DON'T WORRY ABOUT US!
W-WHAT...?
MY BROTHERS ARE IDIOTS!
WHO THE HELL PUT THEM IN CHARGE, ANYWAY?!
VRRRROOM

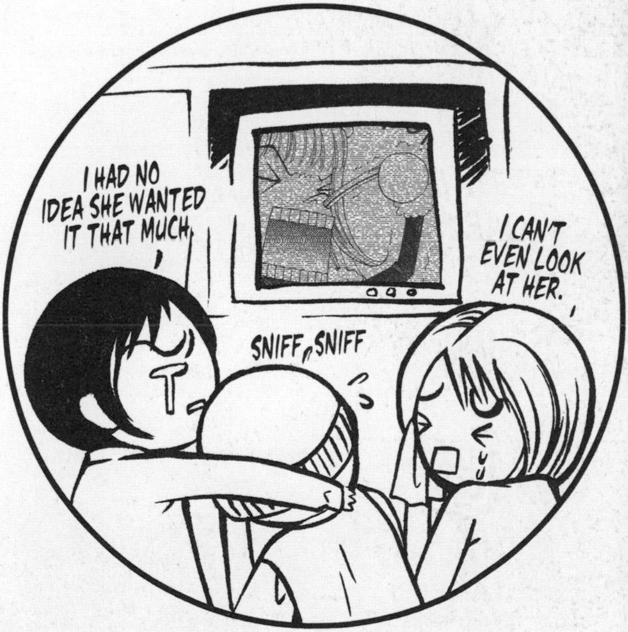
I HAD NO IDEA SHE WANTED IT THAT MUCH.
SNIFF, SNIFF
I CAN'T EVEN LOOK AT HER.

STAR PROJECT
CHIRO 치로

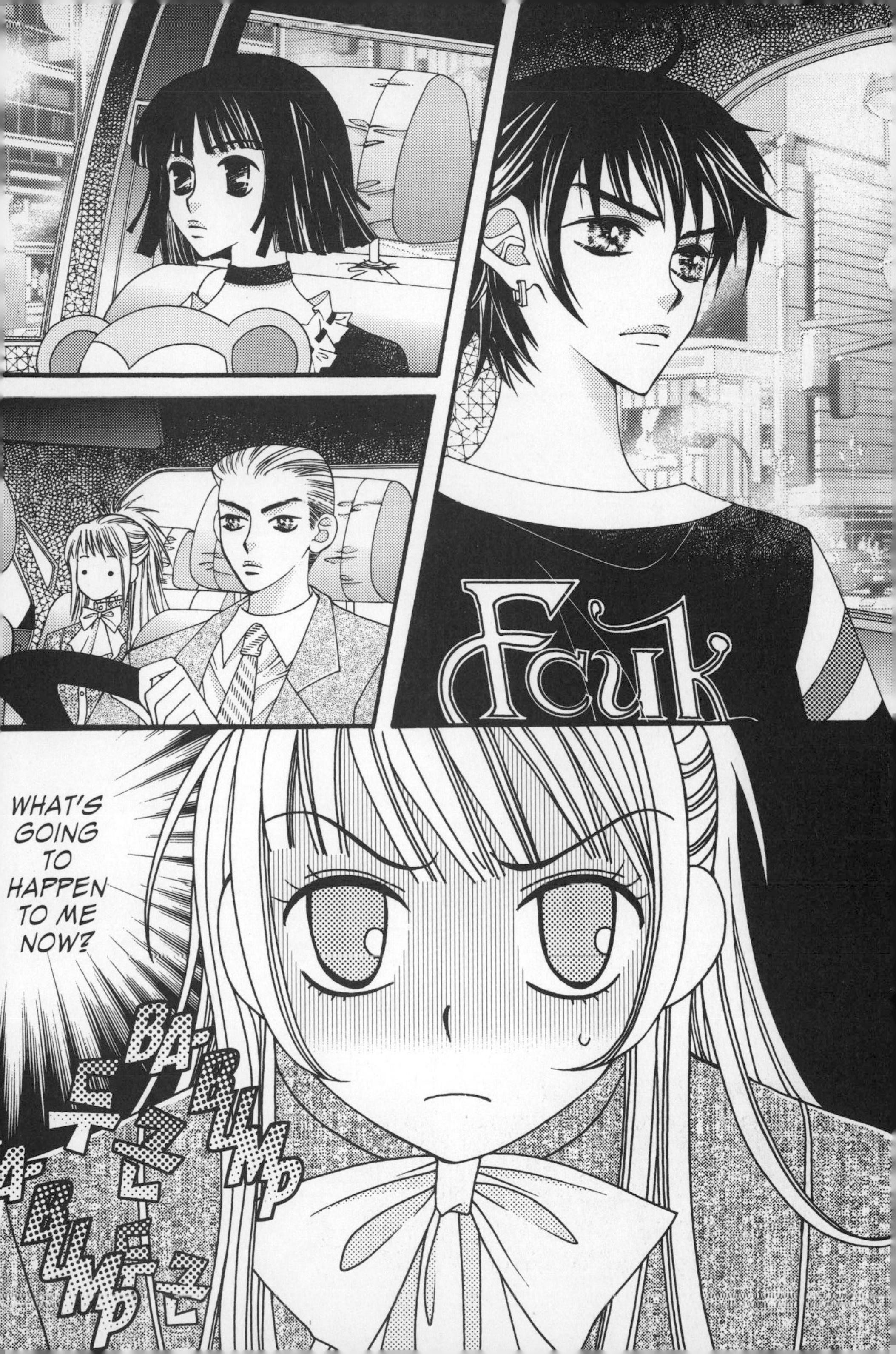
Fcuk
WHAT'S GOING TO HAPPEN TO ME NOW?
BA-BUMP

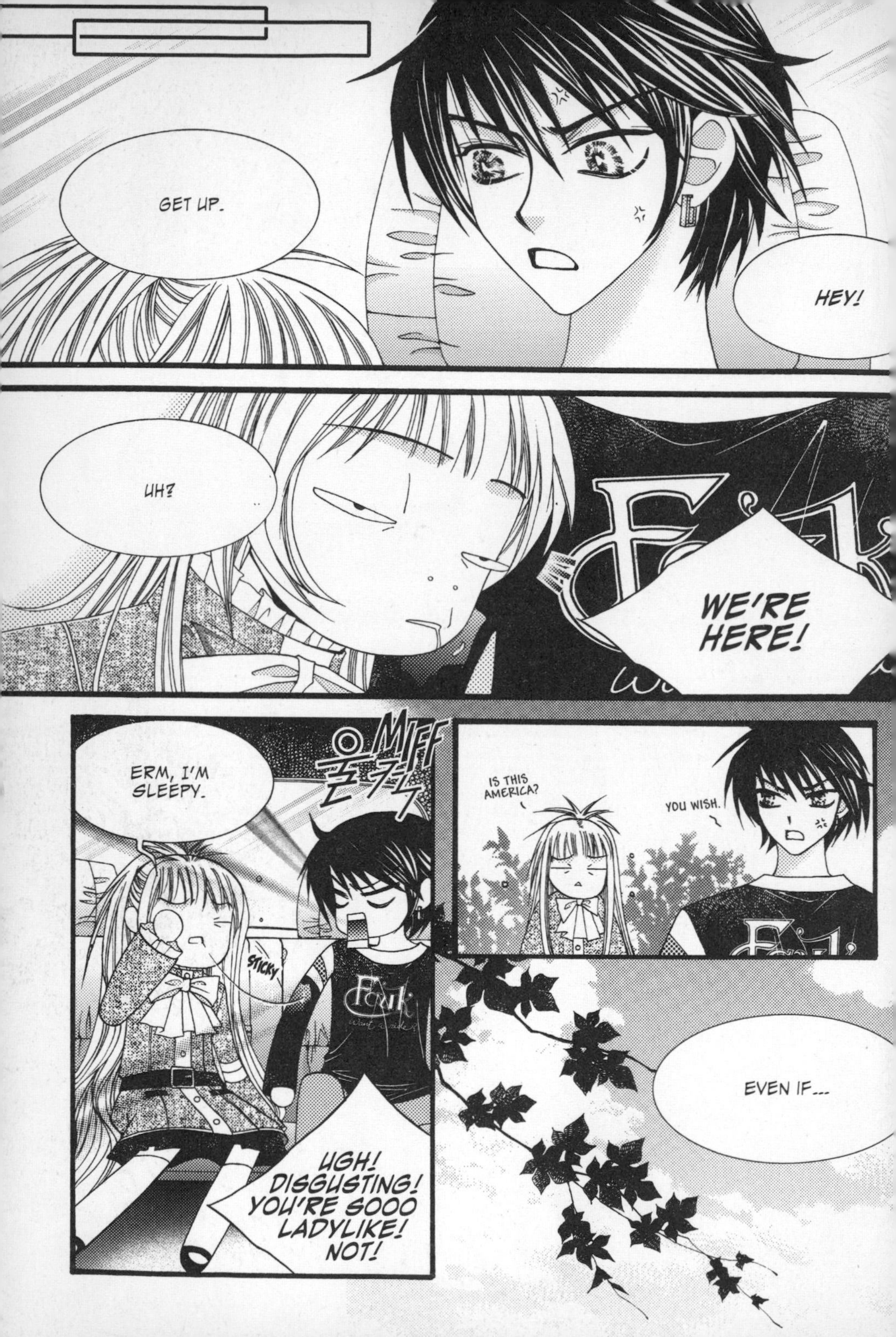
HEY!
GET UP.
UH?
WE'RE HERE!
ERM, I'M SLEEPY.
MIFF
STICKY
UGH! DISGUSTING! YOU'RE SOOO LADYLIKE! NOT!
IS THIS AMERICA?
YOU WISH.
EVEN IF...

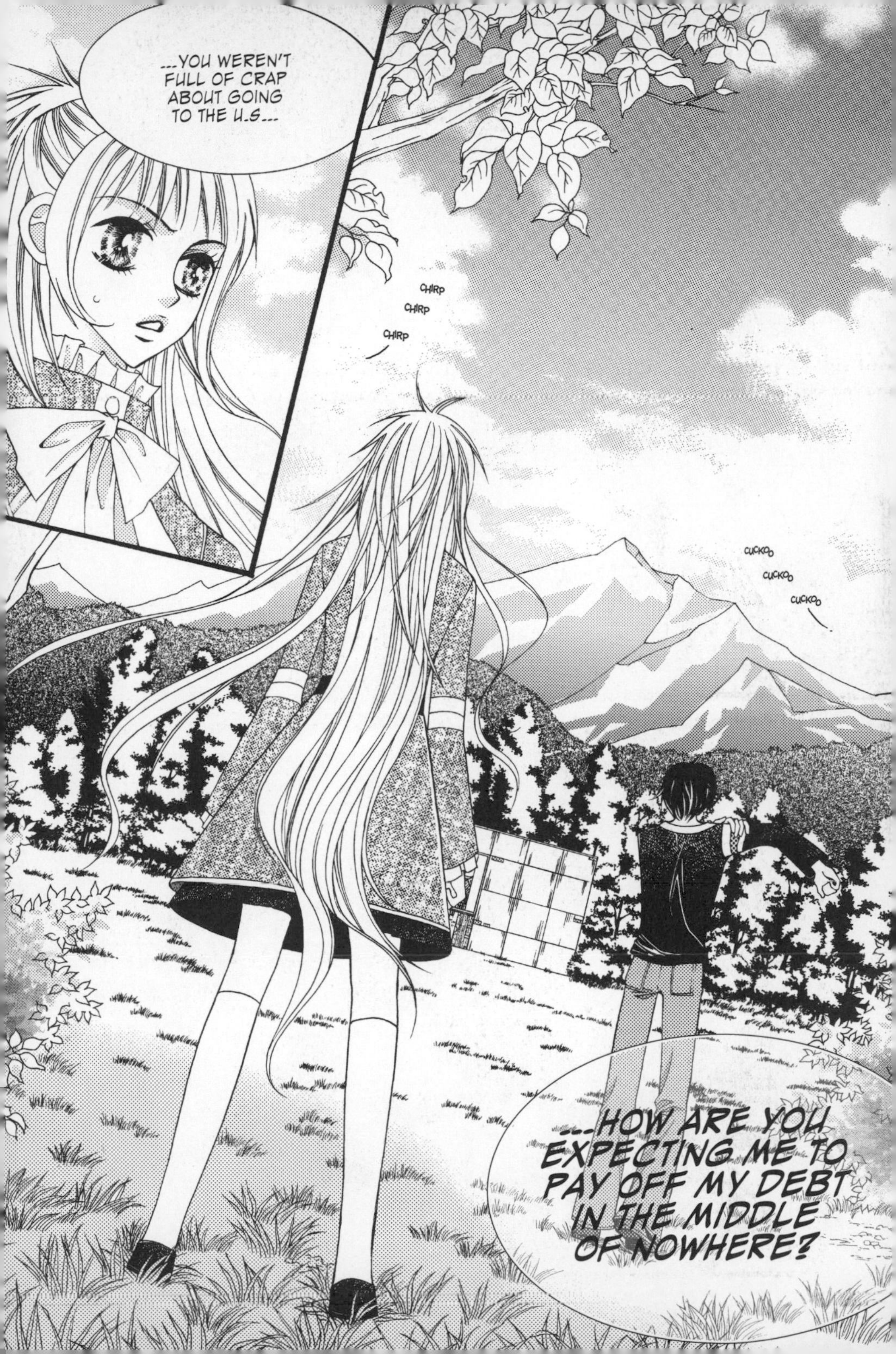
...YOU WEREN'T FULL OF CRAP ABOUT GOING TO THE U.S...
CHIRP
CHIRP
CHIRP
CUCKOO
CUCKOO
CUCKOO
...HOW ARE YOU EXPECTING ME TO PAY OFF MY DEBT IN THE MIDDLE OF NOWHERE?

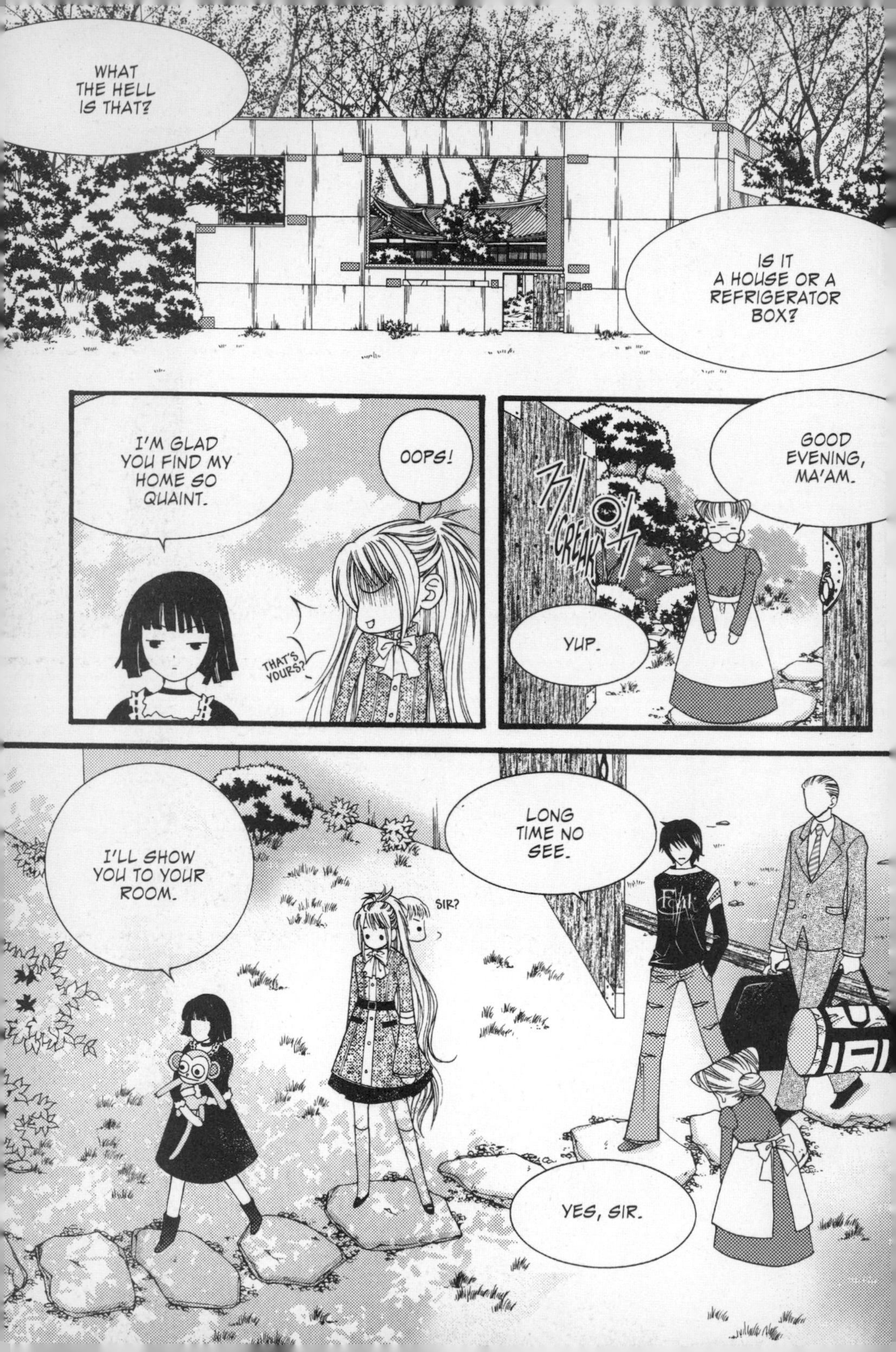
WHAT THE HELL IS THAT?
IS IT A HOUSE OR A REFRIGERATOR BOX?
I'M GLAD YOU FIND MY HOME SO QUAINT.
OOPS!
THAT'S YOURS?
CREAK
GOOD EVENING, MA'AM.
YUP.
I'LL SHOW YOU TO YOUR ROOM.
SIR?
LONG TIME NO SEE.
YES, SIR.

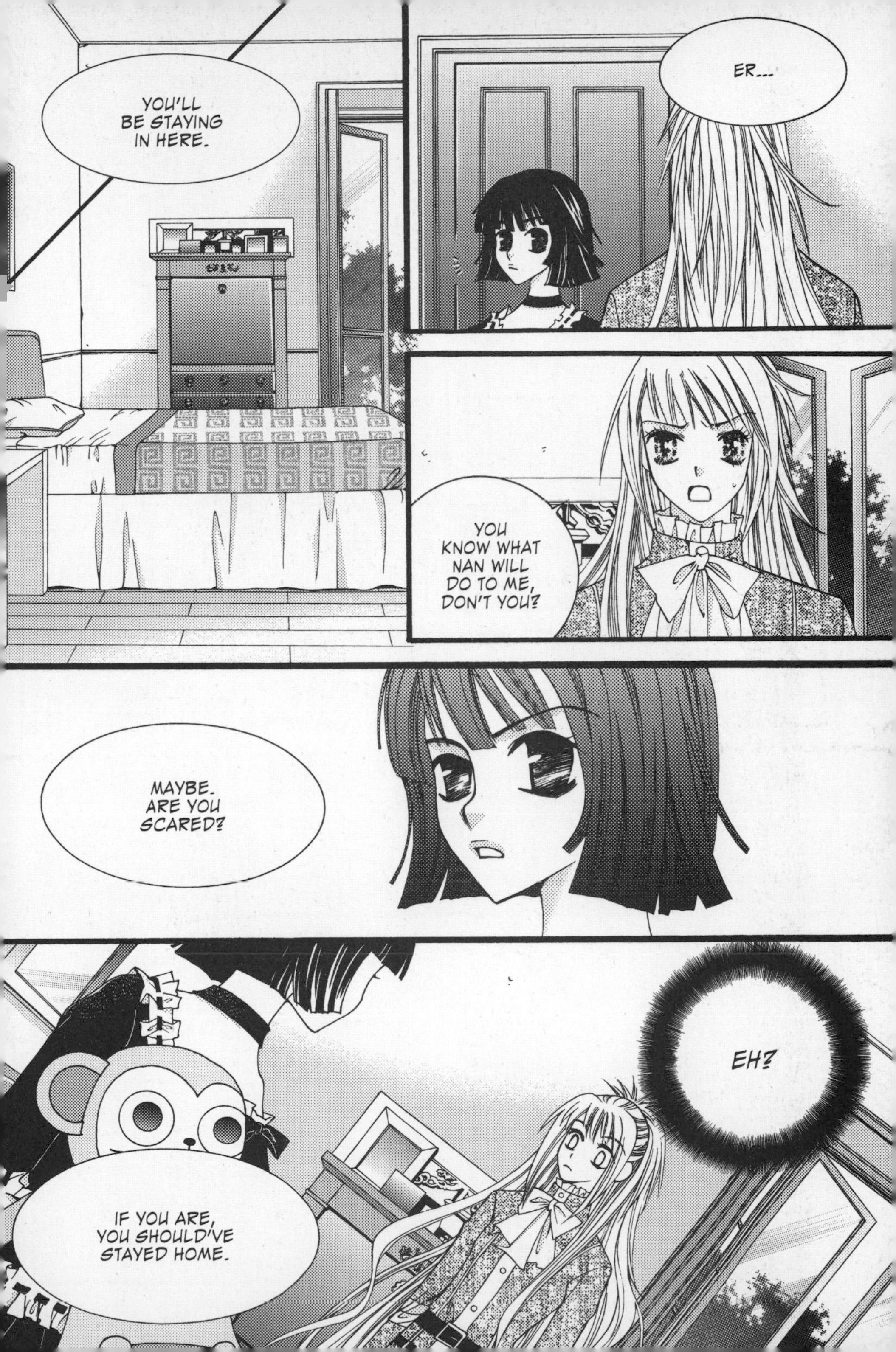
YOU'LL BE STAYING IN HERE.
ER...
YOU KNOW WHAT NAN WILL DO TO ME, DON'T YOU?
MAYBE. ARE YOU SCARED?
IF YOU ARE, YOU SHOULD'VE STAYED HOME.
EH?

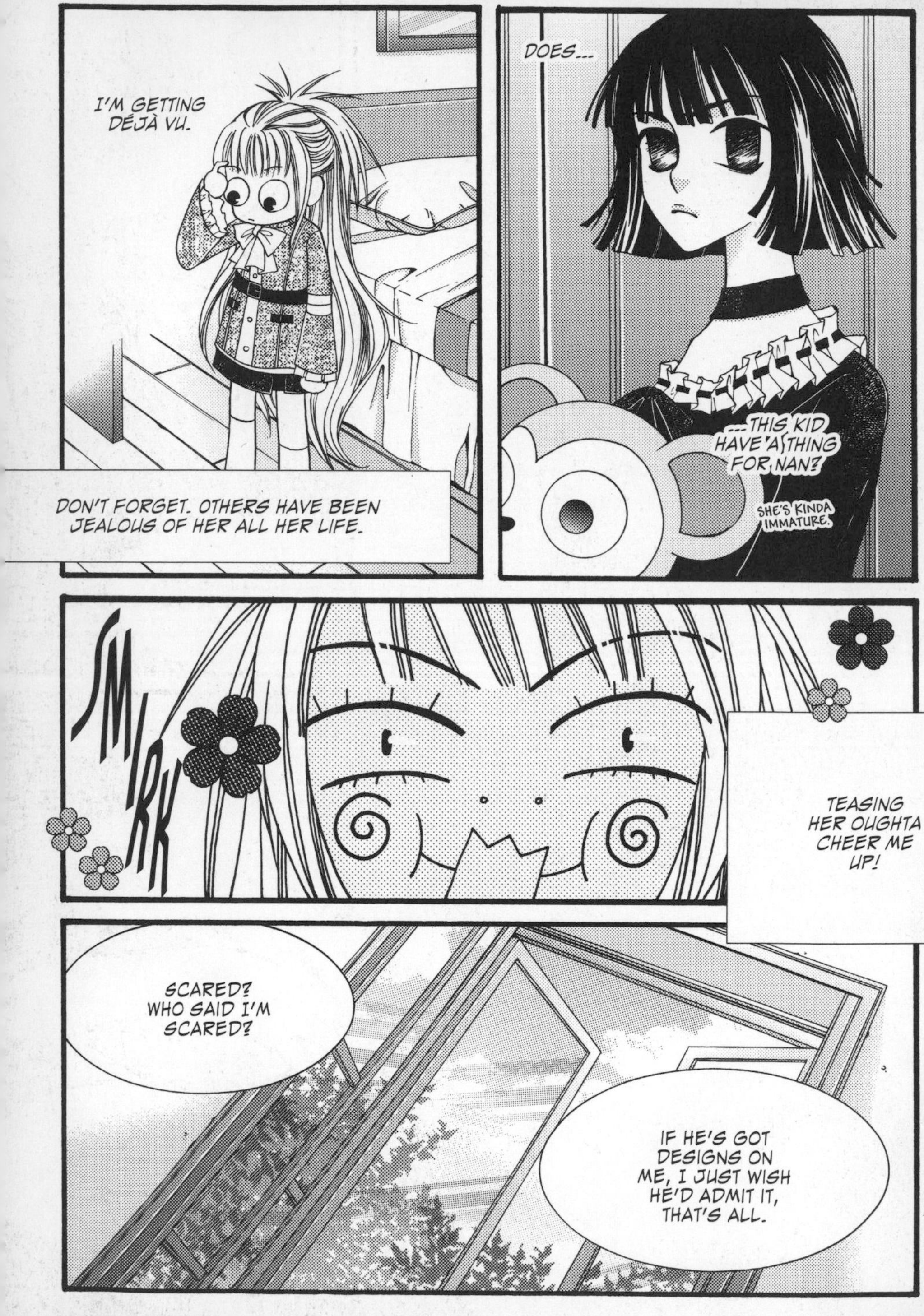
DOES...
I'M GETTING DÉJÀ VU.
...THIS KID HAVE A THING FOR NAN?
SHE'S KINDA IMMATURE.
DON'T FORGET. OTHERS HAVE BEEN JEALOUS OF HER ALL HER LIFE.
TEASING HER OUGHTA CHEER ME UP!
SMIRK
SCARED? WHO SAID I'M SCARED?
IF HE'S GOT DESIGNS ON ME, I JUST WISH HE'D ADMIT IT, THAT'S ALL.

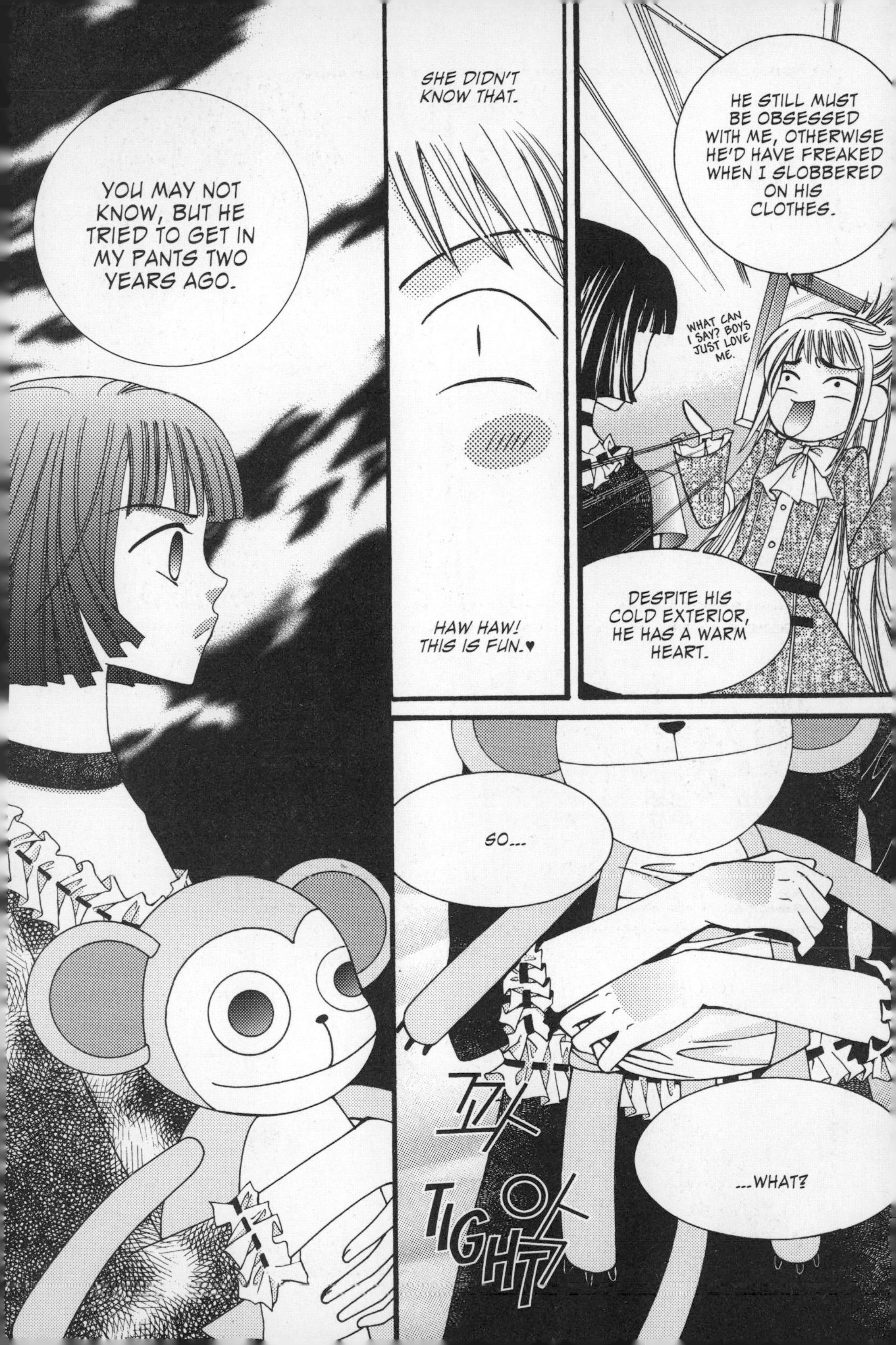
HE STILL MUST BE OBSESSED WITH ME, OTHERWISE HE'D HAVE FREAKED WHEN I SLOBBERED ON HIS CLOTHES.
WHAT CAN I SAY? BOYS JUST LOVE ME.
DESPITE HIS COLD EXTERIOR, HE HAS A WARM HEART.
SHE DIDN'T KNOW THAT.
HAW HAW! THIS IS FUN.♥
SO...
...WHAT?
TIGHT
YOU MAY NOT KNOW, BUT HE TRIED TO GET IN MY PANTS TWO YEARS AGO.

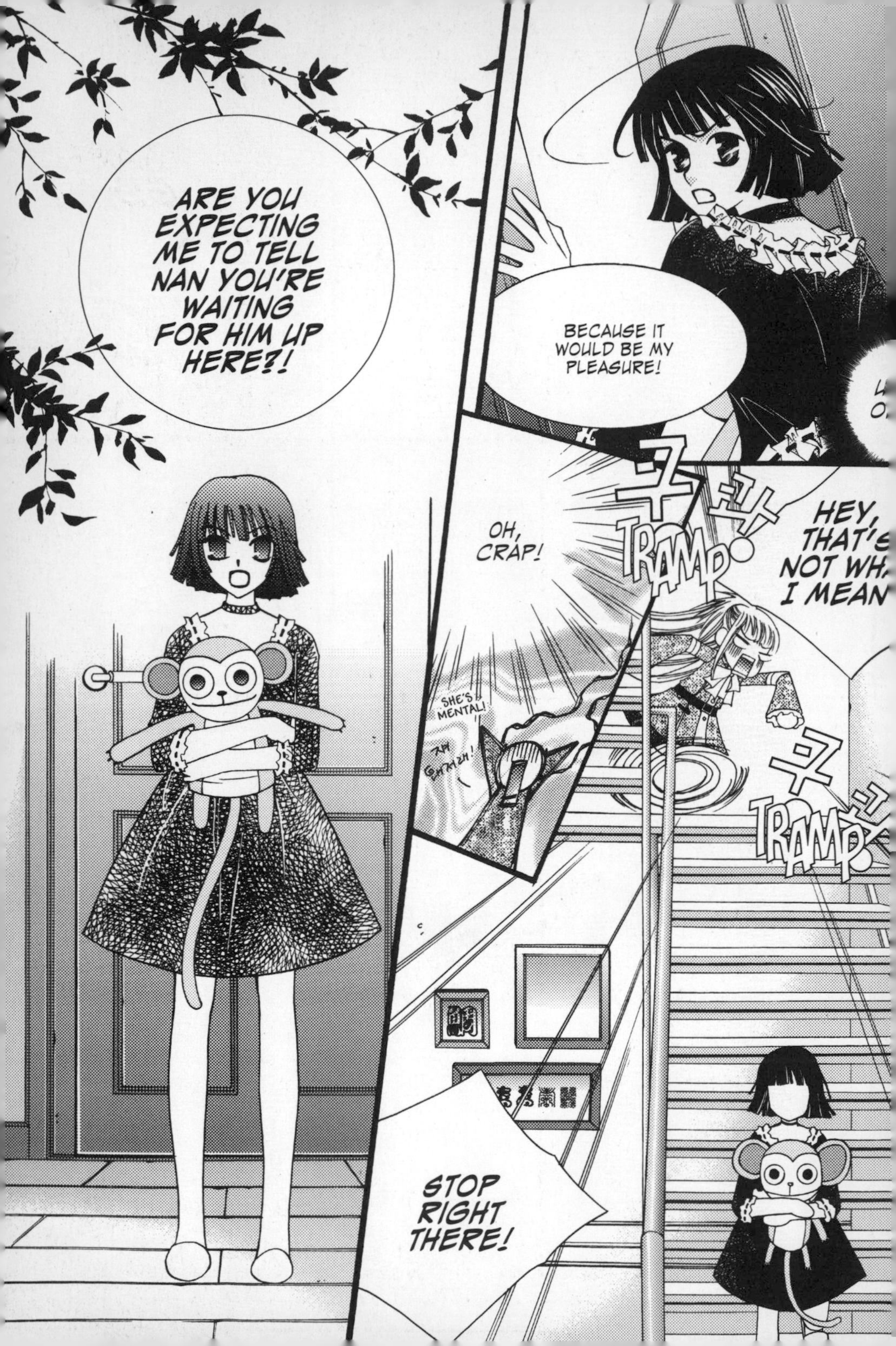

ARE YOU EXPECTING ME TO TELL NAN YOU'RE WAITING FOR HIM UP HERE?!
BECAUSE IT WOULD BE MY PLEASURE!
HEY, THAT'S NOT WHA I MEAN
TRAMP!
OH, CRAP!
SHE'S MENTAL!
TRAMP
STOP RIGHT THERE!

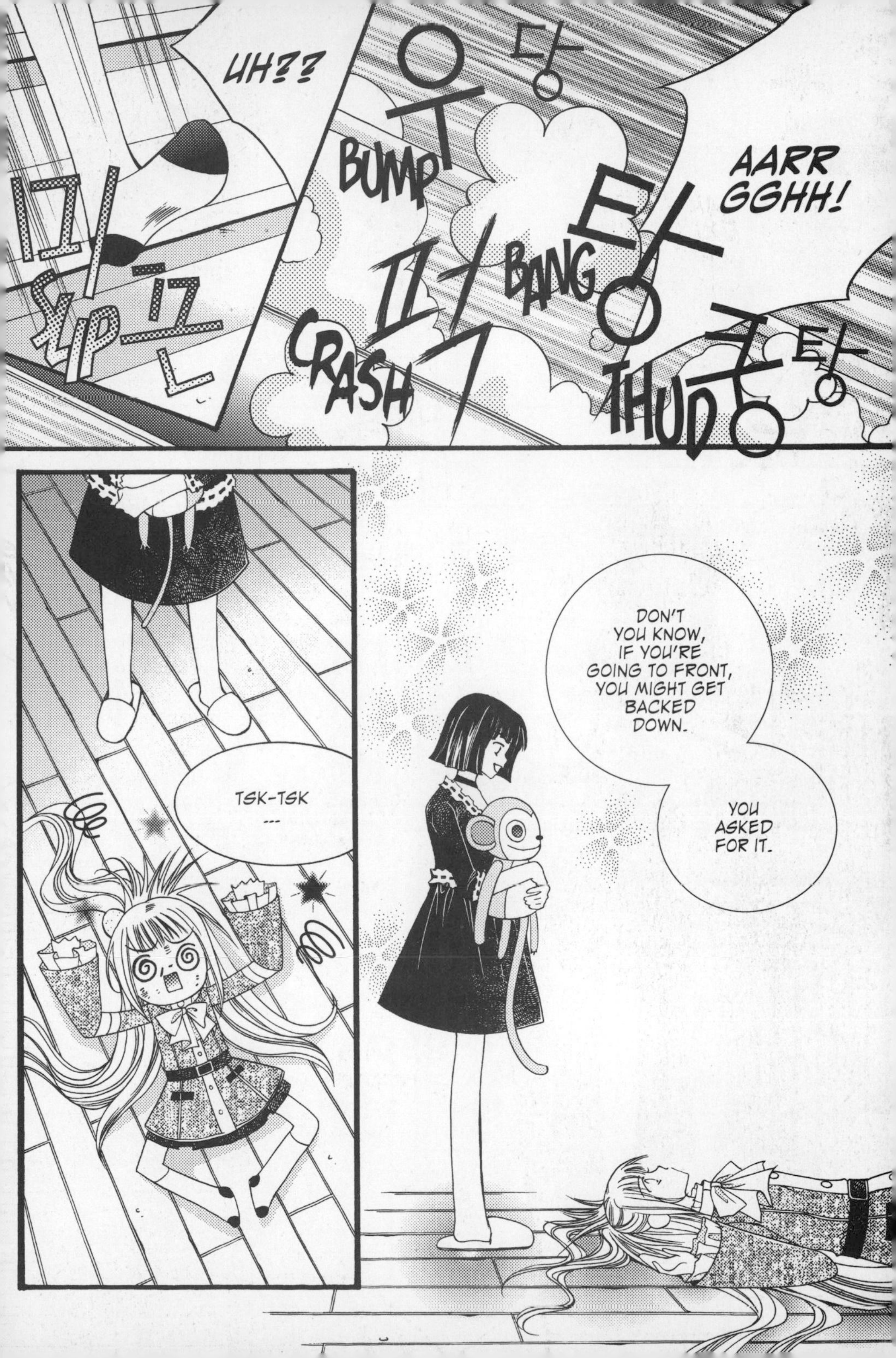
UH??
SLIP
BUMP
CRASH
BANG
AARR GGHH!
THUD
TSK-TSK ---
DON'T YOU KNOW, IF YOU'RE GOING TO FRONT, YOU MIGHT GET BACKED DOWN.
YOU ASKED FOR IT.

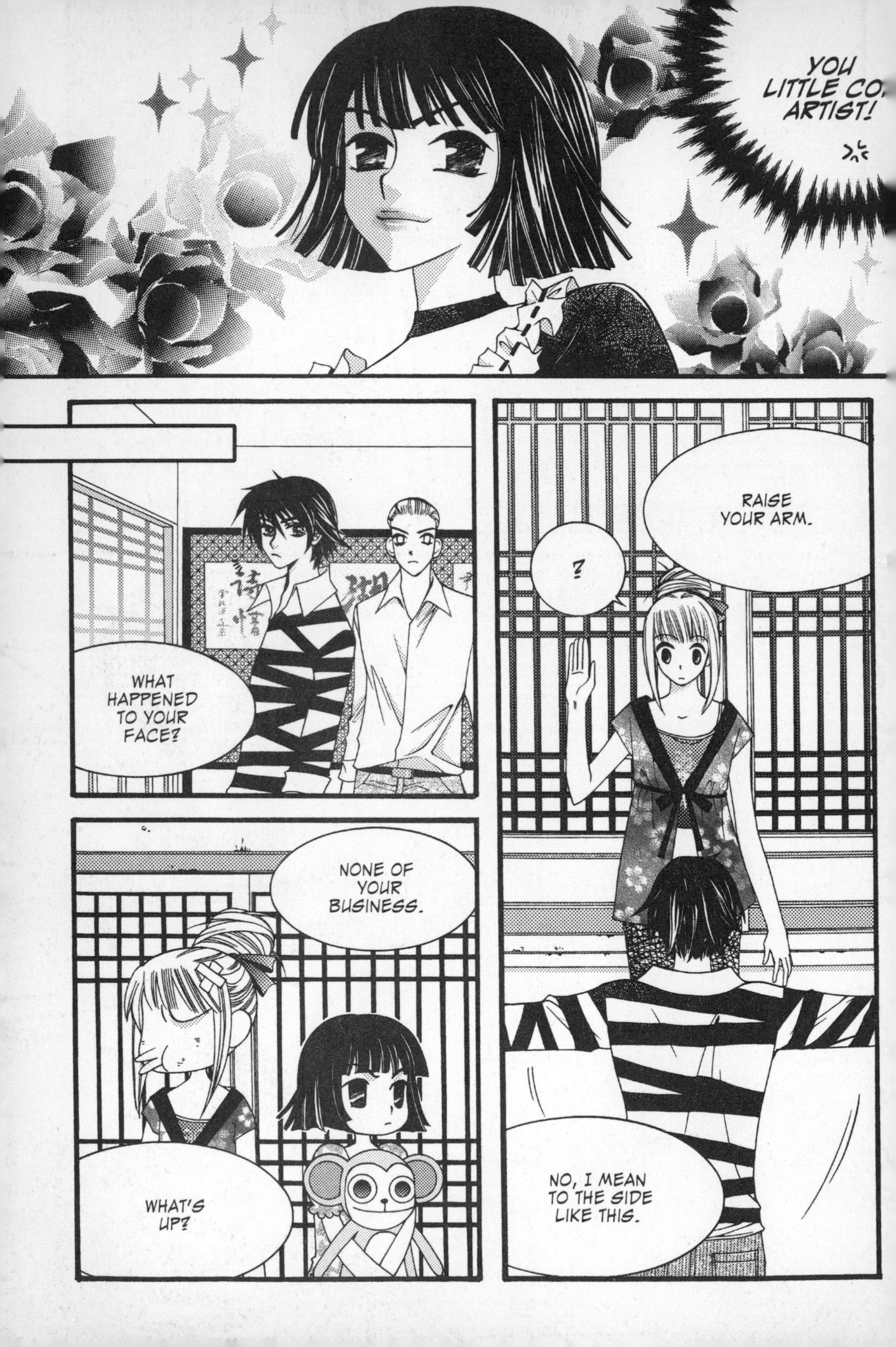
YOU LITTLE CO ARTIST!
WHAT HAPPENED TO YOUR FACE?
NONE OF YOUR BUSINESS.
WHAT'S UP?
?
RAISE YOUR ARM.
NO, I MEAN TO THE SIDE LIKE THIS.

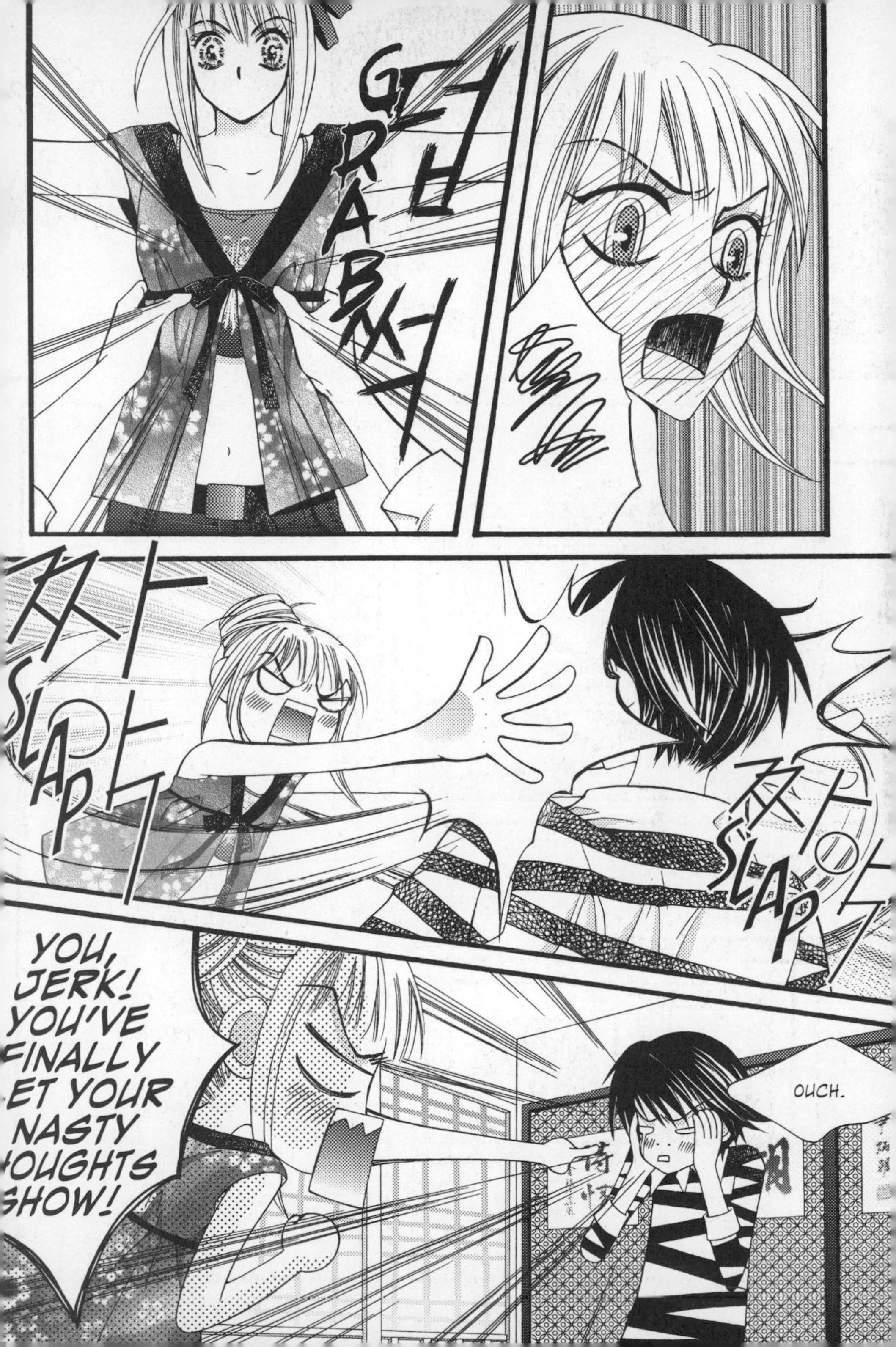
GRAB
SLAP
SLAP
OUCH.
YOU, JERK! YOU'VE FINALLY ET YOUR NASTY OUGHTS SHOW!

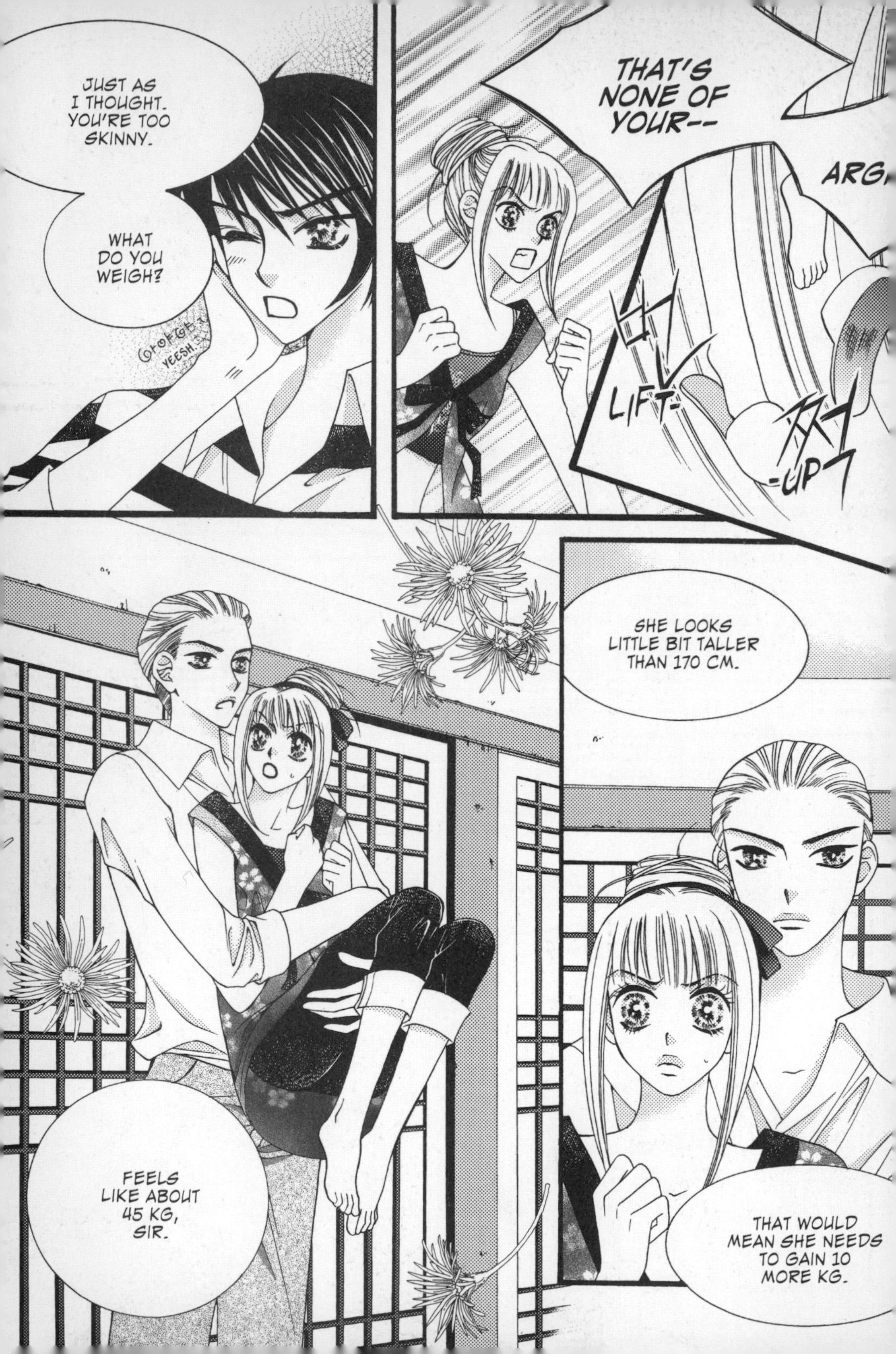
JUST AS I THOUGHT. YOU'RE TOO SKINNY.
WHAT DO YOU WEIGH?
YEESH.
THAT'S NONE OF YOUR--
ARG
LIFT-
-UP
FEELS LIKE ABOUT 45 KG, SIR.
SHE LOOKS LITTLE BIT TALLER THAN 170 CM.
THAT WOULD MEAN SHE NEEDS TO GAIN 10 MORE KG.

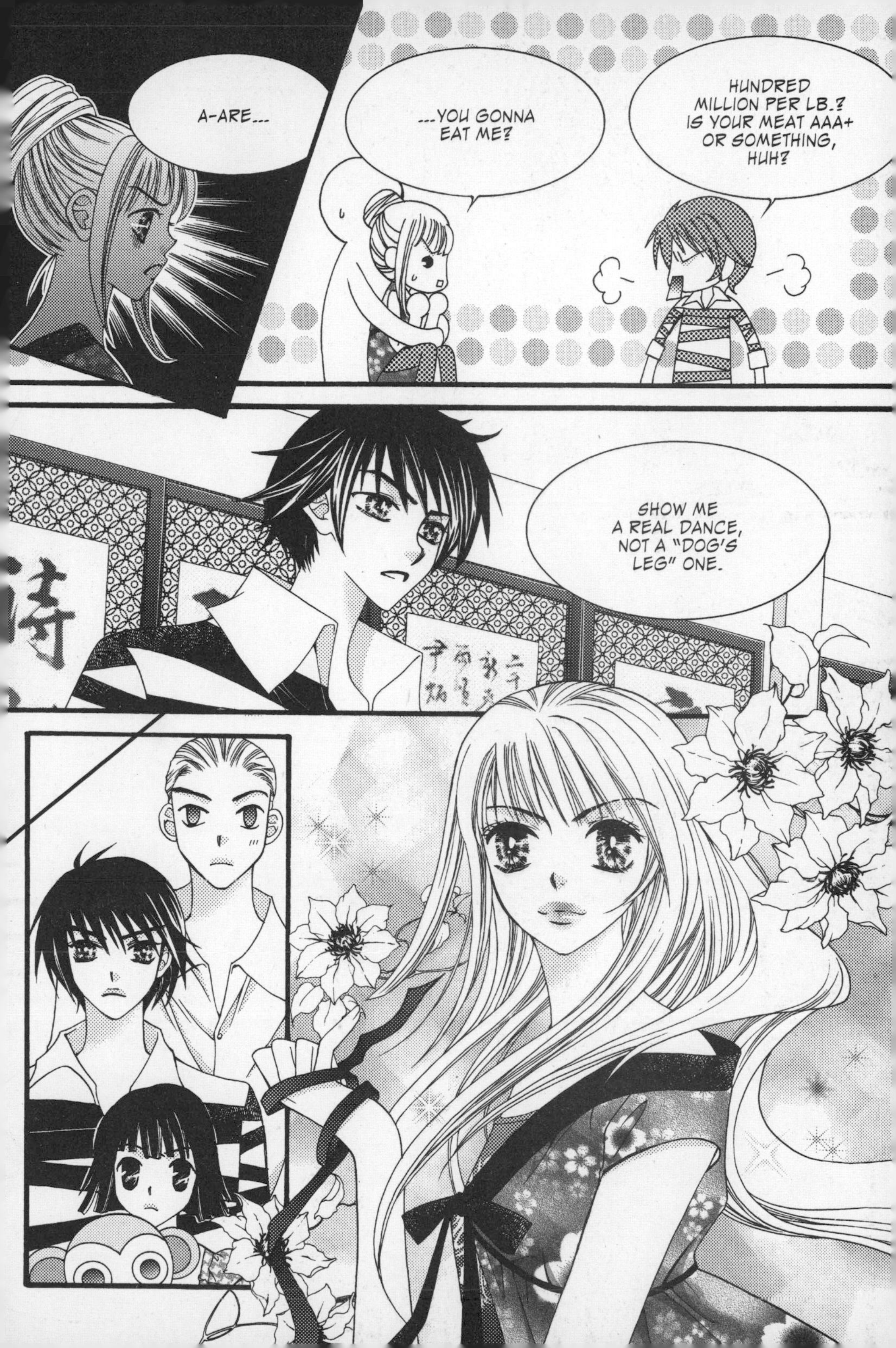
A-ARE...
...YOU GONNA EAT ME?
HUNDRED MILLION PER LB.? IS YOUR MEAT AAA+ OR SOMETHING, HUH?
SHOW ME A REAL DANCE, NOT A "DOG'S LEG" ONE.
詩

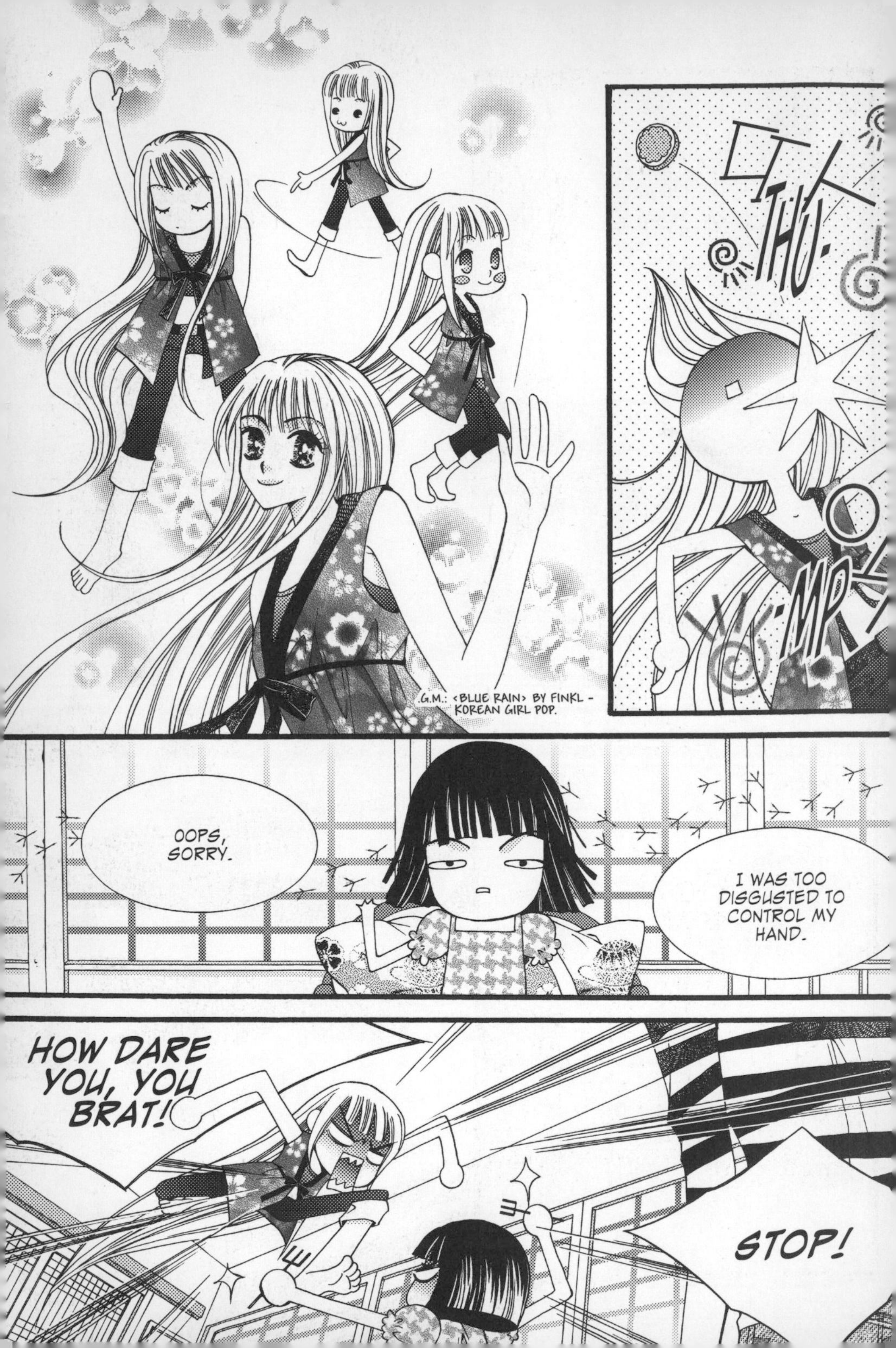
G.M.: <BLUE RAIN> BY FINKL - KOREAN GIRL POP.
THU-
-MP
OOPS, SORRY.
I WAS TOO DISGUSTED TO CONTROL MY HAND.
HOW DARE YOU, YOU BRAT!
STOP!

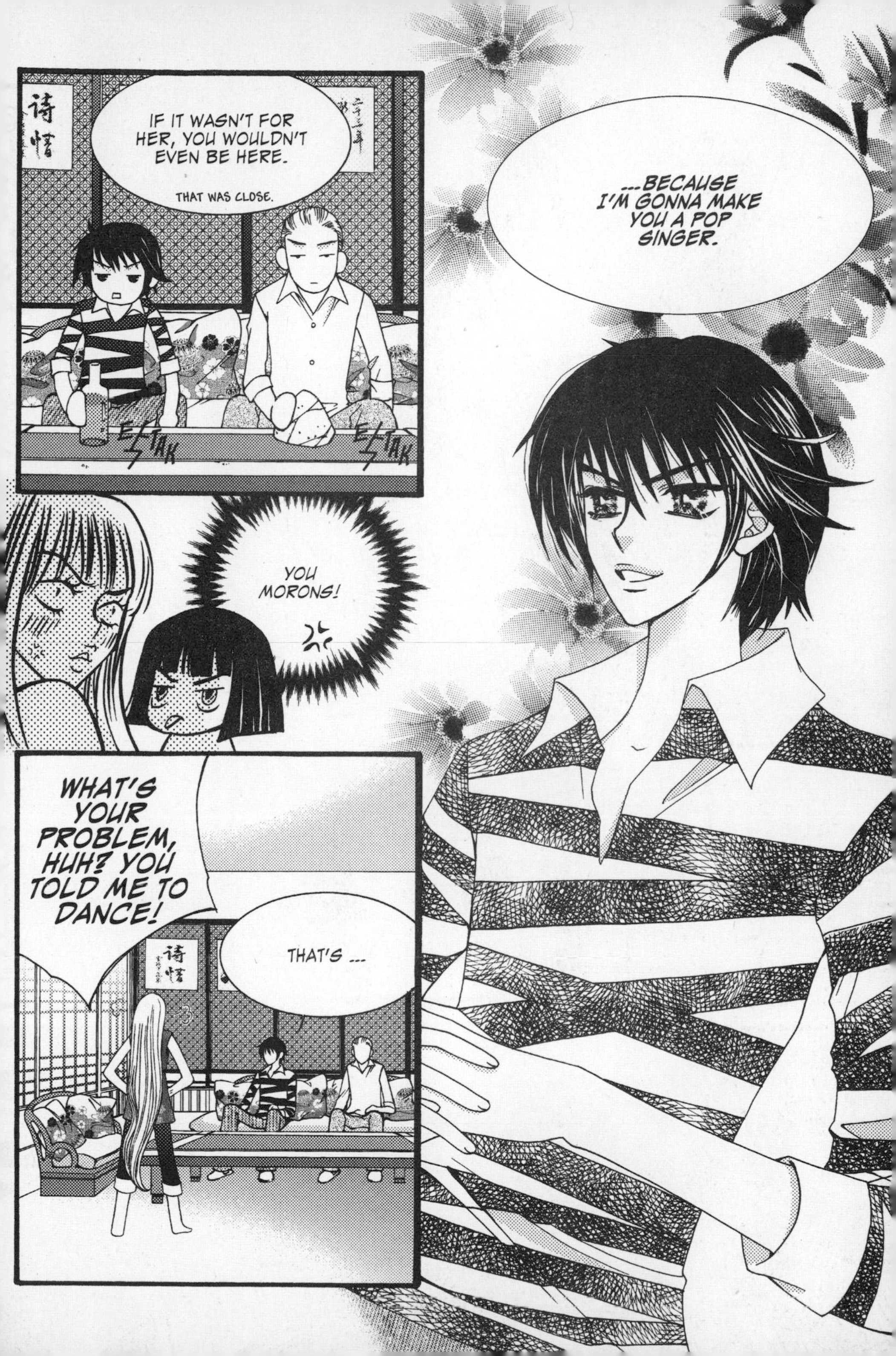

詩情
IF IT WASN'T FOR HER, YOU WOULDN'T EVEN BE HERE.
THAT WAS CLOSE.
YOU MORONS!
WHAT'S YOUR PROBLEM, HUH? YOU TOLD ME TO DANCE!
THAT'S ...
...BECAUSE I'M GONNA MAKE YOU A POP SINGER.

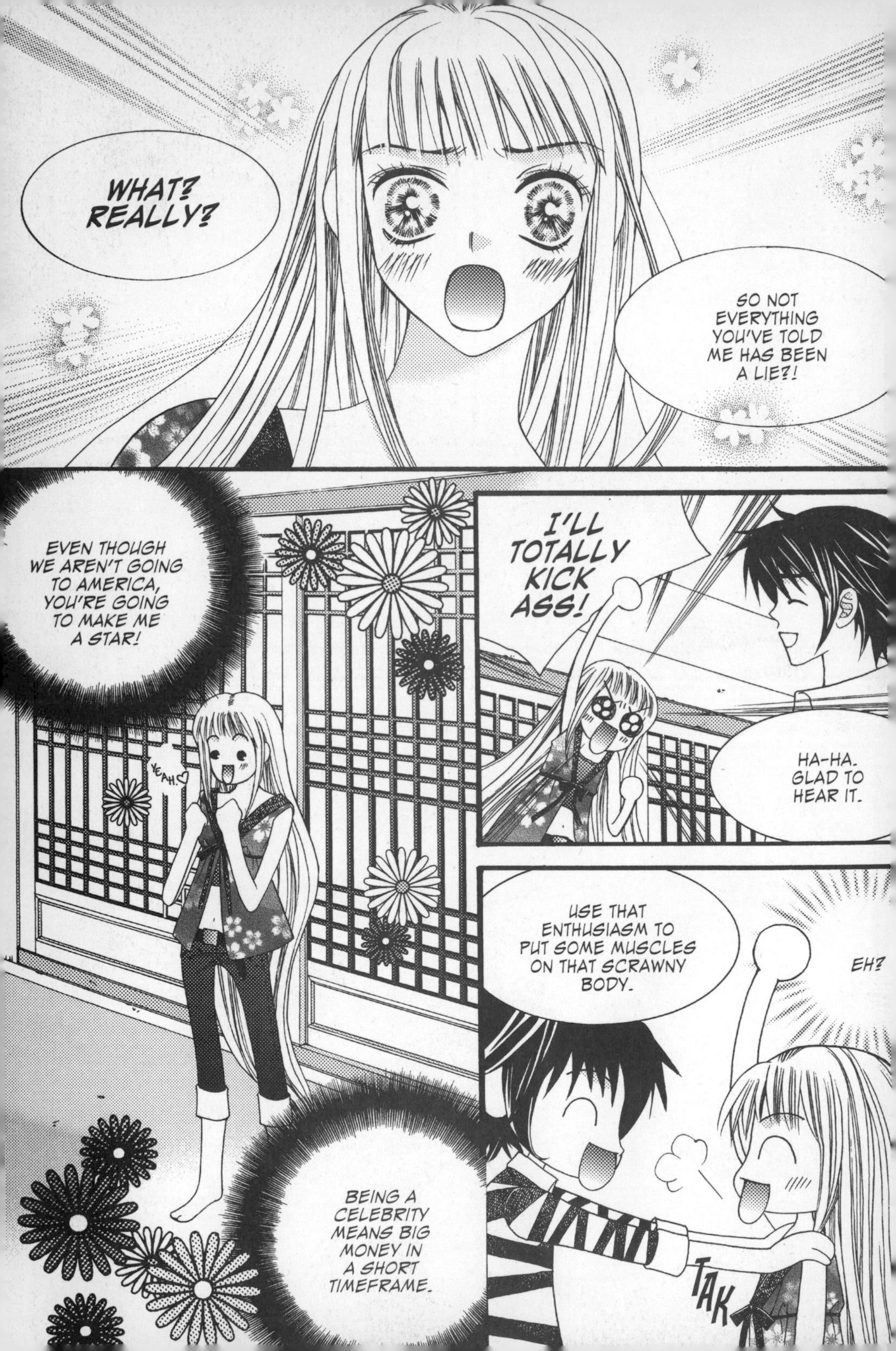
WHAT? REALLY?
SO NOT EVERYTHING YOU'VE TOLD ME HAS BEEN A LIE?!
EVEN THOUGH WE AREN'T GOING TO AMERICA, YOU'RE GOING TO MAKE ME A STAR!
YEAH.♡
BEING A CELEBRITY MEANS BIG MONEY IN A SHORT TIMEFRAME.
I'LL TOTALLY KICK ASS!
HA-HA. GLAD TO HEAR IT.
USE THAT ENTHUSIASM TO PUT SOME MUSCLES ON THAT SCRAWNY BODY.
EH?
TAK

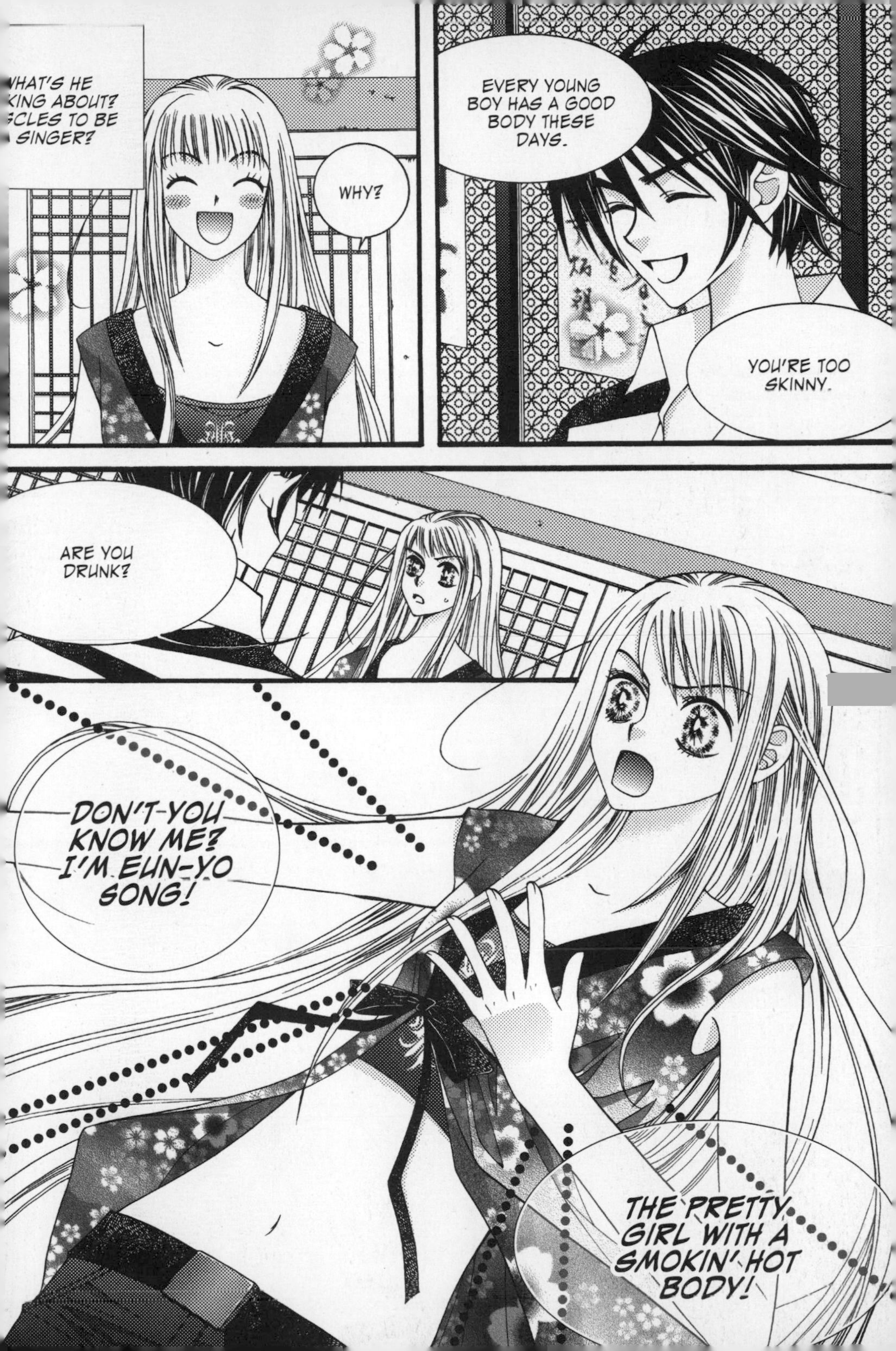
WHAT'S HE KING ABOUT? GCLES TO BE SINGER?
WHY?
EVERY YOUNG BOY HAS A GOOD BODY THESE DAYS.
YOU'RE TOO SKINNY.
ARE YOU DRUNK?
DON'T-YOU KNOW ME? I'M EUN-YO SONG!
THE PRETTY GIRL WITH A SMOKIN' HOT BODY!

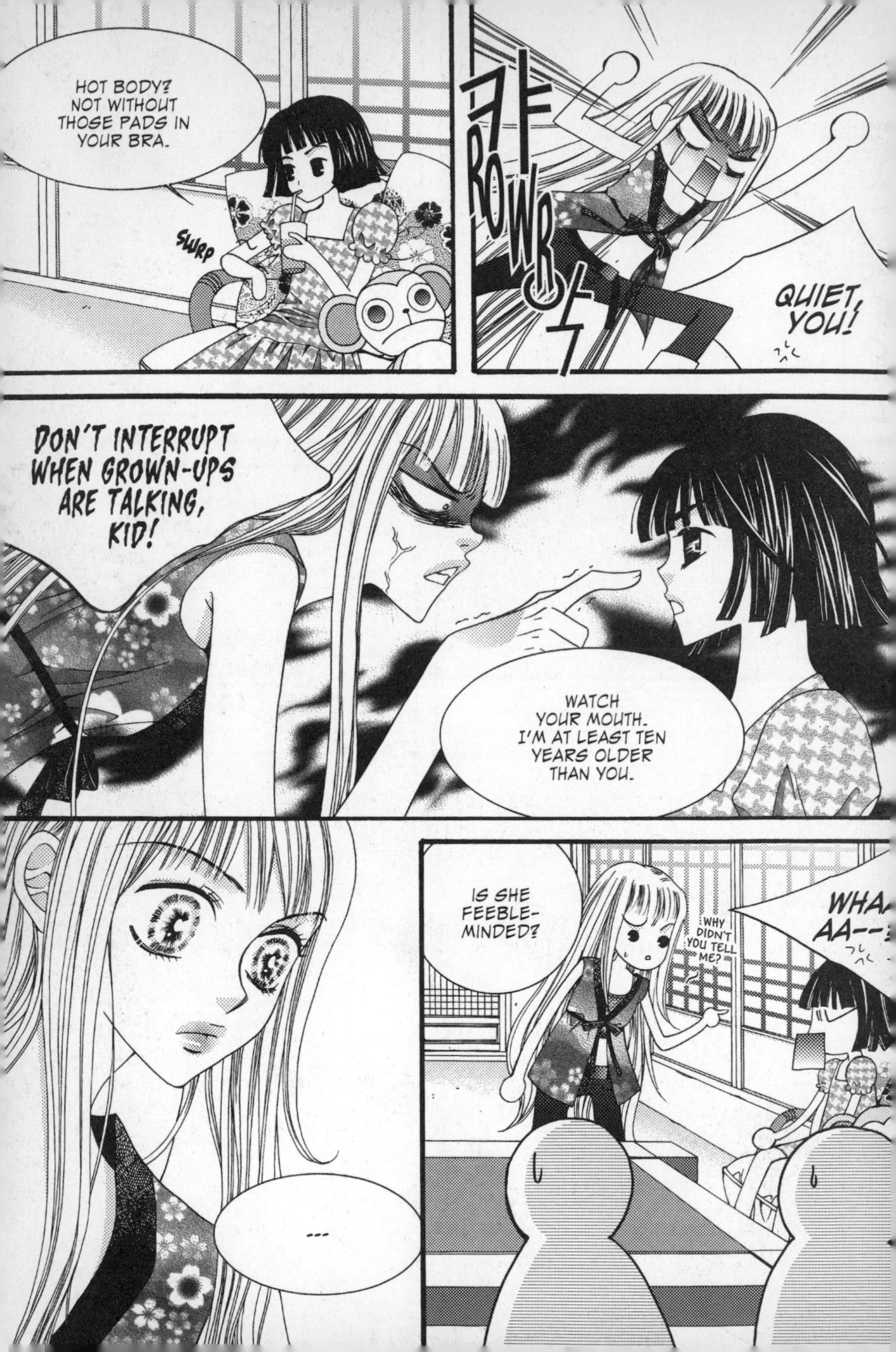
HOT BODY? NOT WITHOUT THOSE PADS IN YOUR BRA.
SLURP
QUIET, YOU!
DON'T INTERRUPT WHEN GROWN-UPS ARE TALKING, KID!
WATCH YOUR MOUTH. I'M AT LEAST TEN YEARS OLDER THAN YOU.
...
IS SHE FEEBLE-MINDED?
WHY DIDN'T YOU TELL ME?
WHAA AA--

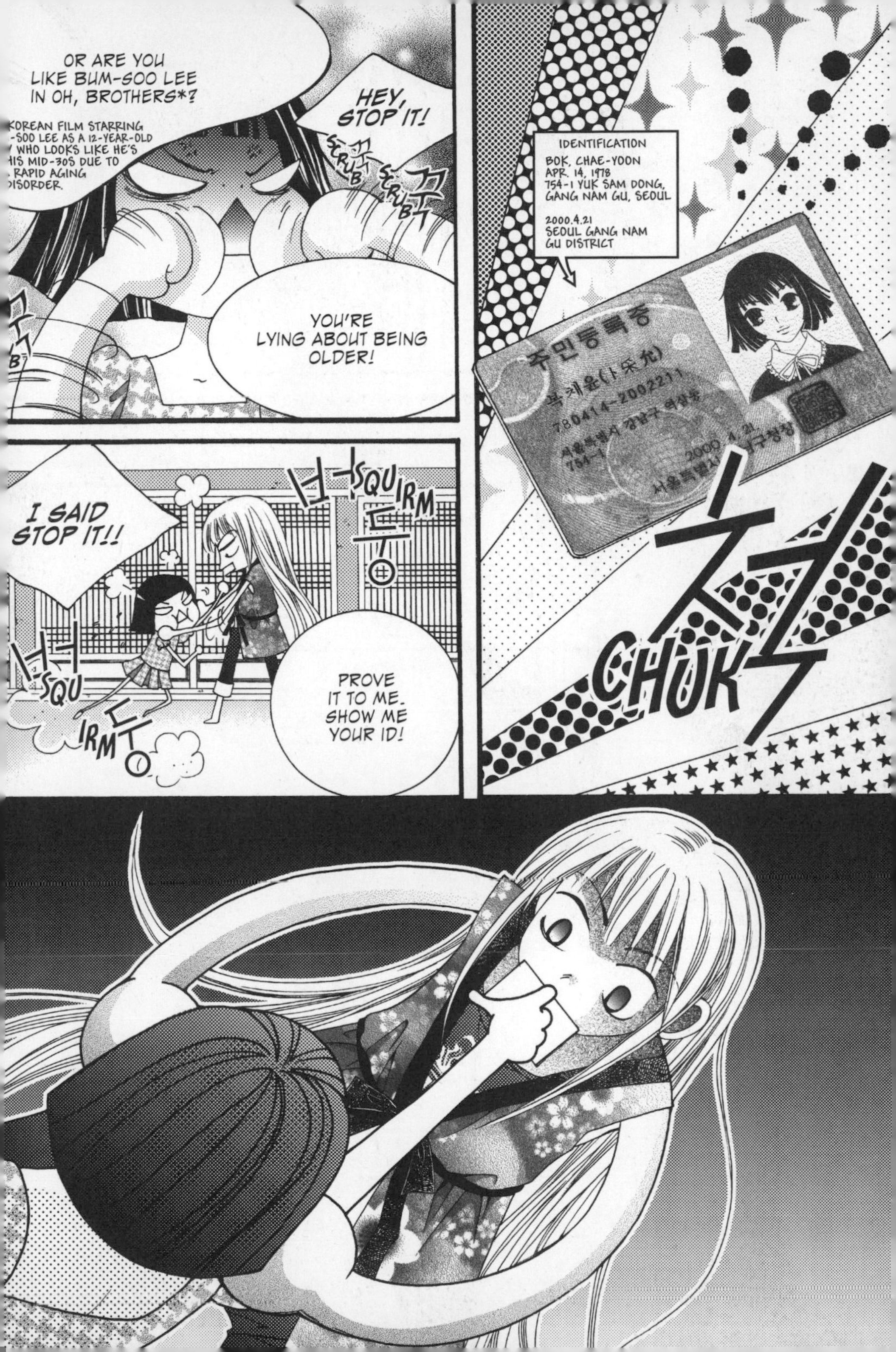
OR ARE YOU LIKE BUM-SOO LEE IN OH, BROTHERS*?
HEY, STOP IT!
SCRUB 꼬 SCRUB 꼬
KOREAN FILM STARRING
-SOO LEE AS A 12-YEAR-OLD
WHO LOOKS LIKE HE'S
HIS MID-30S DUE TO
RAPID AGING
DISORDER.
YOU'RE LYING ABOUT BEING OLDER!
IDENTIFICATION
BOK, CHAE-YOON
APR. 14, 1978
754-1 YUK SAM DONG, GANG NAM GU, SEOUL
2000.4.21
SEOUL GANG NAM GU DISTRICT
주민등록증
I SAID STOP IT!!
SQUIRM
SQUIRM
PROVE IT TO ME. SHOW ME YOUR ID!
CHUK

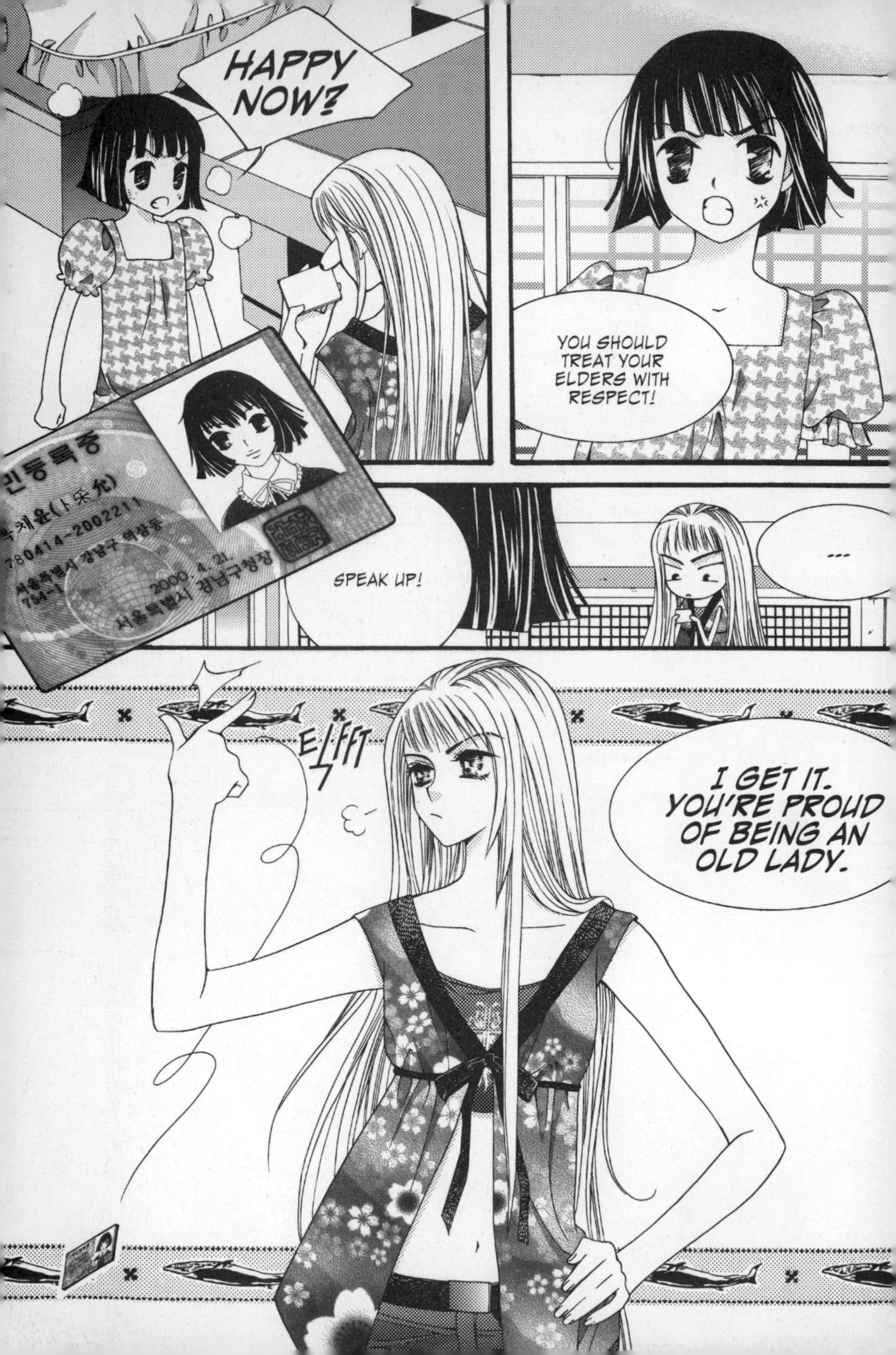
HAPPY NOW?
YOU SHOULD TREAT YOUR ELDERS WITH RESPECT!
780414-2002211
2000. 4. 21.
서울특별시 강남구청장
SPEAK UP!
...
ELFFT
I GET IT. YOU'RE PROUD OF BEING AN OLD LADY.

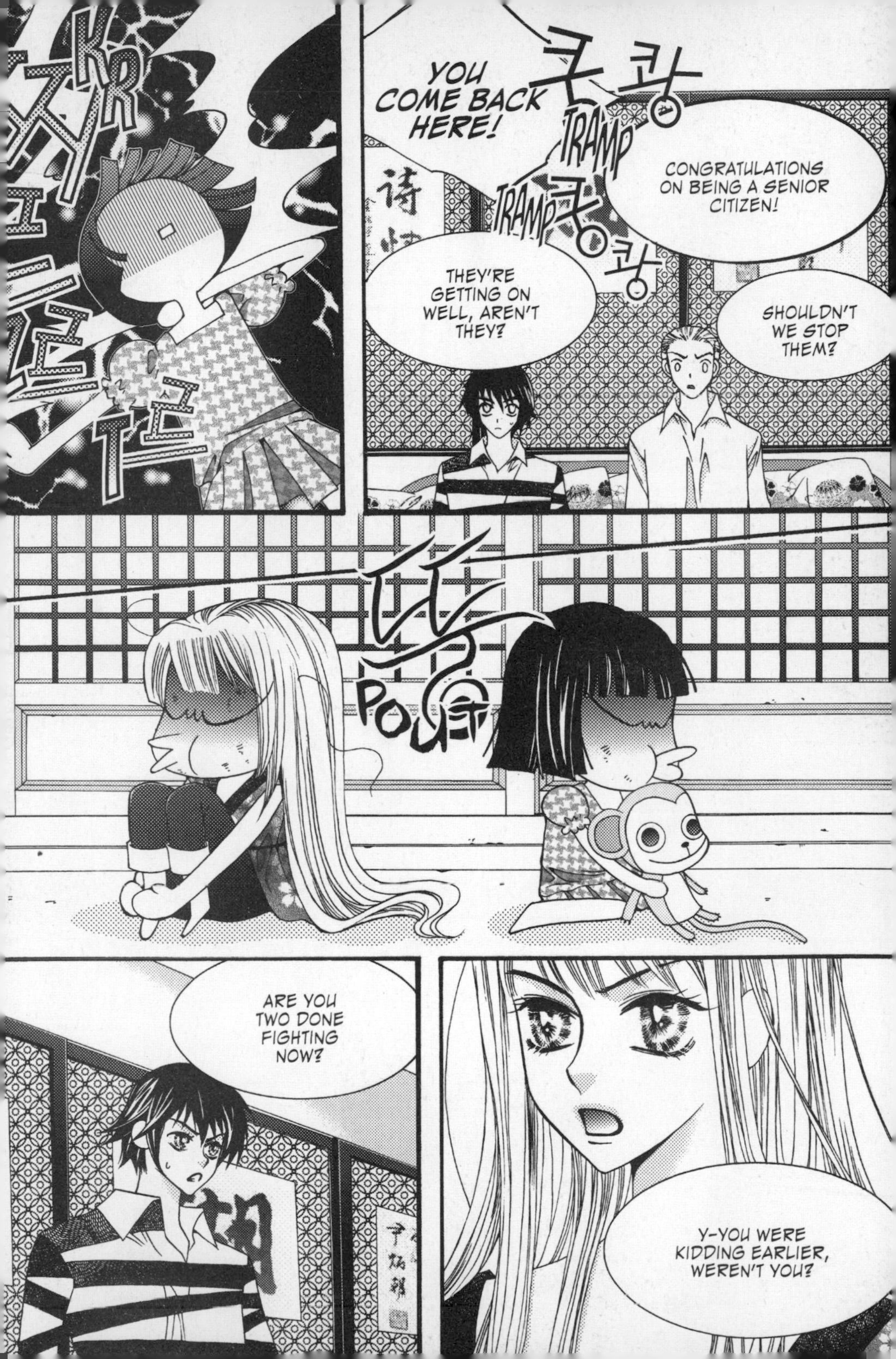
KR
YOU COME BACK HERE!
콩 쾅
TRAMP
TRAMP
콩 쾅
CONGRATULATIONS ON BEING A SENIOR CITIZEN!
THEY'RE GETTING ON WELL, AREN'T THEY?
SHOULDN'T WE STOP THEM?
POUT
ARE YOU TWO DONE FIGHTING NOW?
Y-YOU WERE KIDDING EARLIER, WEREN'T YOU?

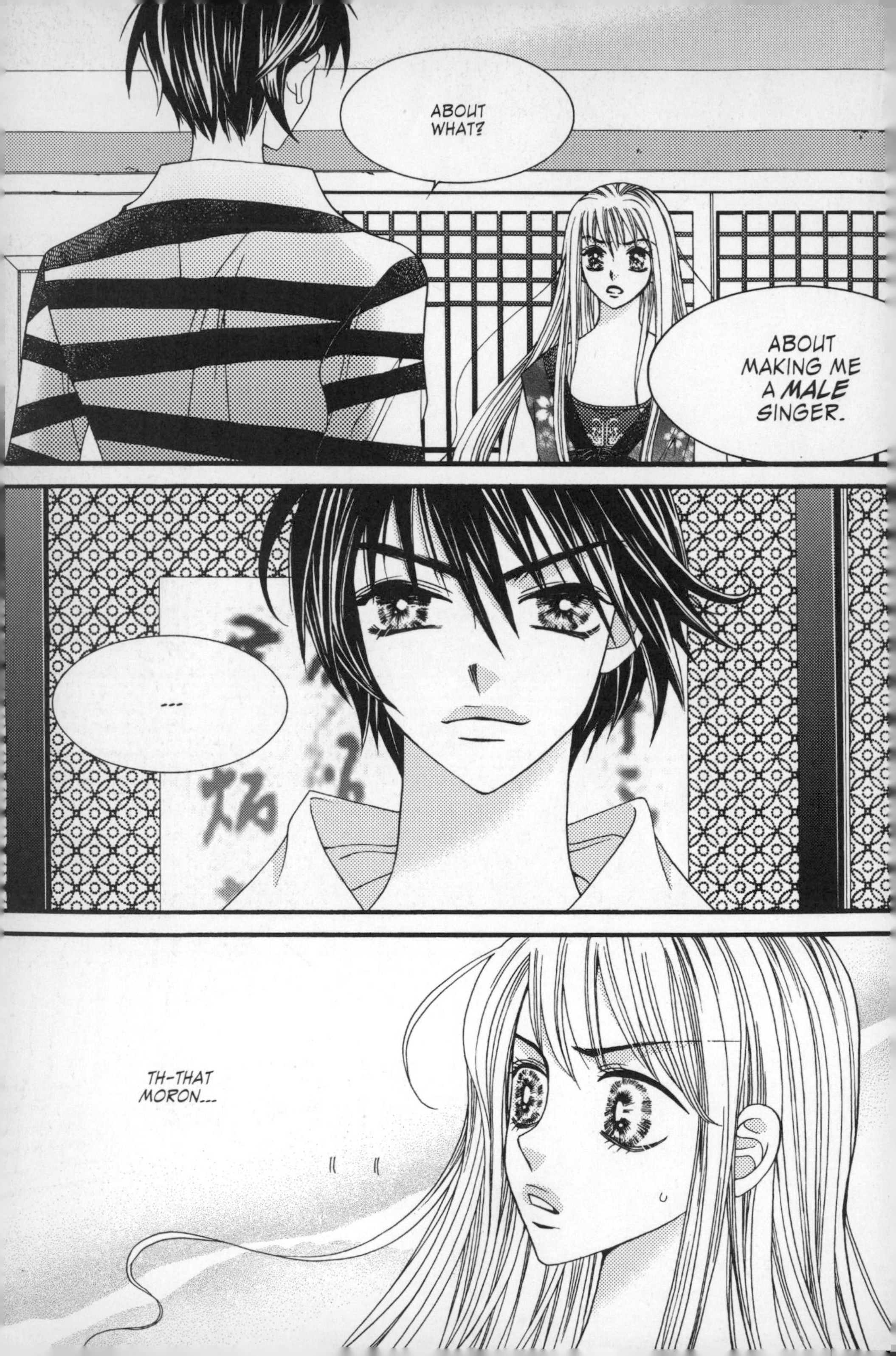
ABOUT WHAT?
ABOUT MAKING ME A MALE SINGER.
...
TH-THAT MORON...

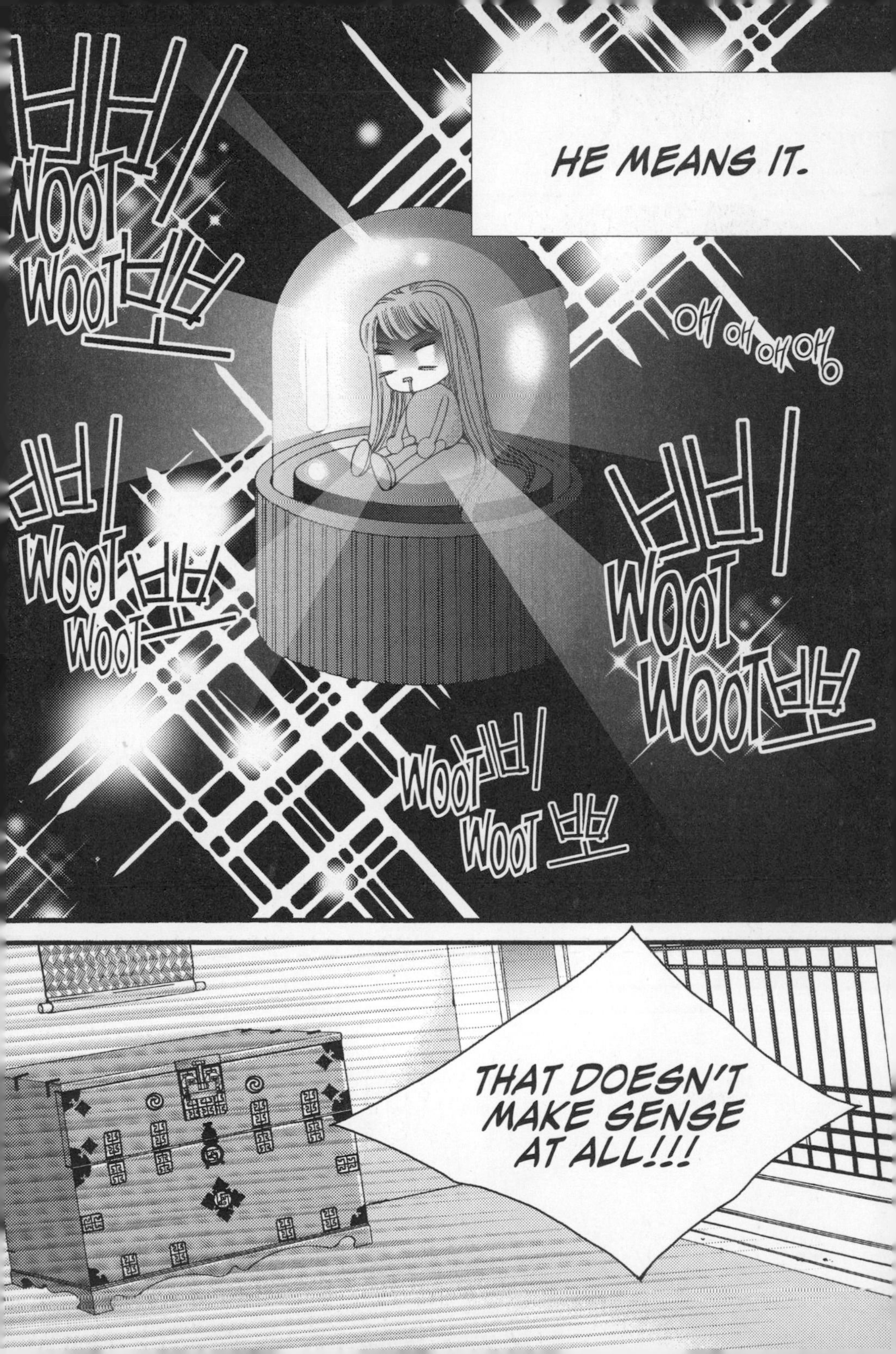
HE MEANS IT.
WOOT WOOT
THAT DOESN'T MAKE SENSE AT ALL!!!

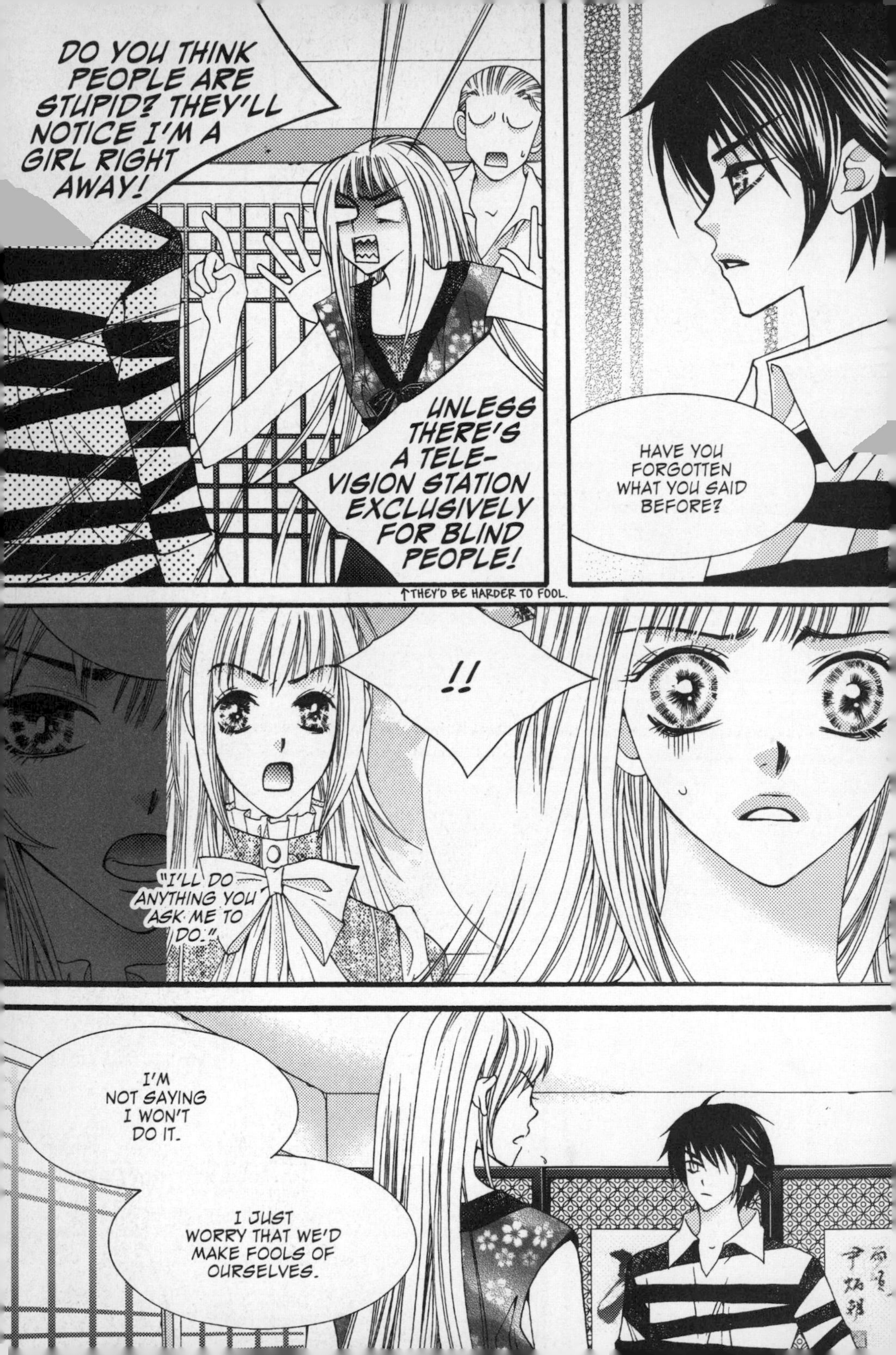

DO YOU THINK PEOPLE ARE STUPID? THEY'LL NOTICE I'M A GIRL RIGHT AWAY!
UNLESS THERE'S A TELE-VISION STATION EXCLUSIVELY FOR BLIND PEOPLE!
↑THEY'D BE HARDER TO FOOL.
HAVE YOU FORGOTTEN WHAT YOU SAID BEFORE?
"I'LL DO ANYTHING YOU ASK ME TO DO."
!!
I'M NOT SAYING I WON'T DO IT.
I JUST WORRY THAT WE'D MAKE FOOLS OF OURSELVES.

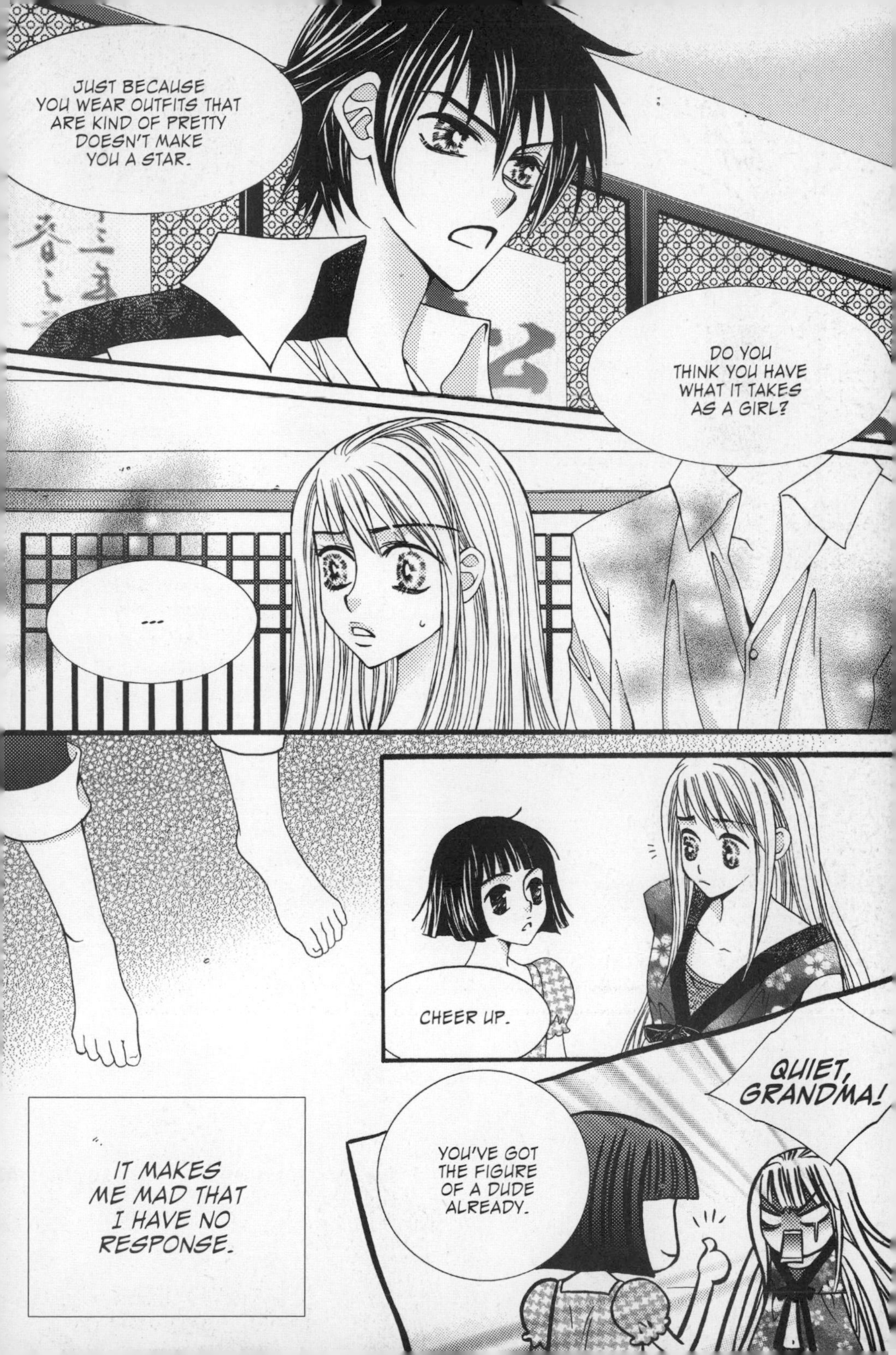
JUST BECAUSE YOU WEAR OUTFITS THAT ARE KIND OF PRETTY DOESN'T MAKE YOU A STAR.
DO YOU THINK YOU HAVE WHAT IT TAKES AS A GIRL?
...
CHEER UP.
YOU'VE GOT THE FIGURE OF A DUDE ALREADY.
QUIET, GRANDMA!
IT MAKES ME MAD THAT I HAVE NO RESPONSE.

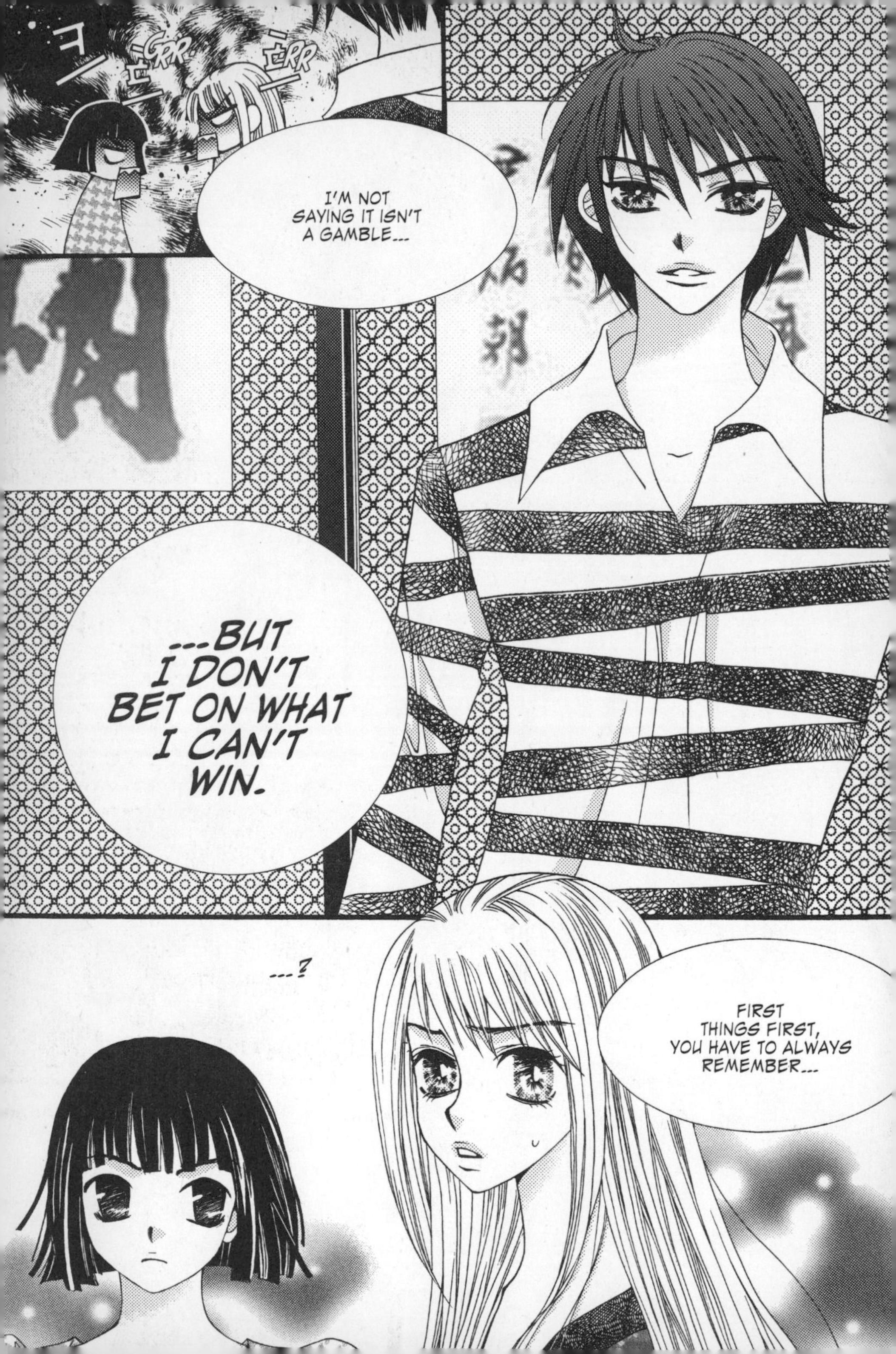
GRR
ERR
I'M NOT SAYING IT ISN'T A GAMBLE...
...BUT I DON'T BET ON WHAT I CAN'T WIN.
...?
FIRST THINGS FIRST, YOU HAVE TO ALWAYS REMEMBER...

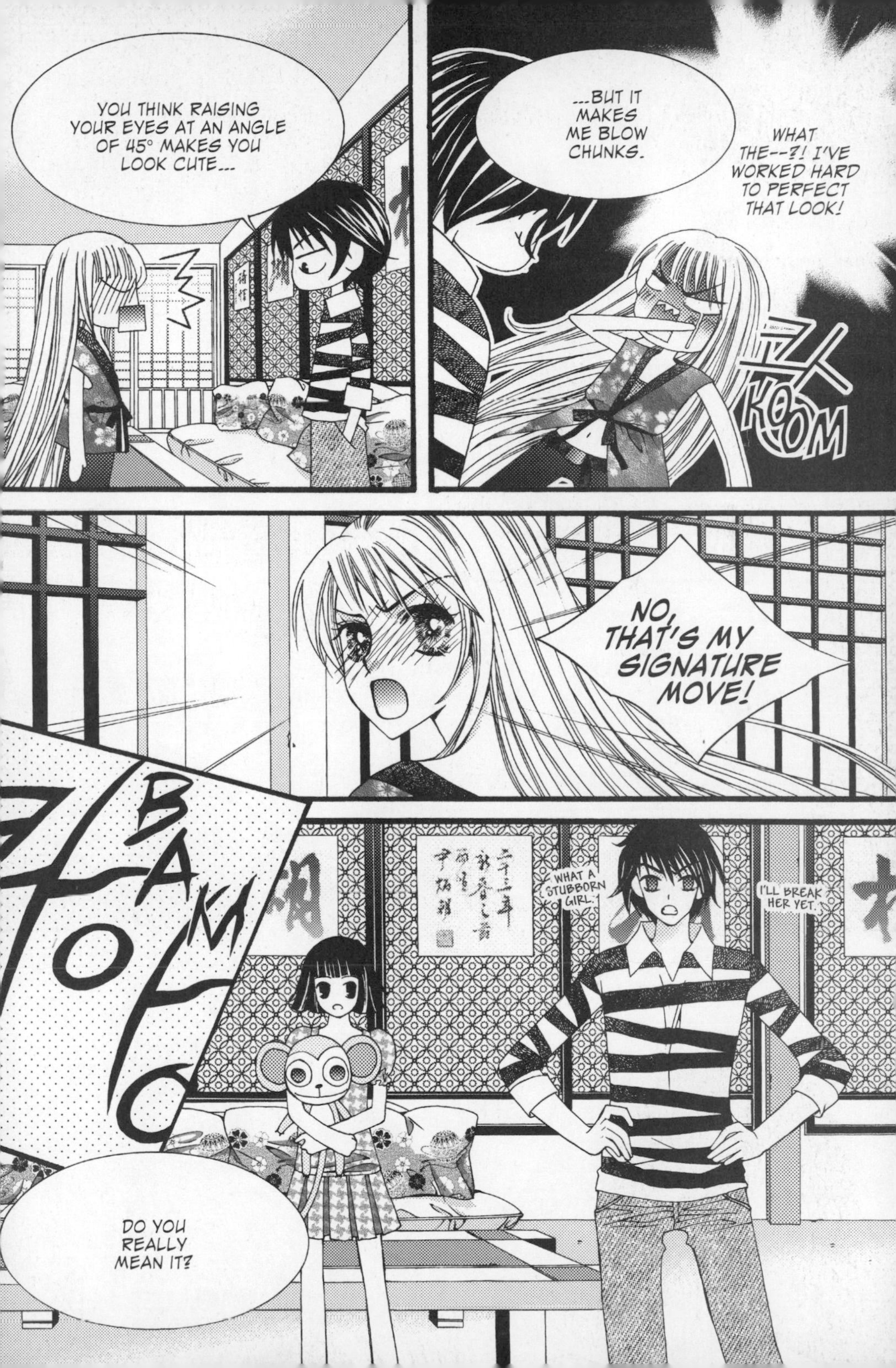
YOU THINK RAISING YOUR EYES AT AN ANGLE OF 45° MAKES YOU LOOK CUTE...
...BUT IT MAKES ME BLOW CHUNKS.
WHAT THE--?! I'VE WORKED HARD TO PERFECT THAT LOOK!
KOOM
NO, THAT'S MY SIGNATURE MOVE!
BAM
WHAT A STUBBORN GIRL.
I'LL BREAK HER YET.
DO YOU REALLY MEAN IT?

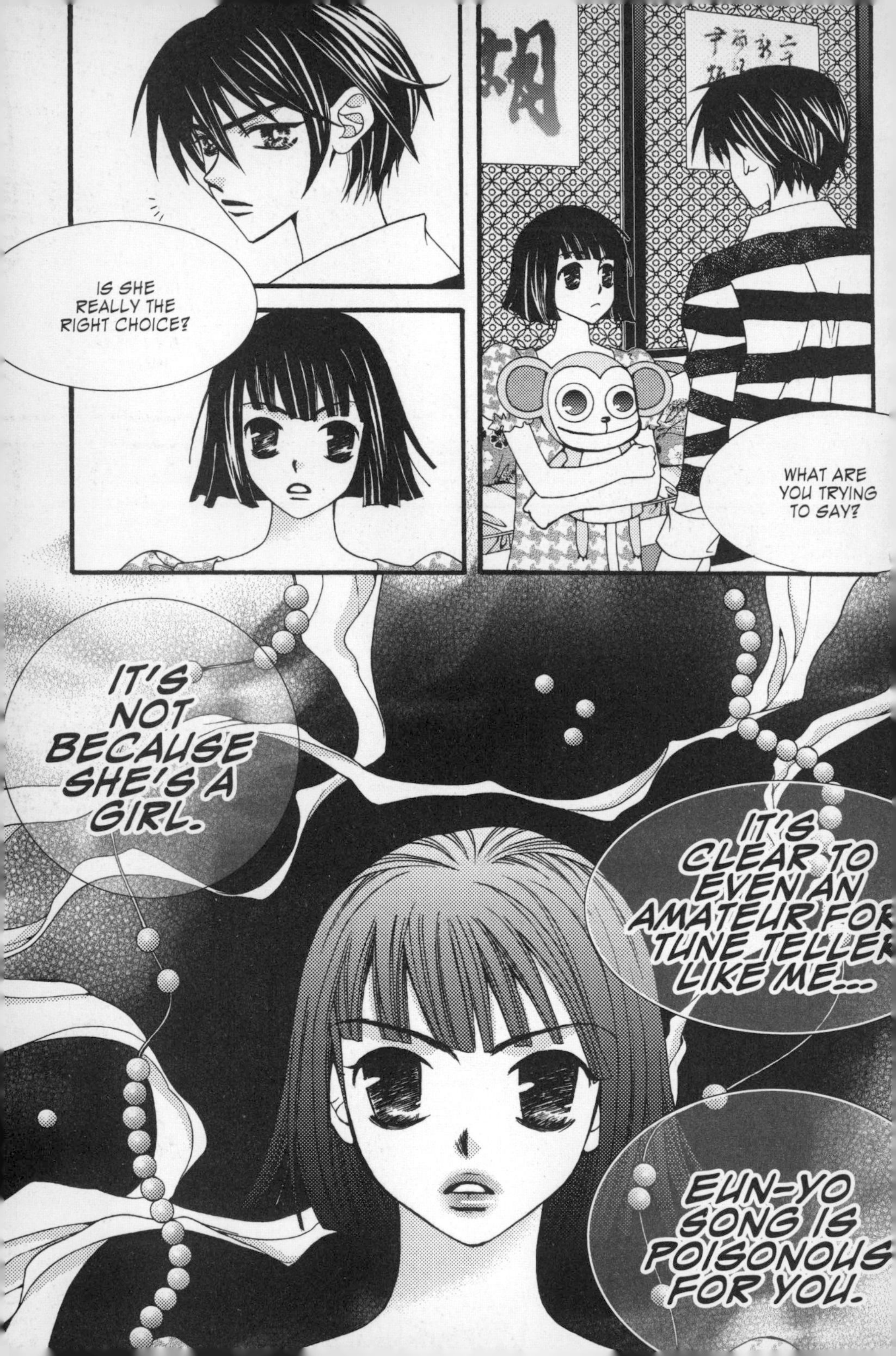
IS SHE REALLY THE RIGHT CHOICE?
WHAT ARE YOU TRYING TO SAY?
IT'S NOT BECAUSE SHE'S A GIRL.
IT'S CLEAR TO EVEN AN AMATEUR FOR TUNE TELLER LIKE ME...
EUN-YO SONG IS POISONOUS FOR YOU.

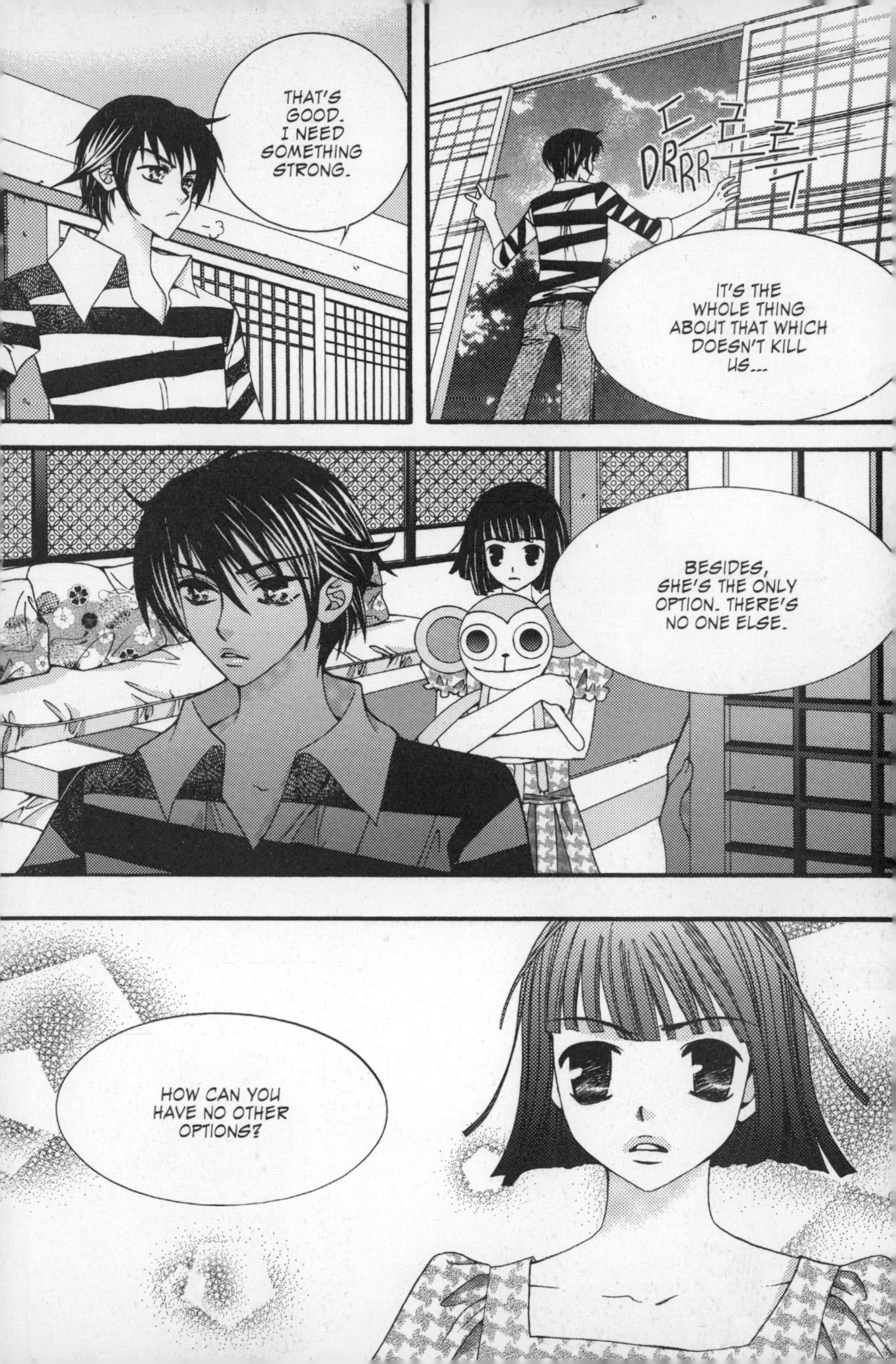
THAT'S GOOD. I NEED SOMETHING STRONG.
DRRR
IT'S THE WHOLE THING ABOUT THAT WHICH DOESN'T KILL US...
BESIDES, SHE'S THE ONLY OPTION. THERE'S NO ONE ELSE.
HOW CAN YOU HAVE NO OTHER OPTIONS?

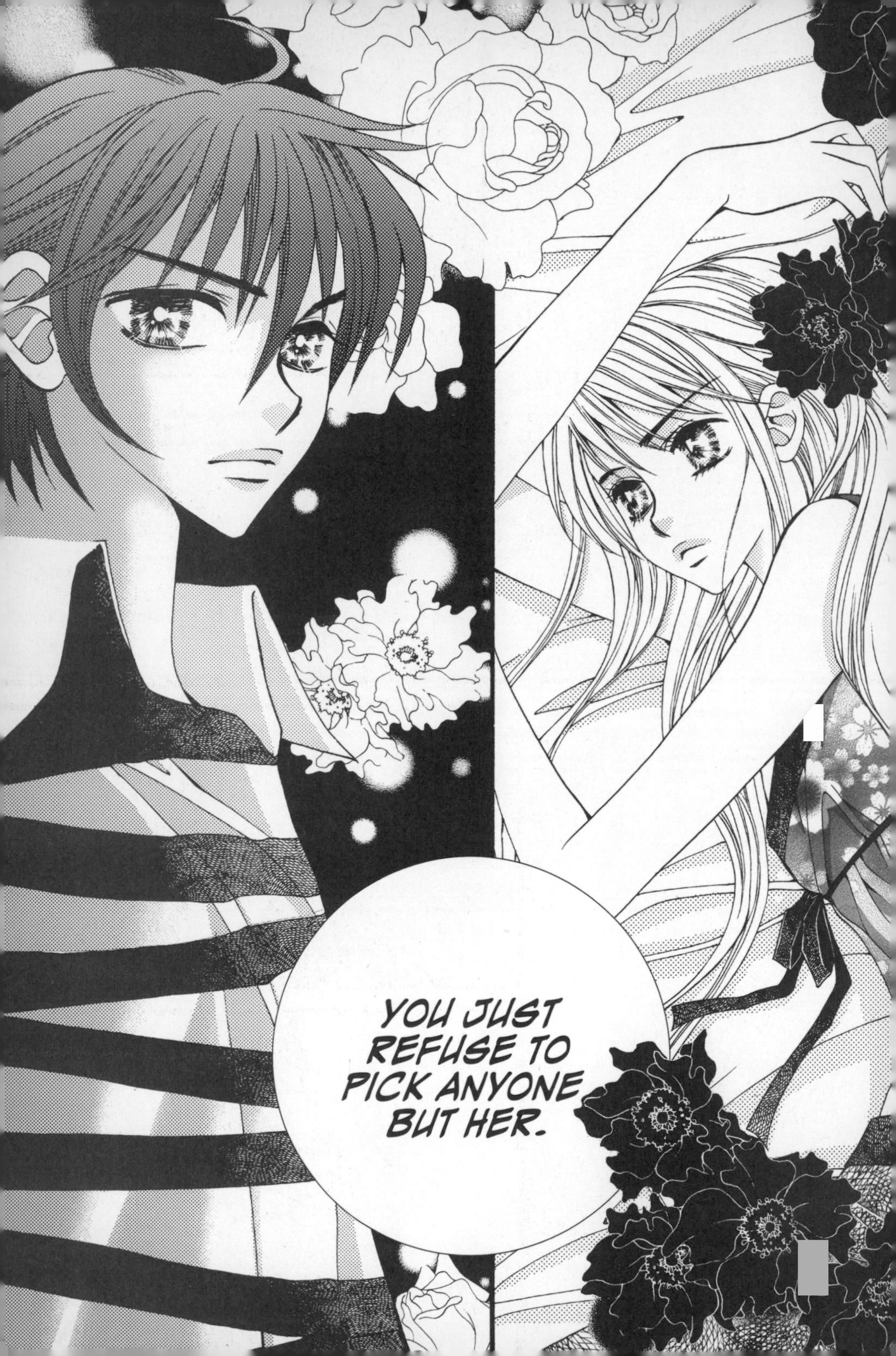
YOU JUST REFUSE TO PICK ANYONE BUT HER.

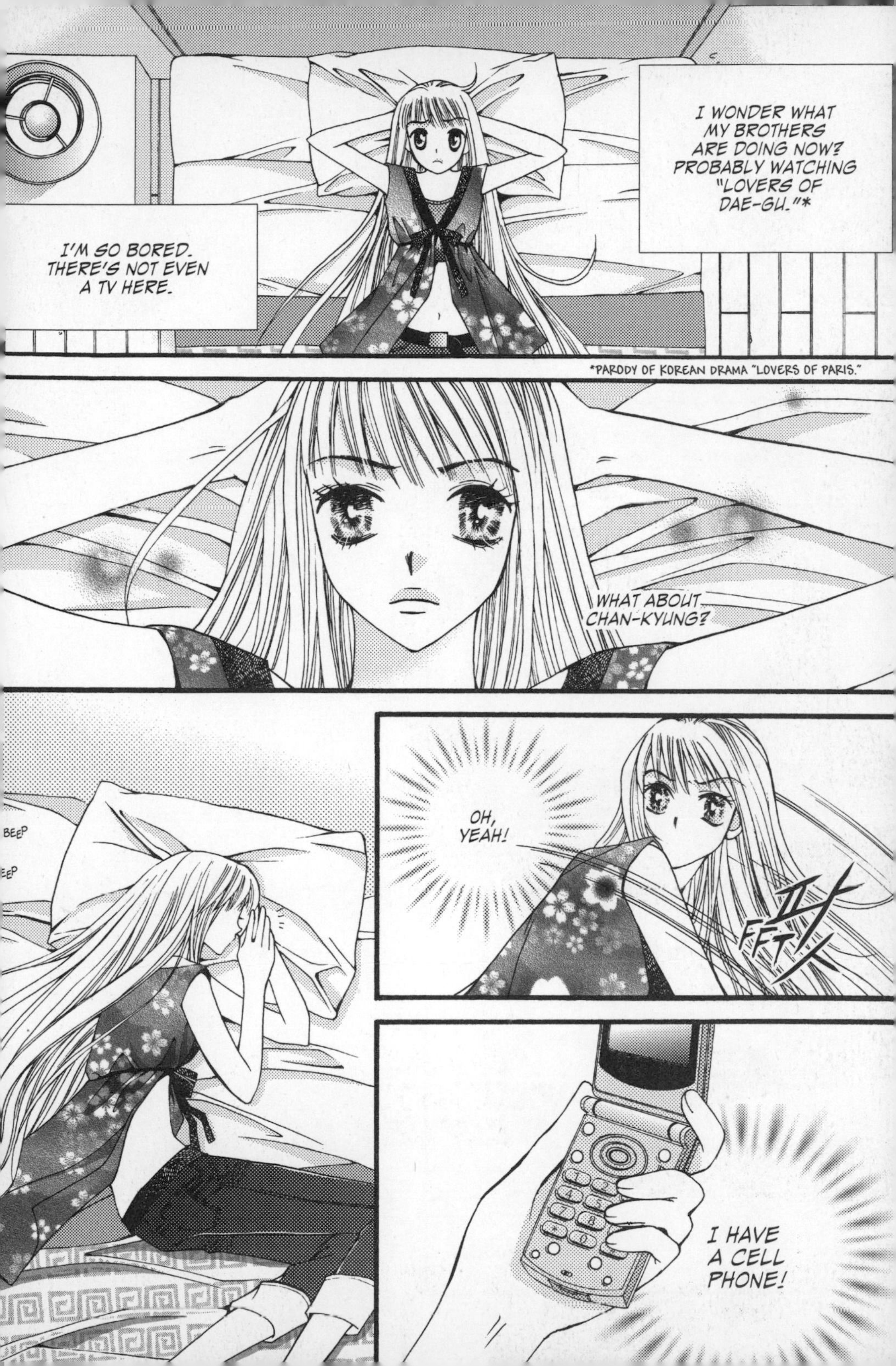
I'M SO BORED. THERE'S NOT EVEN A TV HERE.
I WONDER WHAT MY BROTHERS ARE DOING NOW? PROBABLY WATCHING "LOVERS OF DAE-GU."*
WHAT ABOUT CHAN-KYUNG?
BEEP
EEP
OH, YEAH!
FFT
I HAVE A CELL PHONE!

*PARODY OF KOREAN DRAMA "LOVERS OF PARIS."

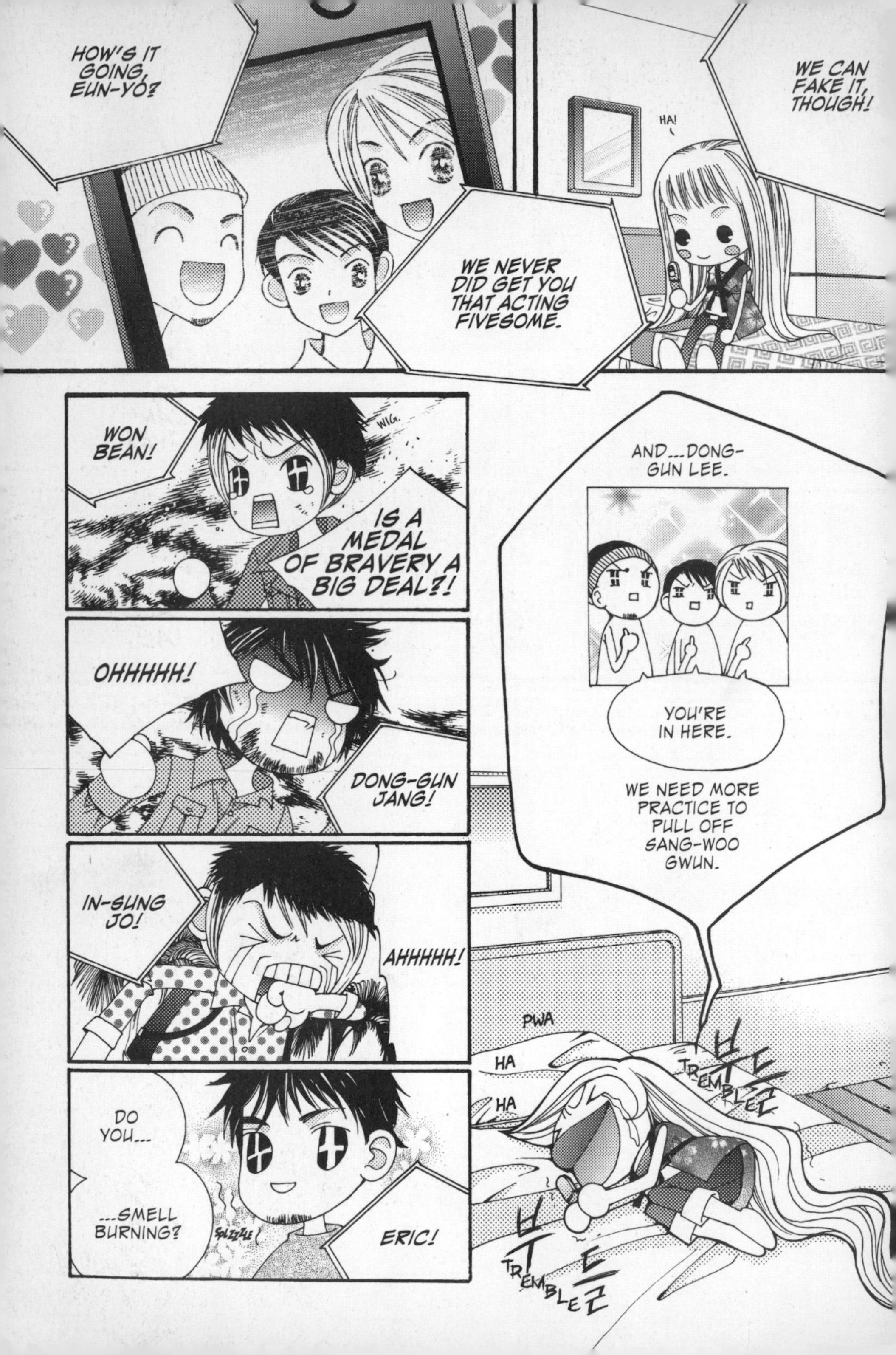

HOW'S IT GOING, EUN-YO?
WE NEVER DID GET YOU THAT ACTING FIVESOME.
HA!
WE CAN FAKE IT, THOUGH!
WON BEAN!
WIG.
IS A MEDAL OF BRAVERY A BIG DEAL?!
OHHHHH!
DONG-GUN JANG!
IN-SUNG JO!
AHHHHH!
DO YOU...
...SMELL BURNING?
SPIZZZLE
ERIC!
AND...DONG-GUN LEE.
YOU'RE IN HERE.
WE NEED MORE PRACTICE TO PULL OFF SANG-WOO GWUN.
PWA
HA
HA
TREMBLE
TREMBLE

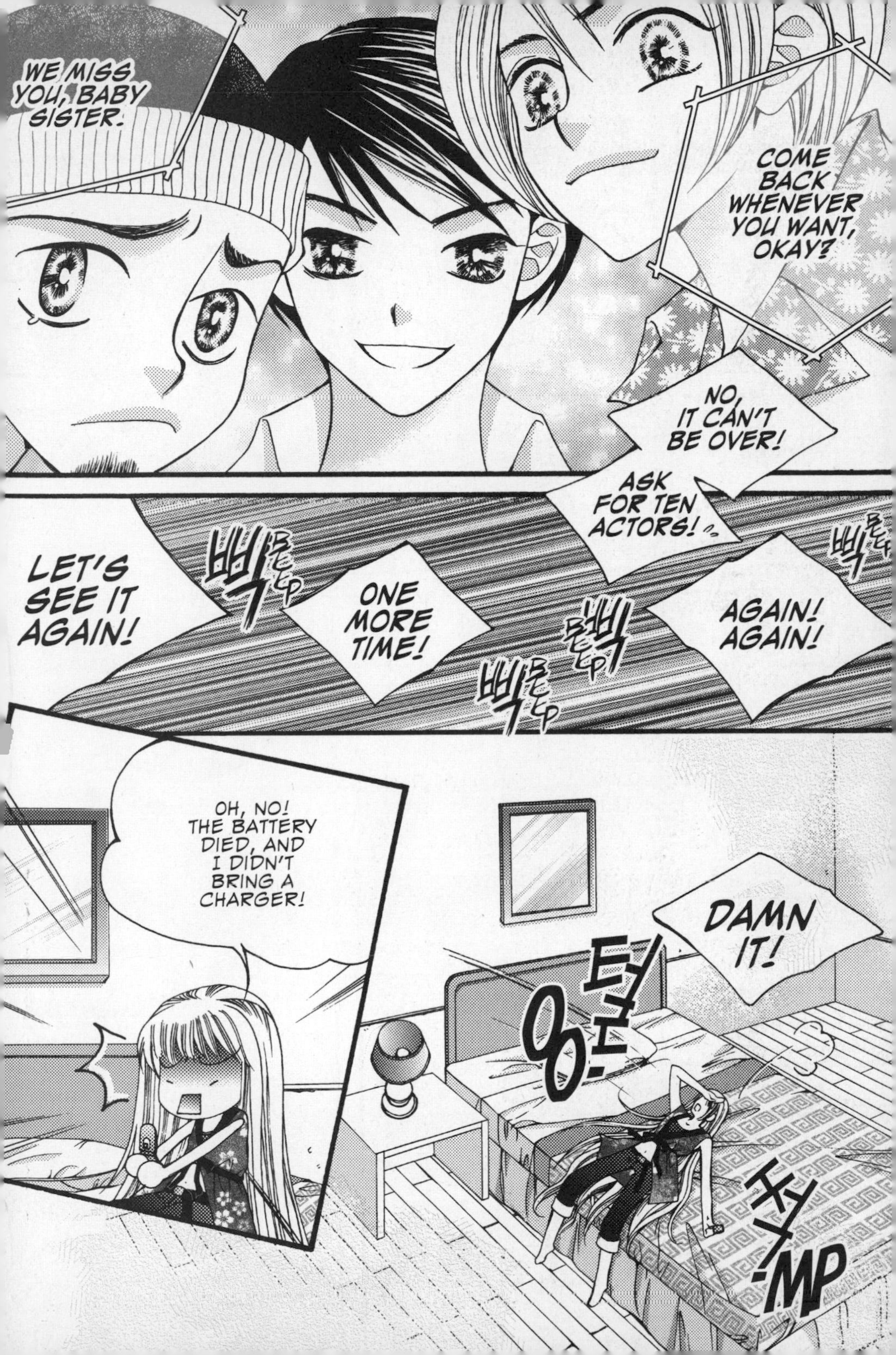
COME BACK WHENEVER YOU WANT, OKAY?
WE MISS YOU, BABY SISTER.
NO, IT CAN'T BE OVER!
ASK FOR TEN ACTORS!
AGAIN! AGAIN!
ONE MORE TIME!
LET'S SEE IT AGAIN!
DAMN IT!
OH, NO! THE BATTERY DIED, AND I DIDN'T BRING A CHARGER!

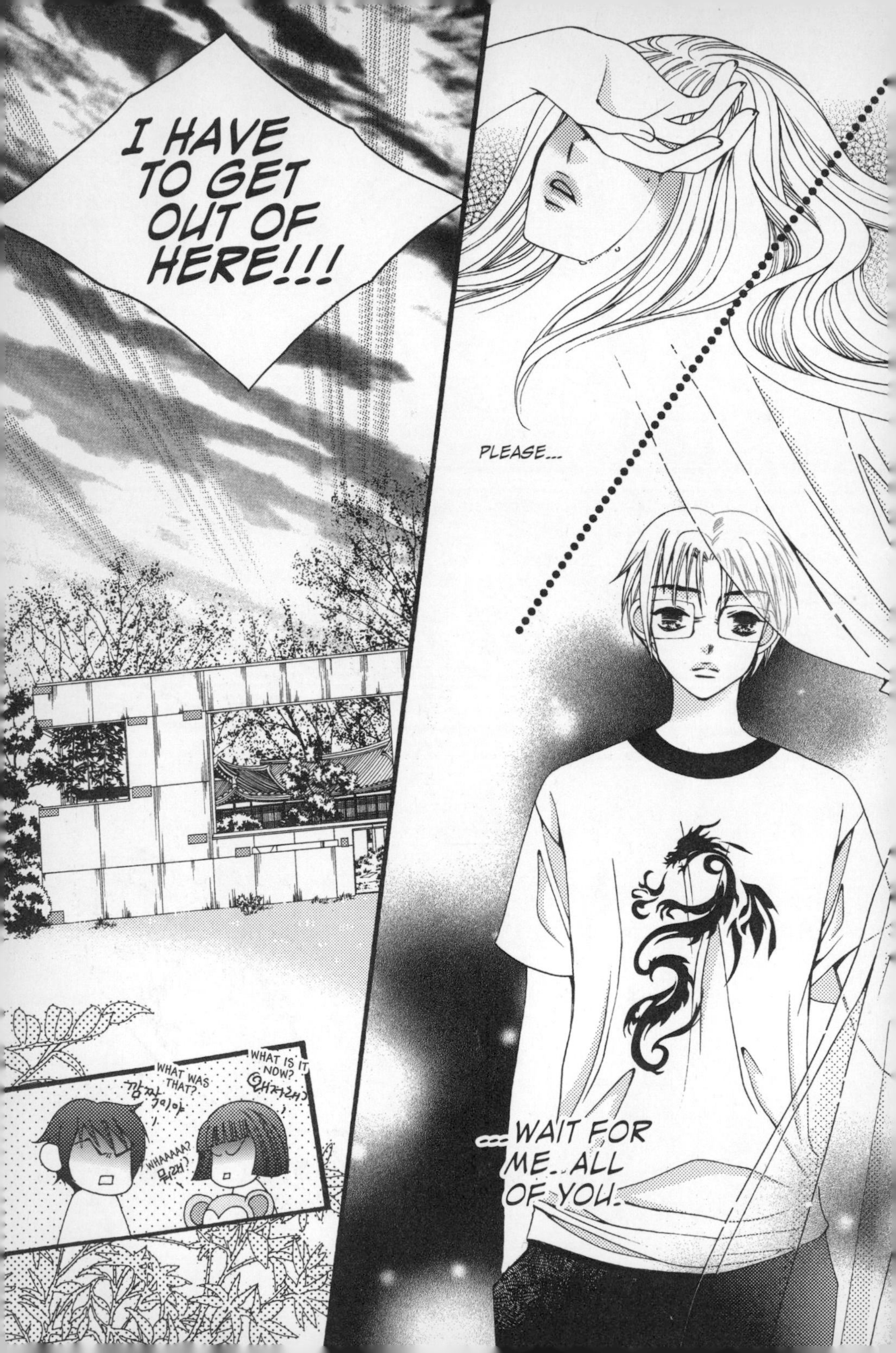
I HAVE TO GET OUT OF HERE!!!
깜짝이야
WHAT WAS THAT?
왜저래?
WHAT IS IT NOW?
뭐래?
WHAAAAAA?
PLEASE...
...WAIT FOR ME...ALL OF YOU.

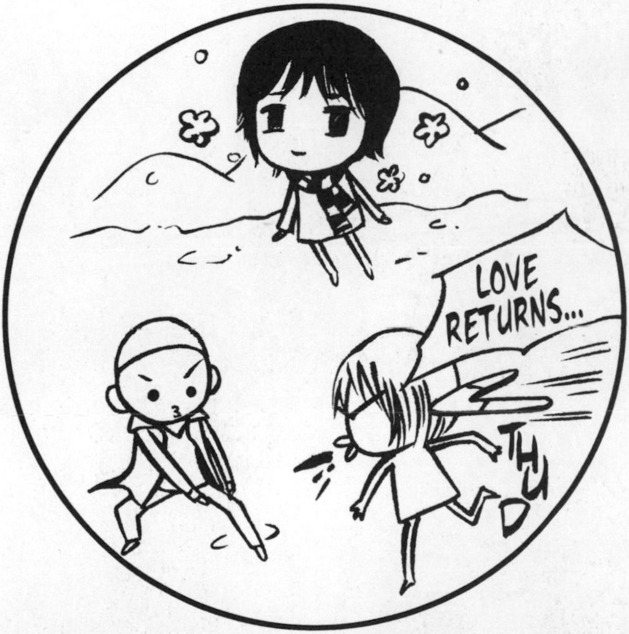
LOVE RETURNS...
THUD

BROTHERS IN A SPARTAN TRAINING PROGRAM
TO BECOME SANG-WOO GWUN.

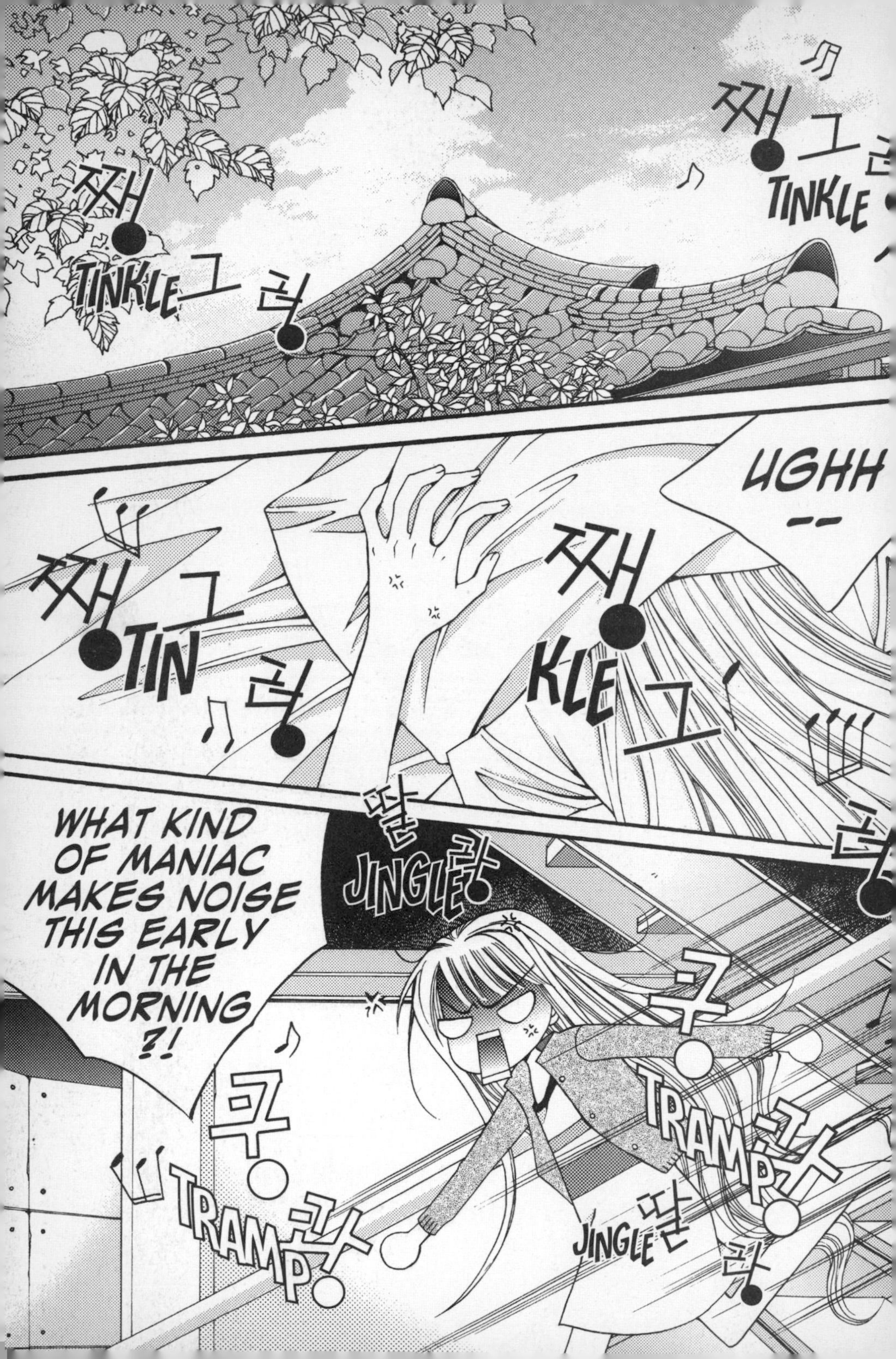
짜그랑
TINKLE
짜그랑
TINKLE
짜그랑
TIN
짜그
KLE
UGHH --
WHAT KIND OF MANIAC MAKES NOISE THIS EARLY IN THE MORNING ?!
딸랑
JINGLE
쿵
TRAMP
쾅
쿵
TRAMP
쾅
딸랑
JINGLE

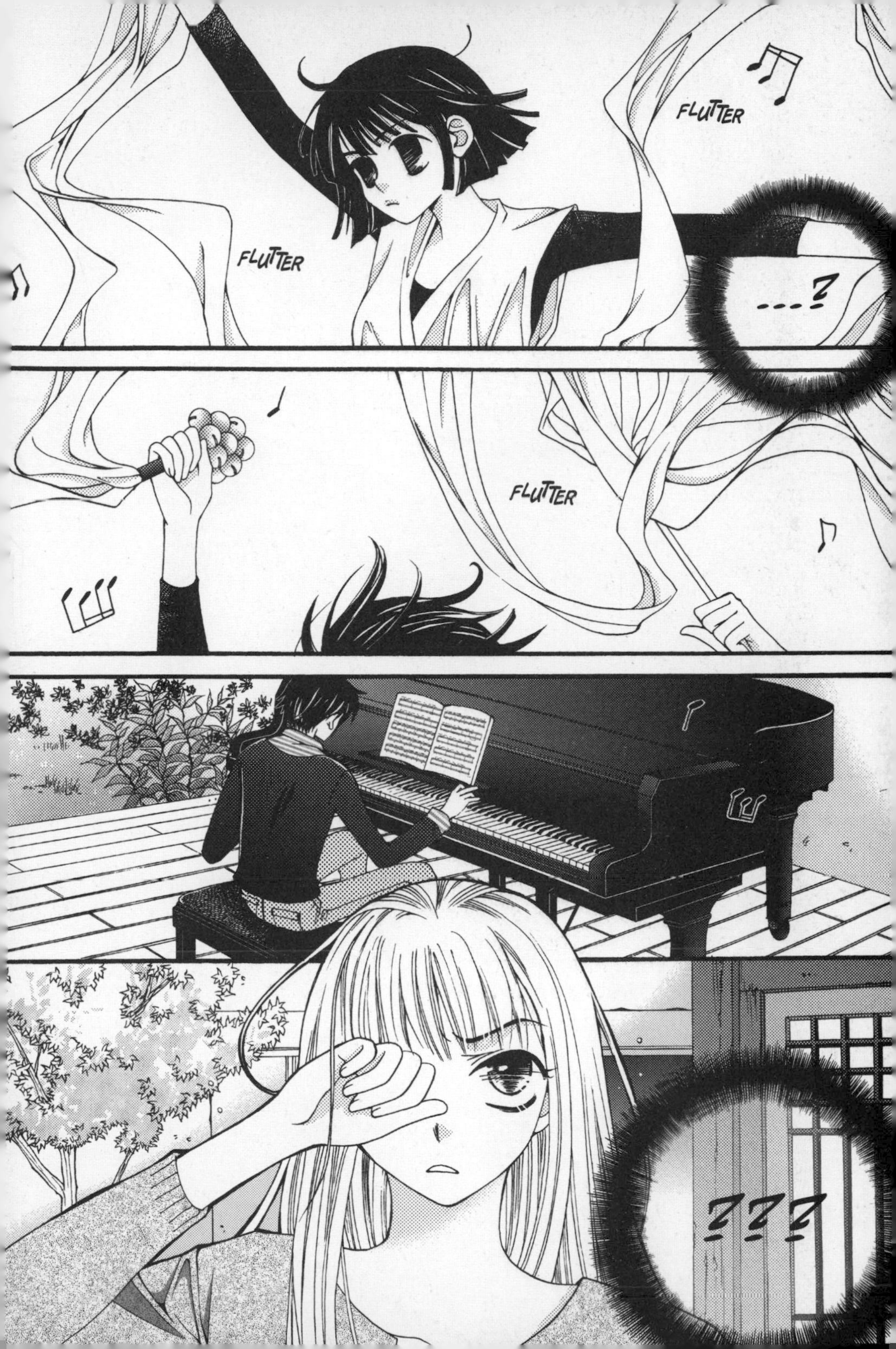

FLUTTER
FLUTTER
...?
FLUTTER
???

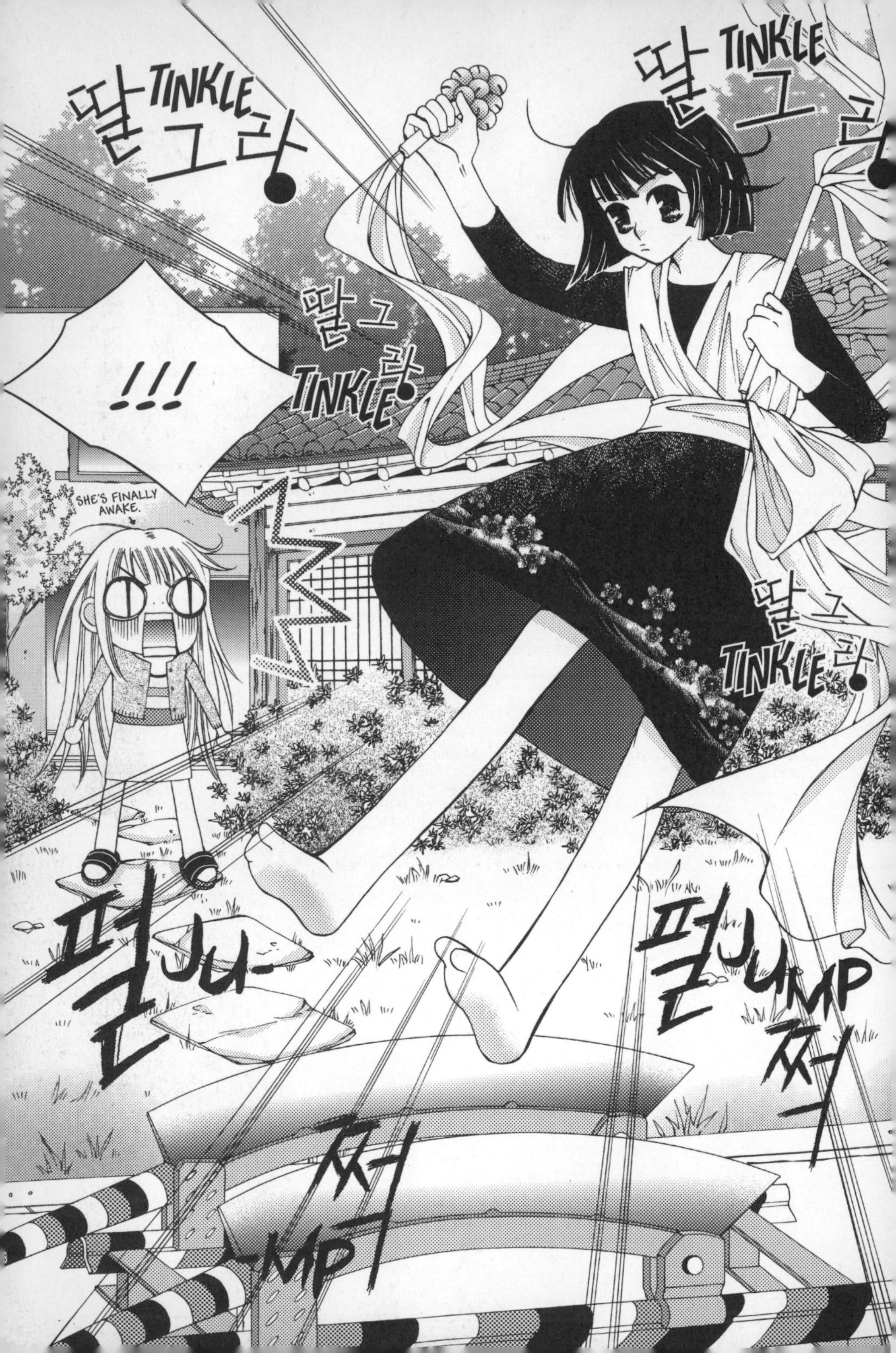
딸그랑 TINKLE
딸그랑 TINKLE
!!!
SHE'S FINALLY AWAKE.
딸그랑 TINKLE
딸그랑 TINKLE
펄쩍 JU-MP
펄쩍 JUMP

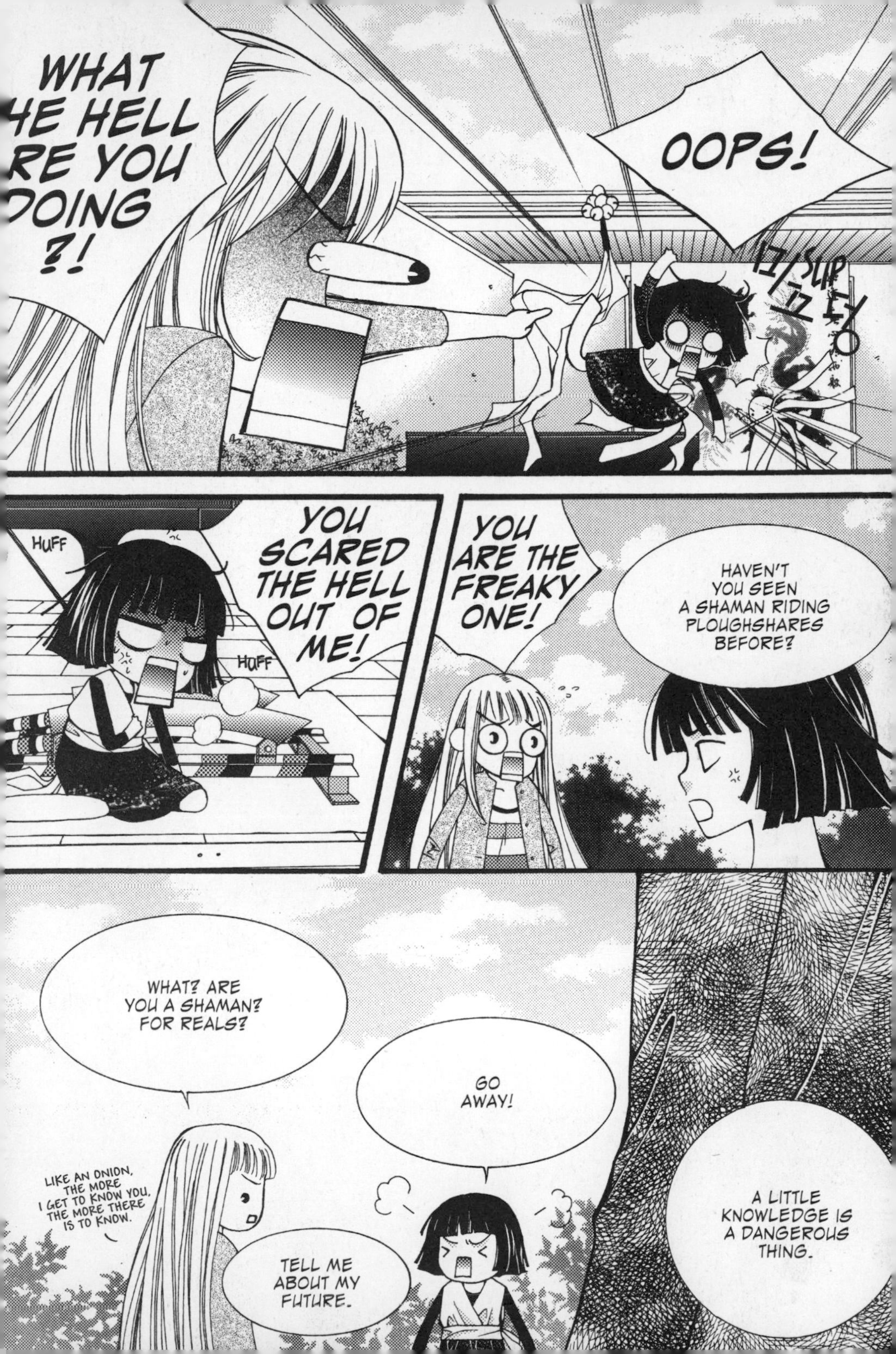

WHAT HE HELL RE YOU DOING ?!
OOPS!
SLIP
HUFF
HUFF
YOU SCARED THE HELL OUT OF ME!
YOU ARE THE FREAKY ONE!
HAVEN'T YOU SEEN A SHAMAN RIDING PLOUGHSHARES BEFORE?
WHAT? ARE YOU A SHAMAN? FOR REALS?
GO AWAY!
LIKE AN ONION, THE MORE I GET TO KNOW YOU, THE MORE THERE IS TO KNOW.
TELL ME ABOUT MY FUTURE.
A LITTLE KNOWLEDGE IS A DANGEROUS THING.

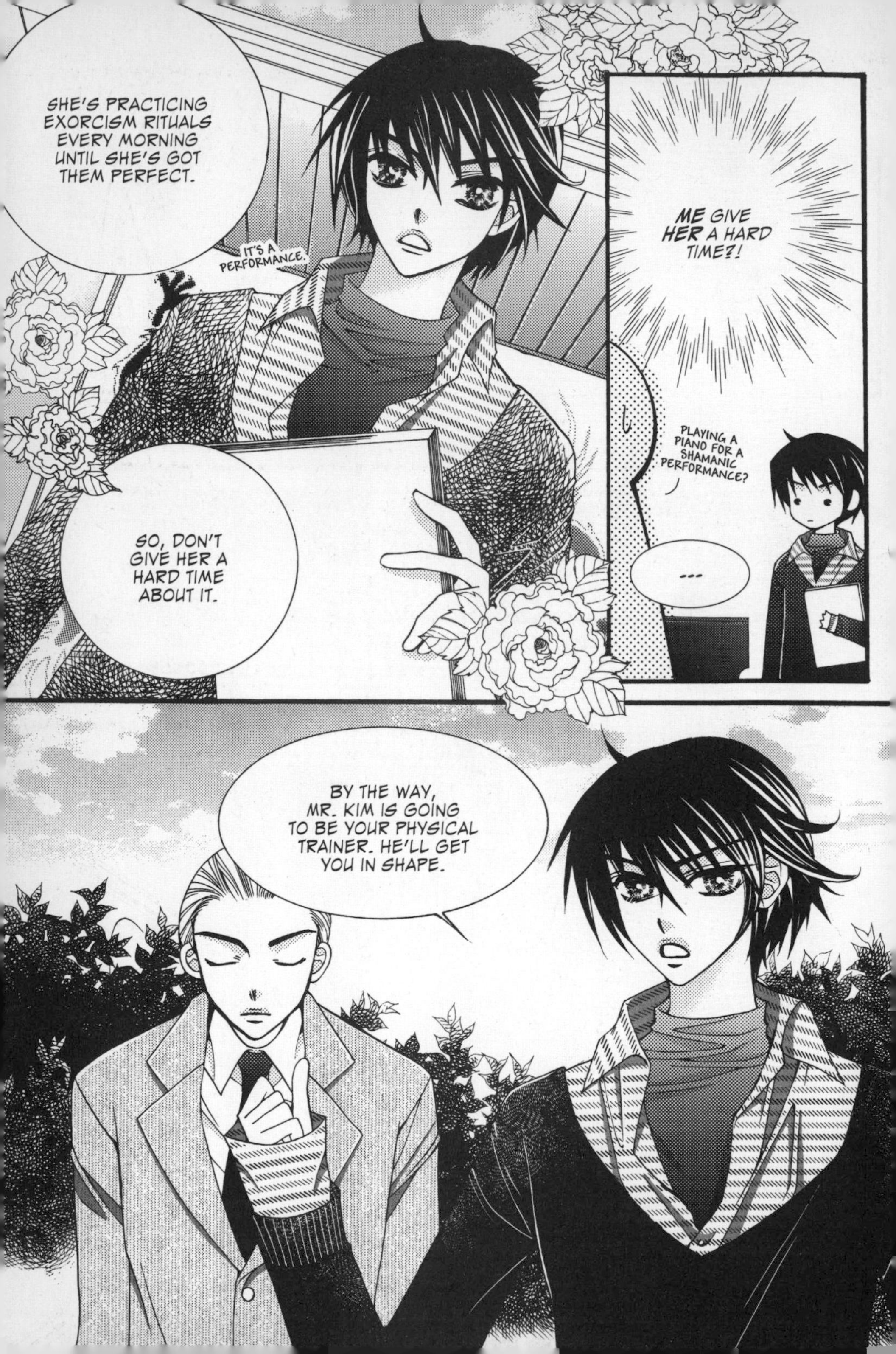
SHE'S PRACTICING EXORCISM RITUALS EVERY MORNING UNTIL SHE'S GOT THEM PERFECT.
IT'S A PERFORMANCE.
SO, DON'T GIVE HER A HARD TIME ABOUT IT.
ME GIVE HER A HARD TIME?!
PLAYING A PIANO FOR A SHAMANIC PERFORMANCE?
...
BY THE WAY, MR. KIM IS GOING TO BE YOUR PHYSICAL TRAINER. HE'LL GET YOU IN SHAPE.

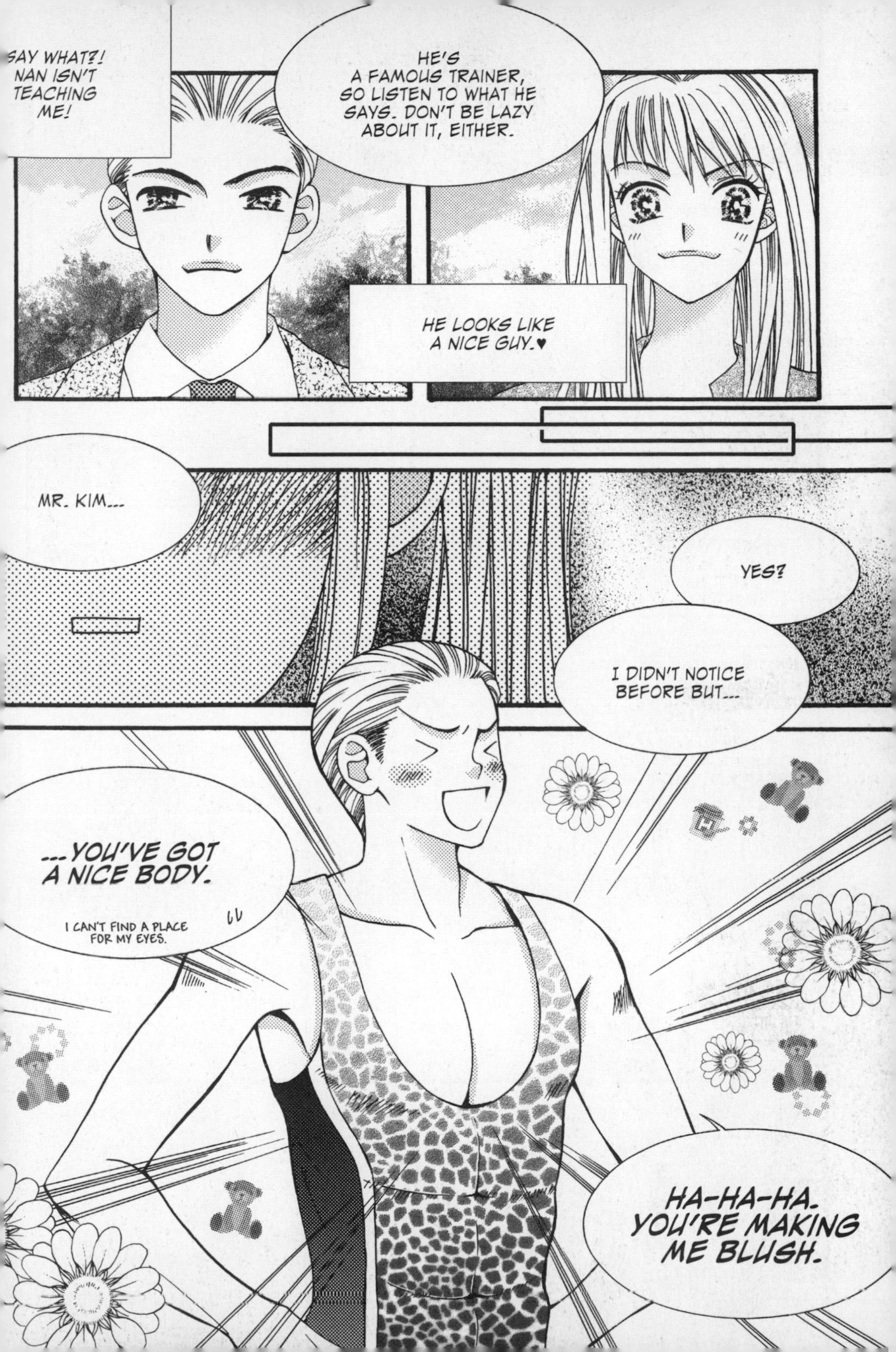
SAY WHAT?! NAN ISN'T TEACHING ME!
HE'S A FAMOUS TRAINER, SO LISTEN TO WHAT HE SAYS. DON'T BE LAZY ABOUT IT, EITHER.
HE LOOKS LIKE A NICE GUY.♥
MR. KIM...
YES?
I DIDN'T NOTICE BEFORE BUT...
...YOU'VE GOT A NICE BODY.
I CAN'T FIND A PLACE FOR MY EYES.
HA-HA-HA. YOU'RE MAKING ME BLUSH.

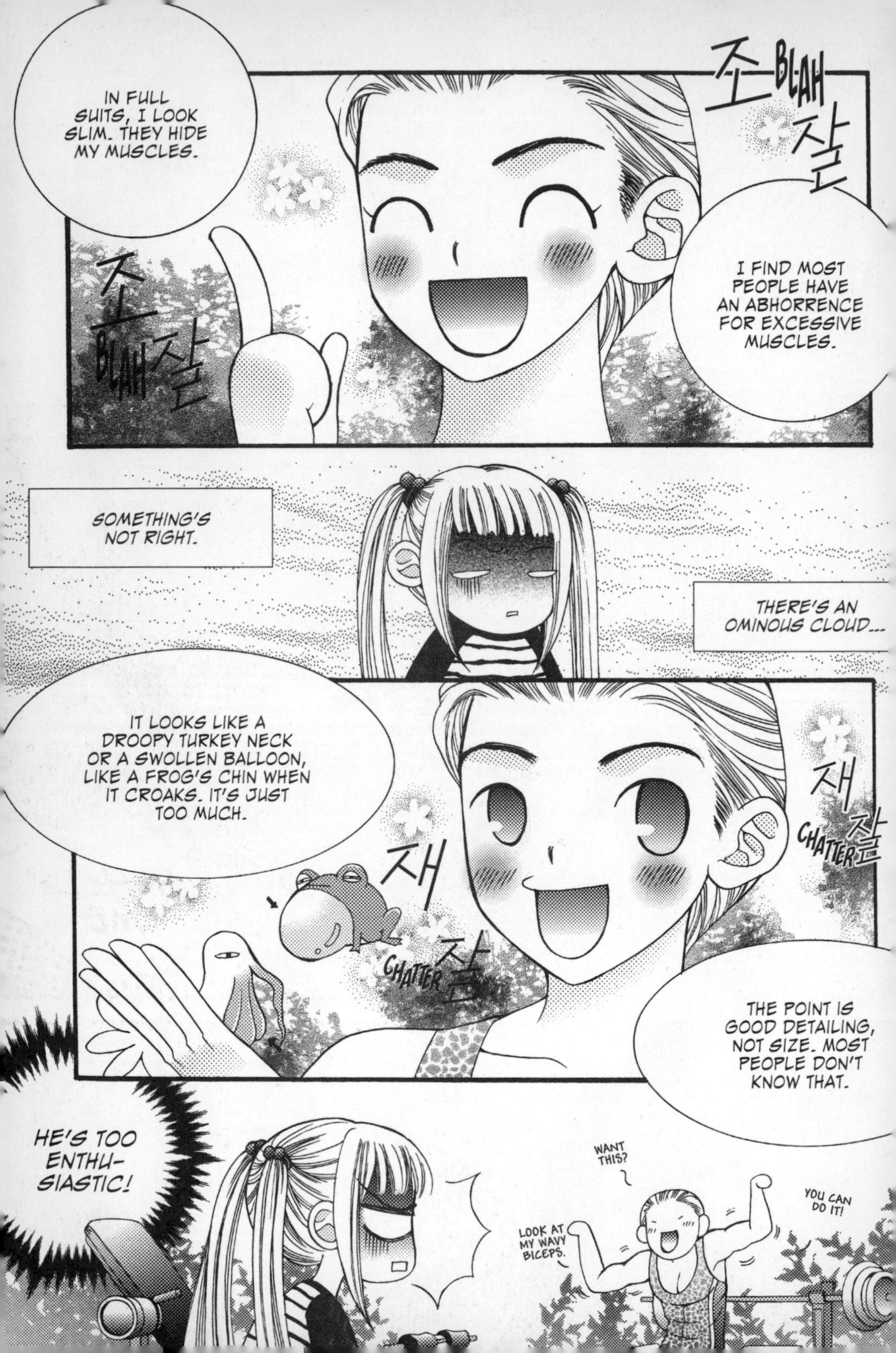

IN FULL SUITS, I LOOK SLIM. THEY HIDE MY MUSCLES.
BLAH
I FIND MOST PEOPLE HAVE AN ABHORRENCE FOR EXCESSIVE MUSCLES.
BLAH
SOMETHING'S NOT RIGHT.
THERE'S AN OMINOUS CLOUD...
IT LOOKS LIKE A DROOPY TURKEY NECK OR A SWOLLEN BALLOON, LIKE A FROG'S CHIN WHEN IT CROAKS. IT'S JUST TOO MUCH.
CHATTER
CHATTER
THE POINT IS GOOD DETAILING, NOT SIZE. MOST PEOPLE DON'T KNOW THAT.
HE'S TOO ENTHU-SIASTIC!
WANT THIS?
YOU CAN DO IT!
LOOK AT MY WAVY BICEPS.

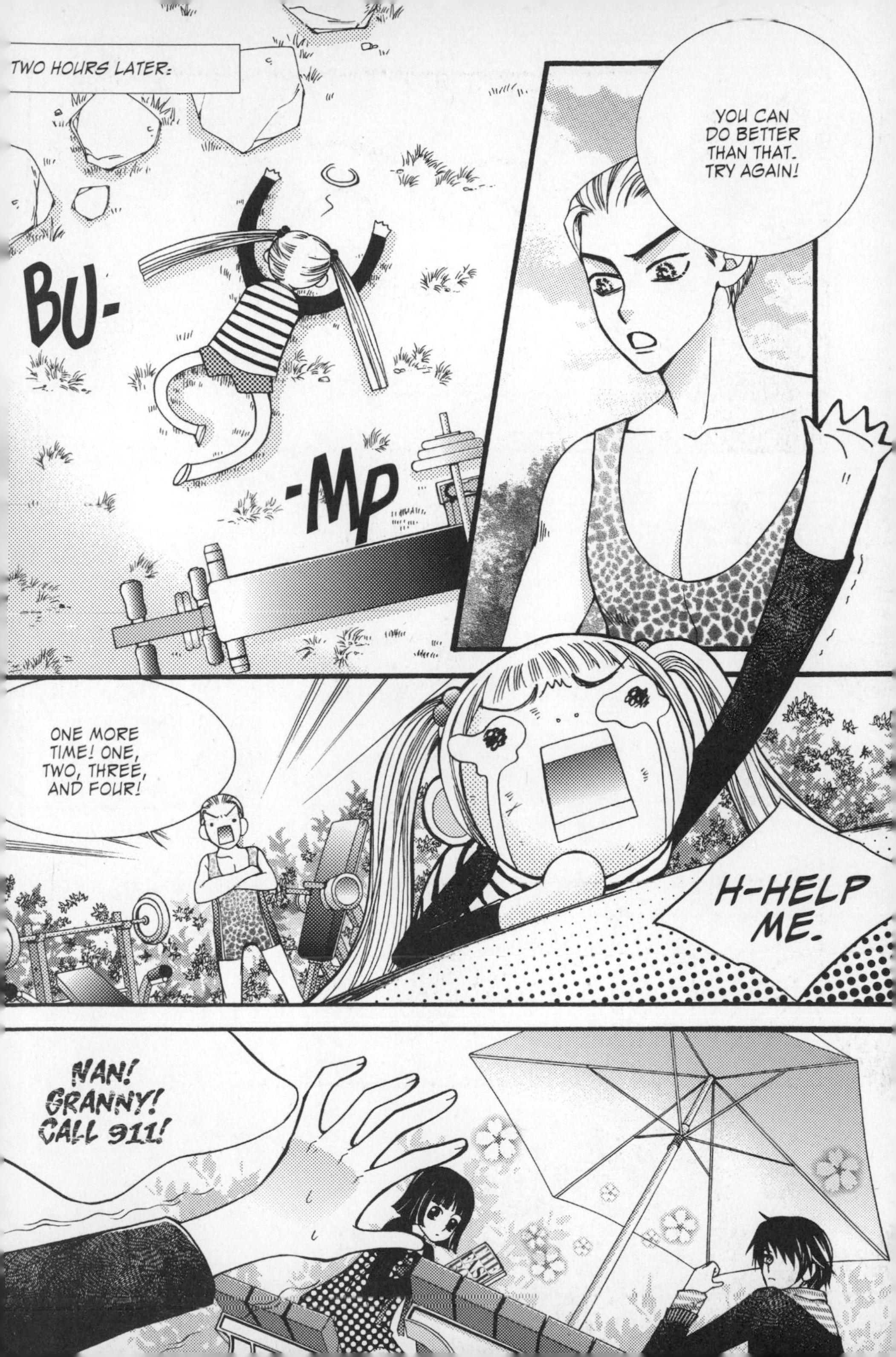
TWO HOURS LATER:
BU-
-MP
YOU CAN DO BETTER THAN THAT. TRY AGAIN!
ONE MORE TIME! ONE, TWO, THREE, AND FOUR!
H-HELP ME.
NAN! GRANNY! CALL 911!

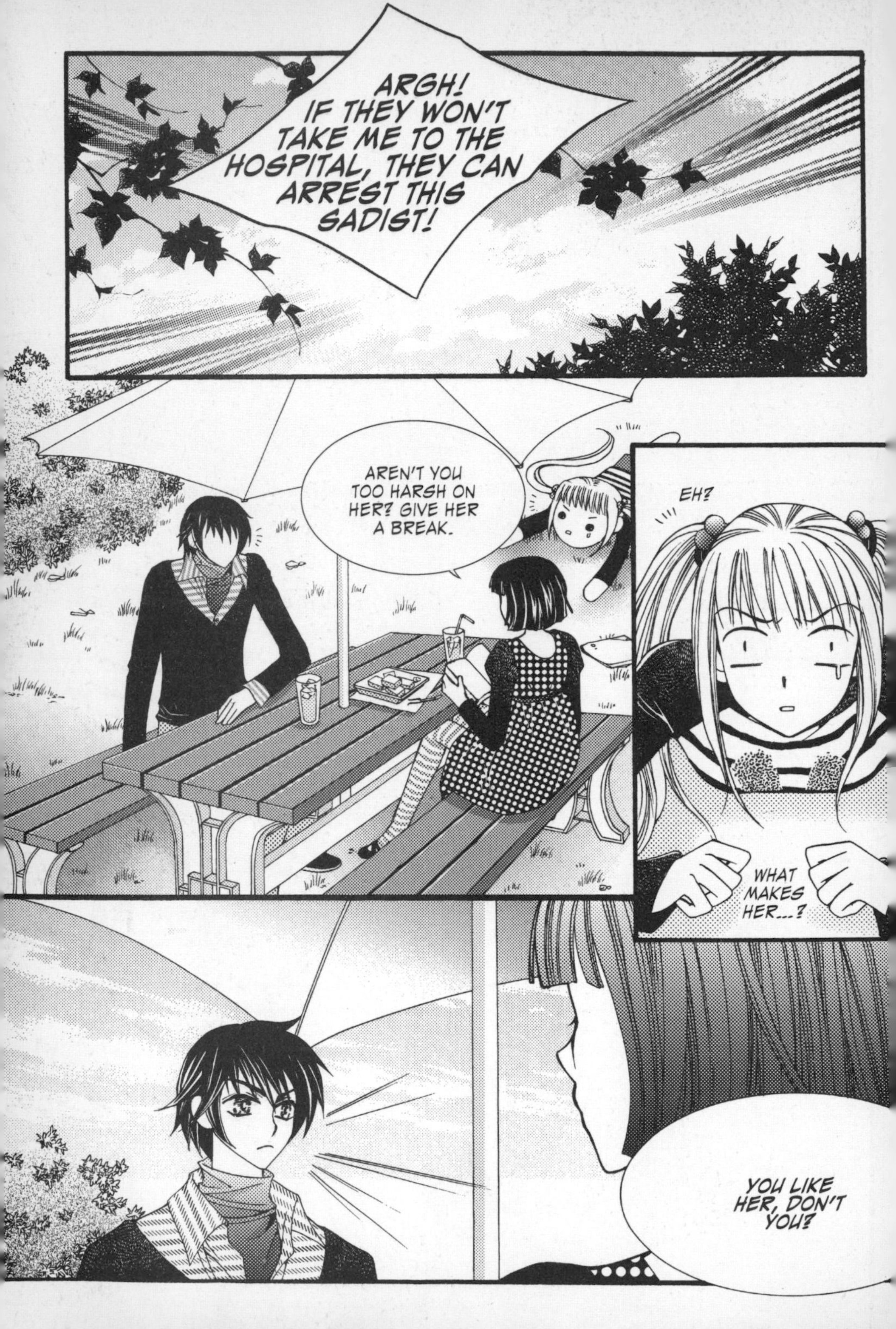
ARGH! IF THEY WON'T TAKE ME TO THE HOSPITAL, THEY CAN ARREST THIS SADIST!
EH?
WHAT MAKES HER...?
AREN'T YOU TOO HARSH ON HER? GIVE HER A BREAK.
YOU LIKE HER, DON'T YOU?

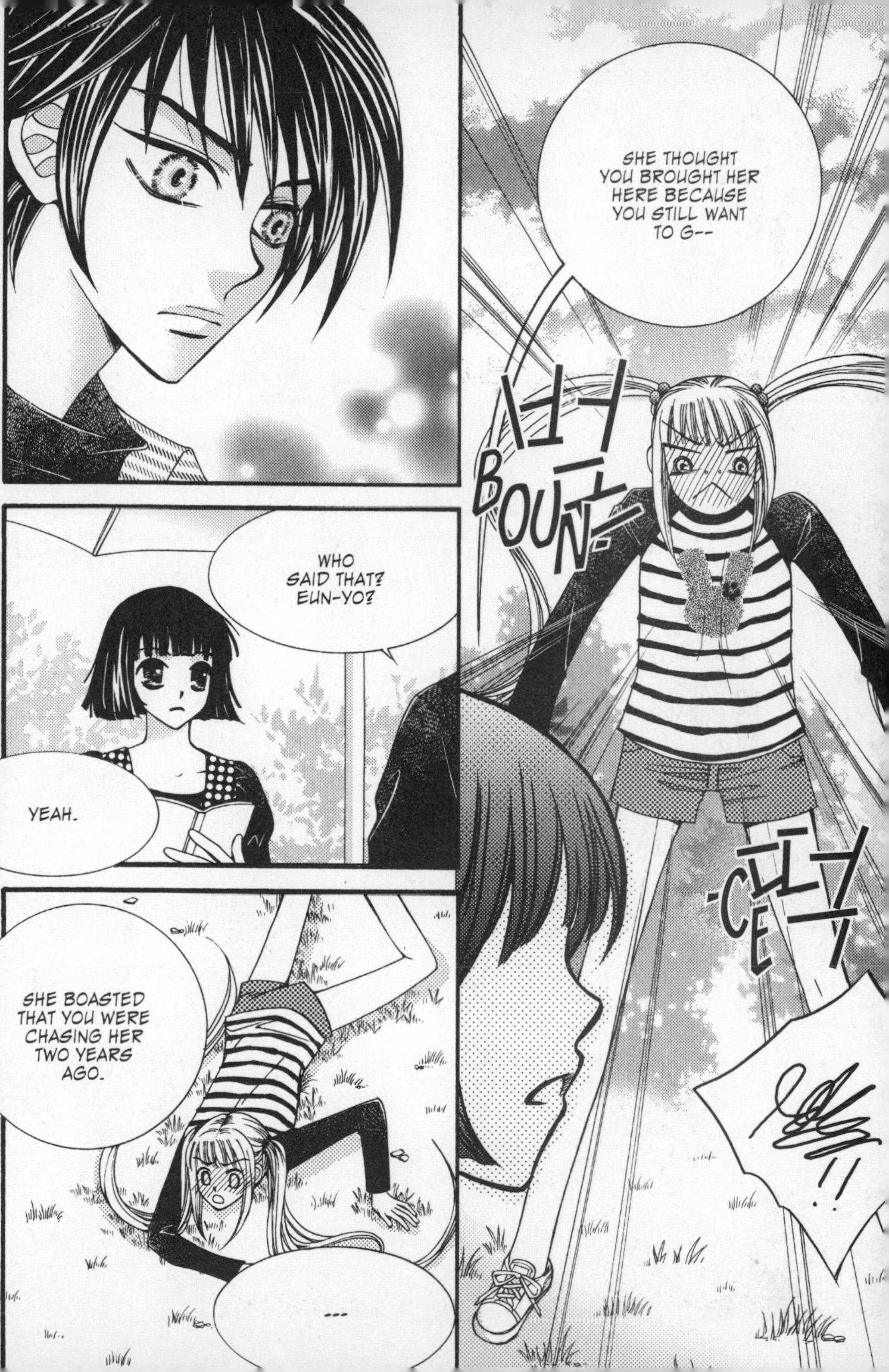
SHE THOUGHT YOU BROUGHT HER HERE BECAUSE YOU STILL WANT TO G--
BOUN-
-CE
WHO SAID THAT? EUN-YO?
YEAH.
SHE BOASTED THAT YOU WERE CHASING HER TWO YEARS AGO.
...

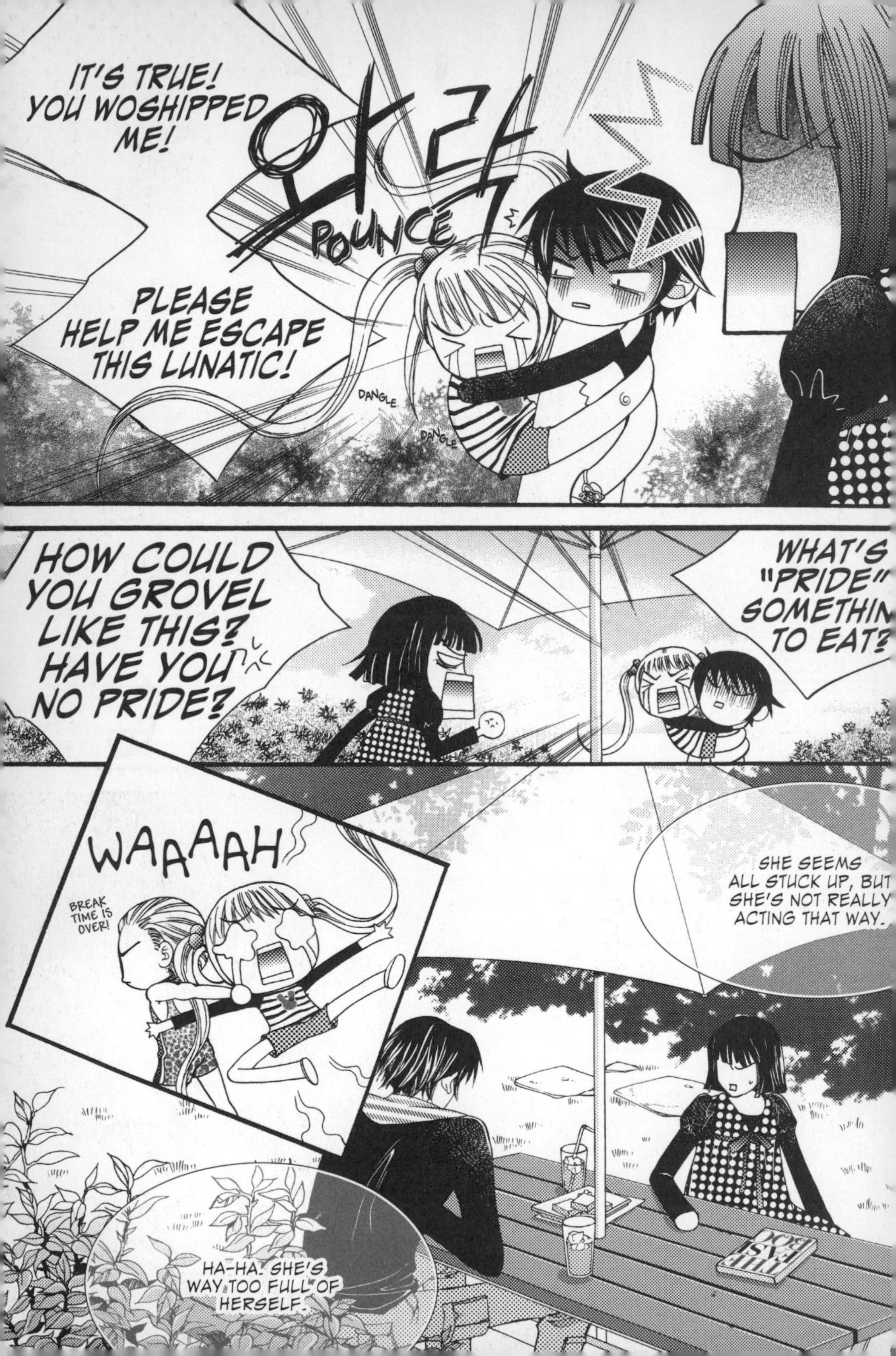
IT'S TRUE! YOU WOSHIPPED ME!
POUNCE
PLEASE HELP ME ESCAPE THIS LUNATIC!
DANGLE
DANGLE
WHAT'S "PRIDE" SOMETHIN TO EAT?
HOW COULD YOU GROVEL LIKE THIS? HAVE YOU NO PRIDE?
SHE SEEMS ALL STUCK UP, BUT SHE'S NOT REALLY ACTING THAT WAY.
WAAAAH
BREAK TIME IS OVER!
HA-HA. SHE'S WAY TOO FULL OF HERSELF.

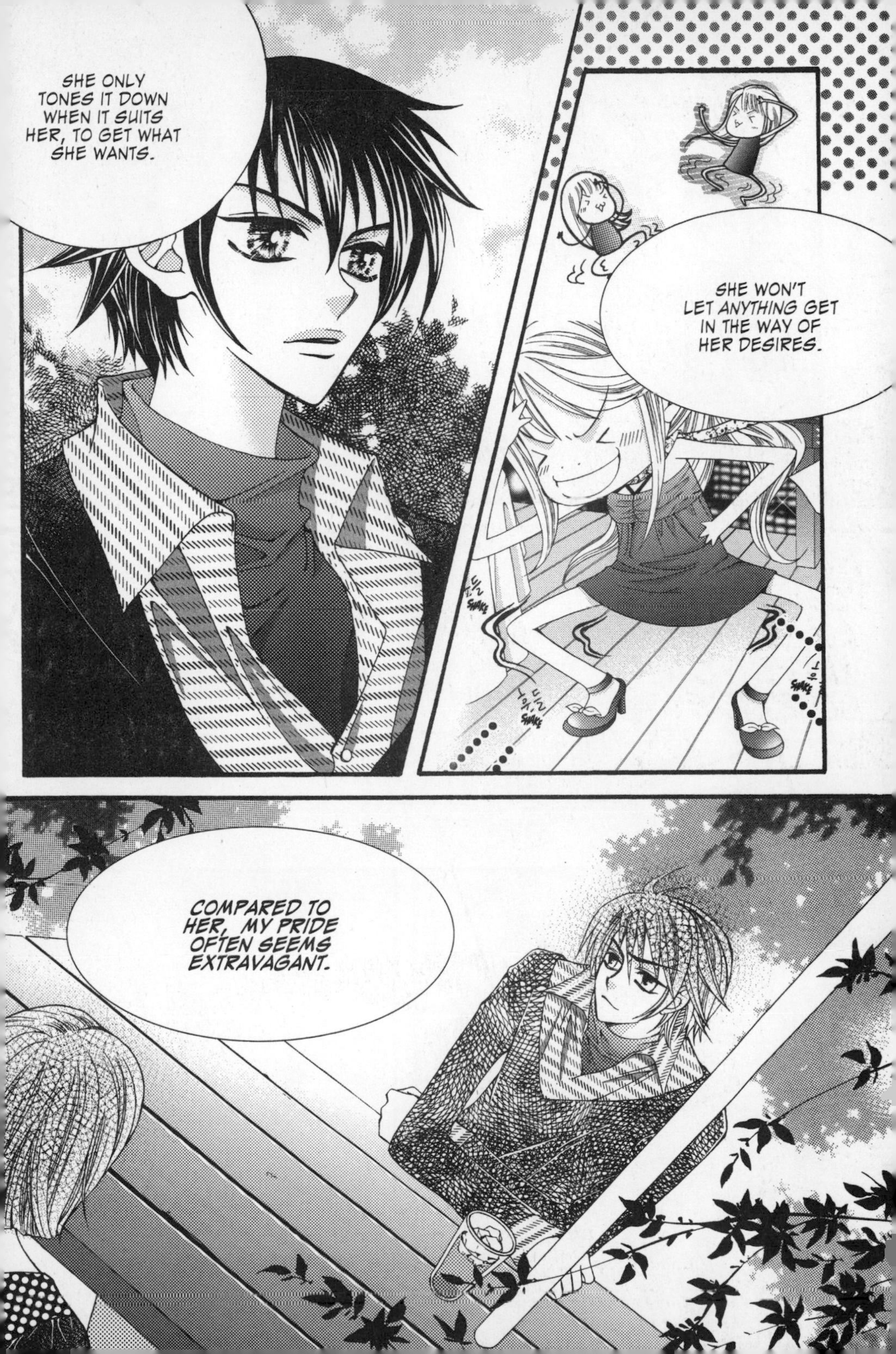
SHE ONLY TONES IT DOWN WHEN IT SUITS HER, TO GET WHAT SHE WANTS.
SHE WON'T LET ANYTHING GET IN THE WAY OF HER DESIRES.
SHAKE
SHAKE
SHAKE
COMPARED TO HER, MY PRIDE OFTEN SEEMS EXTRAVAGANT.

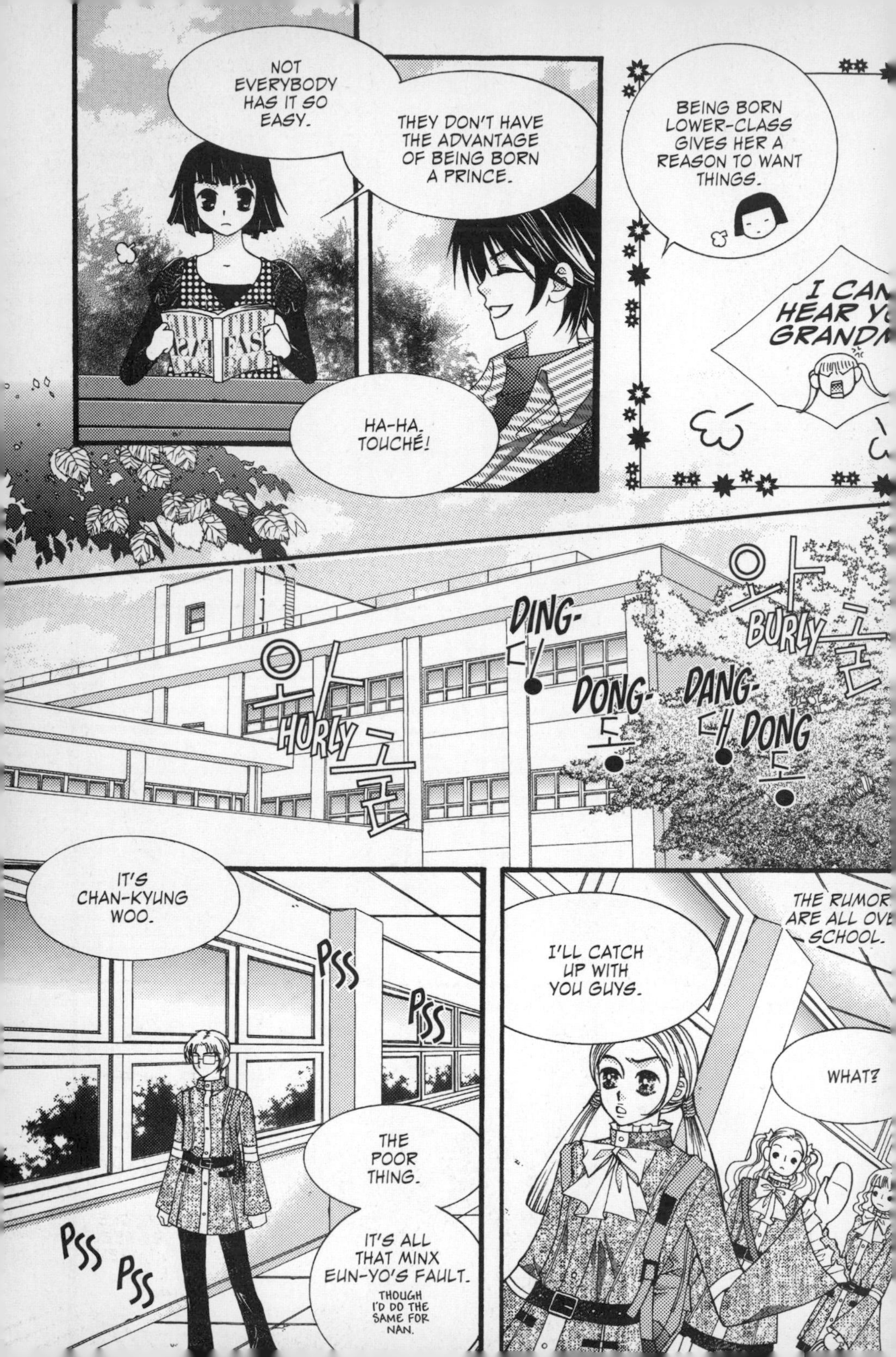

NOT EVERYBODY HAS IT SO EASY.
THEY DON'T HAVE THE ADVANTAGE OF BEING BORN A PRINCE.
HA-HA. TOUCHÉ!
BEING BORN LOWER-CLASS GIVES HER A REASON TO WANT THINGS.
I CAN
HEAR YO
GRANDM
HURLY
DING-
DONG-
DANG-
DONG
BURLY
IT'S CHAN-KYUNG WOO.
PSS
PSS
PSS
PSS
THE POOR THING.
IT'S ALL THAT MINX EUN-YO'S FAULT.
THOUGH I'D DO THE SAME FOR NAN.
I'LL CATCH UP WITH YOU GUYS.
THE RUMOR
ARE ALL OVE
SCHOOL.
WHAT?

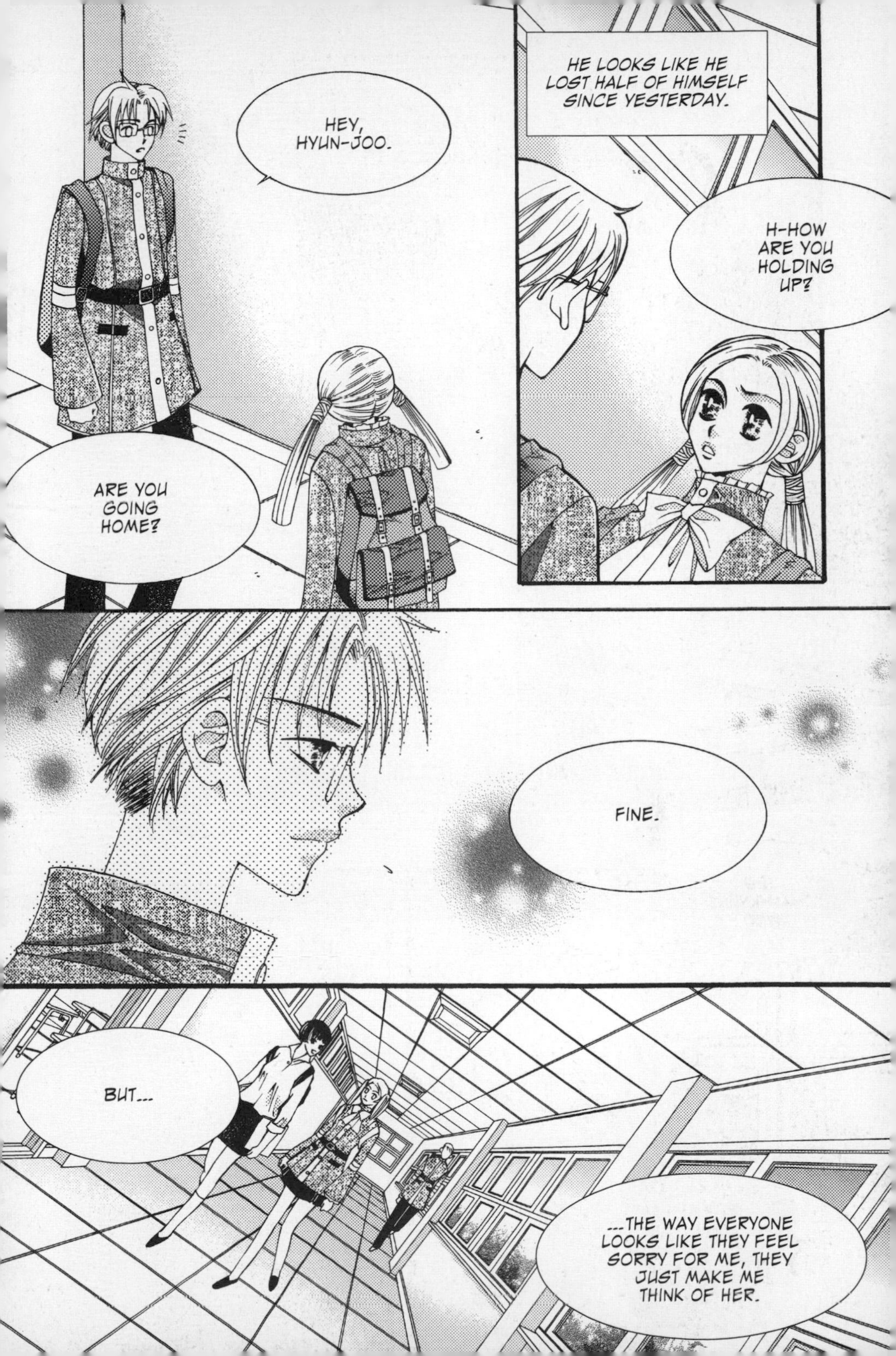
HEY, HYUN-JOO.
ARE YOU GOING HOME?
HE LOOKS LIKE HE LOST HALF OF HIMSELF SINCE YESTERDAY.
H-HOW ARE YOU HOLDING UP?
FINE.
BUT...
...THE WAY EVERYONE LOOKS LIKE THEY FEEL SORRY FOR ME, THEY JUST MAKE ME THINK OF HER.

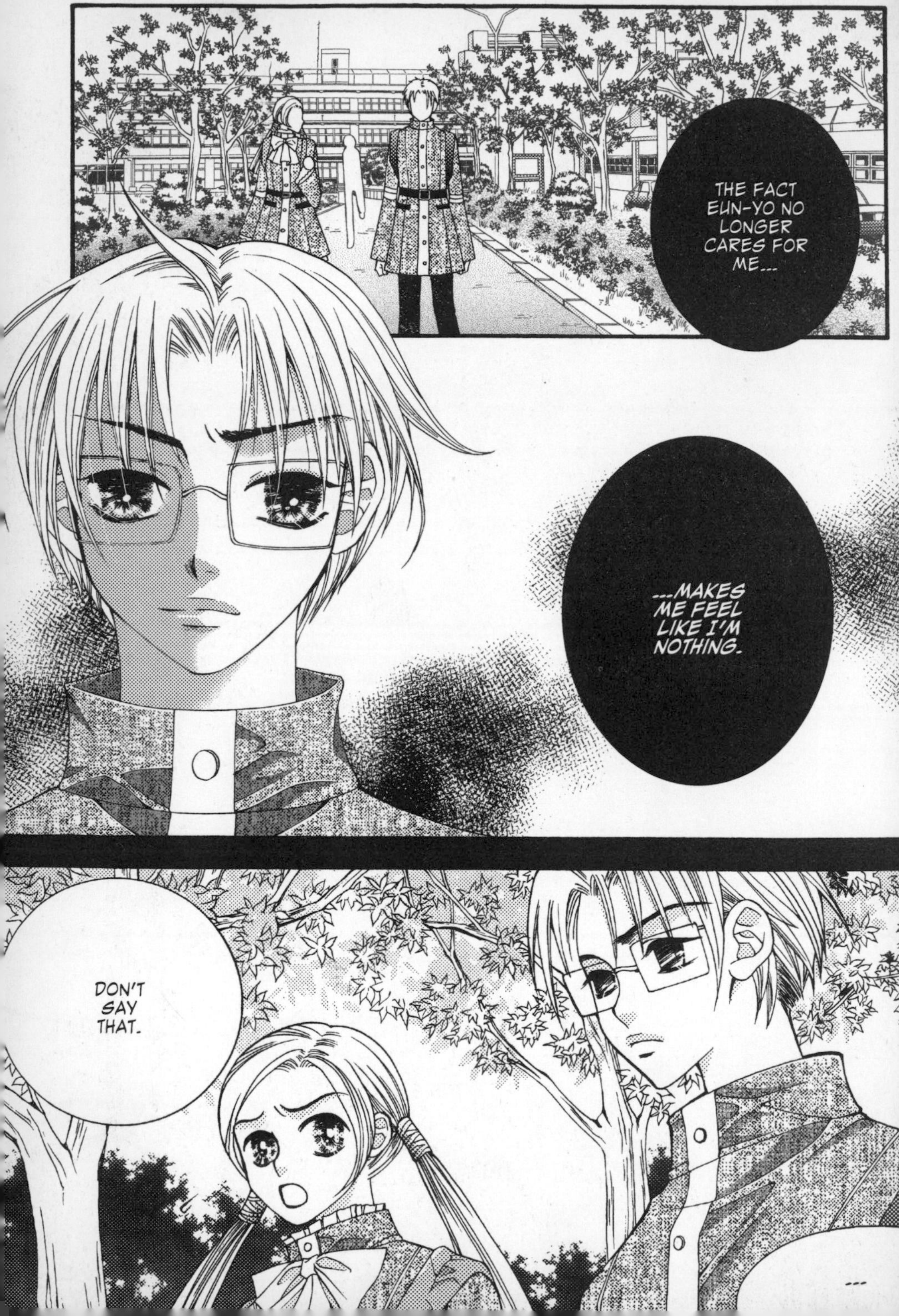
THE FACT EUN-YO NO LONGER CARES FOR ME...
...MAKES ME FEEL LIKE I'M NOTHING.
DON'T SAY THAT.
...

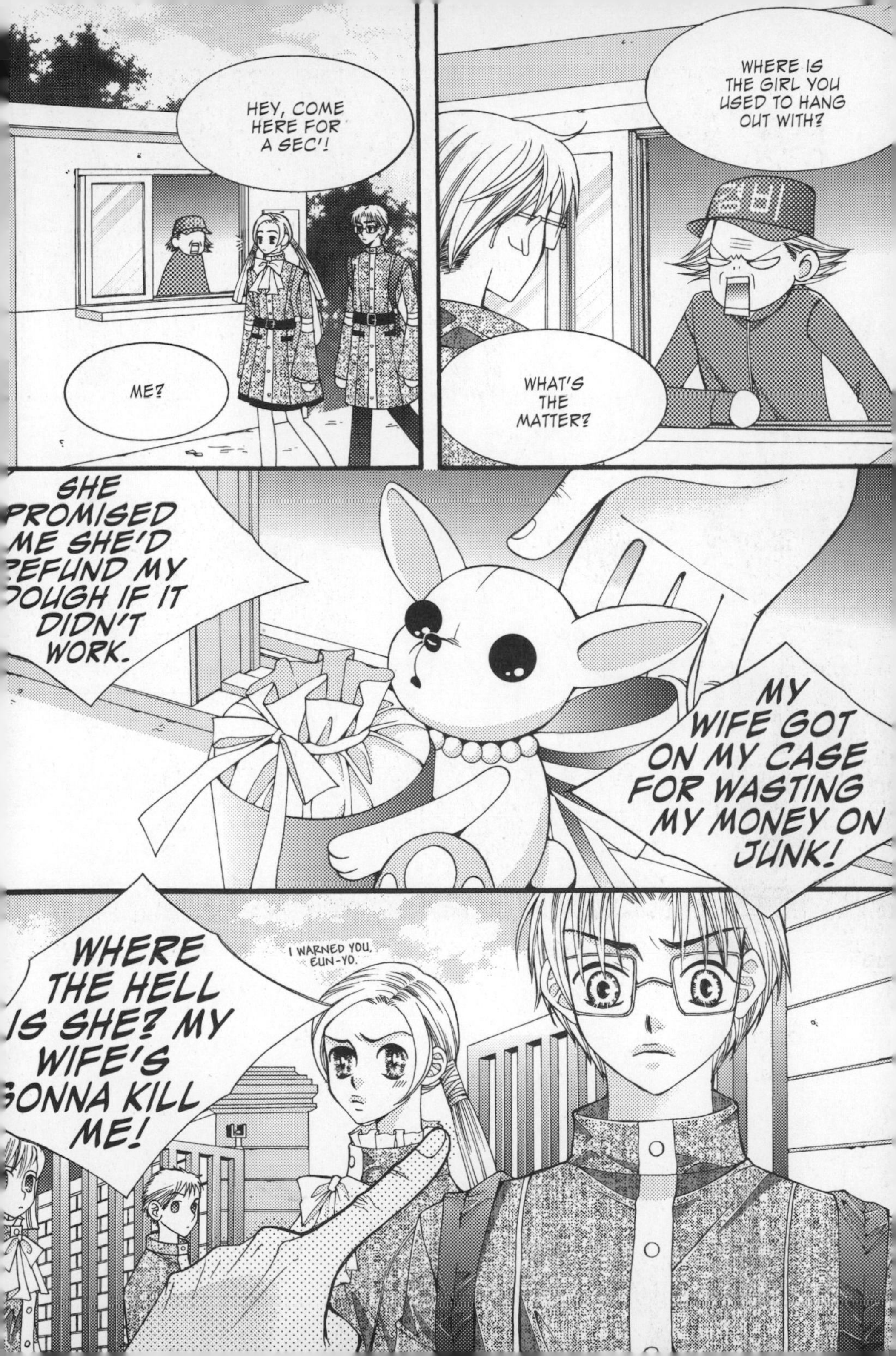
HEY, COME HERE FOR A SEC'!
ME?
WHERE IS THE GIRL YOU USED TO HANG OUT WITH?
WHAT'S THE MATTER?
SHE PROMISED ME SHE'D REFUND MY DOUGH IF IT DIDN'T WORK.
MY WIFE GOT ON MY CASE FOR WASTING MY MONEY ON JUNK!
WHERE THE HELL IS SHE? MY WIFE'S GONNA KILL ME!
I WARNED YOU, EUN-YO.

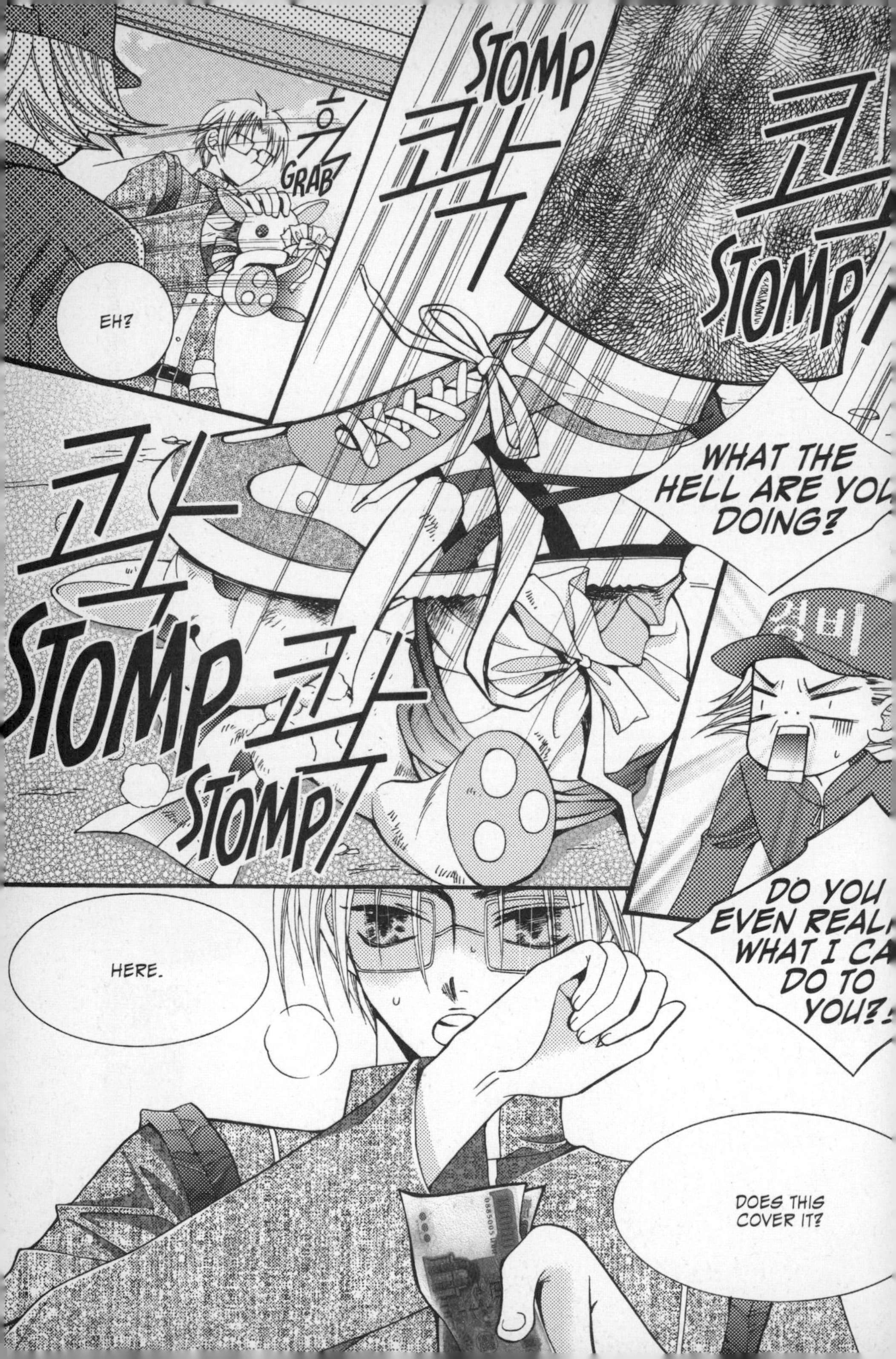
GRAB
EH?
STOMP
STOMP
STOMP
STOMP
WHAT THE HELL ARE YOU DOING?
DO YOU EVEN REAL WHAT I CA DO TO YOU?!
HERE.
DOES THIS COVER IT?

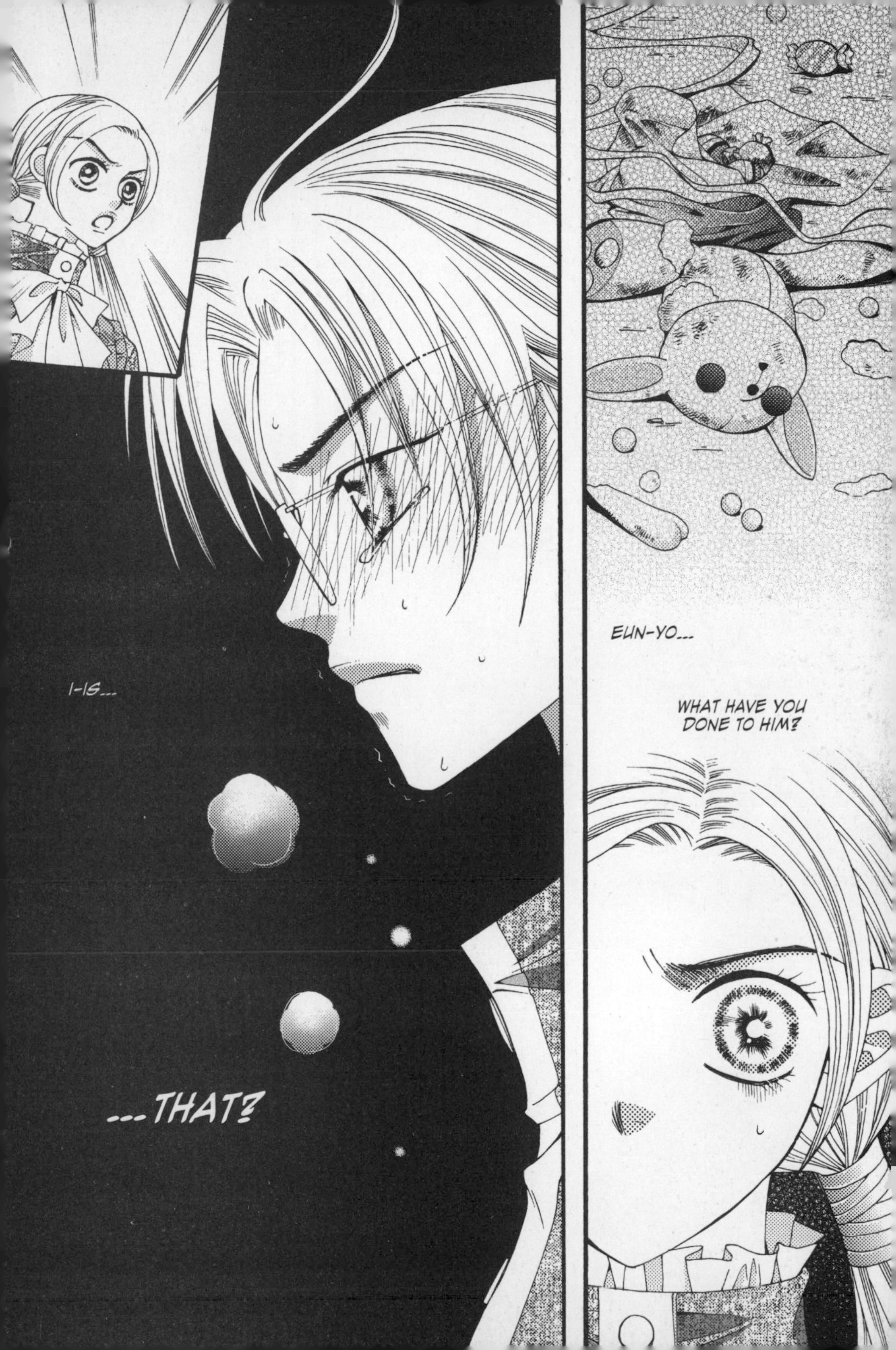
EUN-YO...
WHAT HAVE YOU DONE TO HIM?
I-IS...
...THAT?

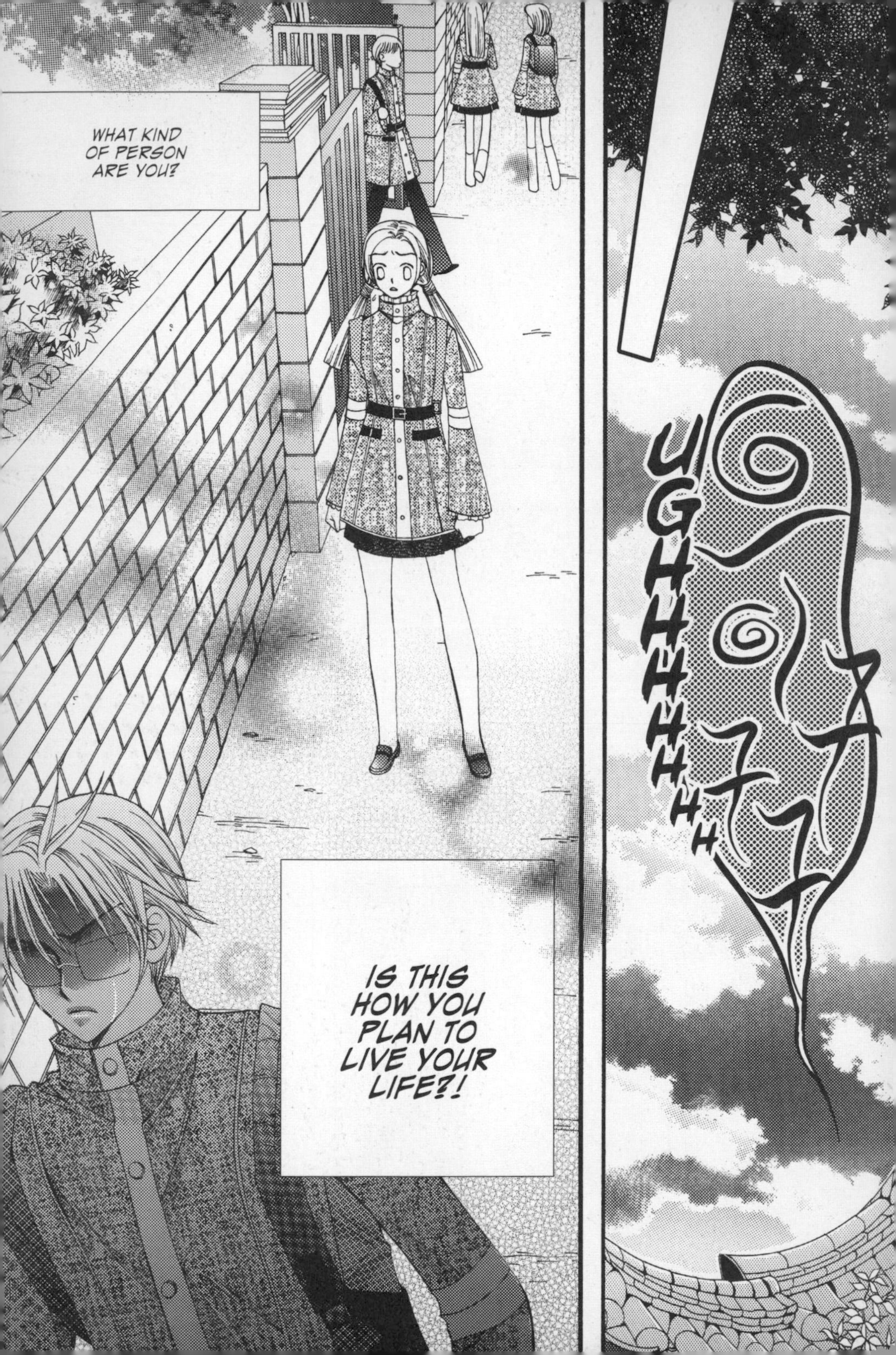
UGHHHHHHHH
WHAT KIND OF PERSON ARE YOU?
IS THIS HOW YOU PLAN TO LIVE YOUR LIFE?!

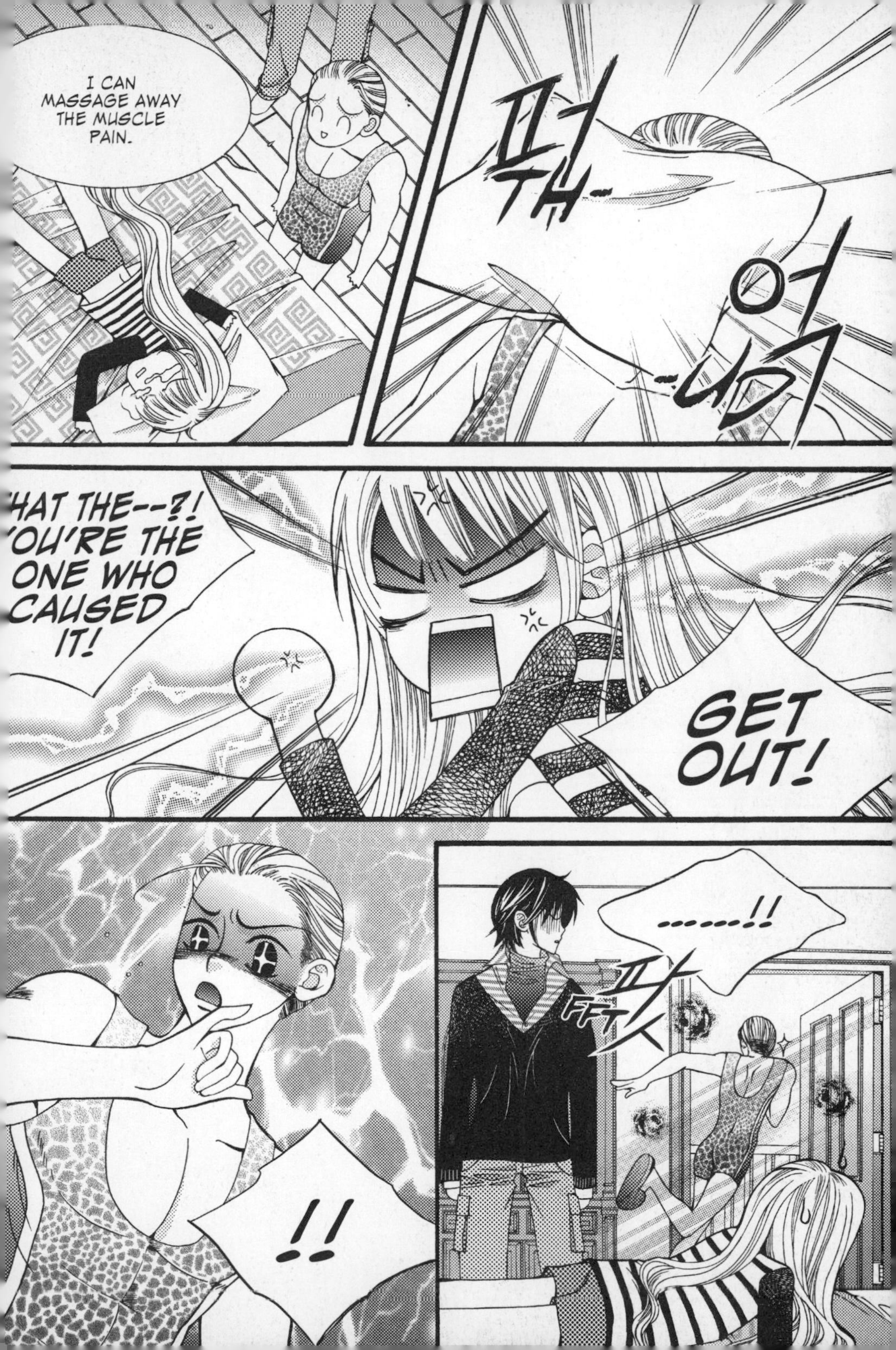
I CAN MASSAGE AWAY THE MUSCLE PAIN.
퍼억
TH--
--UD
HAT THE--?! YOU'RE THE ONE WHO CAUSED IT!
GET OUT!
!!
......!!
파앗
FFFT

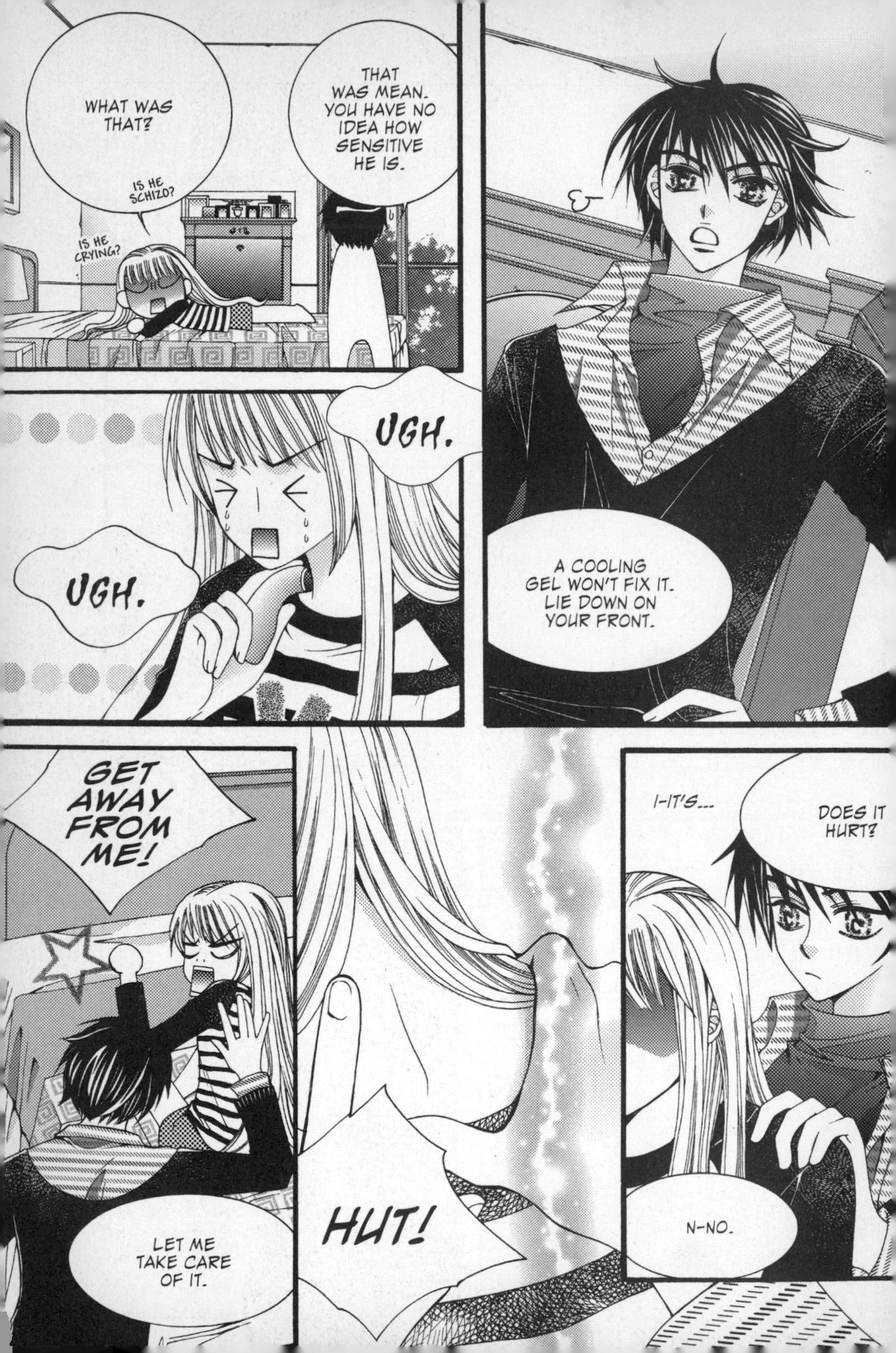
WHAT WAS THAT?
IS HE SCHIZO?
IS HE CRYING?
THAT WAS MEAN. YOU HAVE NO IDEA HOW SENSITIVE HE IS.
UGH.
UGH.
A COOLING GEL WON'T FIX IT. LIE DOWN ON YOUR FRONT.
GET AWAY FROM ME!
LET ME TAKE CARE OF IT.
HUT!
I-IT'S...
DOES IT HURT?
N-NO.

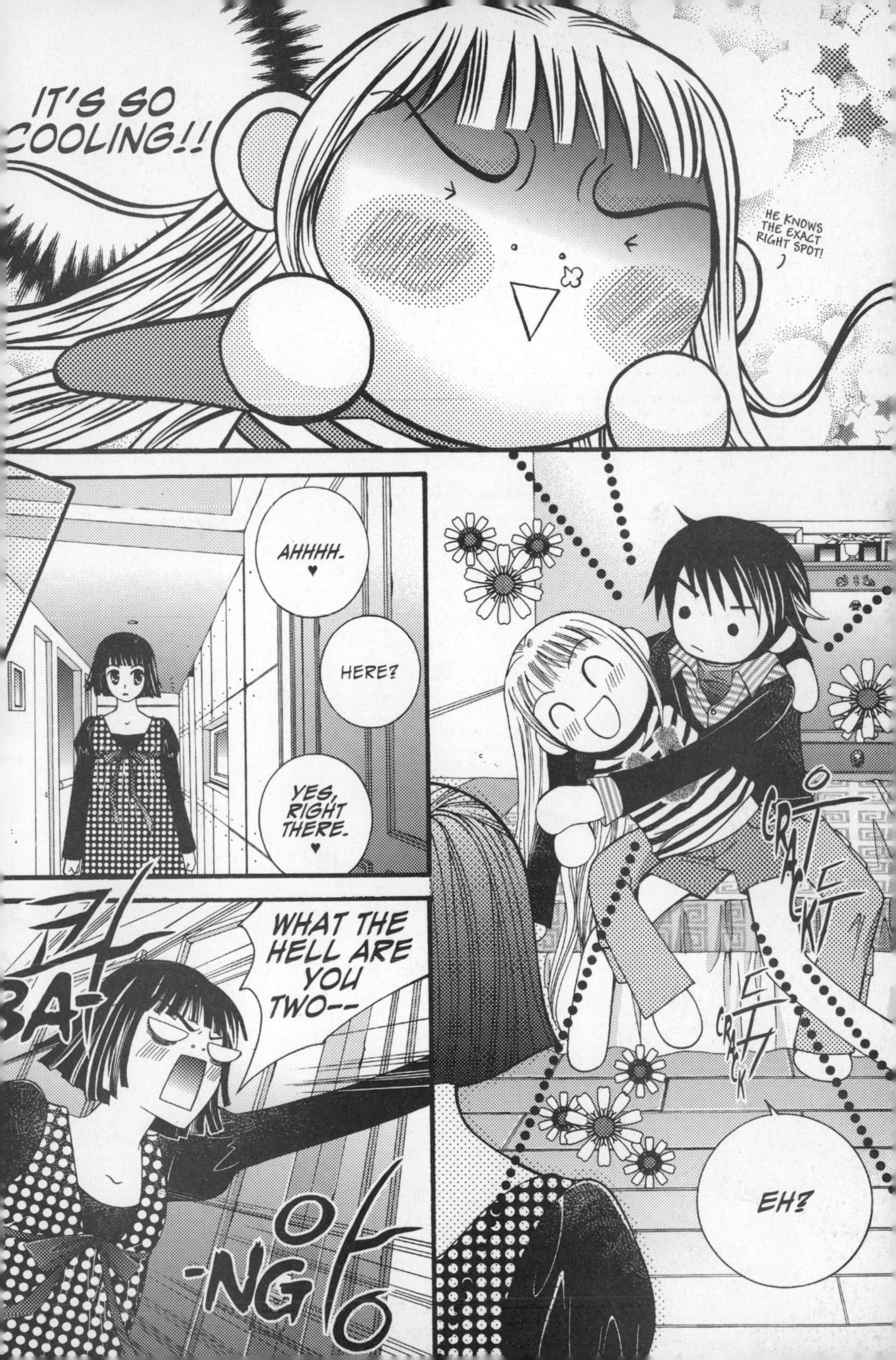
HE KNOWS THE EXACT RIGHT SPOT!
IT'S SO COOLING!!
AHHHH.♥
HERE?
YES, RIGHT THERE.♥
CRACK
CRACK CRACK
EH?
WHAT THE HELL ARE YOU TWO--
BA-
-NG

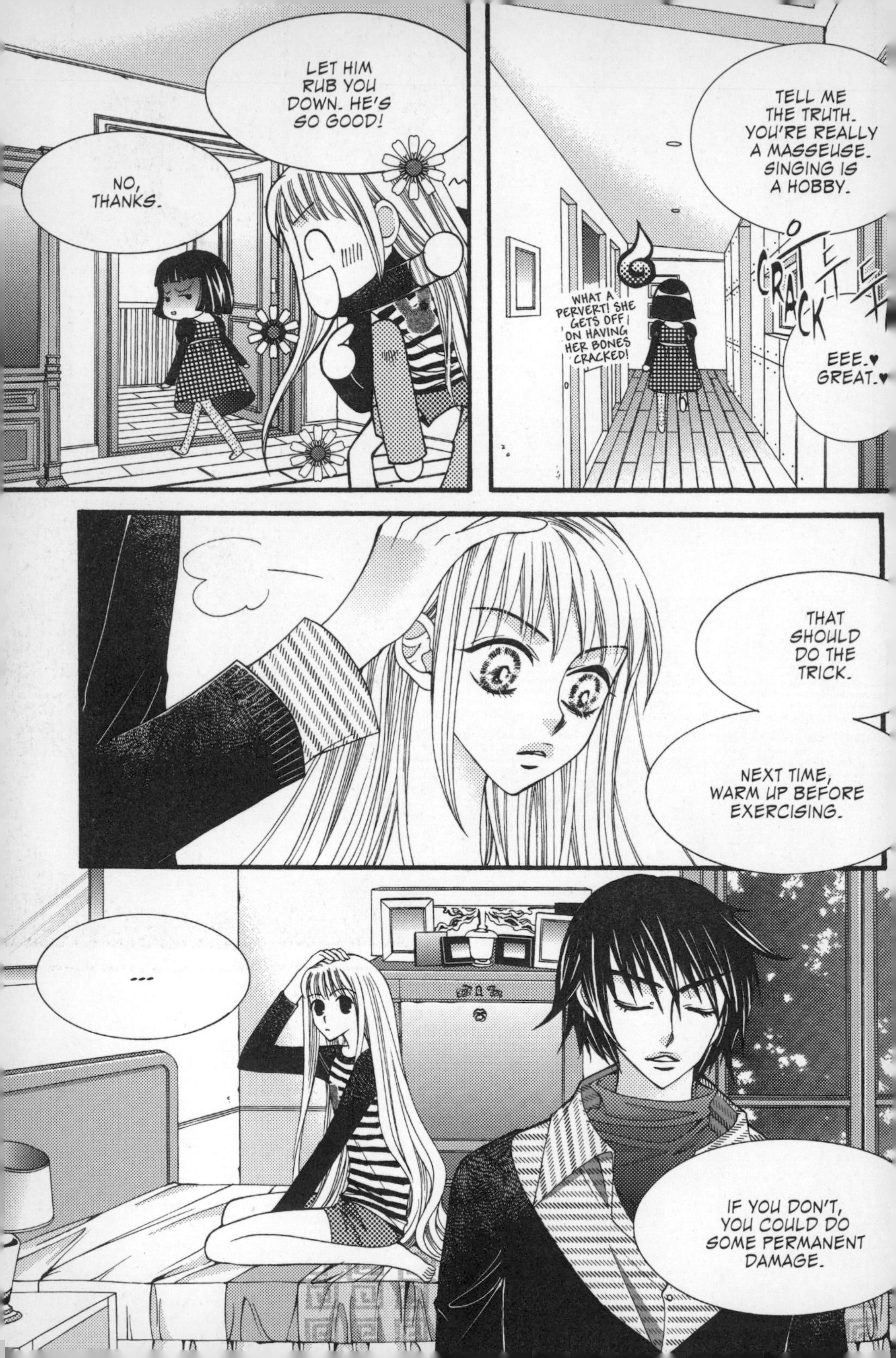
LET HIM RUB YOU DOWN. HE'S SO GOOD!
NO, THANKS.
TELL ME THE TRUTH. YOU'RE REALLY A MASSEUSE. SINGING IS A HOBBY.
CRACK
EEE.♥ GREAT.♥
WHAT A PERVERT! SHE GETS OFF ON HAVING HER BONES CRACKED!
THAT SHOULD DO THE TRICK.
NEXT TIME, WARM UP BEFORE EXERCISING.
...
IF YOU DON'T, YOU COULD DO SOME PERMANENT DAMAGE.

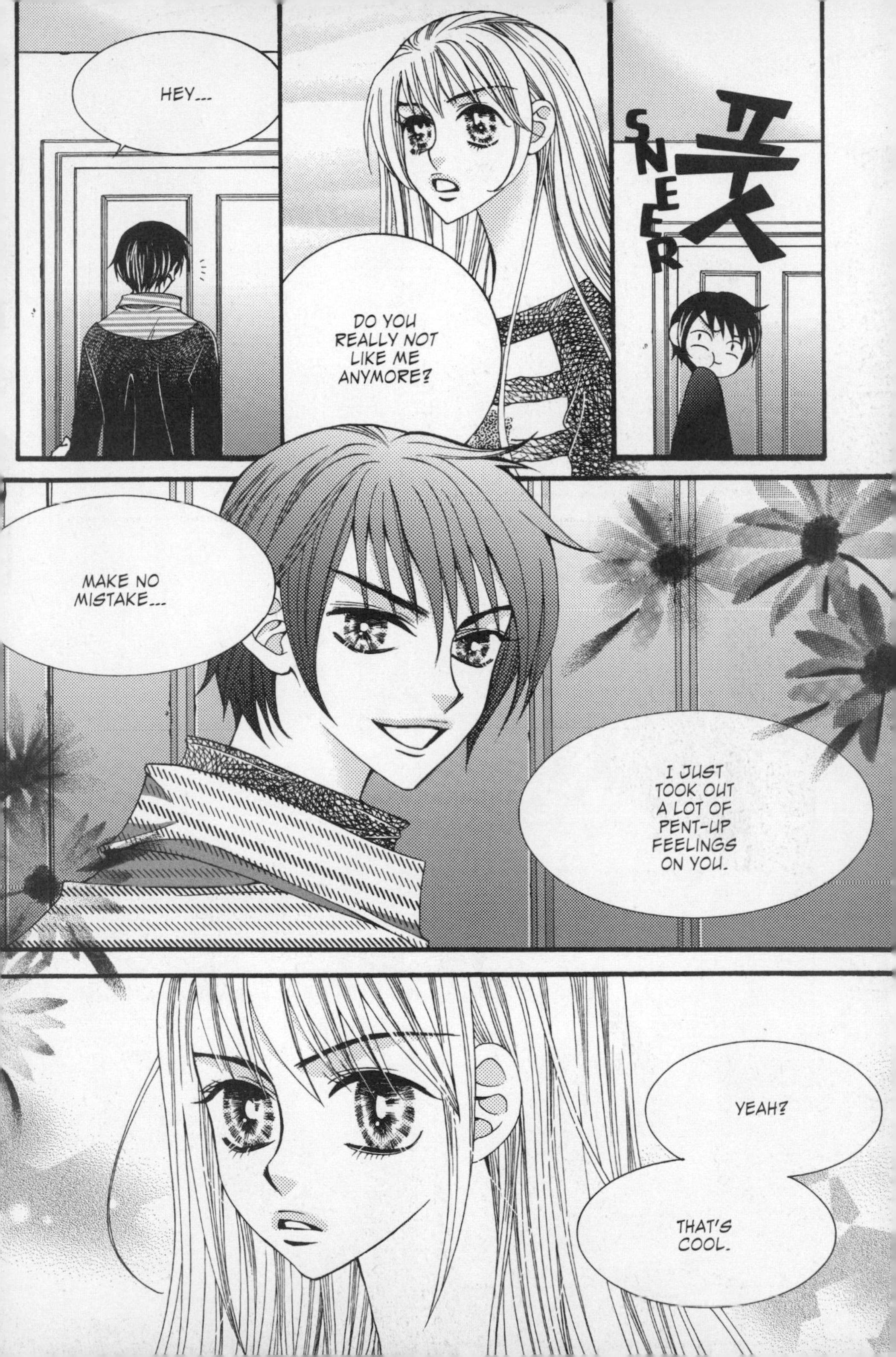
HEY...
DO YOU REALLY NOT LIKE ME ANYMORE?
SNEER
MAKE NO MISTAKE...
I JUST TOOK OUT A LOT OF PENT-UP FEELINGS ON YOU.
YEAH?
THAT'S COOL.

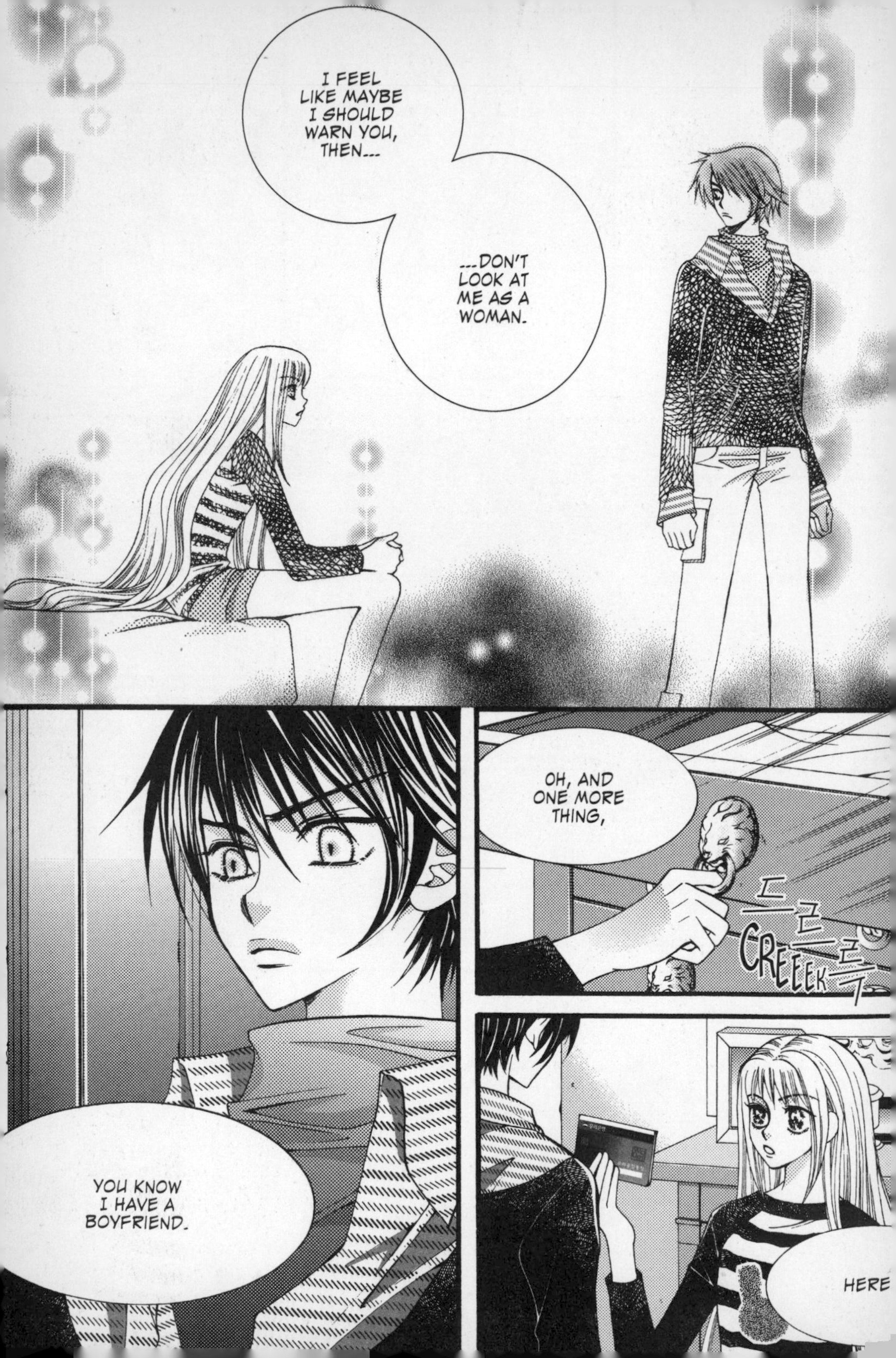
I FEEL LIKE MAYBE I SHOULD WARN YOU, THEN...
...DON'T LOOK AT ME AS A WOMAN.
OH, AND ONE MORE THING,
CREEEK
YOU KNOW I HAVE A BOYFRIEND.
HERE

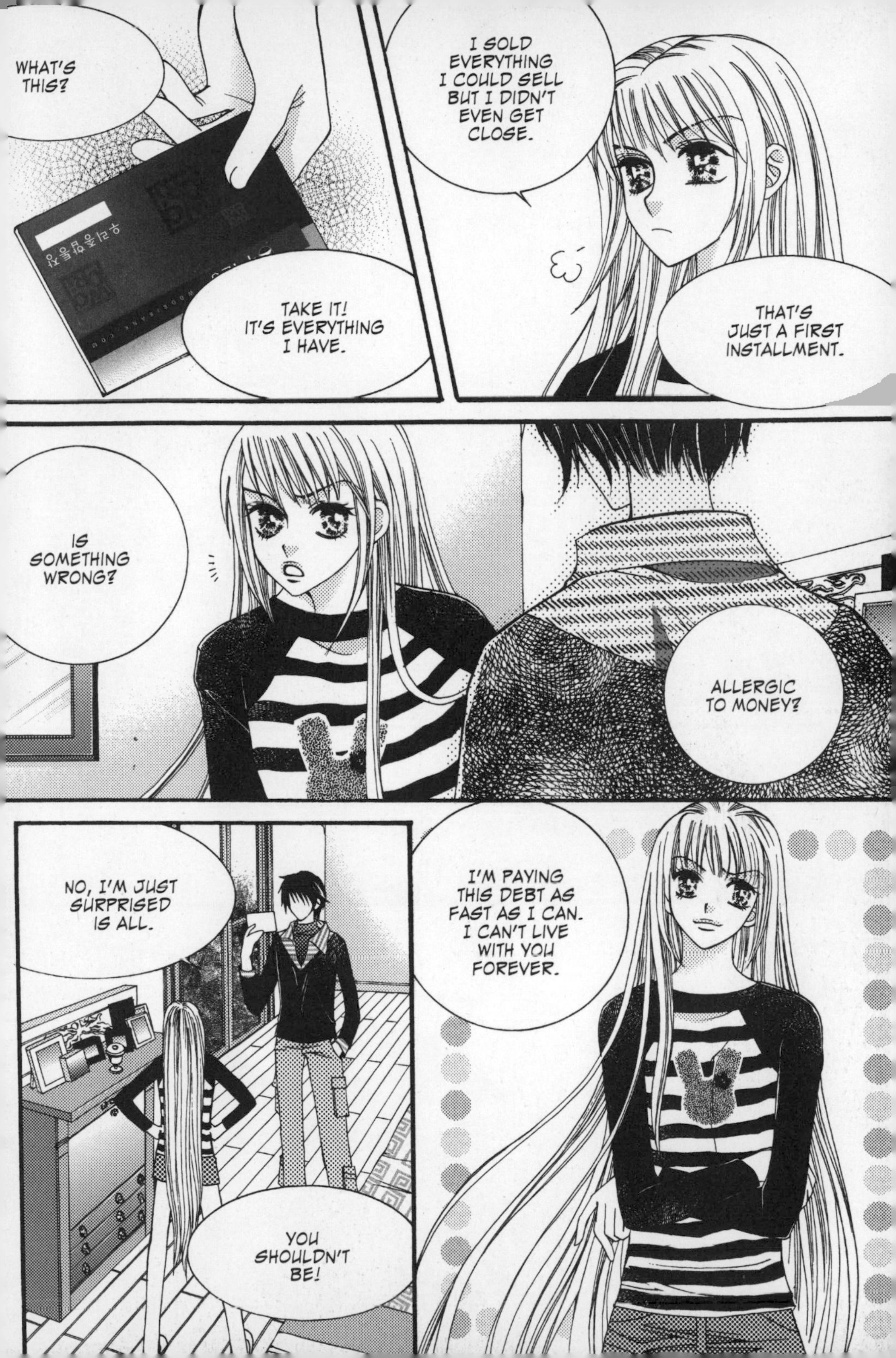
WHAT'S THIS?
TAKE IT! IT'S EVERYTHING I HAVE.
I SOLD EVERYTHING I COULD SELL BUT I DIDN'T EVEN GET CLOSE.
THAT'S JUST A FIRST INSTALLMENT.
IS SOMETHING WRONG?
ALLERGIC TO MONEY?
NO, I'M JUST SURPRISED IS ALL.
YOU SHOULDN'T BE!
I'M PAYING THIS DEBT AS FAST AS I CAN. I CAN'T LIVE WITH YOU FOREVER.

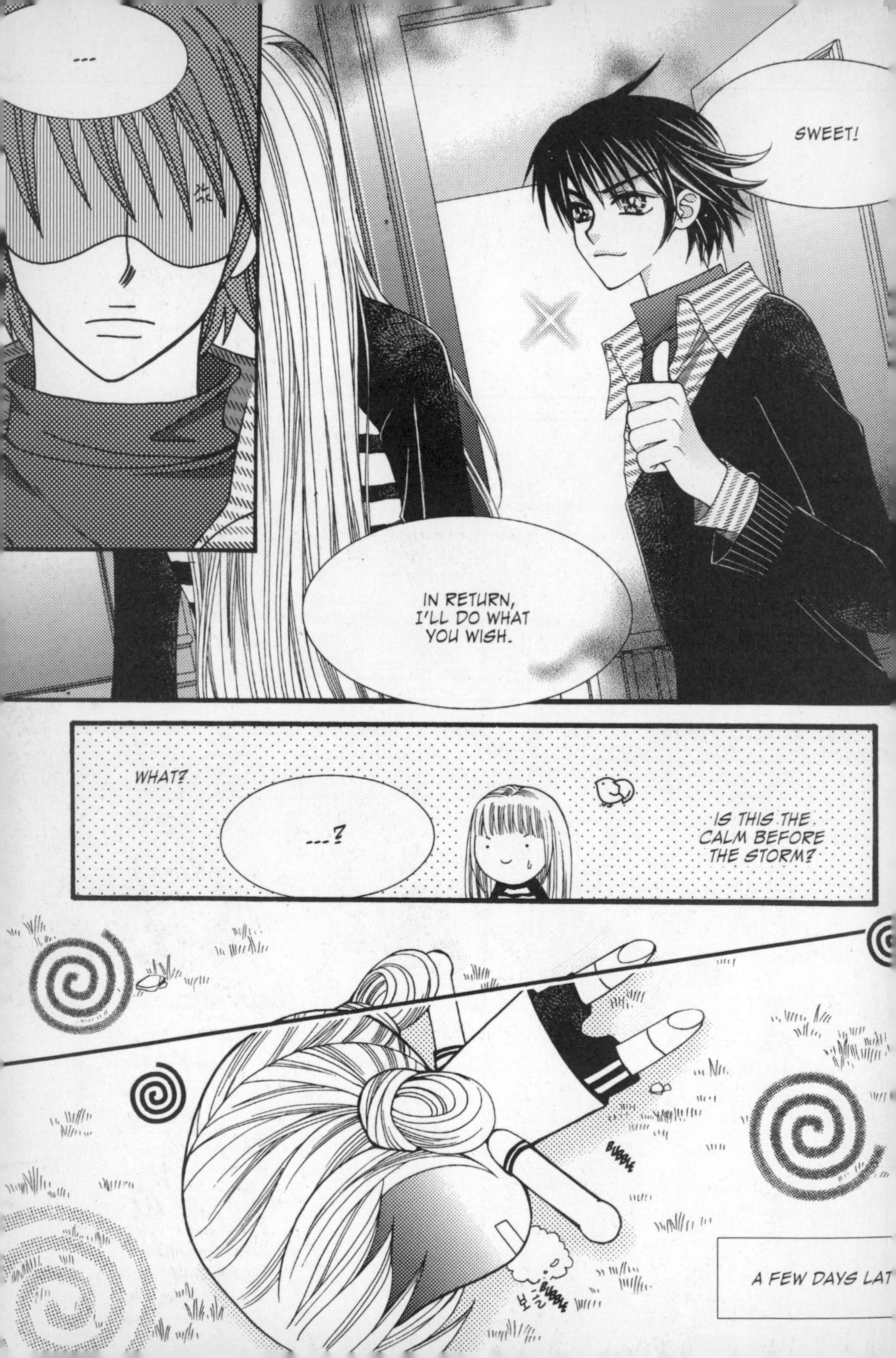
SWEET!
IN RETURN, I'LL DO WHAT YOU WISH.
...
IS THIS THE CALM BEFORE THE STORM?
...?
WHAT?
BUBBLE
BUBBLE
A FEW DAYS LAT

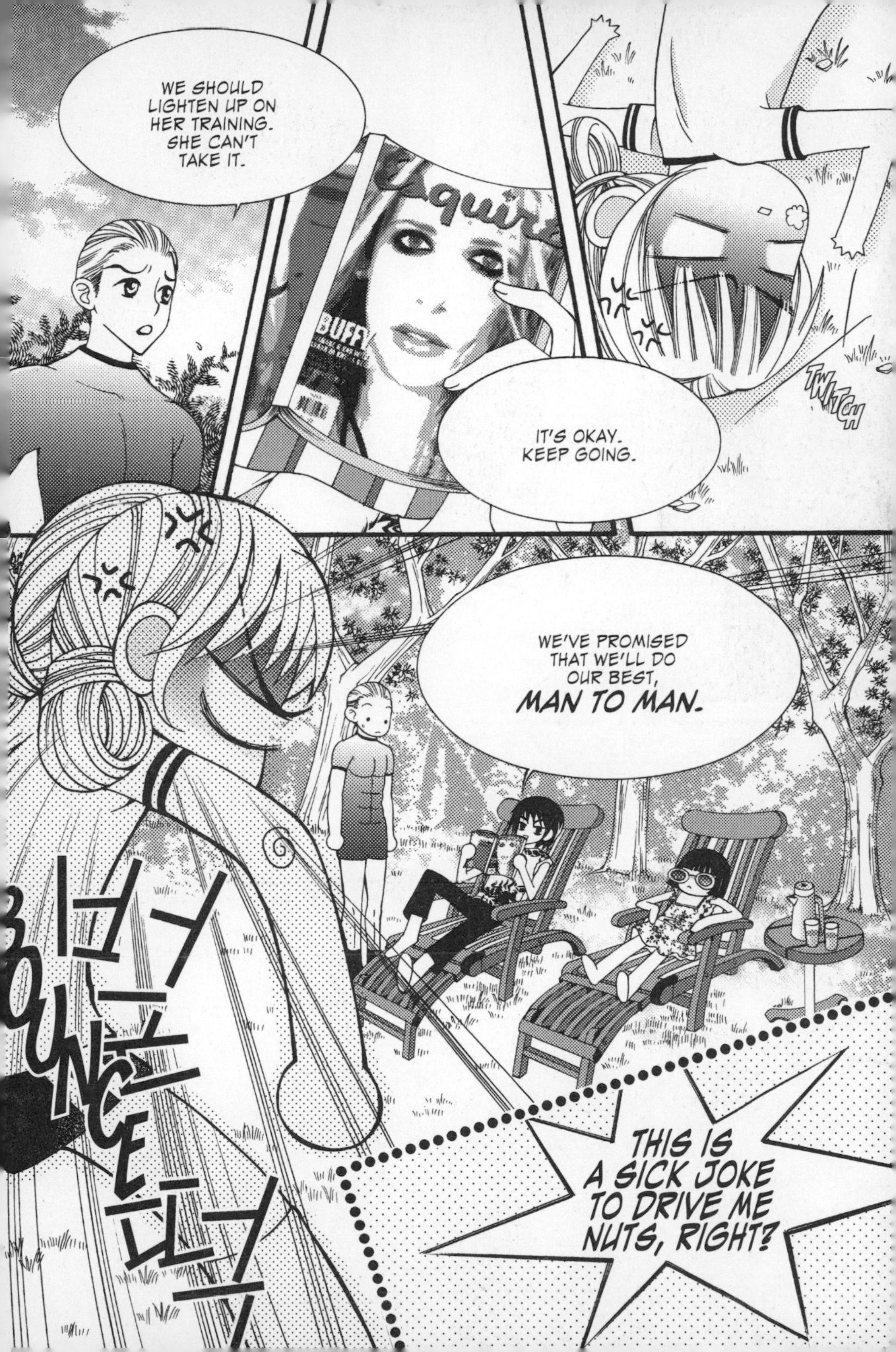
TWITCH
WE SHOULD LIGHTEN UP ON HER TRAINING. SHE CAN'T TAKE IT.
IT'S OKAY. KEEP GOING.
WE'VE PROMISED THAT WE'LL DO OUR BEST, MAN TO MAN.
BOUNCE
THIS IS A SICK JOKE TO DRIVE ME NUTS, RIGHT?

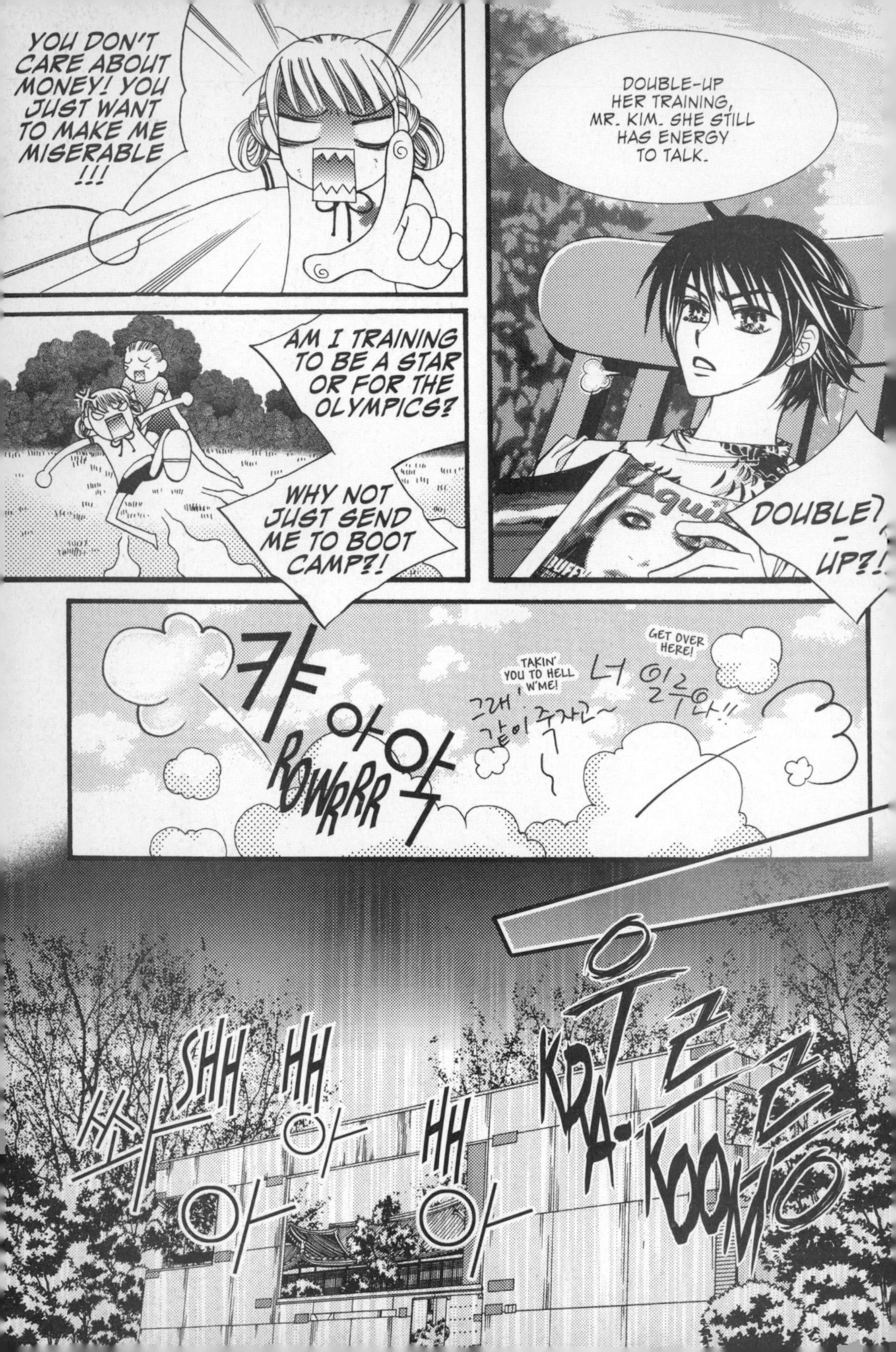

YOU DON'T CARE ABOUT MONEY! YOU JUST WANT TO MAKE ME MISERABLE !!!
DOUBLE-UP HER TRAINING, MR. KIM. SHE STILL HAS ENERGY TO TALK.
AM I TRAINING TO BE A STAR OR FOR THE OLYMPICS?
WHY NOT JUST SEND ME TO BOOT CAMP?!
DOUBLE-UP?!
캬아아악
ROWRRR
그래, 같이 죽자고~
TAKIN' YOU TO HELL W'ME!
너 일루 와라!!
GET OVER HERE!
SHHHHHH
우르르
KRA-KOOM

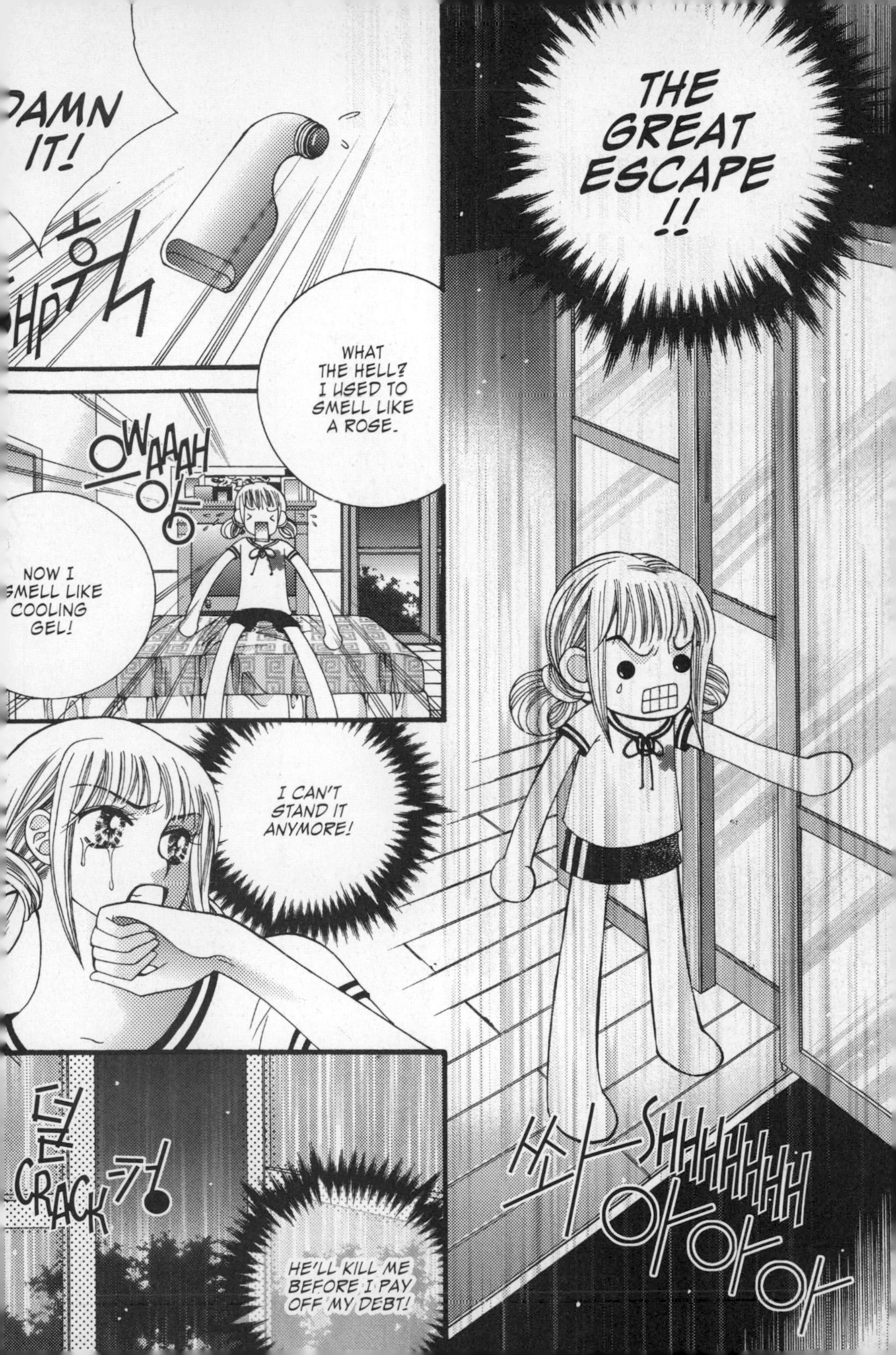
DAMN IT!
SHP
WHAT THE HELL? I USED TO SMELL LIKE A ROSE.
OWAAAH
NOW I SMELL LIKE COOLING GEL!
I CAN'T STAND IT ANYMORE!
CRACK
HE'LL KILL ME BEFORE I PAY OFF MY DEBT!
THE GREAT ESCAPE!!
SHHHHHHH

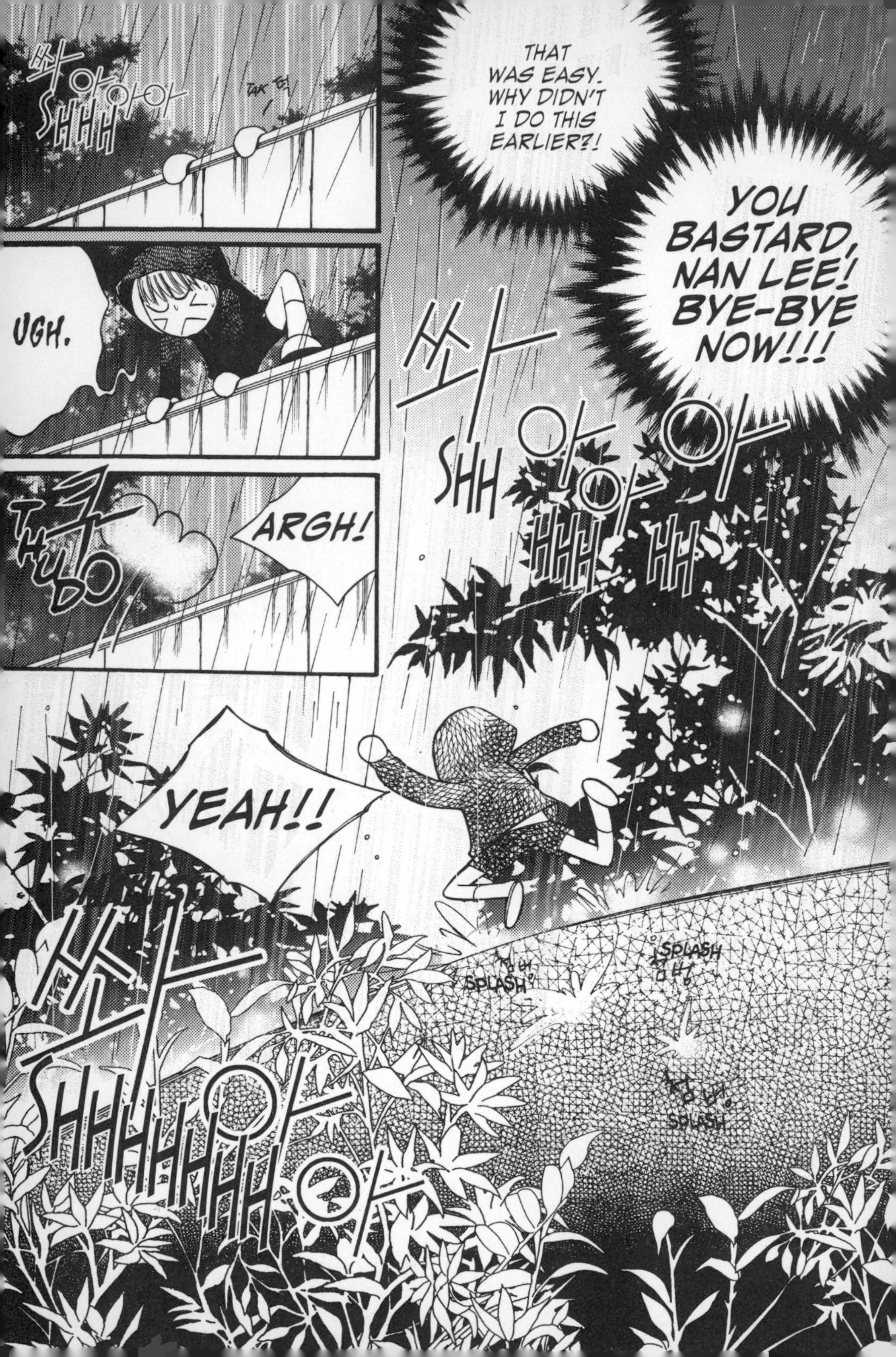
SHHH
TAK
UGH.
THUD
ARGH!
THAT WAS EASY. WHY DIDN'T I DO THIS EARLIER?!
YOU BASTARD, NAN LEE! BYE-BYE NOW!!!
SHHHHHH
YEAH!!
SHHHHHHHH
SPLASH
SPLASH
SPLASH

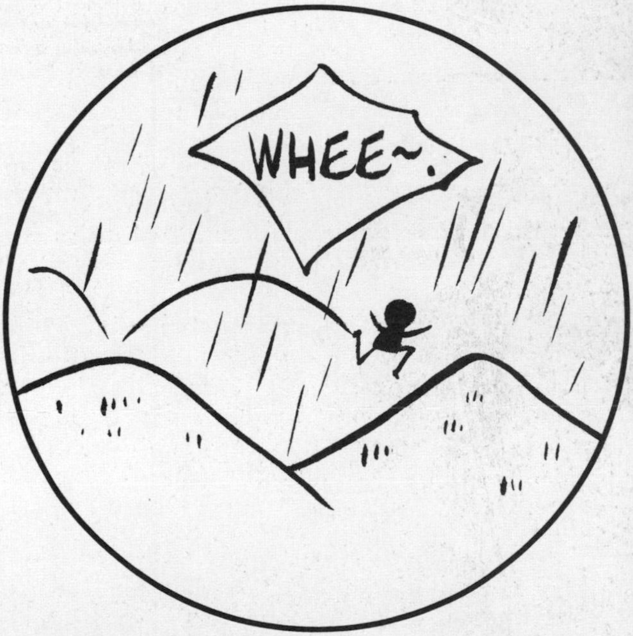
WHEE~.

THE TRAINING WAS USEFUL AFTER ALL.

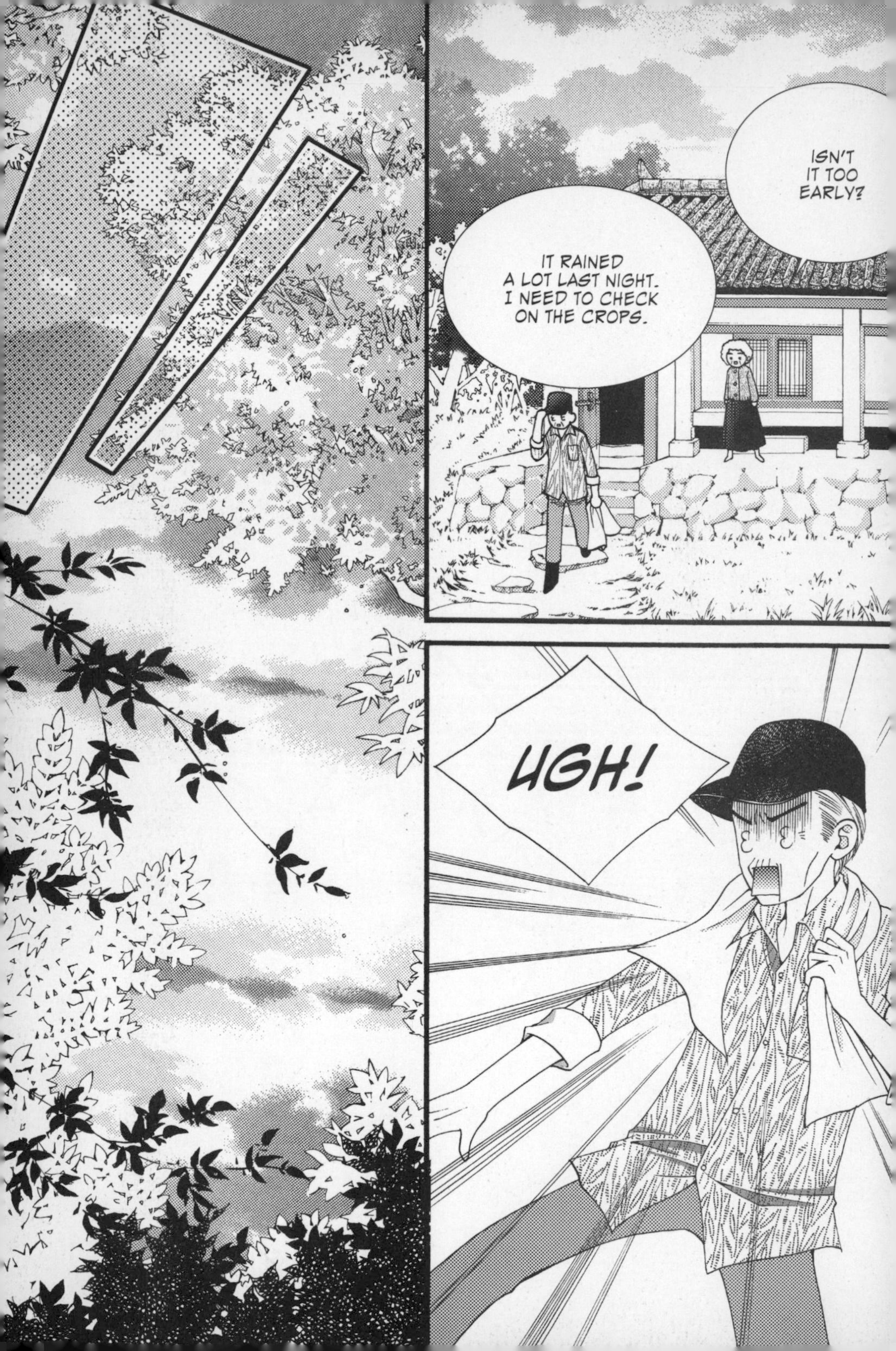
ISN'T IT TOO EARLY?
IT RAINED A LOT LAST NIGHT. I NEED TO CHECK ON THE CROPS.
UGH!

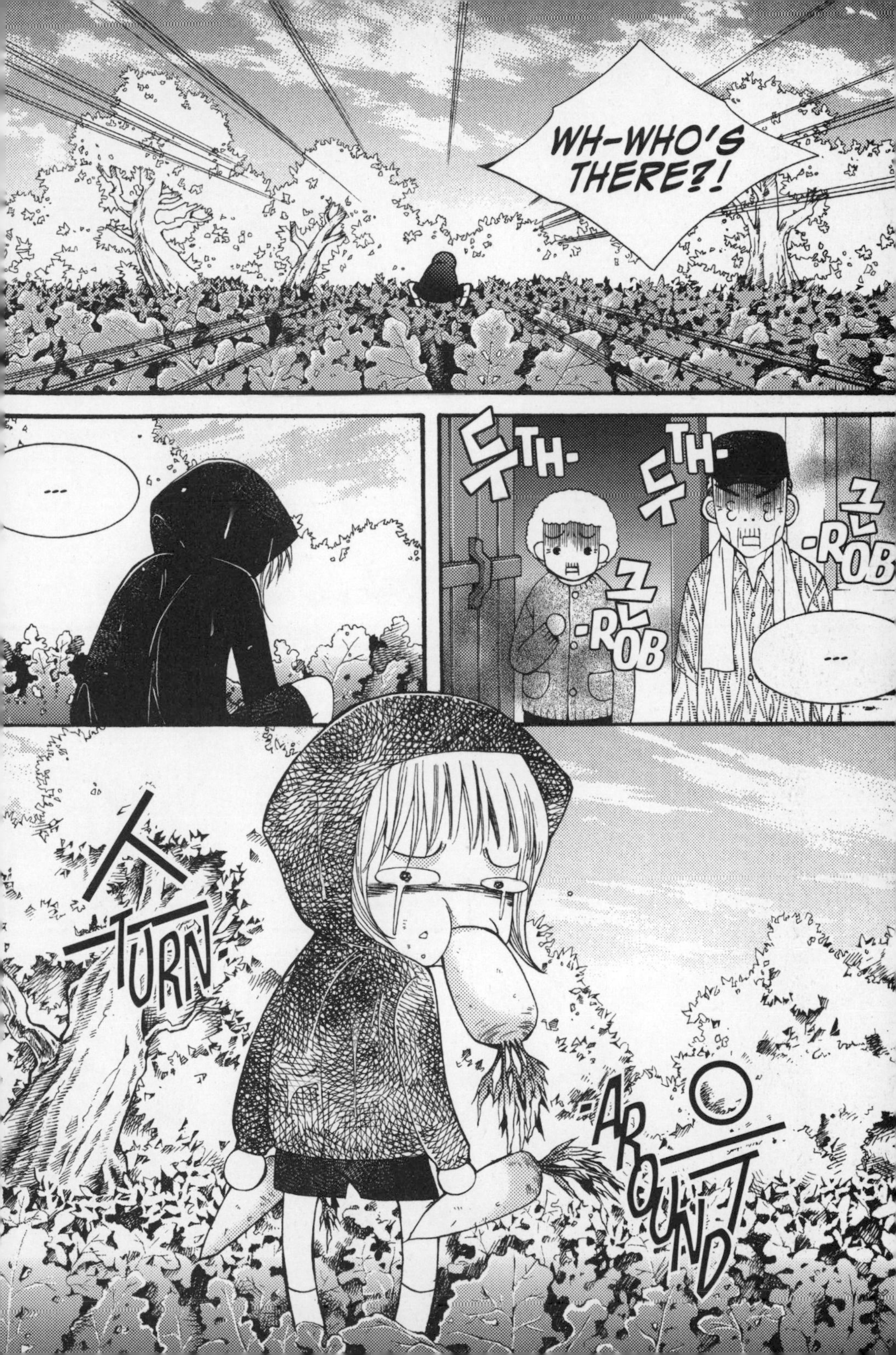

WH-WHO'S THERE?!
...
TH-
TH-
-ROB
-ROB
...
TURN-
-AROUND

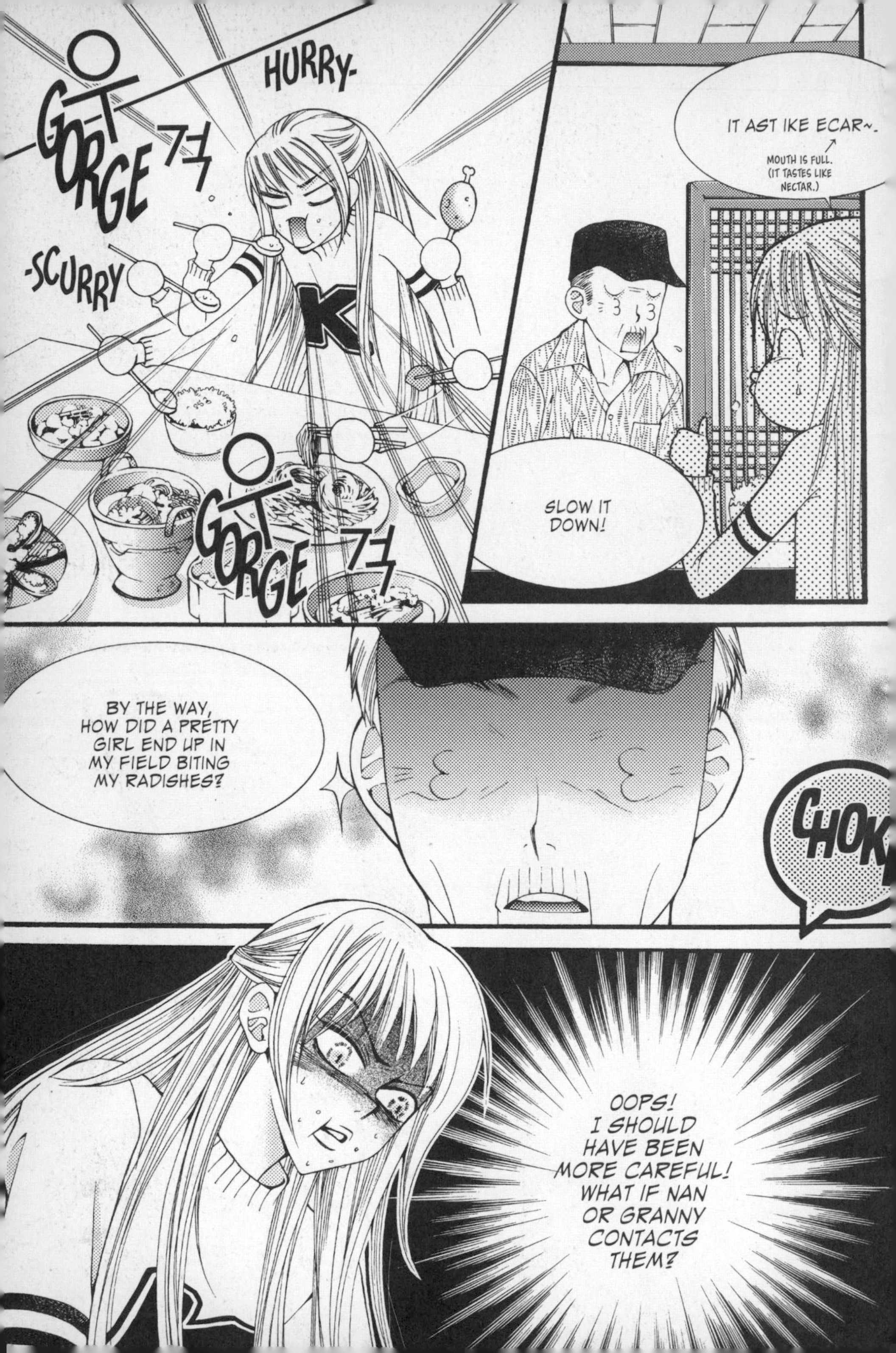
GORGE
HURRY-
-SCURRY
GORGE
IT AST IKE ECAR~.
MOUTH IS FULL. (IT TASTES LIKE NECTAR.)
SLOW IT DOWN!
BY THE WAY, HOW DID A PRETTY GIRL END UP IN MY FIELD BITING MY RADISHES?
CHOK
OOPS! I SHOULD HAVE BEEN MORE CAREFUL! WHAT IF NAN OR GRANNY CONTACTS THEM?

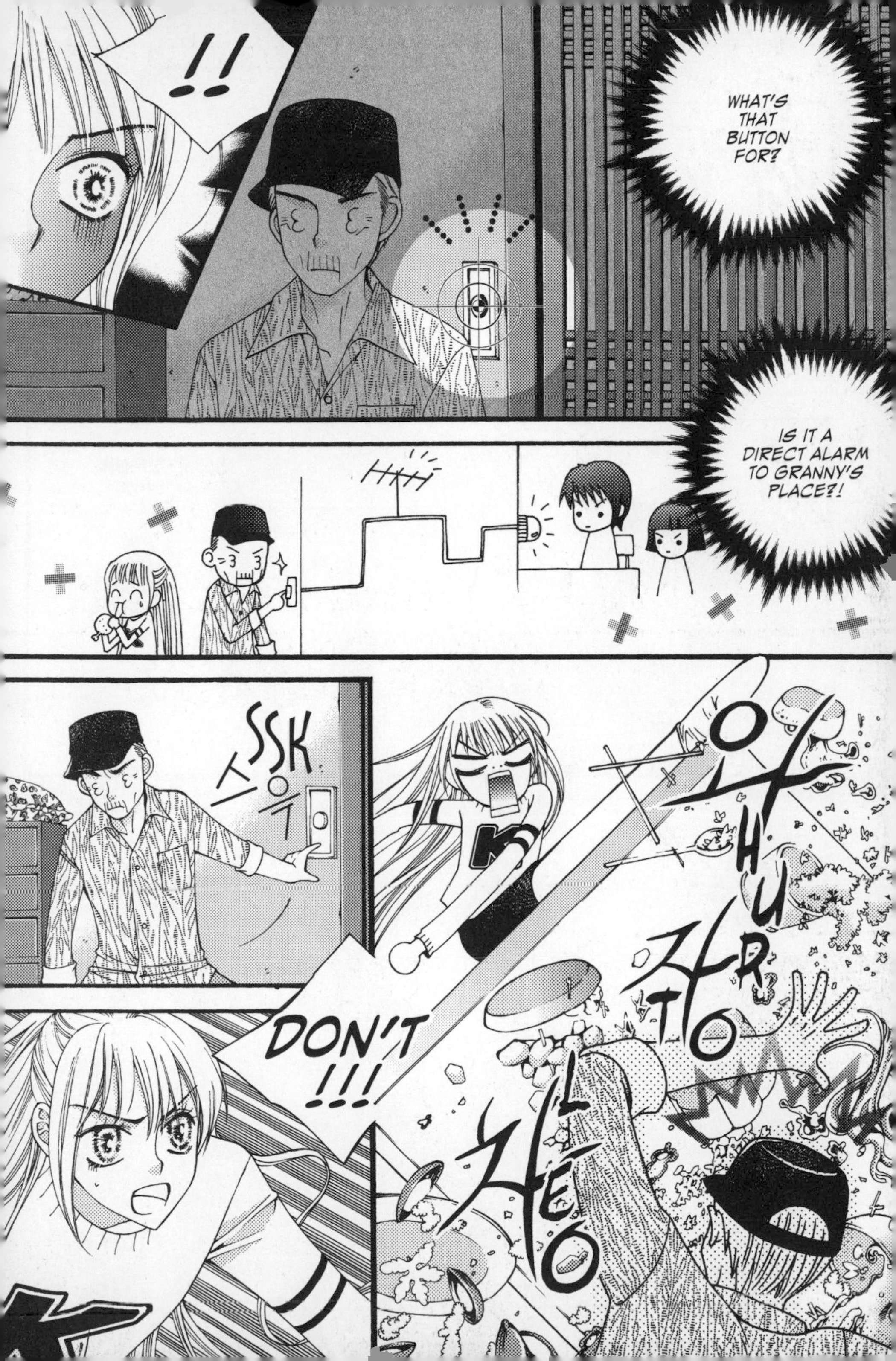
WHAT'S THAT BUTTON FOR?
!!
IS IT A DIRECT ALARM TO GRANNY'S PLACE?!
SSK
DON'T !!!

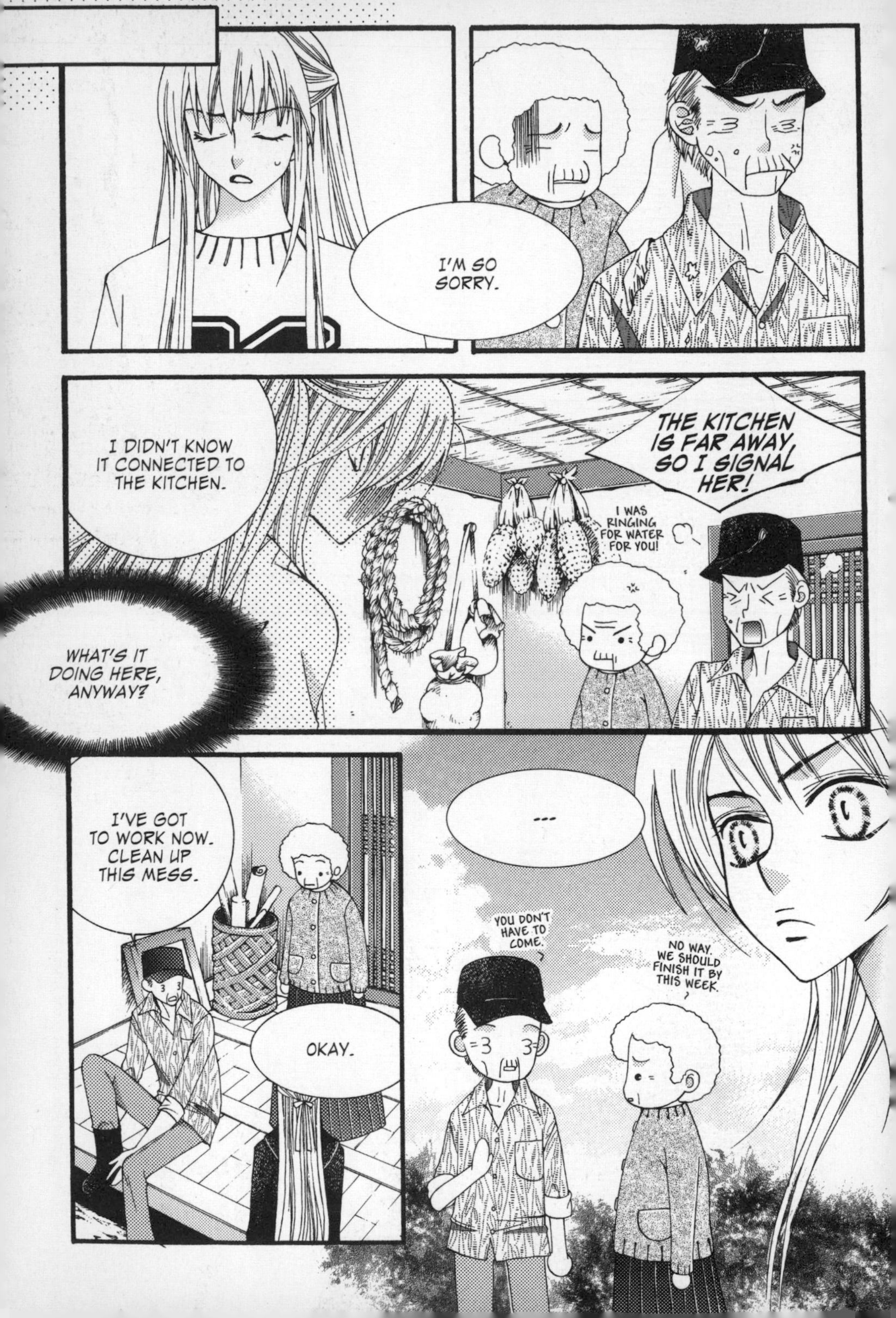
I'M SO SORRY.
I DIDN'T KNOW IT CONNECTED TO THE KITCHEN.
THE KITCHEN IS FAR AWAY, SO I SIGNAL HER!
I WAS RINGING FOR WATER FOR YOU!
WHAT'S IT DOING HERE, ANYWAY?
I'VE GOT TO WORK NOW. CLEAN UP THIS MESS.
OKAY.
...
YOU DON'T HAVE TO COME.
NO WAY. WE SHOULD FINISH IT BY THIS WEEK.

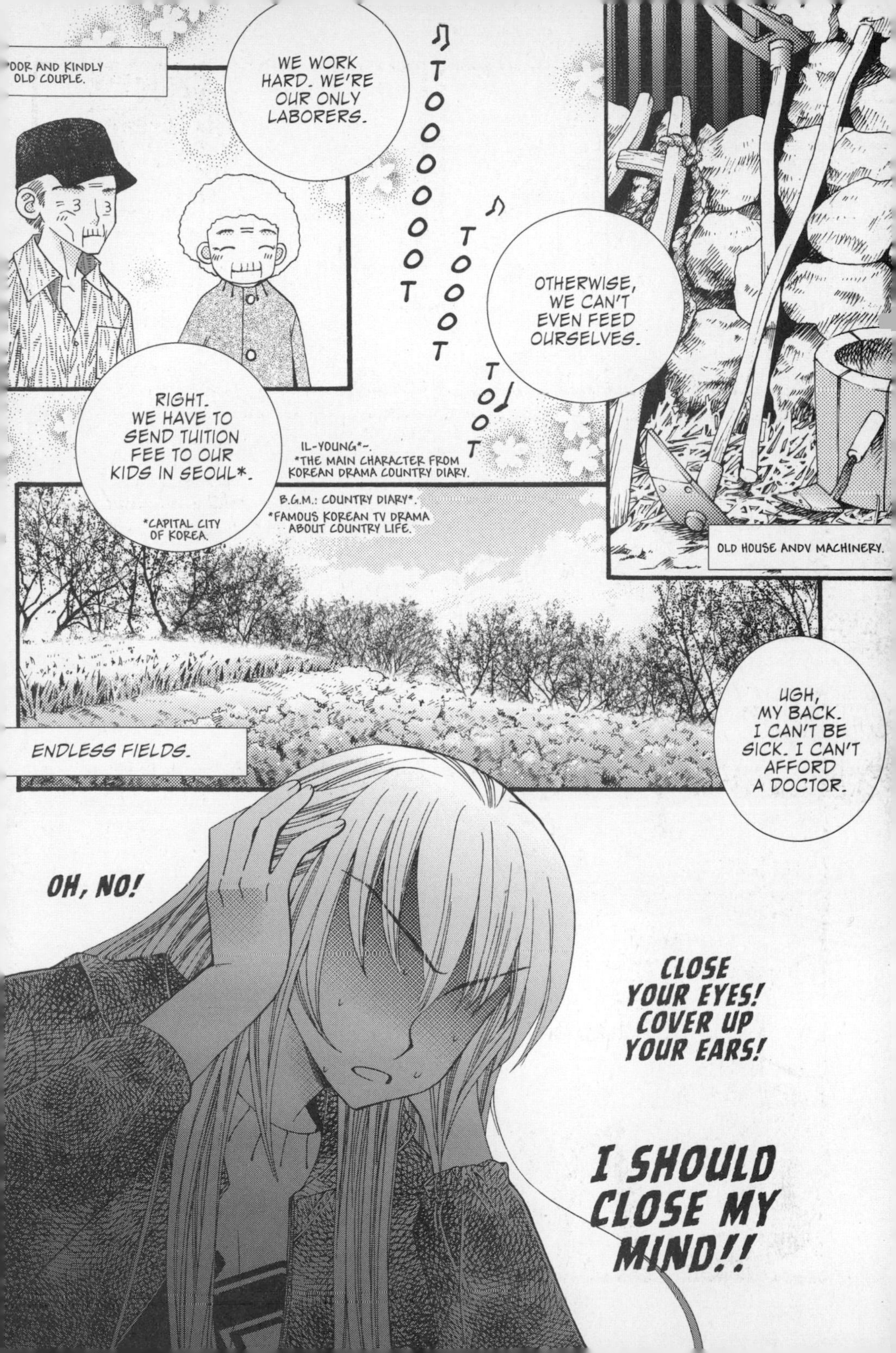
POOR AND KINDLY OLD COUPLE.
WE WORK HARD. WE'RE OUR ONLY LABORERS.
♫TOOOOOOOOT TOOOOT TOOOT
OTHERWISE, WE CAN'T EVEN FEED OURSELVES.
RIGHT. WE HAVE TO SEND TUITION FEE TO OUR KIDS IN SEOUL*.
*CAPITAL CITY OF KOREA.
IL-YOUNG*-.
*THE MAIN CHARACTER FROM KOREAN DRAMA COUNTRY DIARY.
B.G.M.: COUNTRY DIARY*.
*FAMOUS KOREAN TV DRAMA ABOUT COUNTRY LIFE.
OLD HOUSE ANDV MACHINERY.
ENDLESS FIELDS.
UGH, MY BACK. I CAN'T BE SICK. I CAN'T AFFORD A DOCTOR.
OH, NO!
CLOSE YOUR EYES! COVER UP YOUR EARS!
I SHOULD CLOSE MY MIND!!

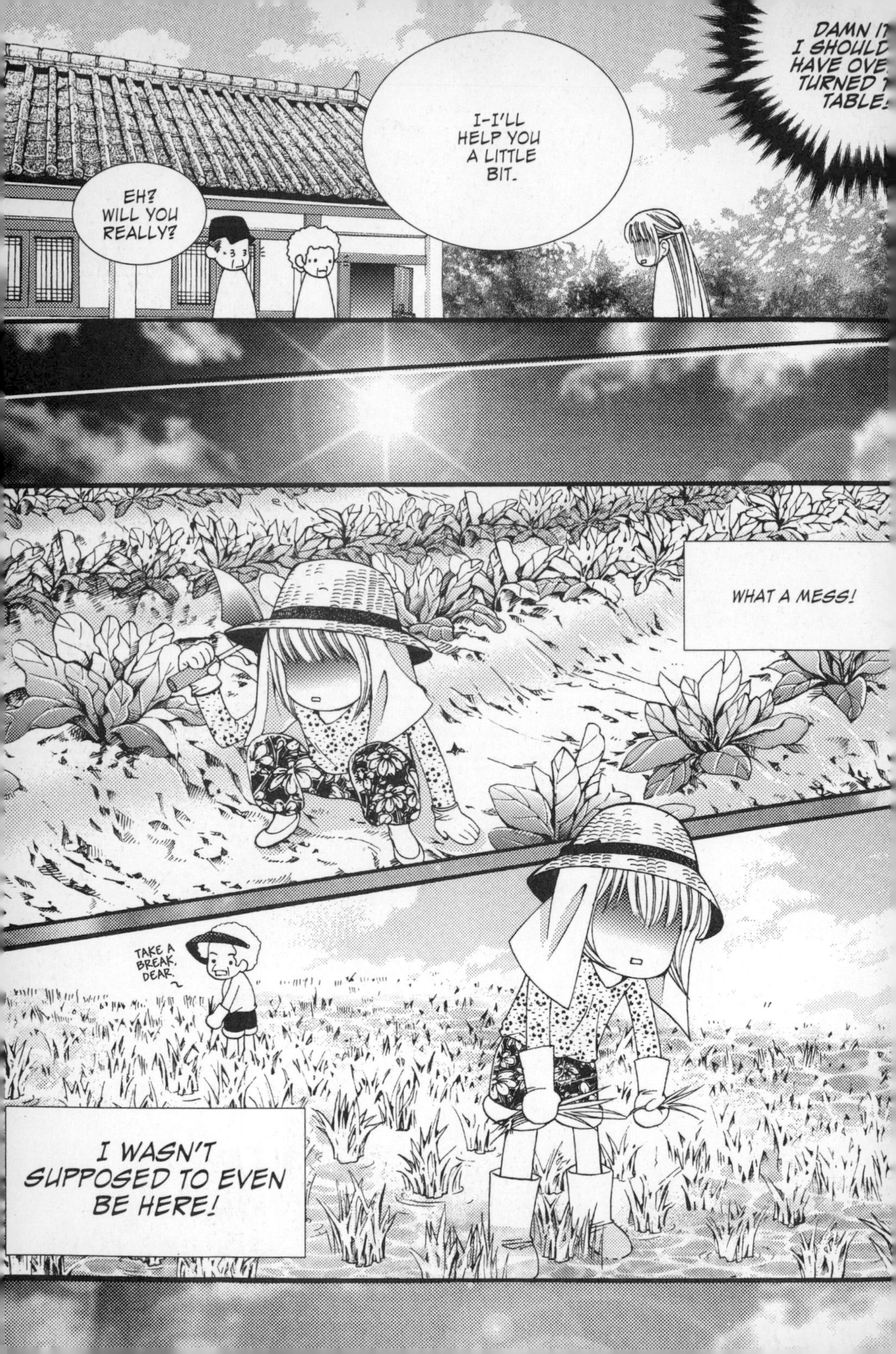
I-I'LL HELP YOU A LITTLE BIT.
EH? WILL YOU REALLY?
DAMN IT I SHOULD HAVE OVE TURNED T TABLE!
WHAT A MESS!
TAKE A BREAK, DEAR.
I WASN'T SUPPOSED TO EVEN BE HERE!

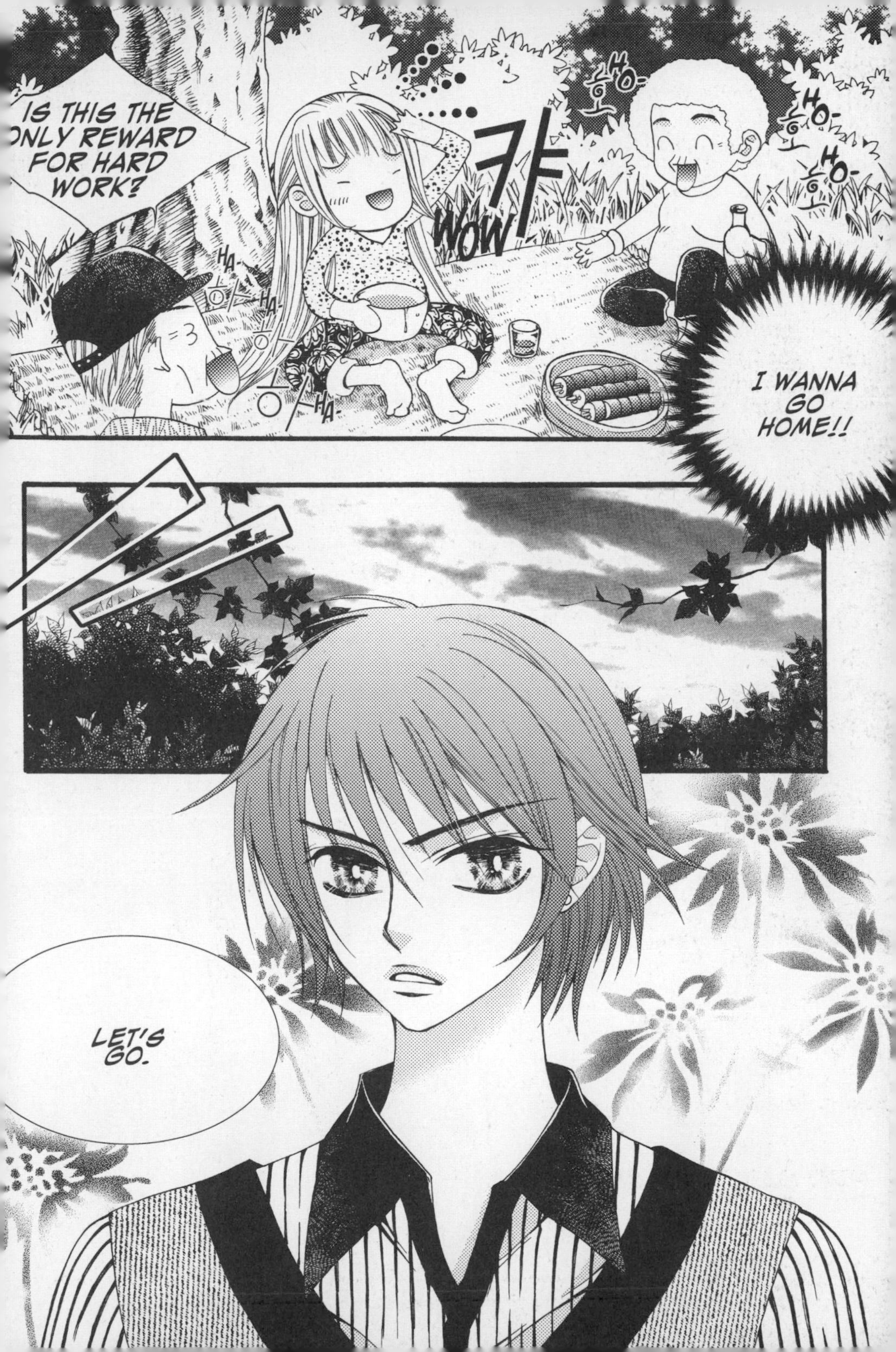
IS THIS THE ONLY REWARD FOR HARD WORK?
......
카
WOW
HO-HO-HO-
HA-HA-HA-
I WANNA GO HOME!!
LET'S GO.

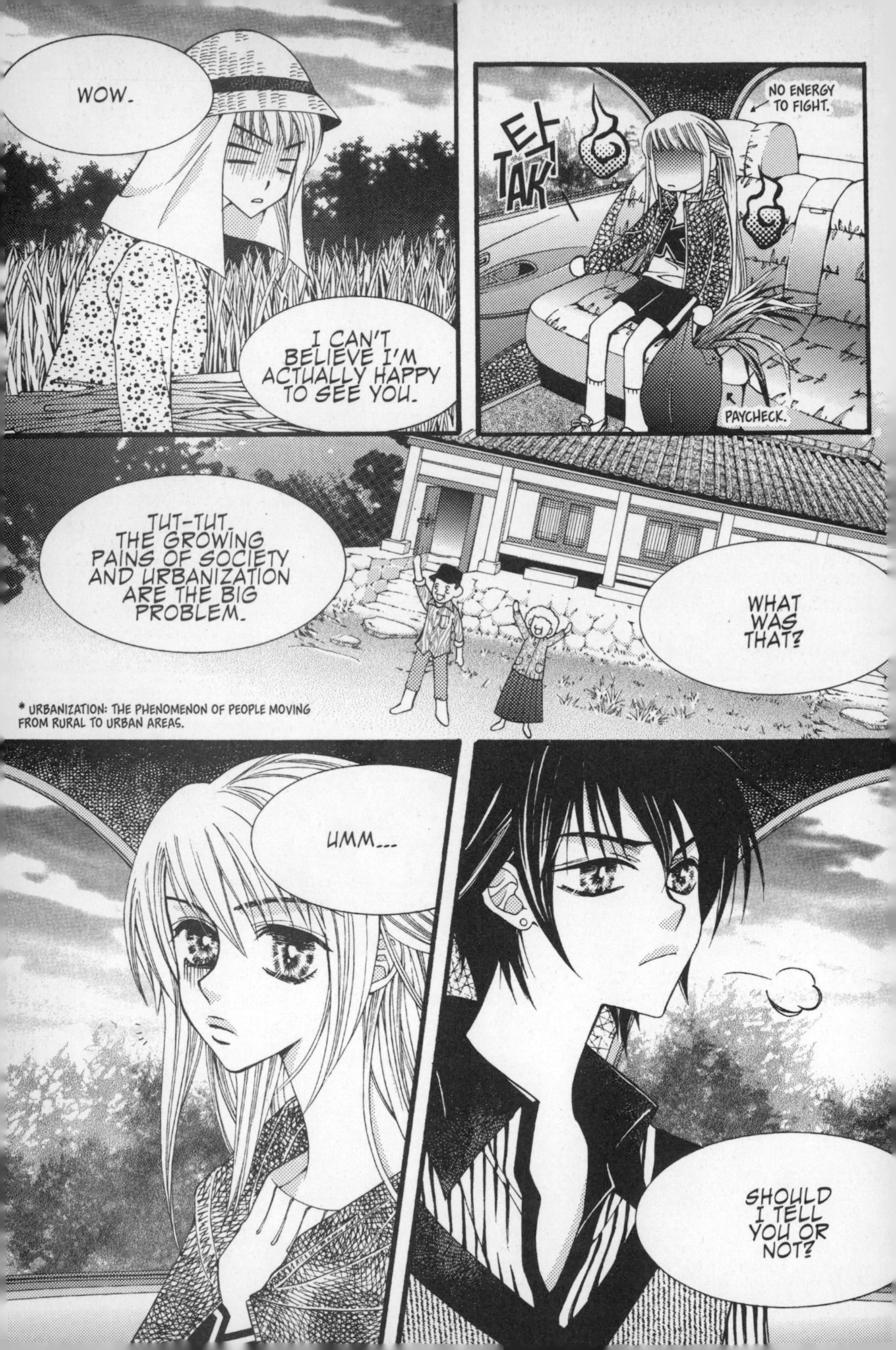
WOW.
I CAN'T BELIEVE I'M ACTUALLY HAPPY TO SEE YOU.
TAK
NO ENERGY TO FIGHT.
PAYCHECK.
TUT-TUT. THE GROWING PAINS OF SOCIETY AND URBANIZATION ARE THE BIG PROBLEM.
WHAT WAS THAT?
* URBANIZATION: THE PHENOMENON OF PEOPLE MOVING FROM RURAL TO URBAN AREAS.
UMM...
SHOULD I TELL YOU OR NOT?

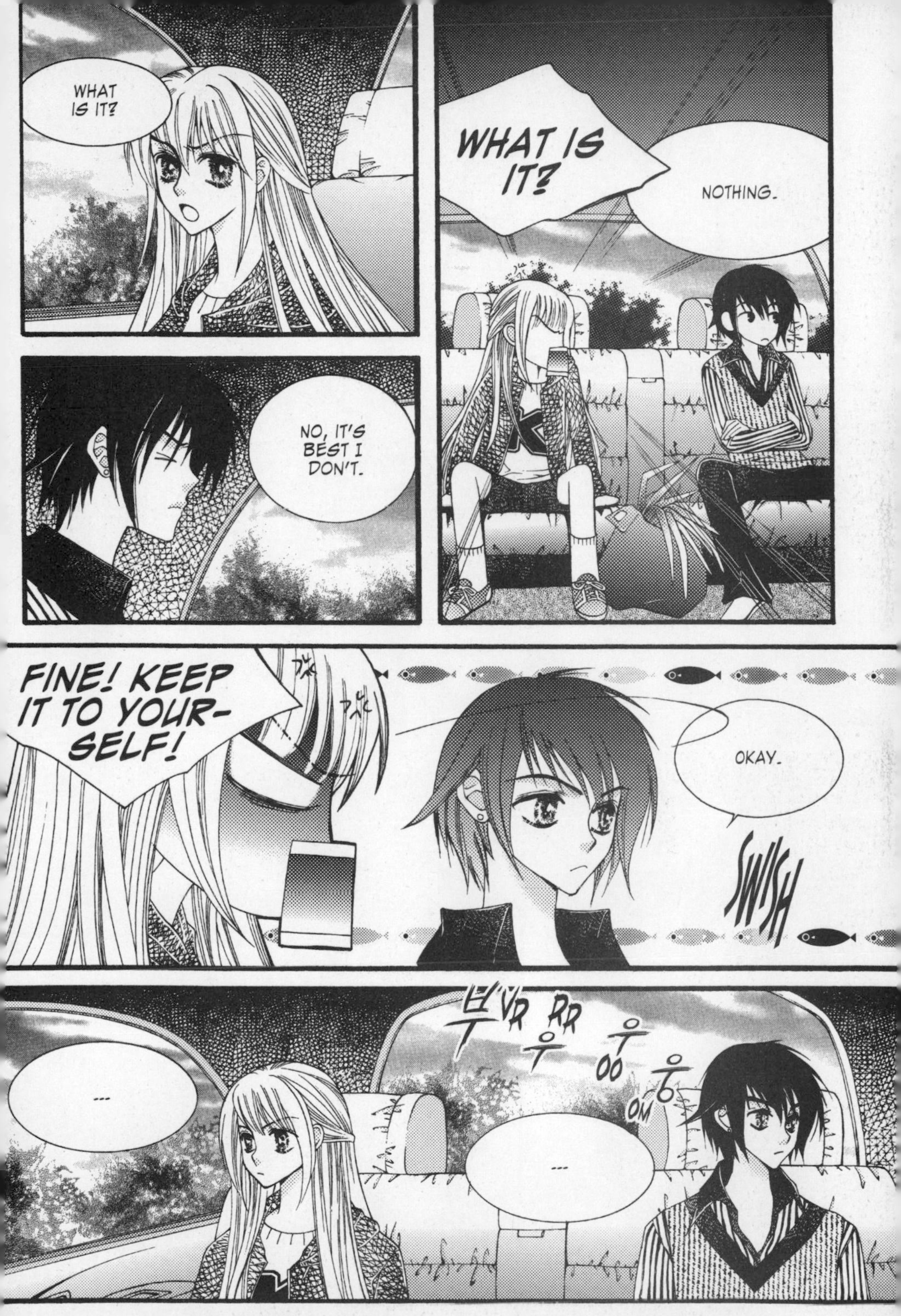
WHAT IS IT?
WHAT IS IT?
NOTHING.
NO, IT'S BEST I DON'T.
FINE! KEEP IT TO YOURSELF!
OKAY.
SWISH
부우우웅
VRRROOOM
...
...

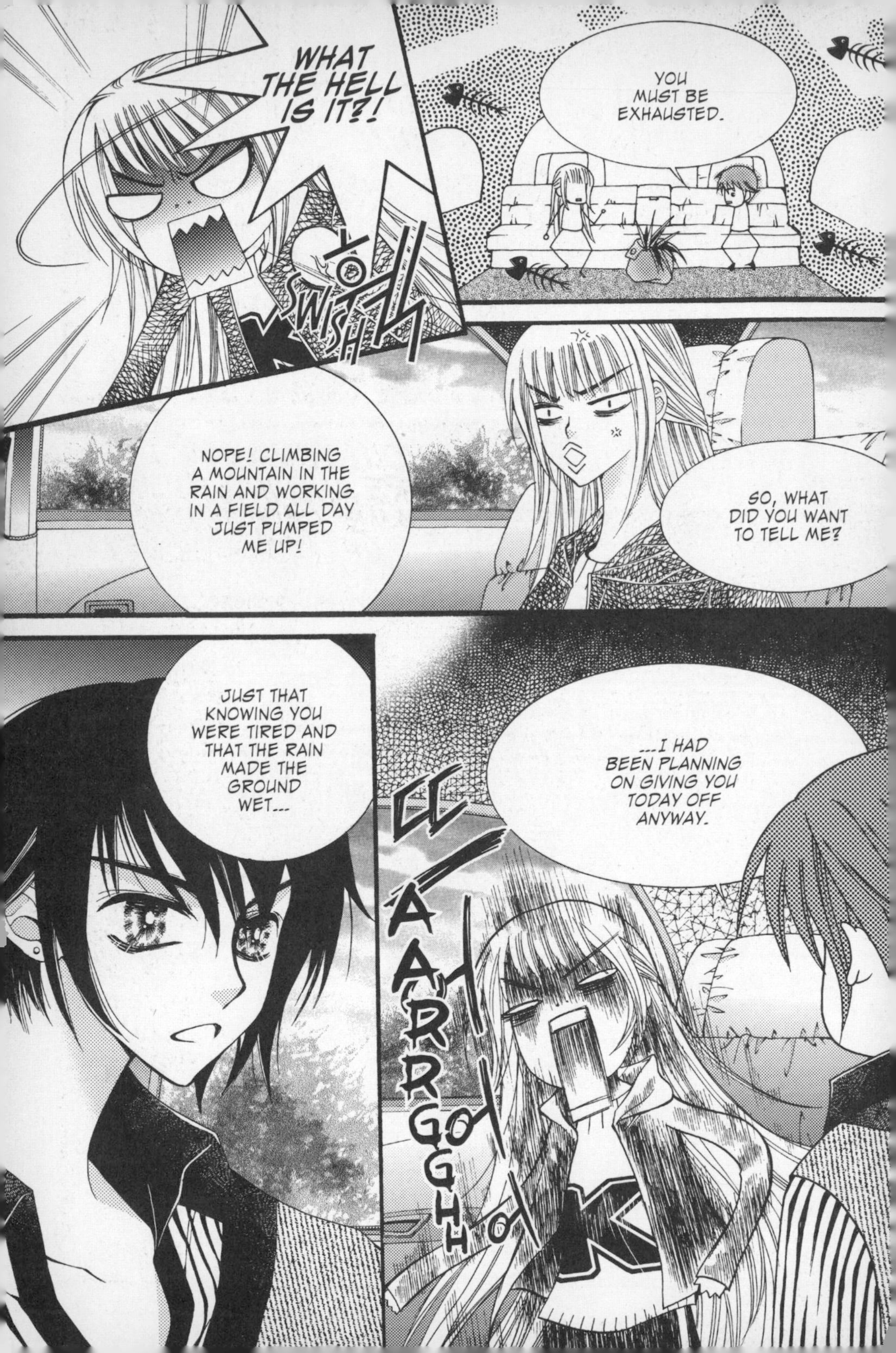
WHAT THE HELL IS IT?!
SWISH
YOU MUST BE EXHAUSTED.
NOPE! CLIMBING A MOUNTAIN IN THE RAIN AND WORKING IN A FIELD ALL DAY JUST PUMPED ME UP!
SO, WHAT DID YOU WANT TO TELL ME?
JUST THAT KNOWING YOU WERE TIRED AND THAT THE RAIN MADE THE GROUND WET...
...I HAD BEEN PLANNING ON GIVING YOU TODAY OFF ANYWAY.
AARRGGH

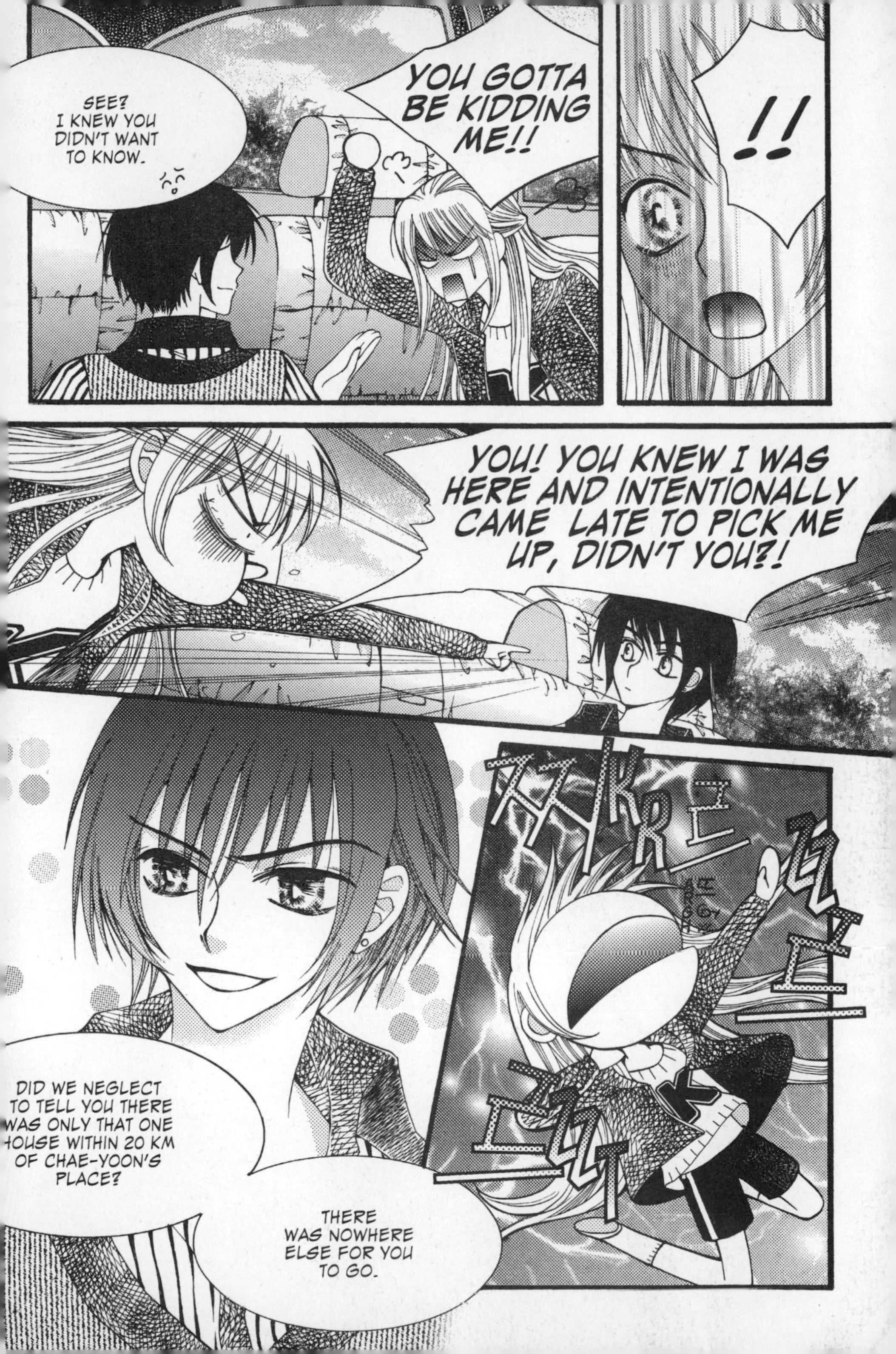
SEE? I KNEW YOU DIDN'T WANT TO KNOW.
YOU GOTTA BE KIDDING ME!!
!!
YOU! YOU KNEW I WAS HERE AND INTENTIONALLY CAME LATE TO PICK ME UP, DIDN'T YOU?!
DID WE NEGLECT TO TELL YOU THERE WAS ONLY THAT ONE HOUSE WITHIN 20 KM OF CHAE-YOON'S PLACE?
THERE WAS NOWHERE ELSE FOR YOU TO GO.

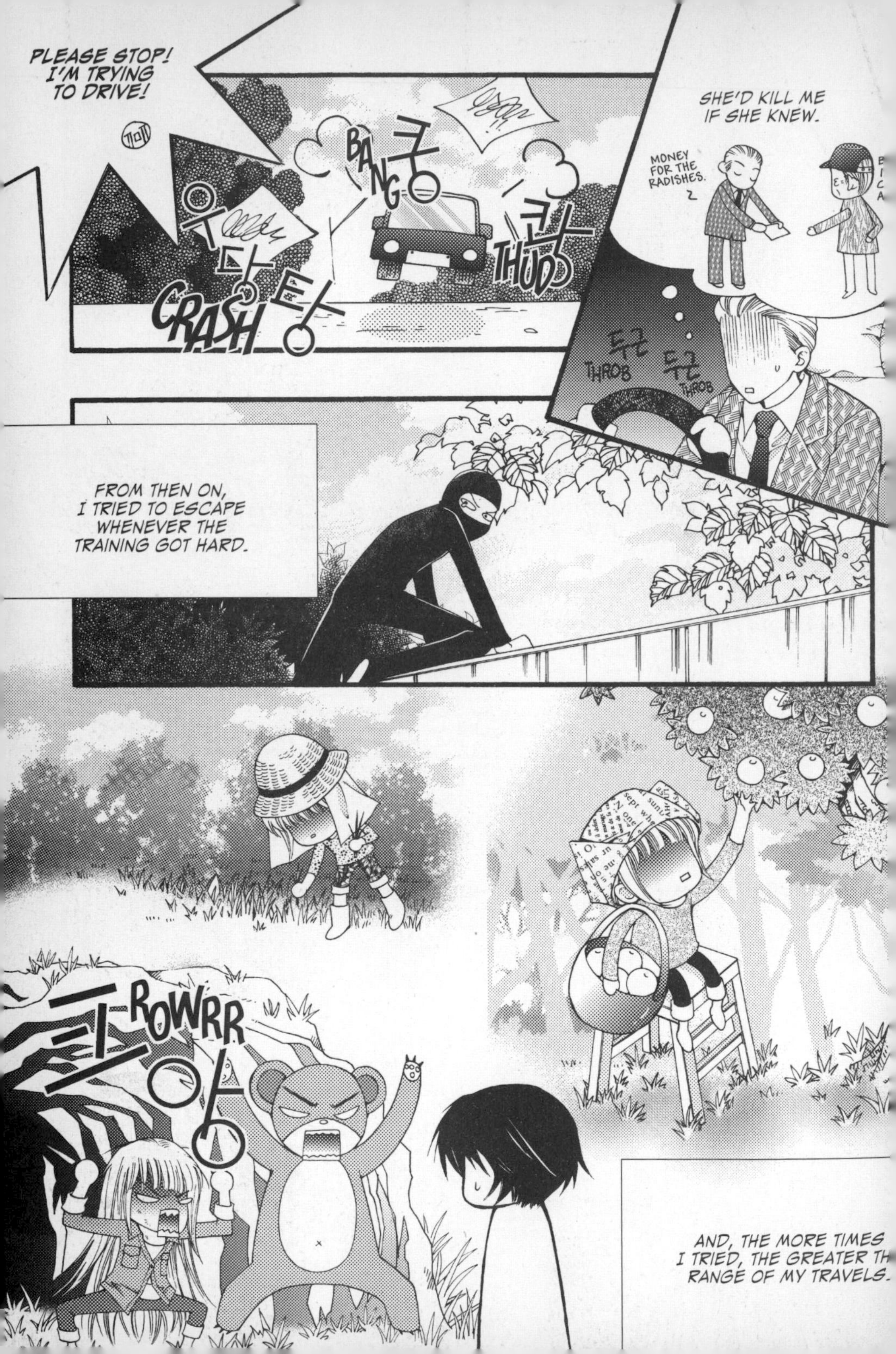

PLEASE STOP! I'M TRYING TO DRIVE!
BANG
CRASH
THUD
SHE'D KILL ME IF SHE KNEW.
MONEY FOR THE RADISHES.
두근
THROB
두근
THROB
FROM THEN ON, I TRIED TO ESCAPE WHENEVER THE TRAINING GOT HARD.
....
ROWRR
AND, THE MORE TIMES I TRIED, THE GREATER TH RANGE OF MY TRAVELS.

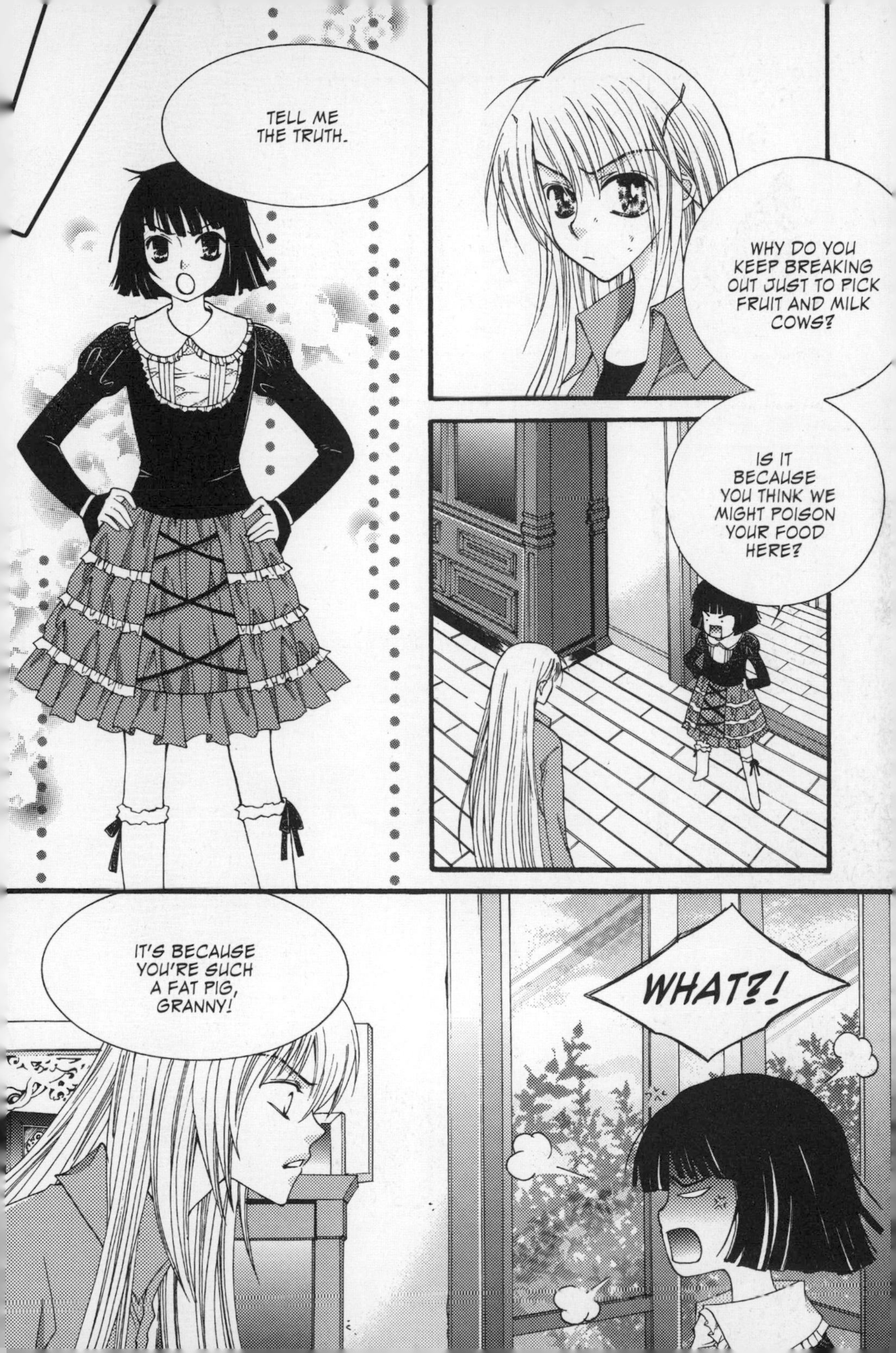
TELL ME THE TRUTH.
WHY DO YOU KEEP BREAKING OUT JUST TO PICK FRUIT AND MILK COWS?
IS IT BECAUSE YOU THINK WE MIGHT POISON YOUR FOOD HERE?
IT'S BECAUSE YOU'RE SUCH A FAT PIG, GRANNY!
WHAT?!

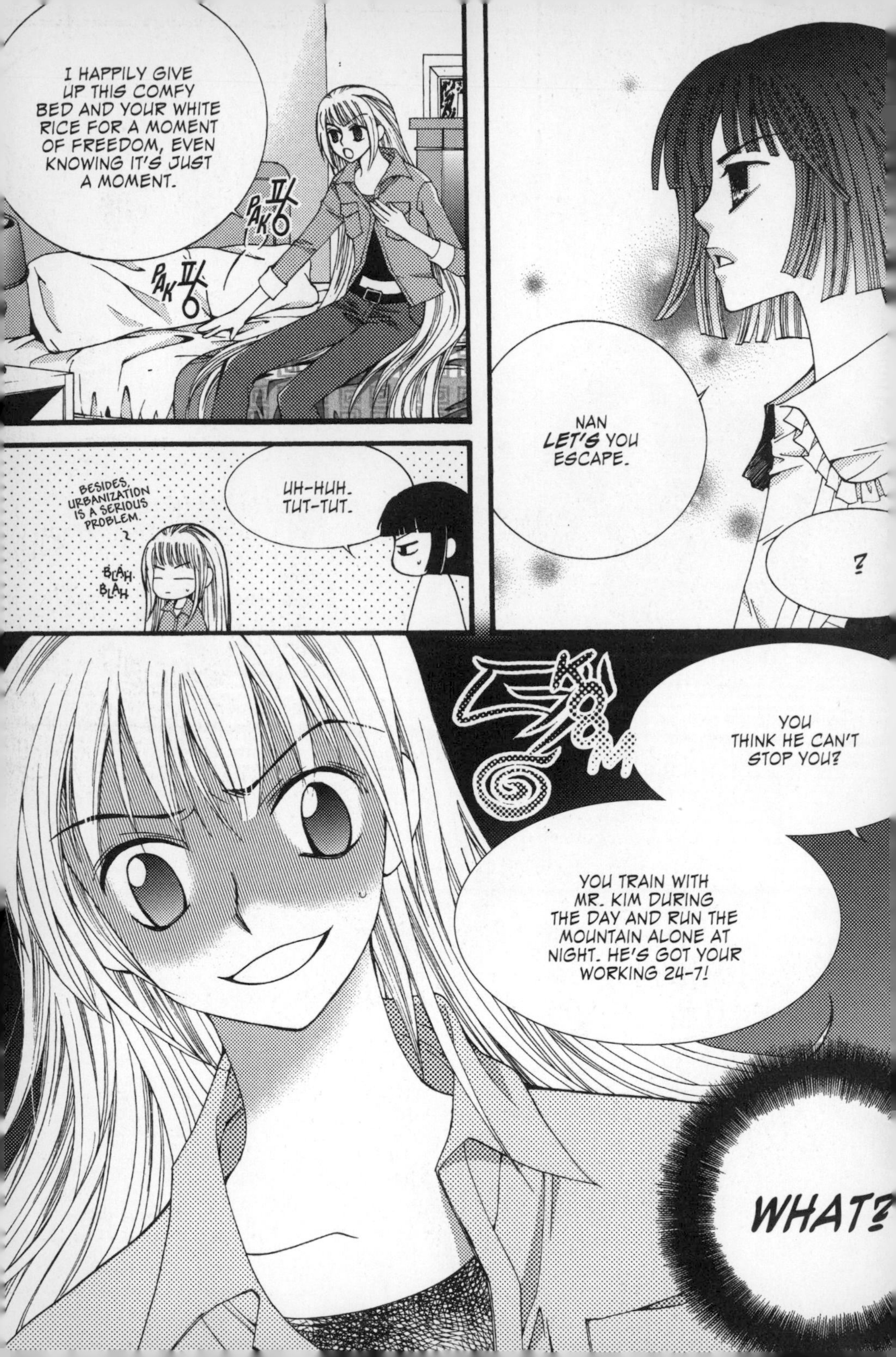
I HAPPILY GIVE UP THIS COMFY BED AND YOUR WHITE RICE FOR A MOMENT OF FREEDOM, EVEN KNOWING IT'S JUST A MOMENT.
PAK
PAK
BESIDES, URBANIZATION IS A SERIOUS PROBLEM.
BLAH. BLAH.
UH-HUH. TUT-TUT.
NAN *LET'S* YOU ESCAPE.
?
YOU THINK HE CAN'T STOP YOU?
YOU TRAIN WITH MR. KIM DURING THE DAY AND RUN THE MOUNTAIN ALONE AT NIGHT. HE'S GOT YOUR WORKING 24-7!
WHAT?

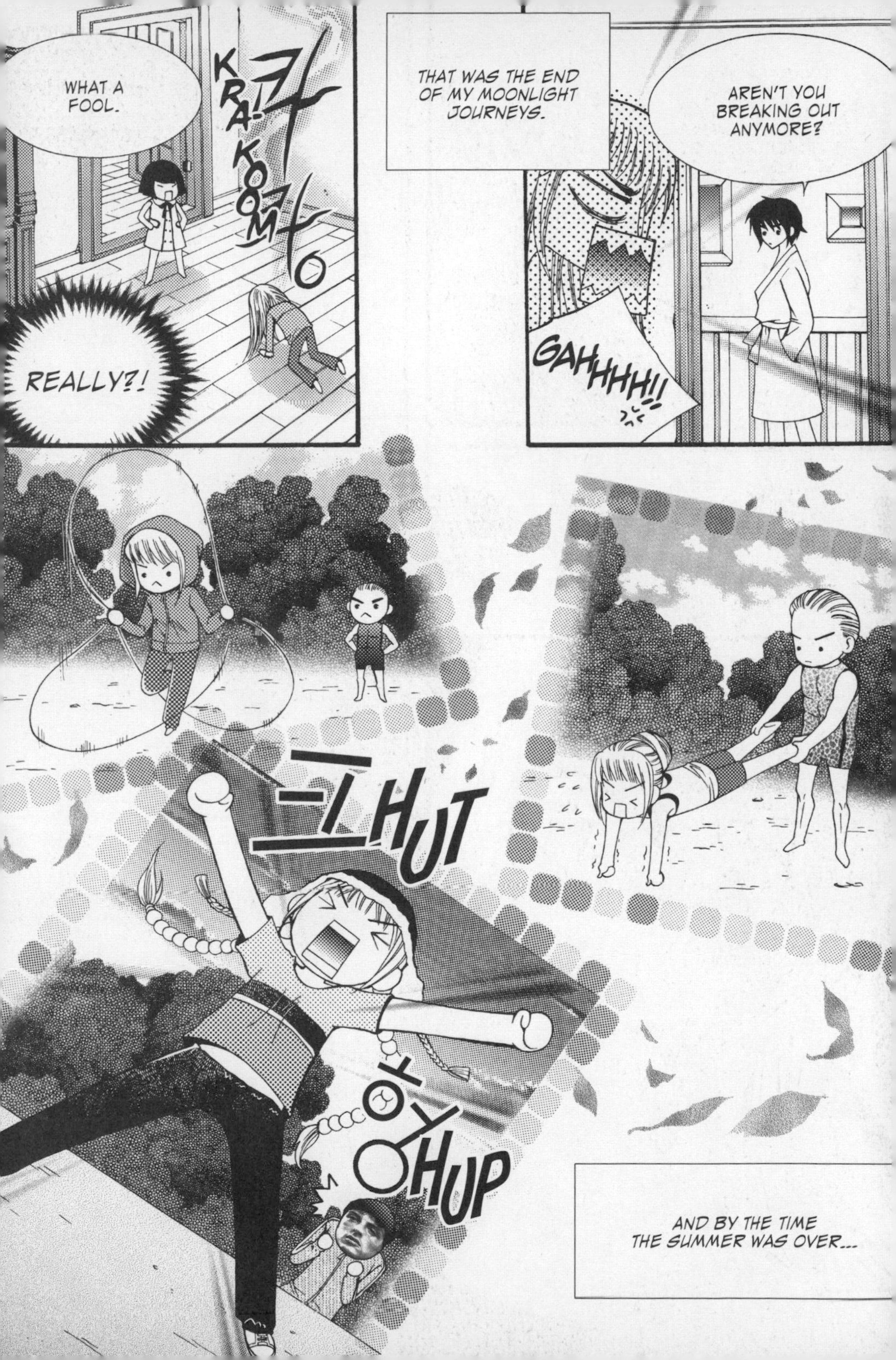
WHAT A FOOL.
KRA-KOOM
REALLY?!
THAT WAS THE END OF MY MOONLIGHT JOURNEYS.
AREN'T YOU BREAKING OUT ANYMORE?
GAHHHH!!
HUT
HUP
AND BY THE TIME THE SUMMER WAS OVER...

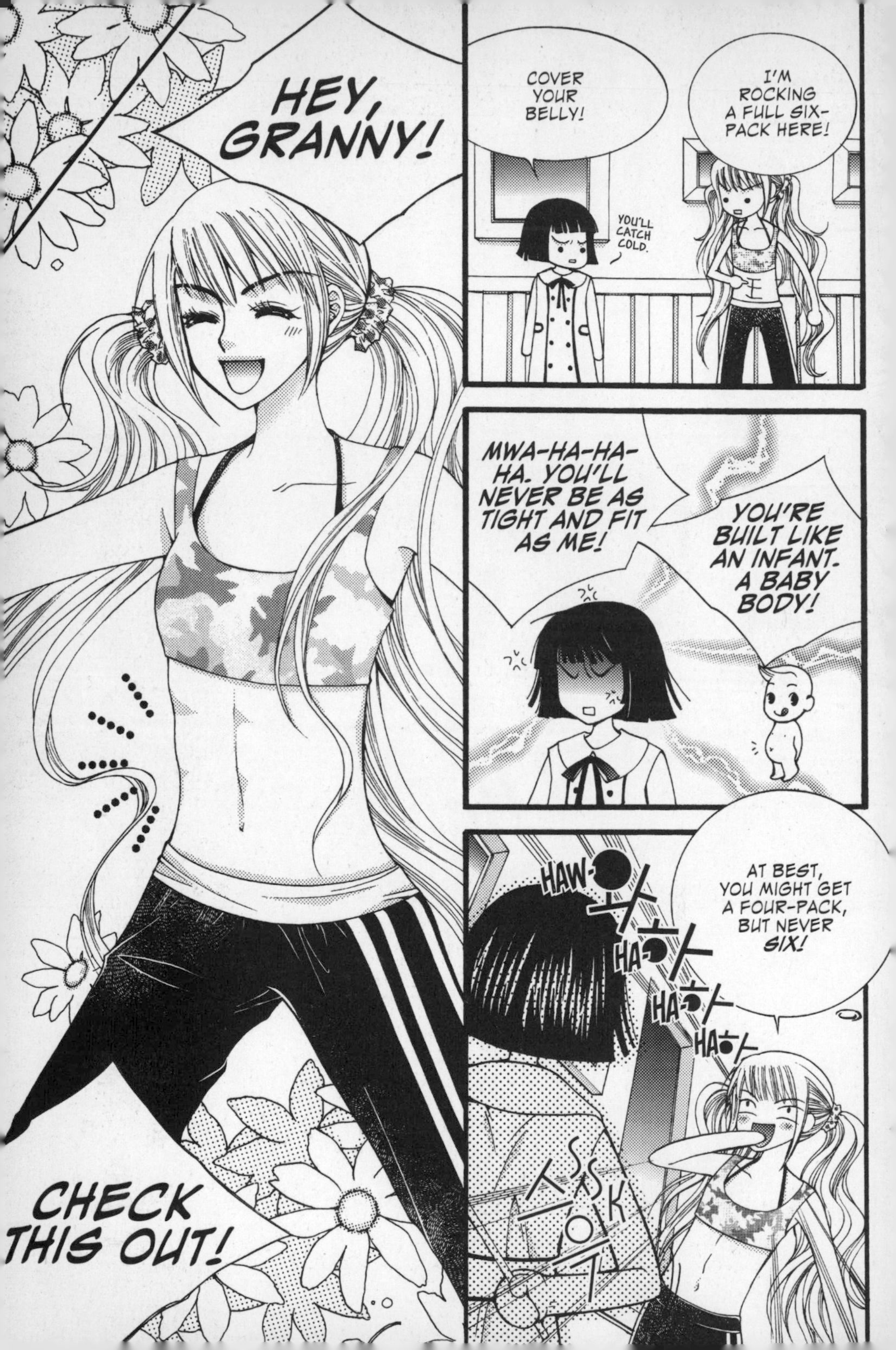
HEY, GRANNY!
CHECK THIS OUT!
COVER YOUR BELLY!
YOU'LL CATCH COLD.
I'M ROCKING A FULL SIX-PACK HERE!
MWA-HA-HA-HA. YOU'LL NEVER BE AS TIGHT AND FIT AS ME!
YOU'RE BUILT LIKE AN INFANT. A BABY BODY!
AT BEST, YOU MIGHT GET A FOUR-PACK, BUT NEVER SIX!
HAW-
HA-
HA-
HA-
SSK

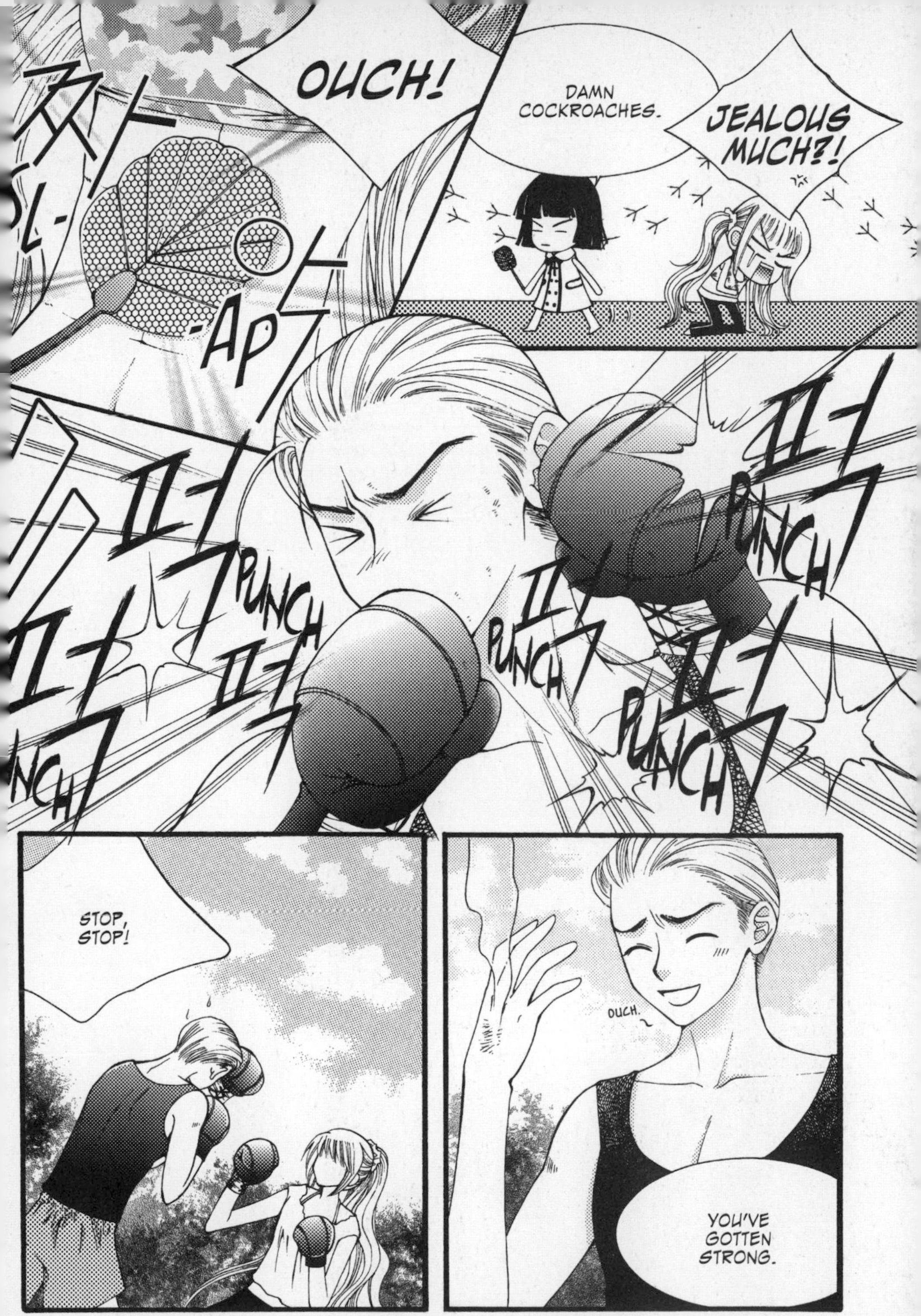
OUCH!
SL-
-AP
DAMN COCKROACHES.
JEALOUS MUCH?!
PUNCH
PUNCH
PUNCH
PUNCH
PUNCH
STOP, STOP!
OUCH.
YOU'VE GOTTEN STRONG.

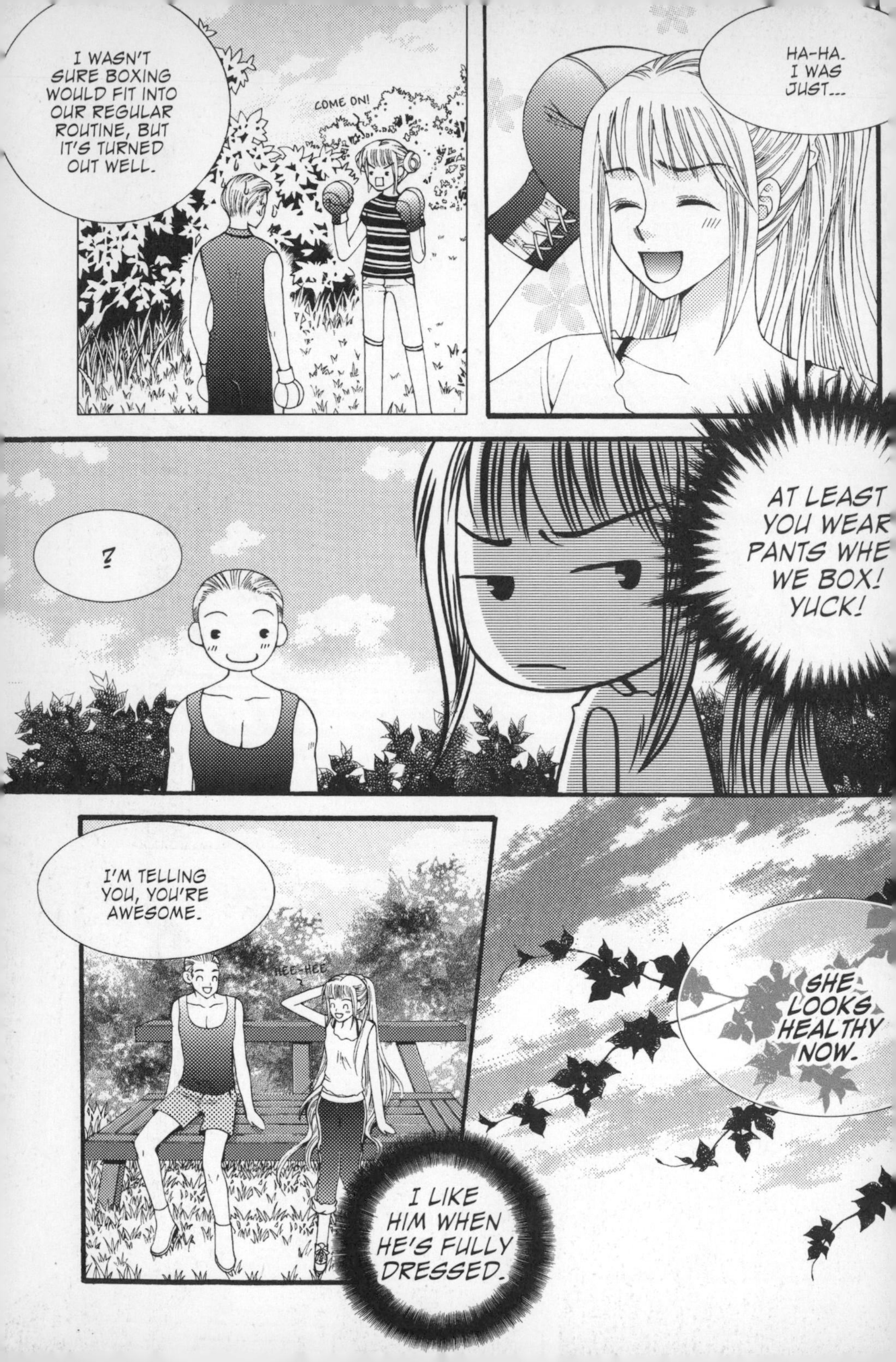
I WASN'T SURE BOXING WOULD FIT INTO OUR REGULAR ROUTINE, BUT IT'S TURNED OUT WELL.
COME ON!
HA-HA. I WAS JUST...
?
AT LEAST YOU WEAR PANTS WHE WE BOX! YUCK!
I'M TELLING YOU, YOU'RE AWESOME.
HEE-HEE
I LIKE HIM WHEN HE'S FULLY DRESSED.
SHE LOOKS HEALTHY NOW.

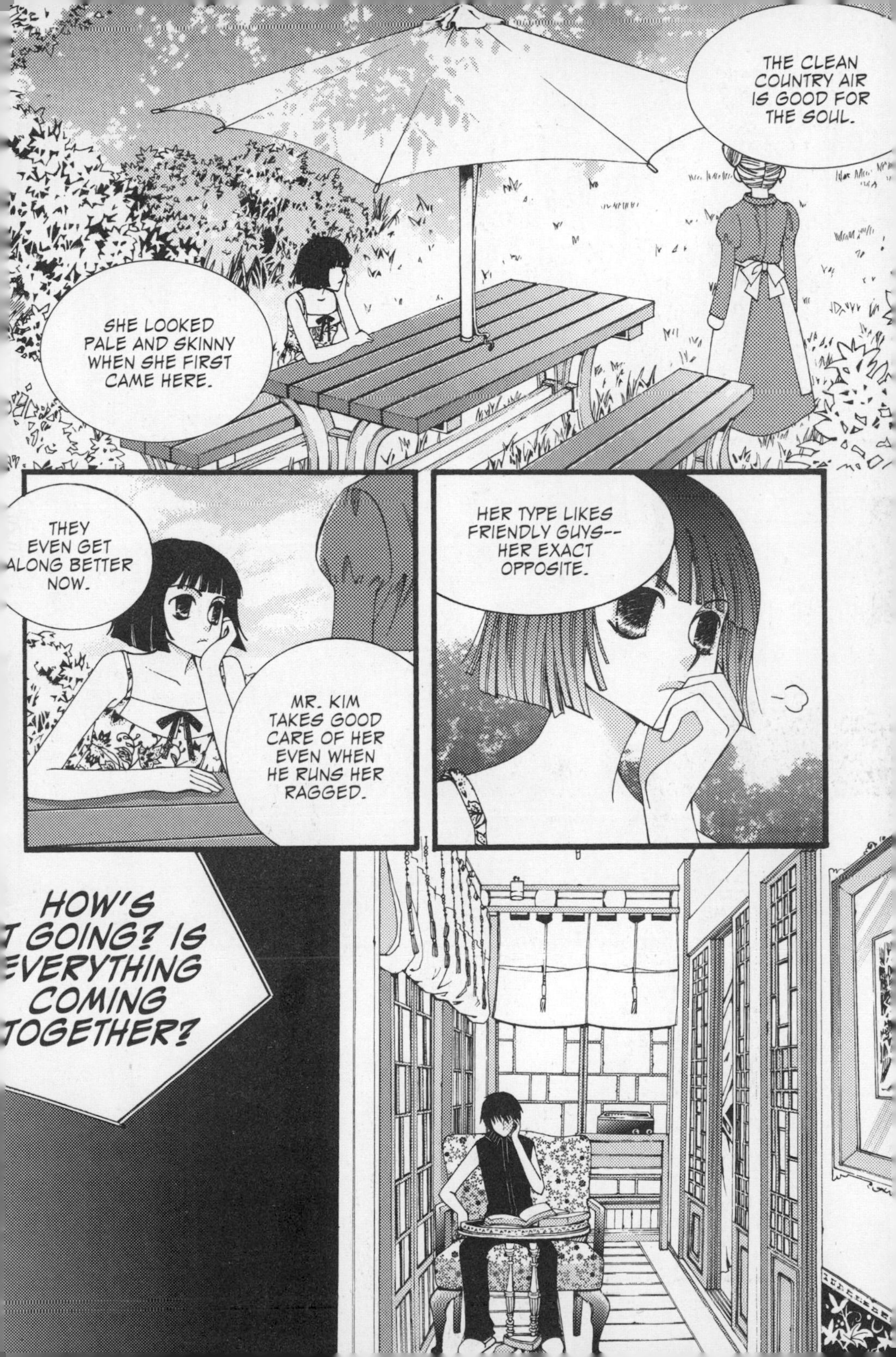
THE CLEAN COUNTRY AIR IS GOOD FOR THE SOUL.
SHE LOOKED PALE AND SKINNY WHEN SHE FIRST CAME HERE.
THEY EVEN GET ALONG BETTER NOW.
MR. KIM TAKES GOOD CARE OF HER EVEN WHEN HE RUNS HER RAGGED.
HER TYPE LIKES FRIENDLY GUYS-- HER EXACT OPPOSITE.
HOW'S T GOING? IS EVERYTHING COMING TOGETHER?

YOUR FATHER'S DEBT...

I KNOW.

SO-SO.

I CAN'T WAIT FOREVER.

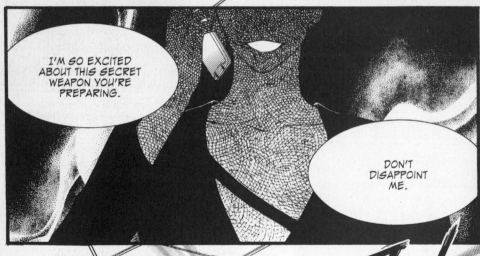

I'M SO EXCITED ABOUT THIS SECRET WEAPON YOU'RE PREPARING.

DON'T DISAPPOINT ME.

FEEL FREE TO GIVE IN AND PAY ME MY WAY ANY TIME YOU WANT.

CRASH

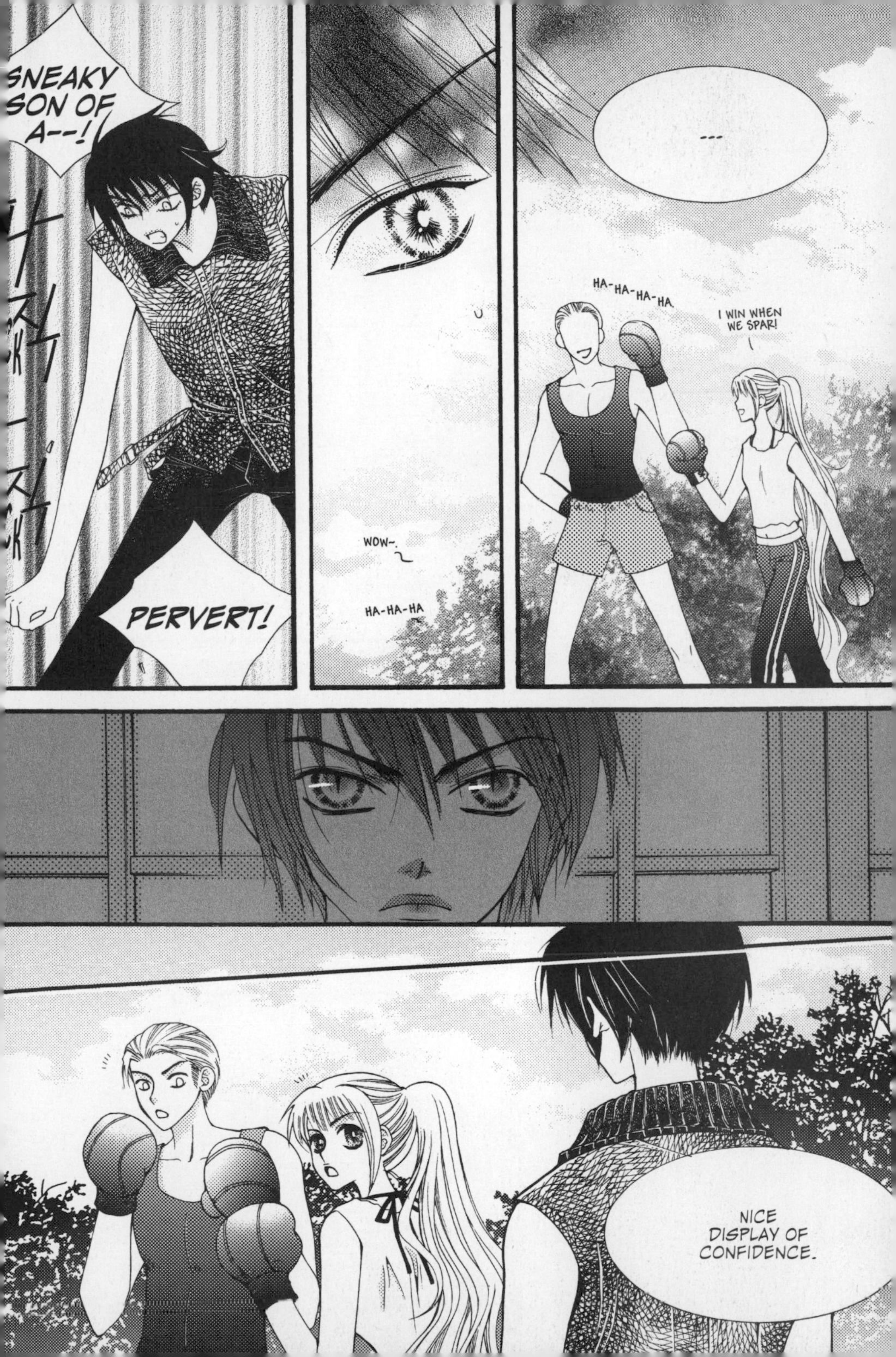

HA-HA-HA-HA.
I WIN WHEN WE SPAR!
WOW~.
HA-HA-HA
SNEAKY SON OF A--!
PERVERT!
NICE DISPLAY OF CONFIDENCE.

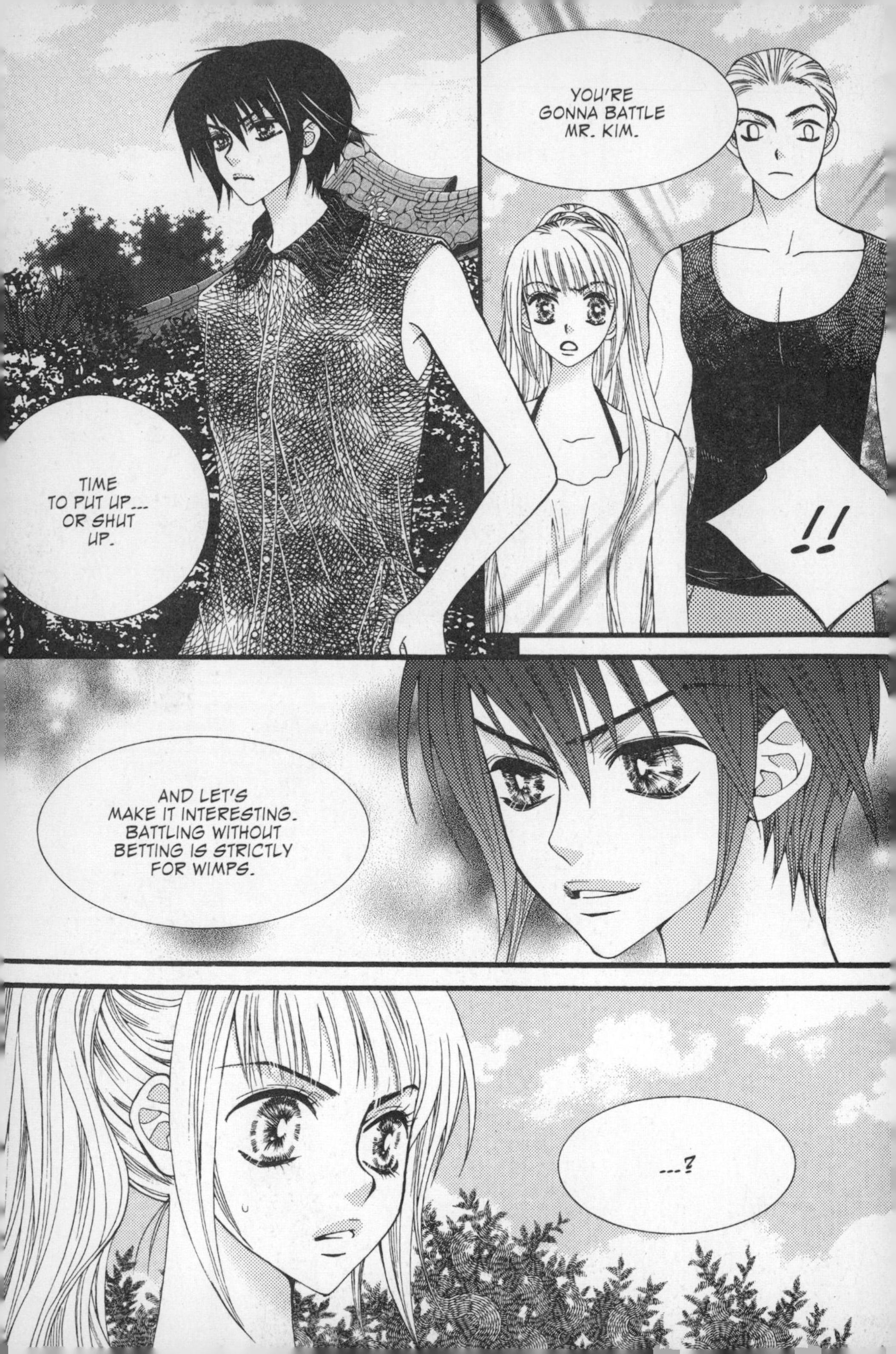
TIME TO PUT UP... OR SHUT UP.
YOU'RE GONNA BATTLE MR. KIM.
!!
AND LET'S MAKE IT INTERESTING. BATTLING WITHOUT BETTING IS STRICTLY FOR WIMPS.
...?

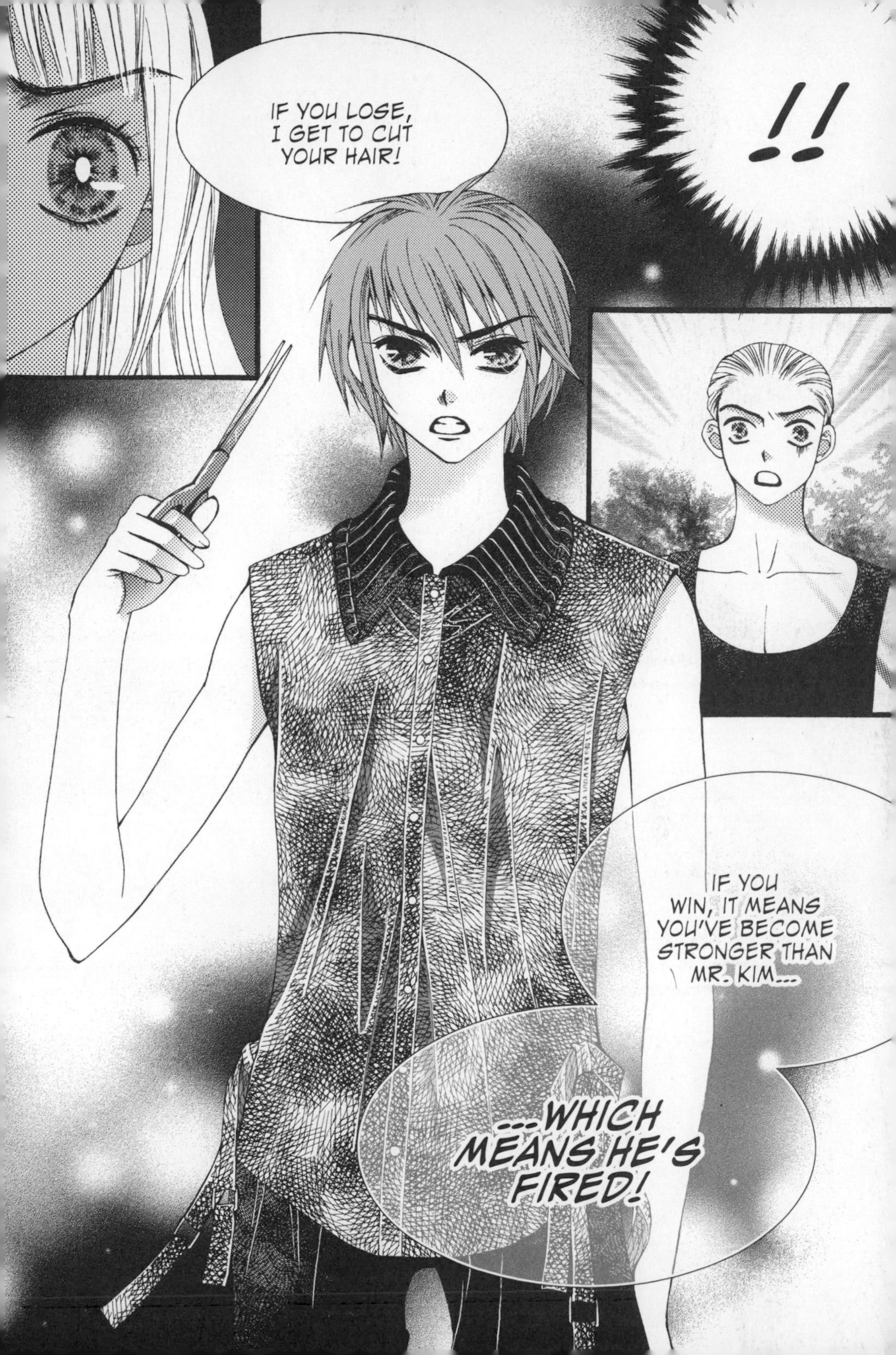
IF YOU LOSE, I GET TO CUT YOUR HAIR!
!!
IF YOU WIN, IT MEANS YOU'VE BECOME STRONGER THAN MR. KIM...
...WHICH MEANS HE'S FIRED!

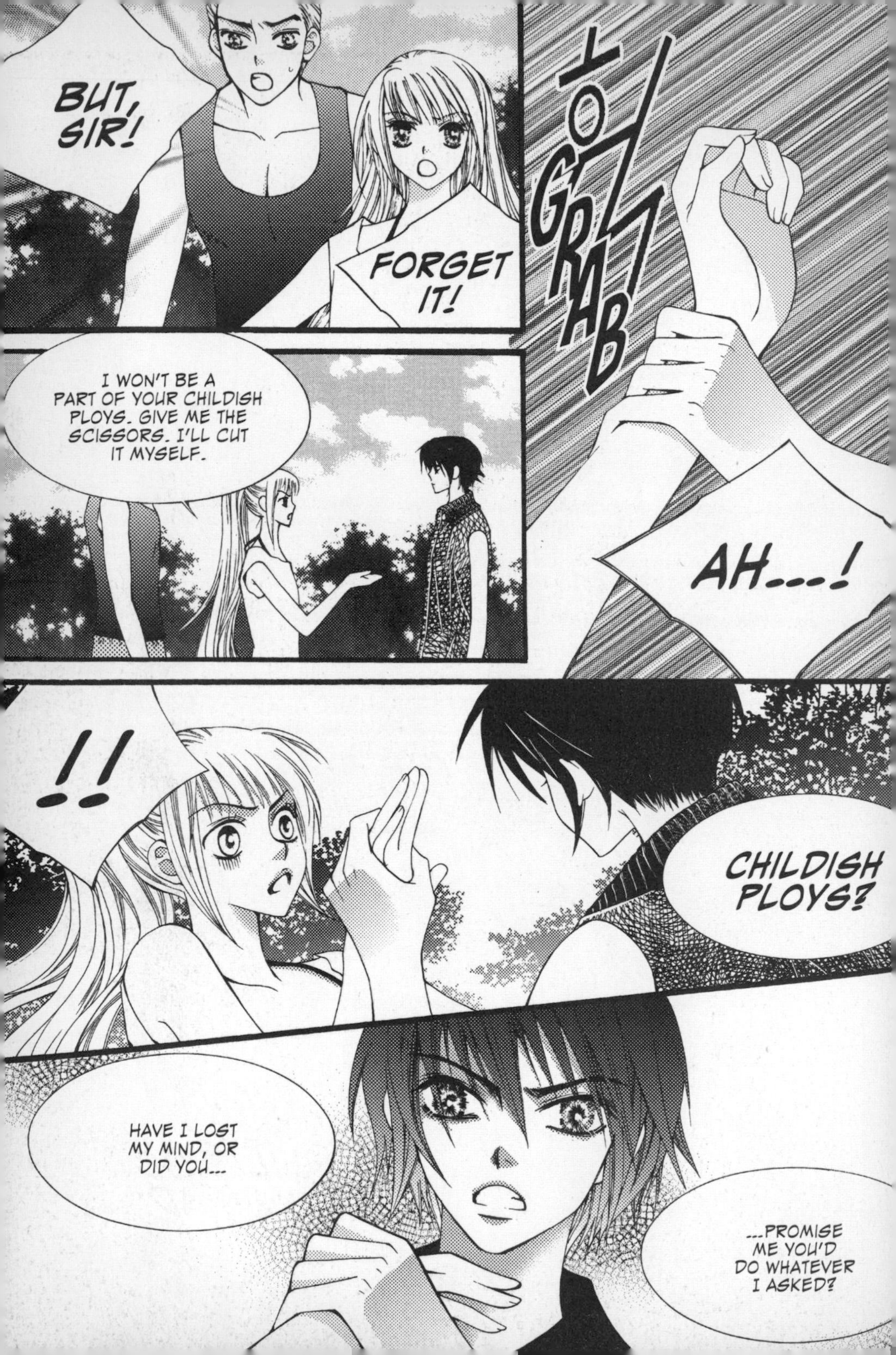
BUT, SIR!
FORGET IT!
I WON'T BE A PART OF YOUR CHILDISH PLOYS. GIVE ME THE SCISSORS. I'LL CUT IT MYSELF.
GRAB
AH...!
!!
CHILDISH PLOYS?
HAVE I LOST MY MIND, OR DID YOU...
...PROMISE ME YOU'D DO WHATEVER I ASKED?

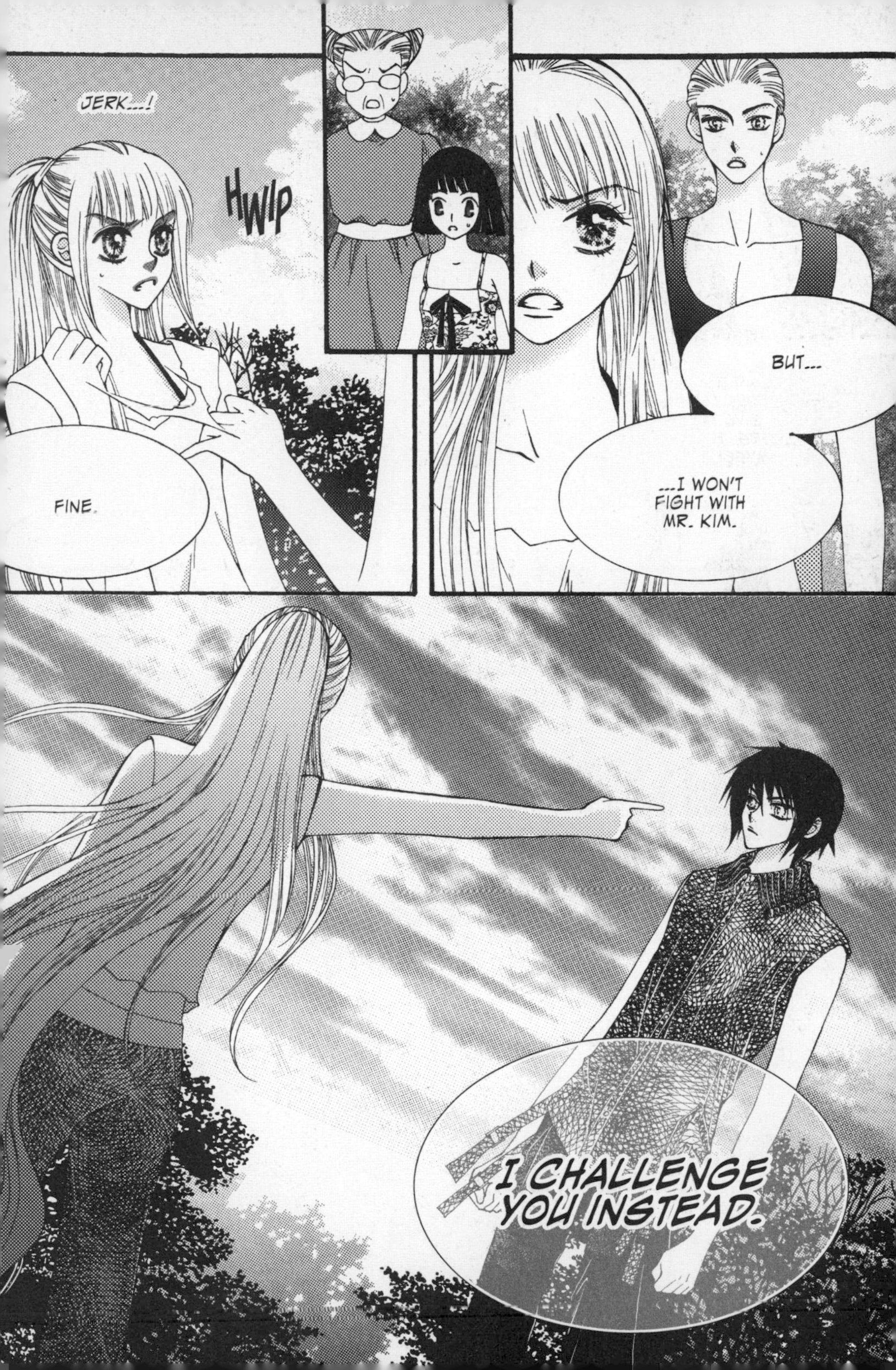
JERK...!
HWIP
FINE.
BUT...
...I WON'T FIGHT WITH MR. KIM.
I CHALLENGE YOU INSTEAD.

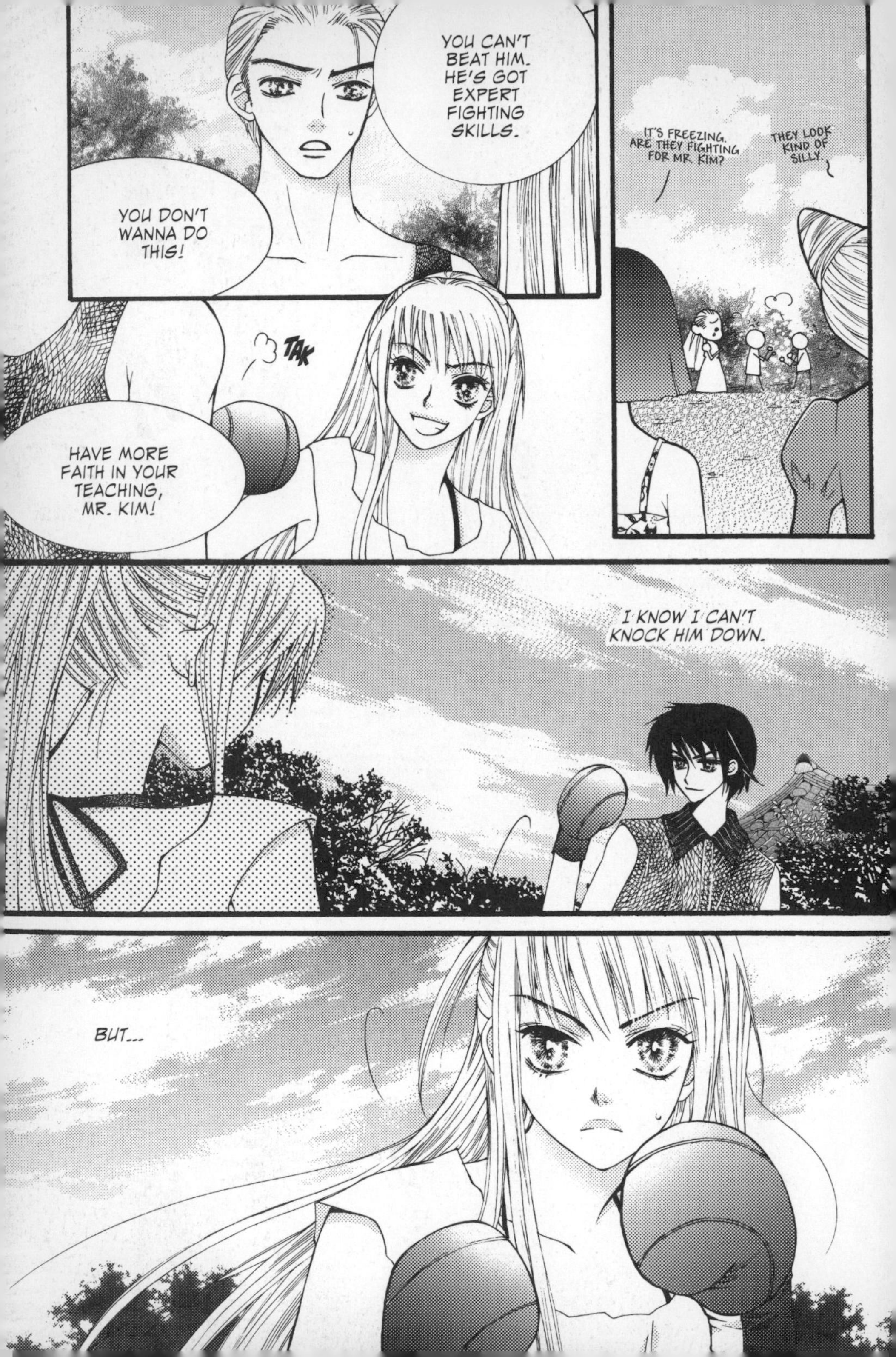
YOU CAN'T BEAT HIM. HE'S GOT EXPERT FIGHTING SKILLS.
YOU DON'T WANNA DO THIS!
IT'S FREEZING. ARE THEY FIGHTING FOR MR. KIM?
THEY LOOK KIND OF SILLY.
TAK
HAVE MORE FAITH IN YOUR TEACHING, MR. KIM!
I KNOW I CAN'T KNOCK HIM DOWN.
BUT...

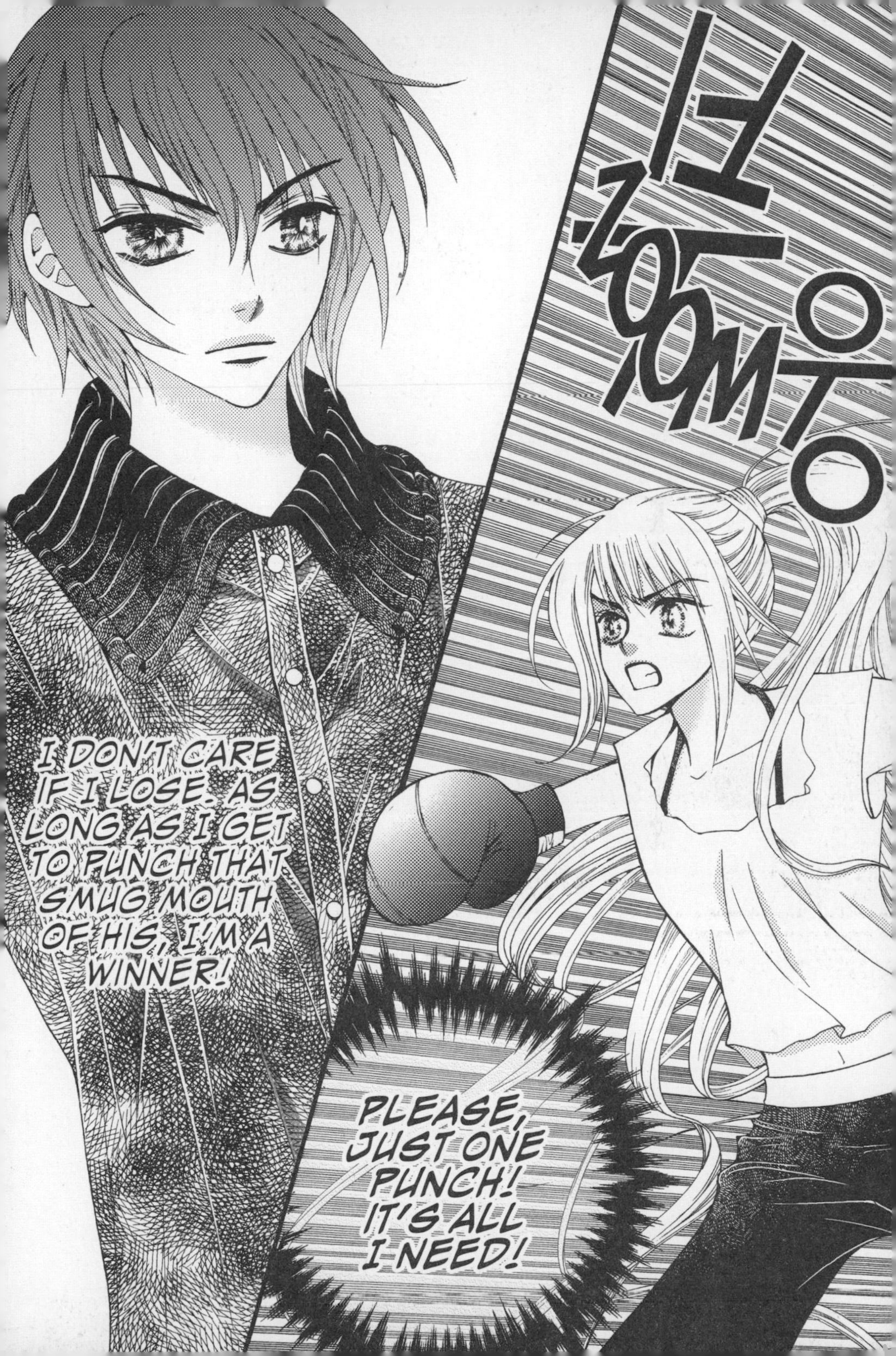
I DON'T CARE IF I LOSE. AS LONG AS I GET TO PUNCH THAT SMUG MOUTH OF HIS, I'M A WINNER!
PLEASE, JUST ONE PUNCH! IT'S ALL I NEED!

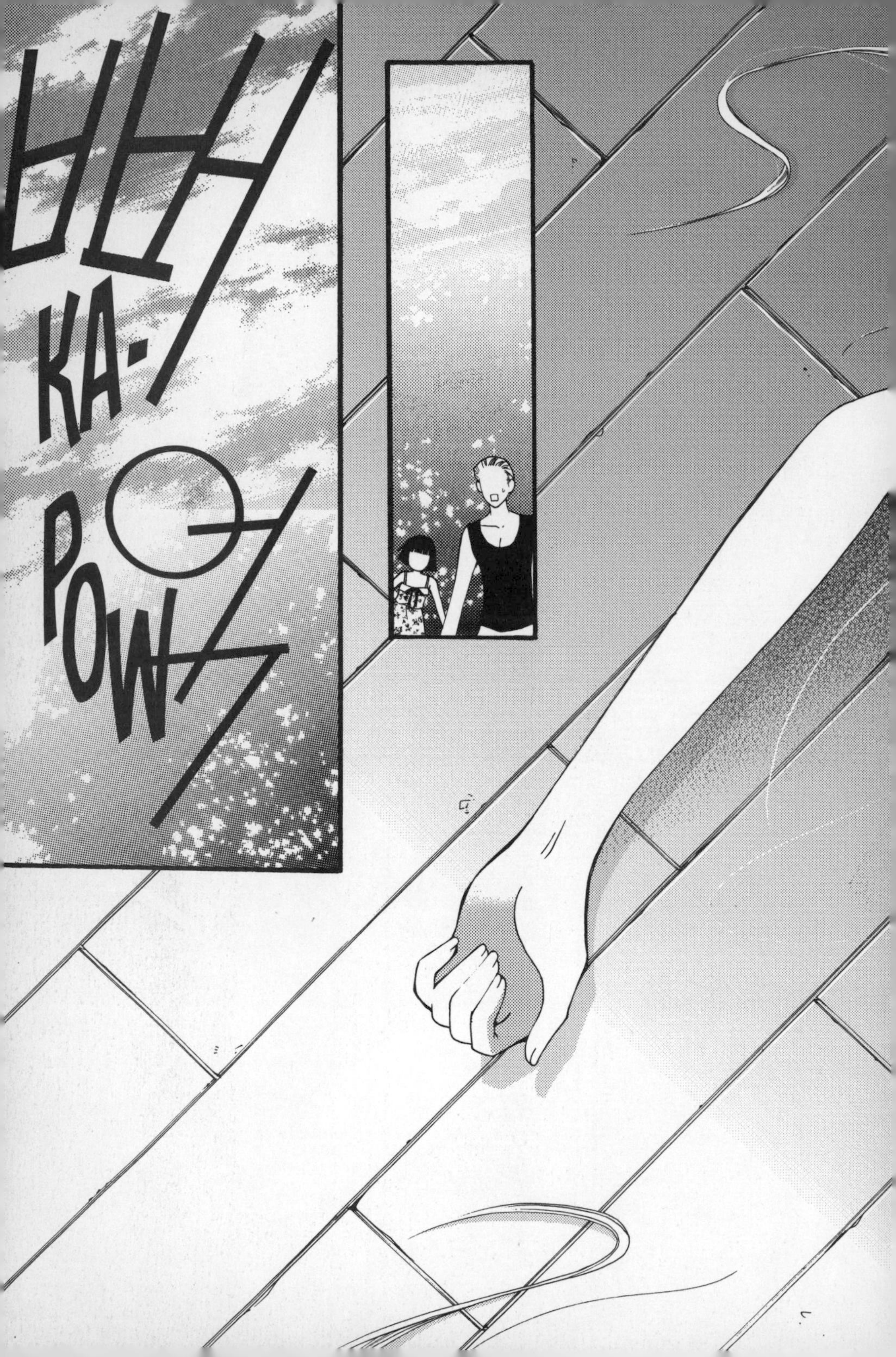

UH
KA-
POW

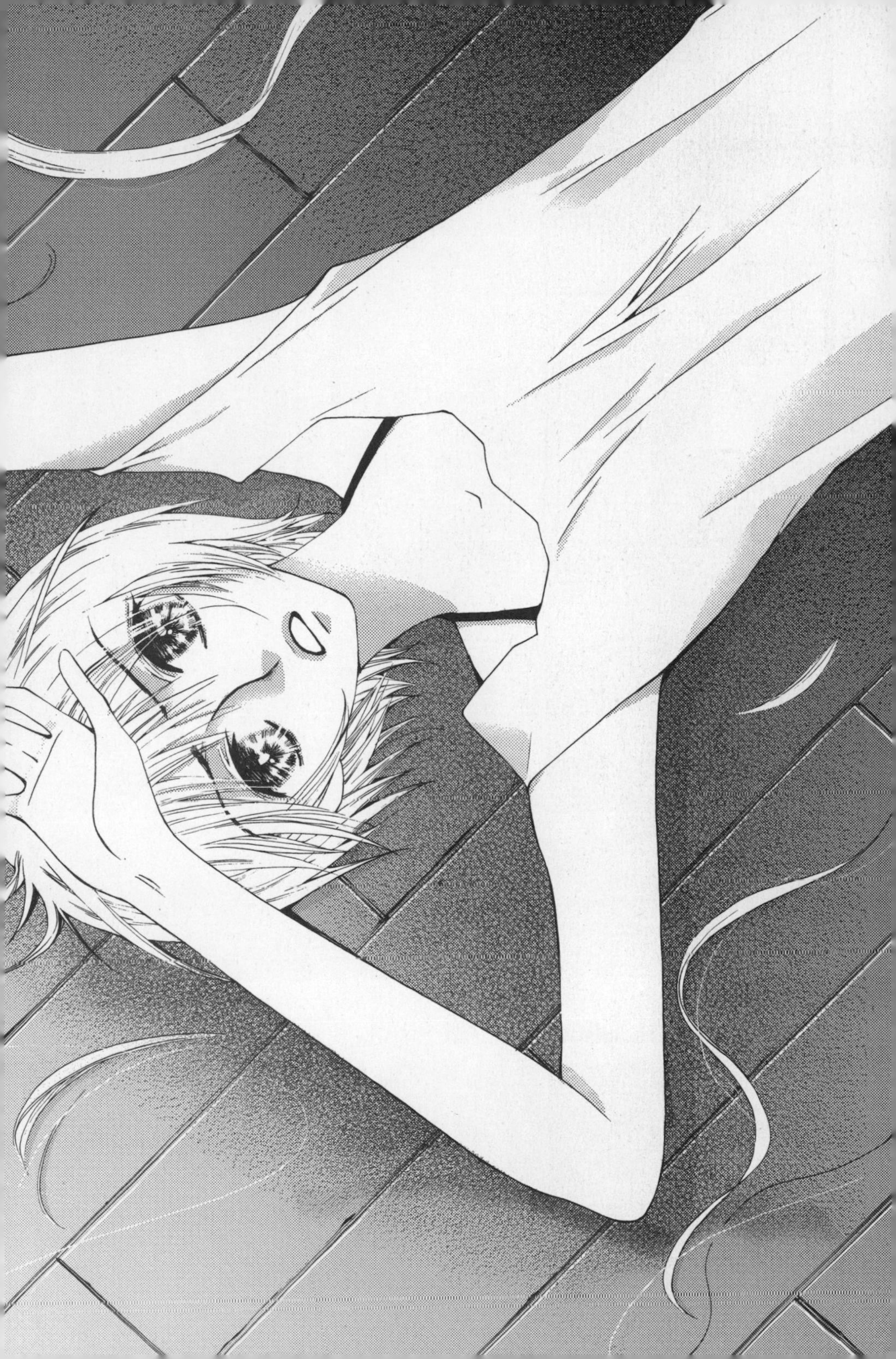

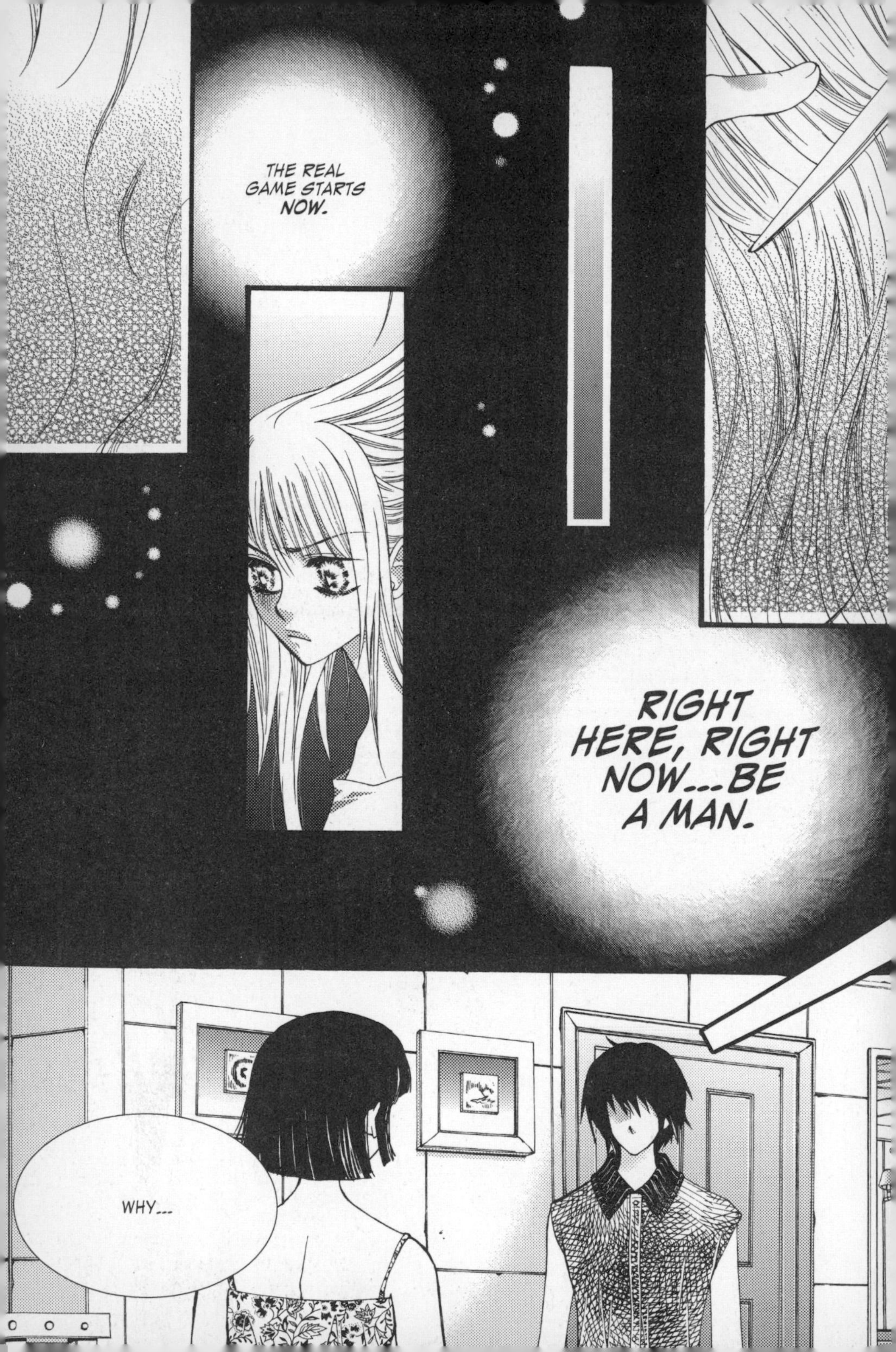
THE REAL GAME STARTS NOW.
RIGHT HERE, RIGHT NOW... BE A MAN.
WHY...

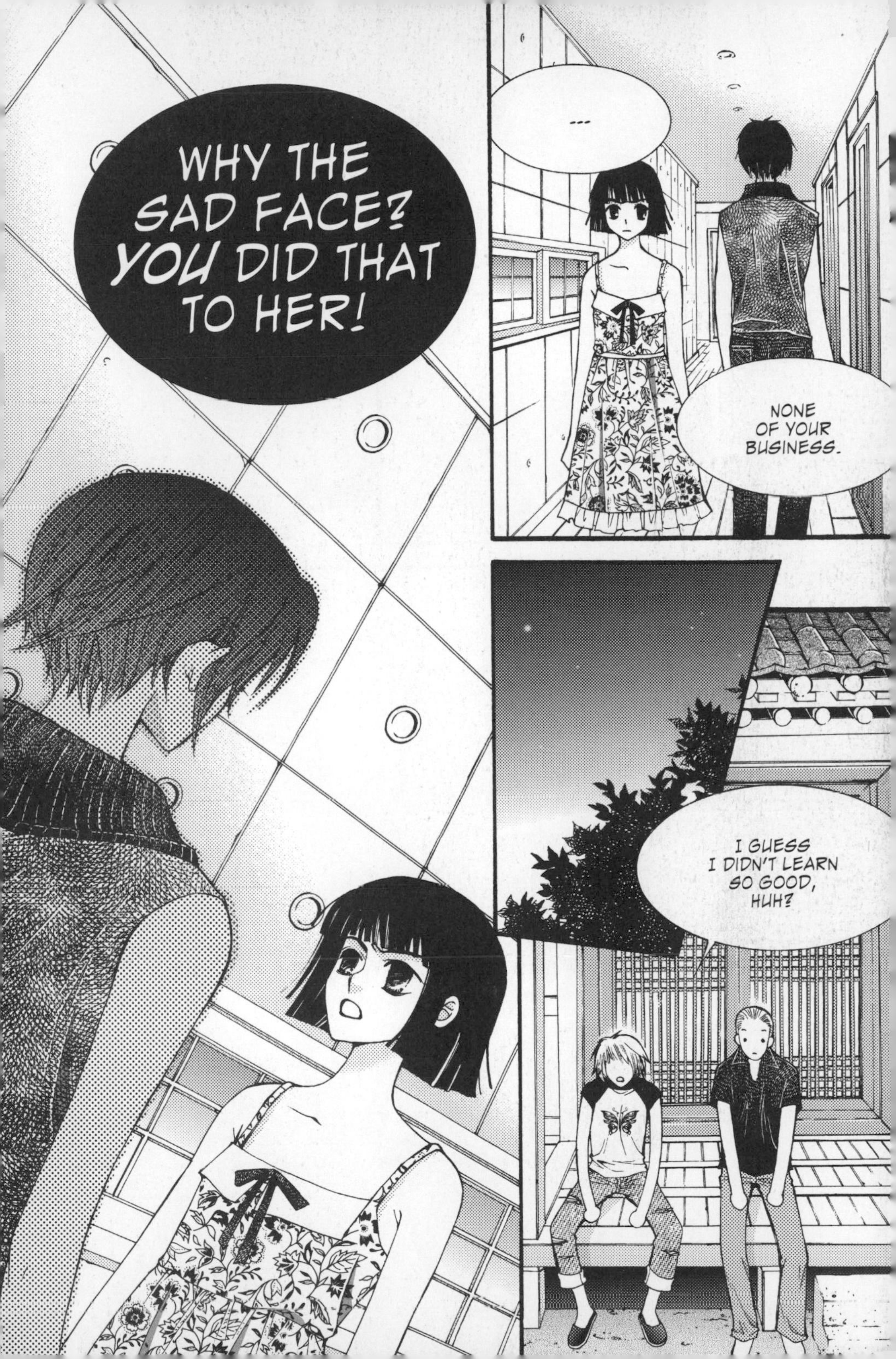
...
NONE OF YOUR BUSINESS.
WHY THE SAD FACE? YOU DID THAT TO HER!
I GUESS I DIDN'T LEARN SO GOOD, HUH?

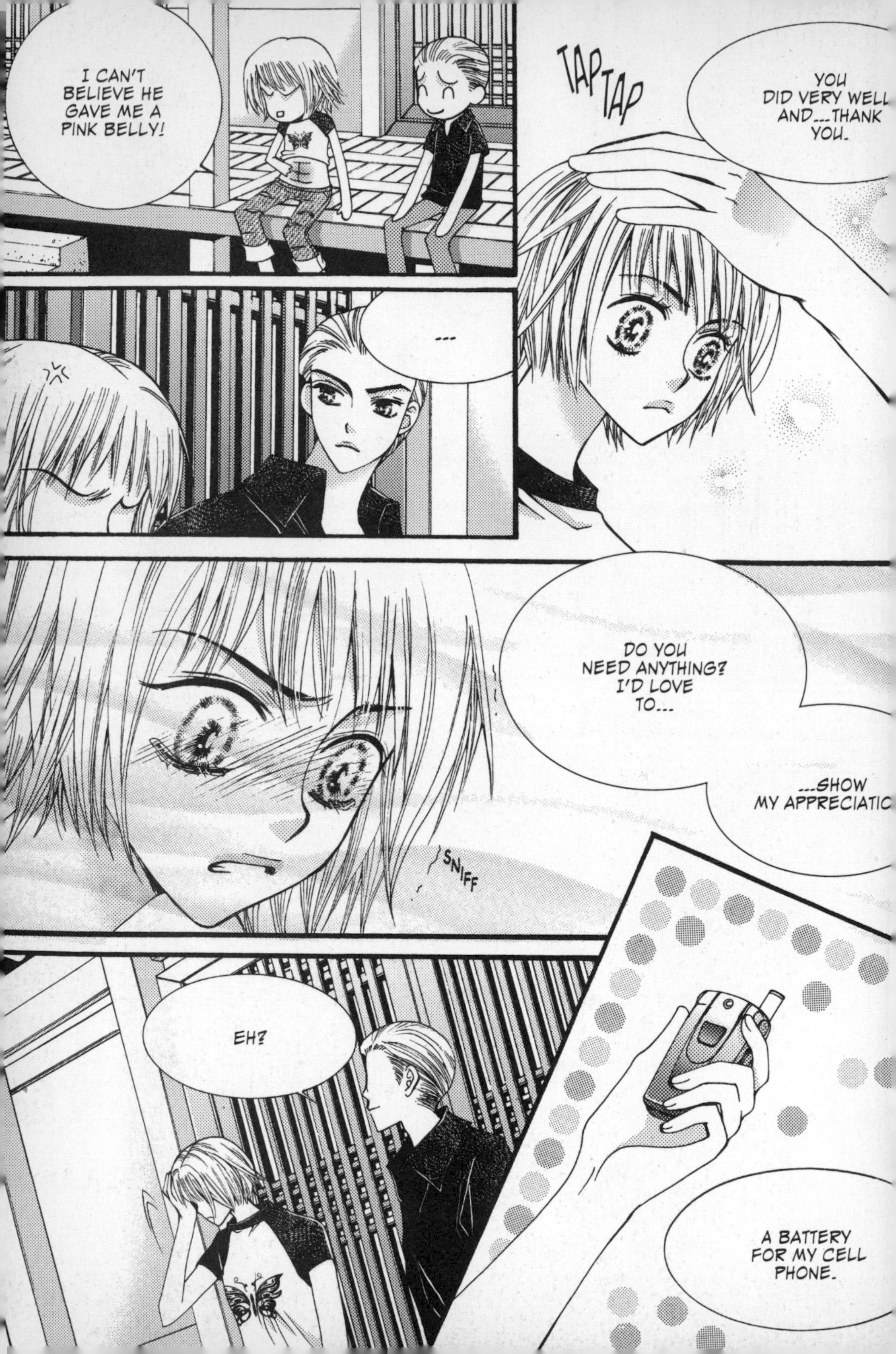
TAP TAP
YOU DID VERY WELL AND...THANK YOU.
I CAN'T BELIEVE HE GAVE ME A PINK BELLY!
...
DO YOU NEED ANYTHING? I'D LOVE TO...
...SHOW MY APPRECIATIC
SNIFF
A BATTERY FOR MY CELL PHONE.
EH?

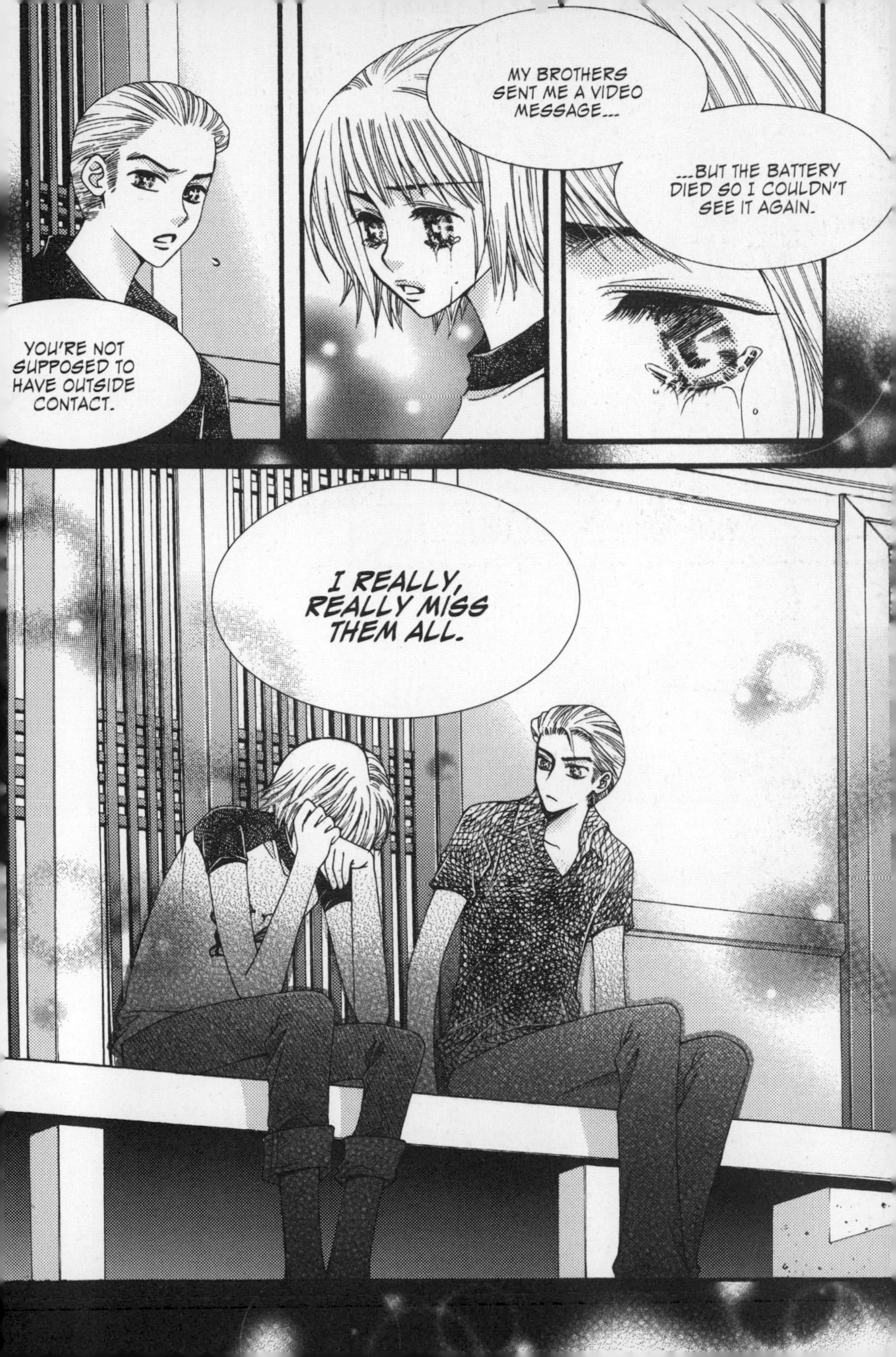
YOU'RE NOT SUPPOSED TO HAVE OUTSIDE CONTACT.
MY BROTHERS SENT ME A VIDEO MESSAGE...
...BUT THE BATTERY DIED SO I COULDN'T SEE IT AGAIN.
I REALLY, REALLY MISS THEM ALL.

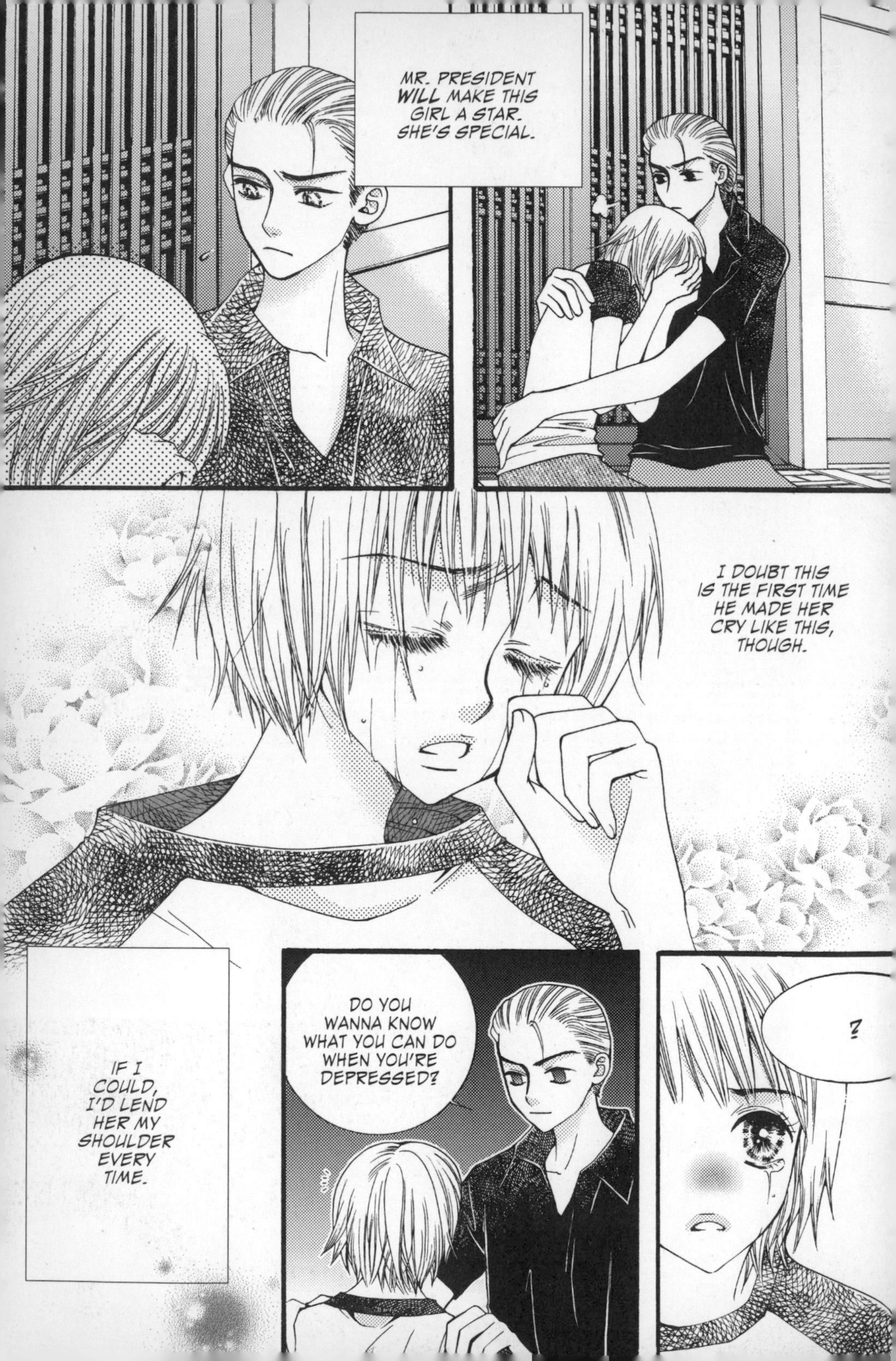
MR. PRESIDENT WILL MAKE THIS GIRL A STAR. SHE'S SPECIAL.
I DOUBT THIS IS THE FIRST TIME HE MADE HER CRY LIKE THIS, THOUGH.
IF I COULD, I'D LEND HER MY SHOULDER EVERY TIME.
DO YOU WANNA KNOW WHAT YOU CAN DO WHEN YOU'RE DEPRESSED?
?

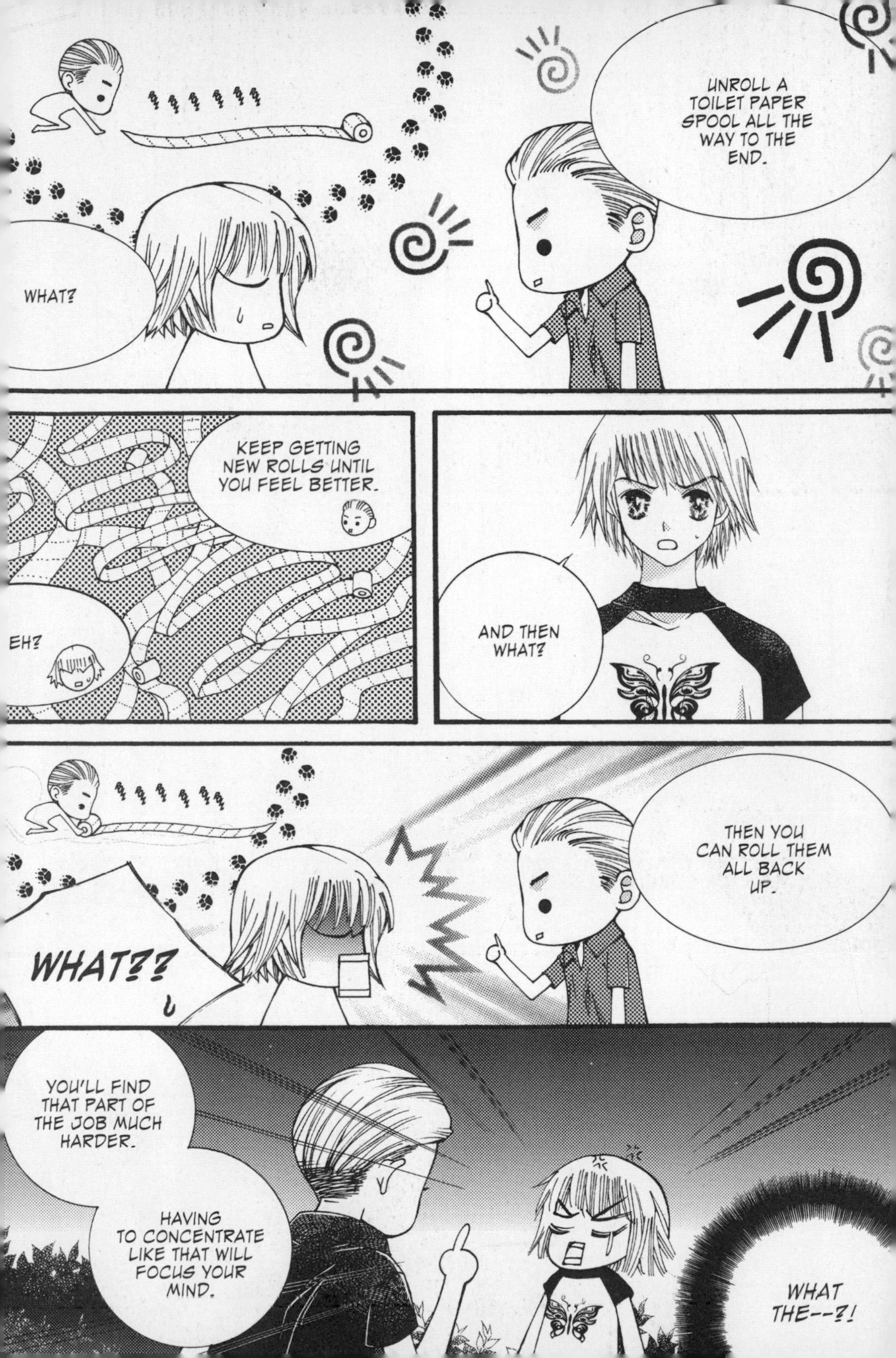

UNROLL A TOILET PAPER SPOOL ALL THE WAY TO THE END.
WHAT?
KEEP GETTING NEW ROLLS UNTIL YOU FEEL BETTER.
EH?
AND THEN WHAT?
THEN YOU CAN ROLL THEM ALL BACK UP.
WHAT??
YOU'LL FIND THAT PART OF THE JOB MUCH HARDER.
HAVING TO CONCENTRATE LIKE THAT WILL FOCUS YOUR MIND.
WHAT THE--?!

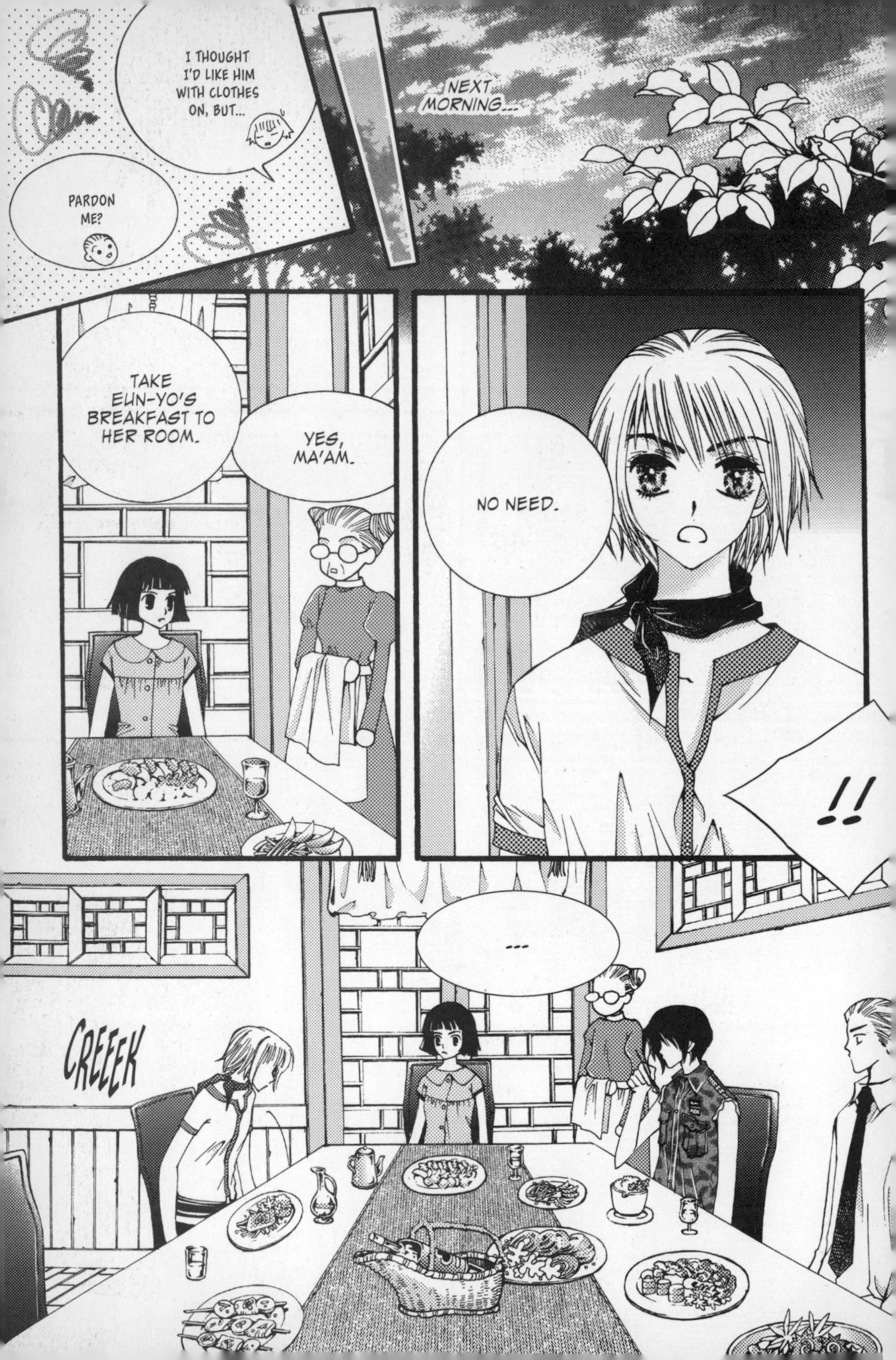
I THOUGHT I'D LIKE HIM WITH CLOTHES ON, BUT...
PARDON ME?
NEXT MORNING...
TAKE EUN-YO'S BREAKFAST TO HER ROOM.
YES, MA'AM.
NO NEED.
!!
...
CREEEK

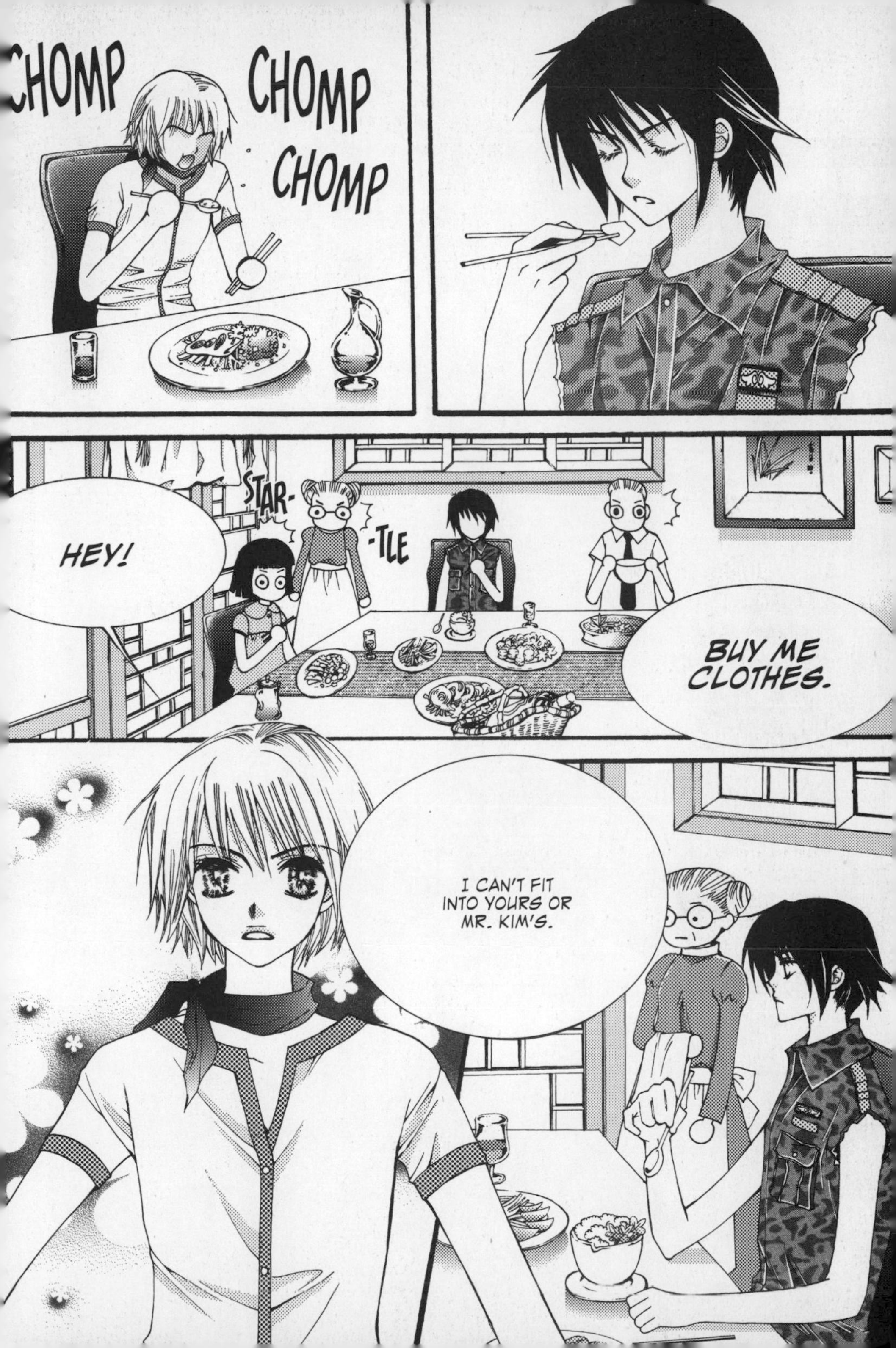
CHOMP
CHOMP
CHOMP
HEY!
STAR-
-TLE
BUY ME CLOTHES.
I CAN'T FIT INTO YOURS OR MR. KIM'S.

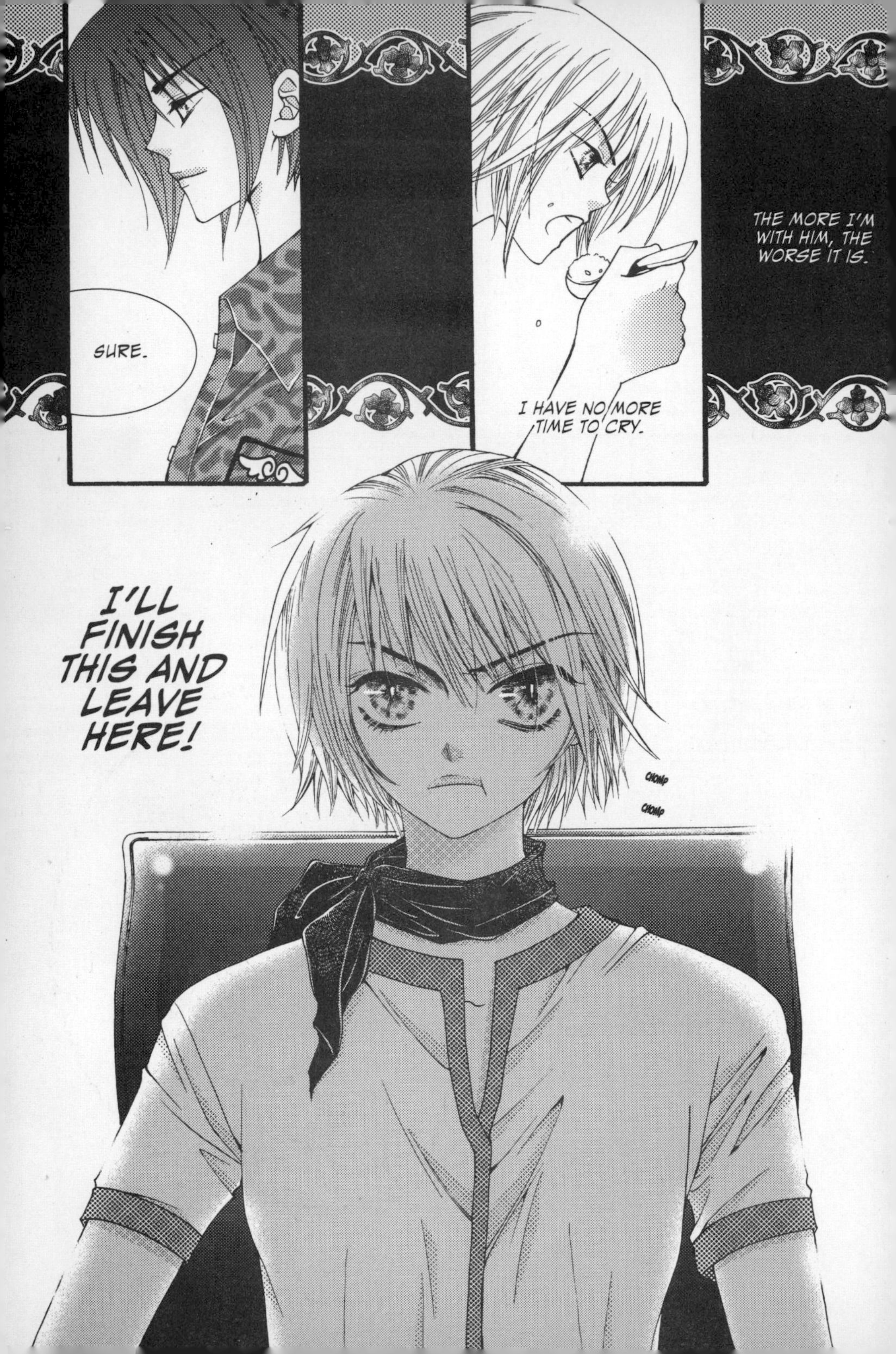
THE MORE I'M WITH HIM, THE WORSE IT IS.
I HAVE NO MORE TIME TO CRY.
SURE.
I'LL FINISH THIS AND LEAVE HERE!
CHOMP
CHOMP

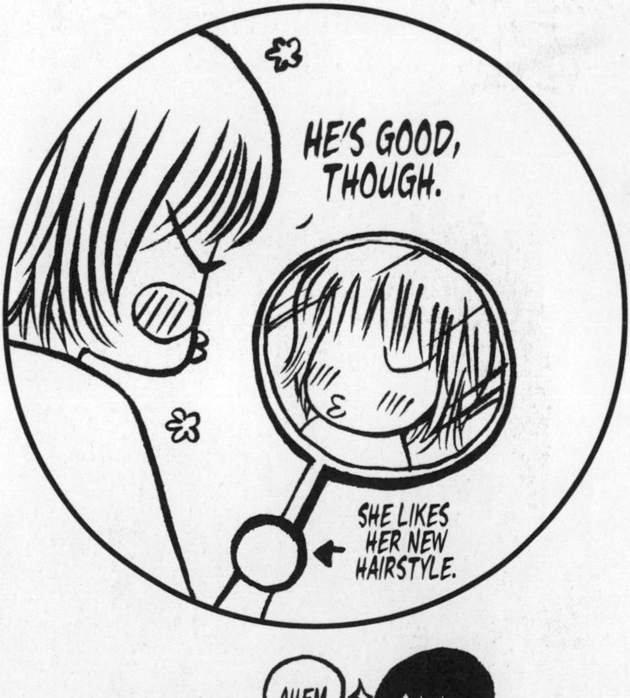
HE'S GOOD, THOUGH.
SHE LIKES HER NEW HAIRSTYLE.
AHEM.

STAR PROJECT
CHIRO 치로

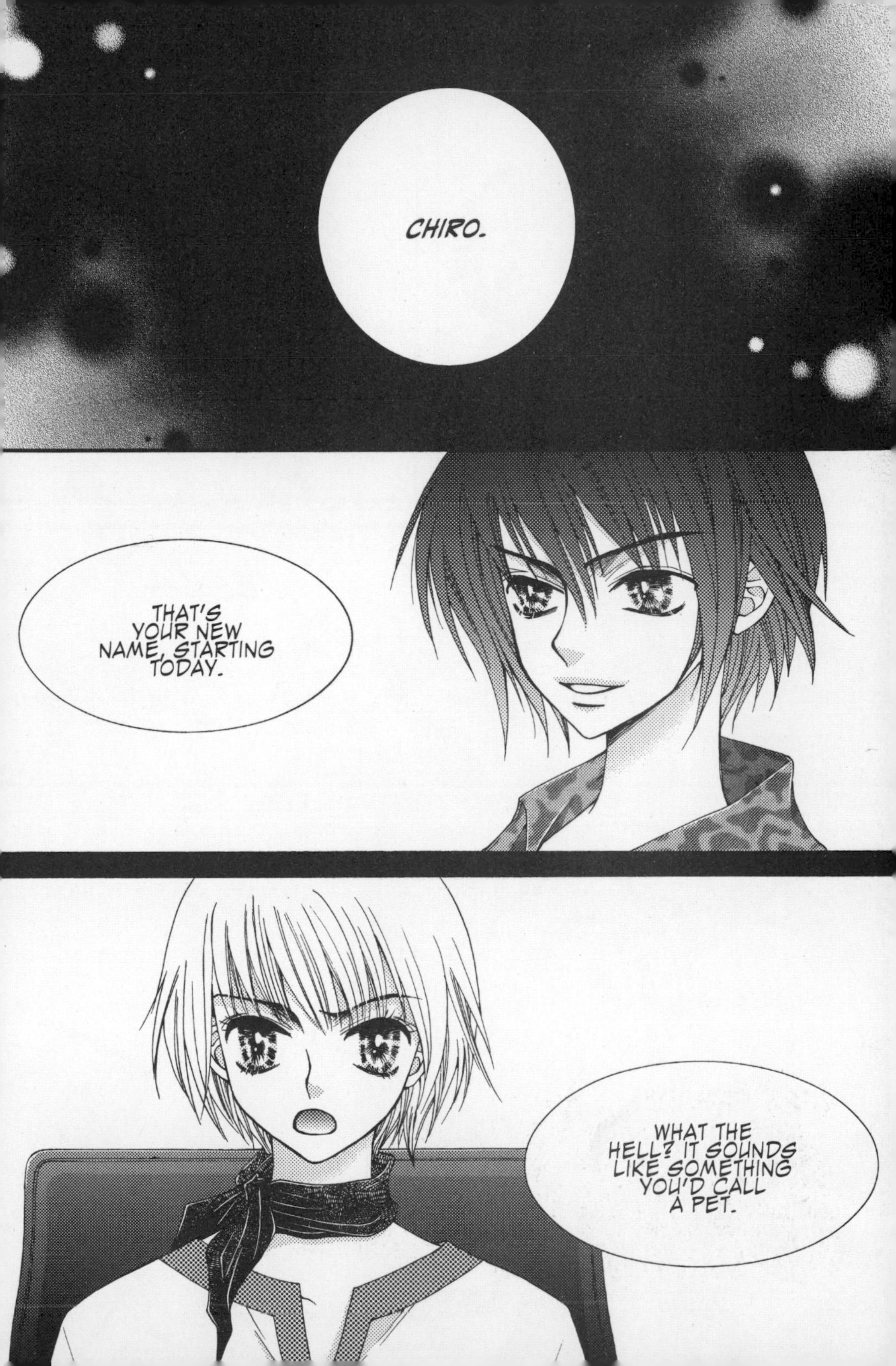
CHIRO.
THAT'S YOUR NEW NAME, STARTING TODAY.
WHAT THE HELL? IT SOUNDS LIKE SOMETHING YOU'D CALL A PET.

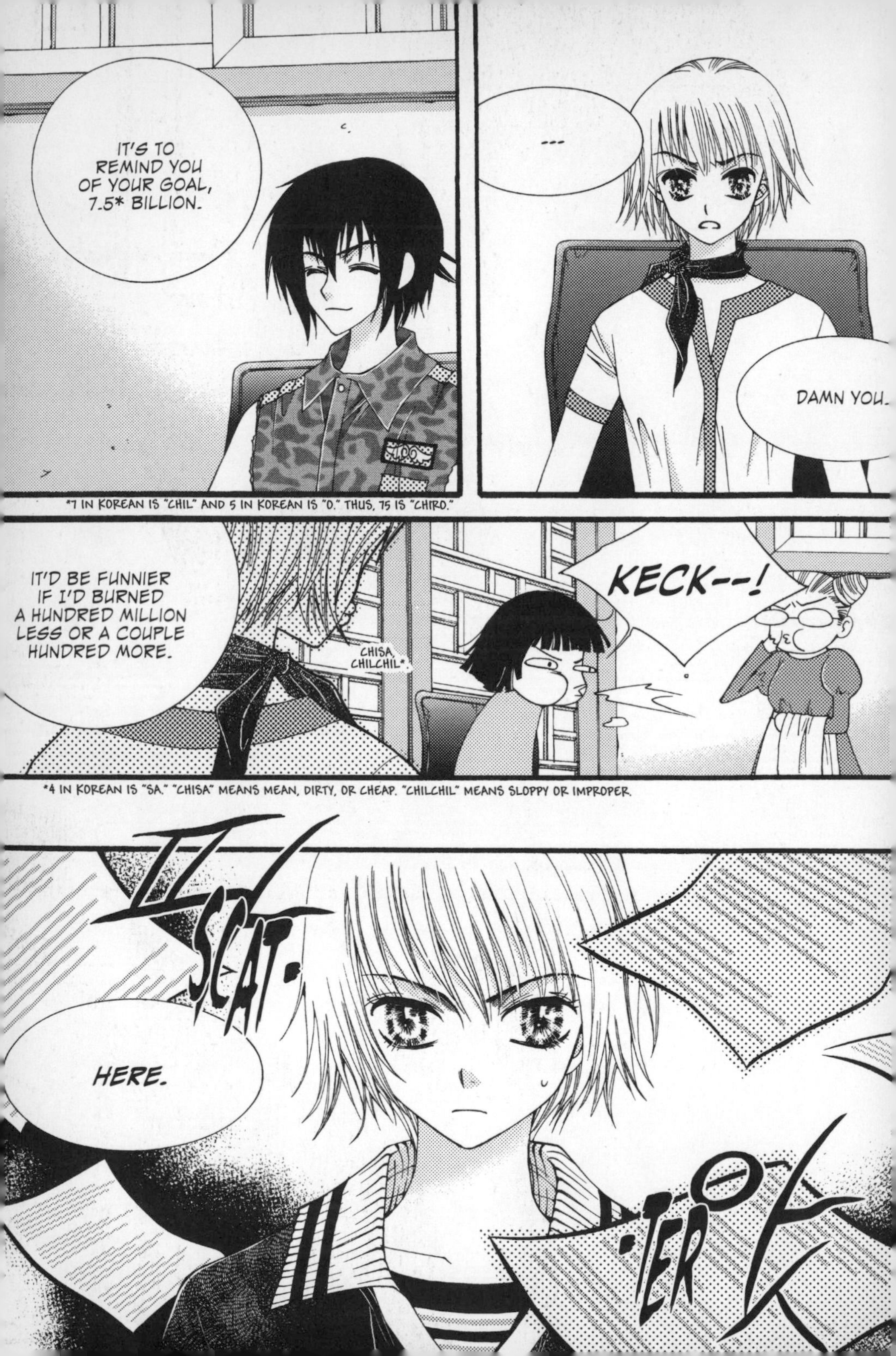
IT'S TO REMIND YOU OF YOUR GOAL, 7.5* BILLION.
...
DAMN YOU.
IT'D BE FUNNIER IF I'D BURNED A HUNDRED MILLION LESS OR A COUPLE HUNDRED MORE.
CHISA, CHILCHIL*.
KECK--!
SCAT
HERE.
-ER-K

*7 IN KOREAN IS "CHIL" AND 5 IN KOREAN IS "O." THUS, 75 IS "CHIRO."

*4 IN KOREAN IS "SA." "CHISA" MEANS MEAN, DIRTY, OR CHEAP. "CHILCHIL" MEANS SLOPPY OR IMPROPER.

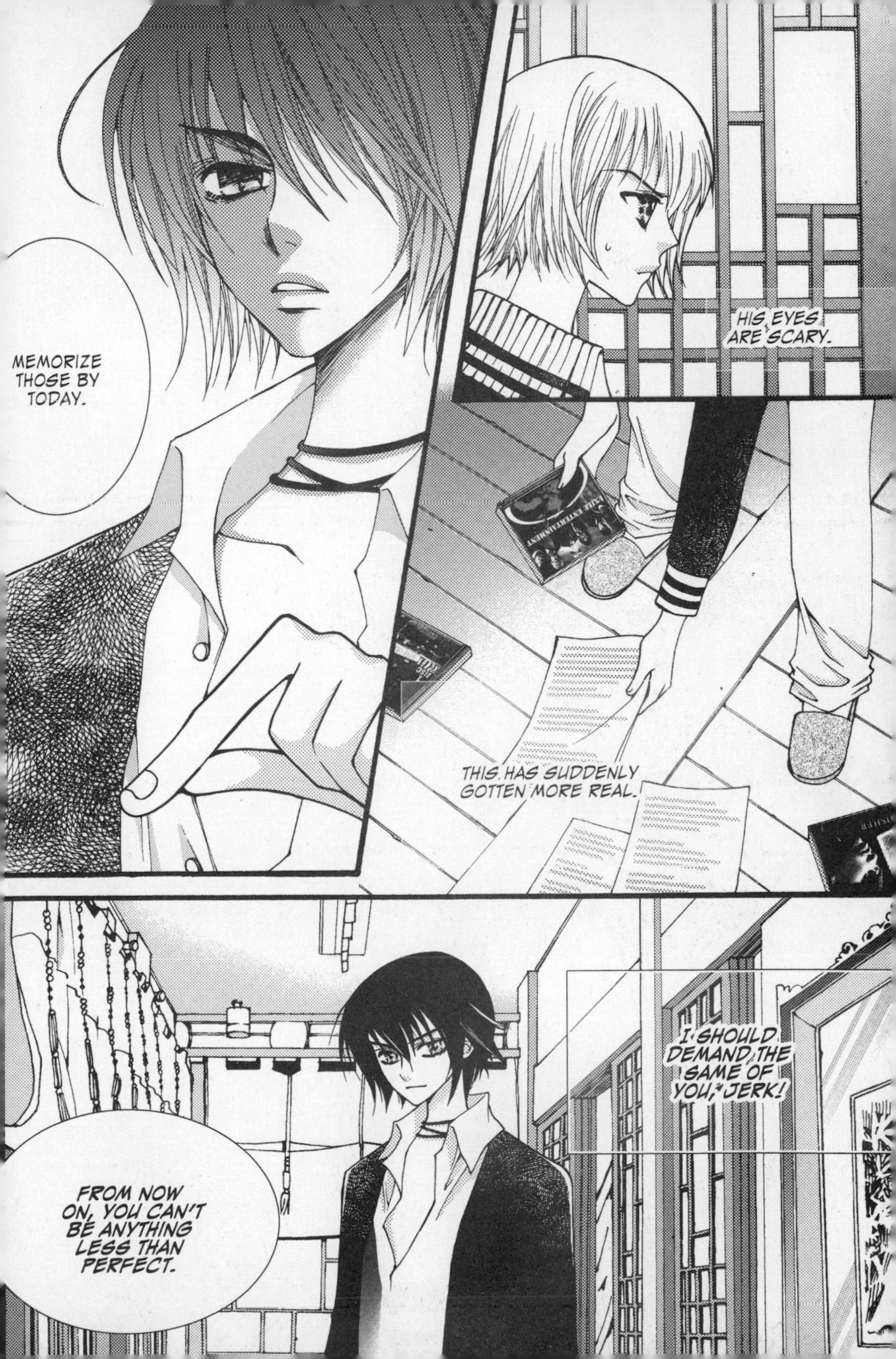
MEMORIZE THOSE BY TODAY.
HIS EYES ARE SCARY.
THIS HAS SUDDENLY GOTTEN MORE REAL.
FROM NOW ON, YOU CAN'T BE ANYTHING LESS THAN PERFECT.
I SHOULD DEMAND THE SAME OF YOU, JERK!

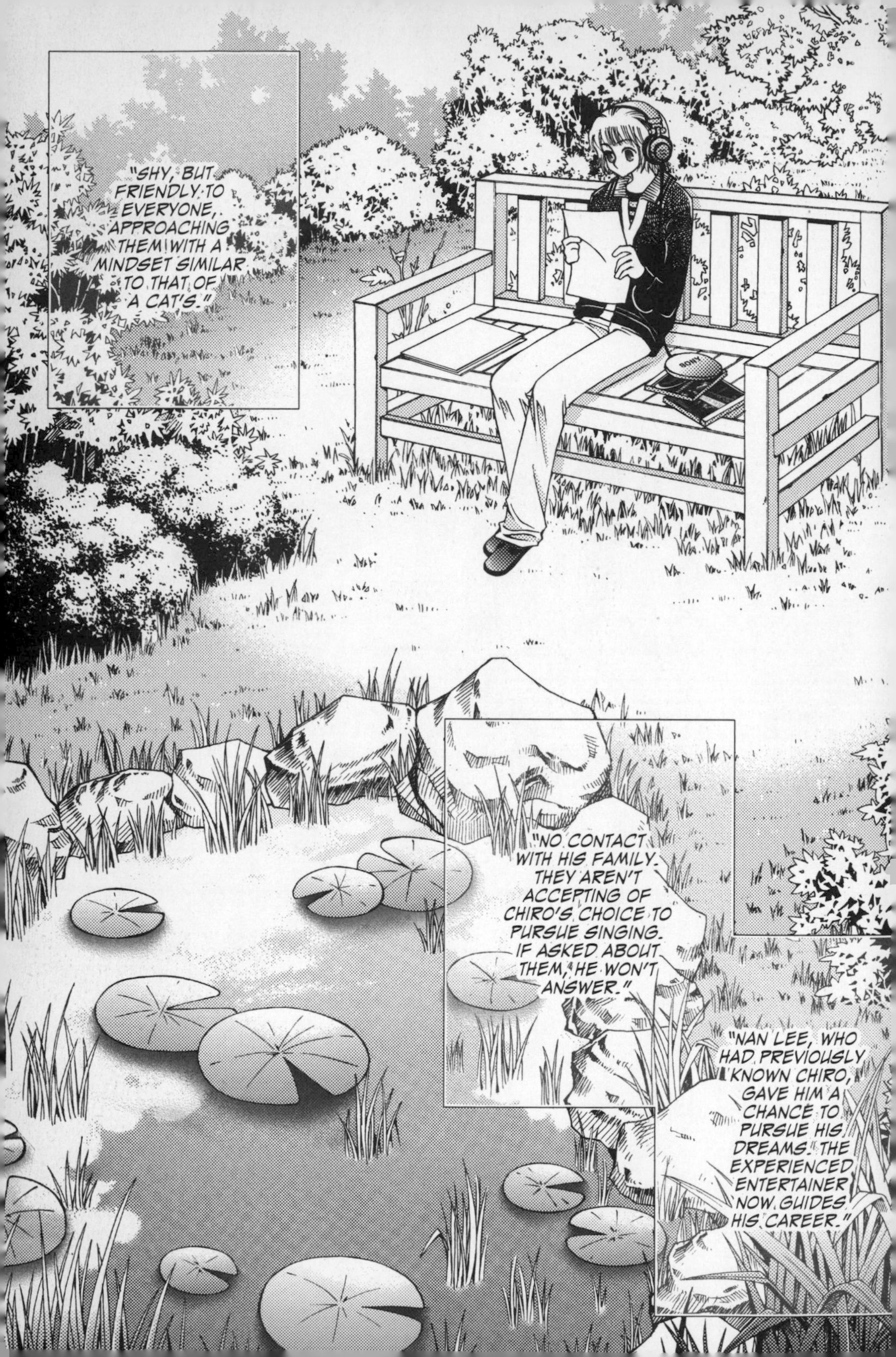
"SHY, BUT FRIENDLY TO EVERYONE, APPROACHING THEM WITH A MINDSET SIMILAR TO THAT OF A CAT'S."
SONY
"NO CONTACT WITH HIS FAMILY. THEY AREN'T ACCEPTING OF CHIRO'S CHOICE TO PURSUE SINGING. IF ASKED ABOUT THEM, HE WON'T ANSWER."
"NAN LEE, WHO HAD PREVIOUSLY KNOWN CHIRO, GAVE HIM A CHANCE TO PURSUE HIS DREAMS. THE EXPERIENCED ENTERTAINER NOW GUIDES HIS CAREER."

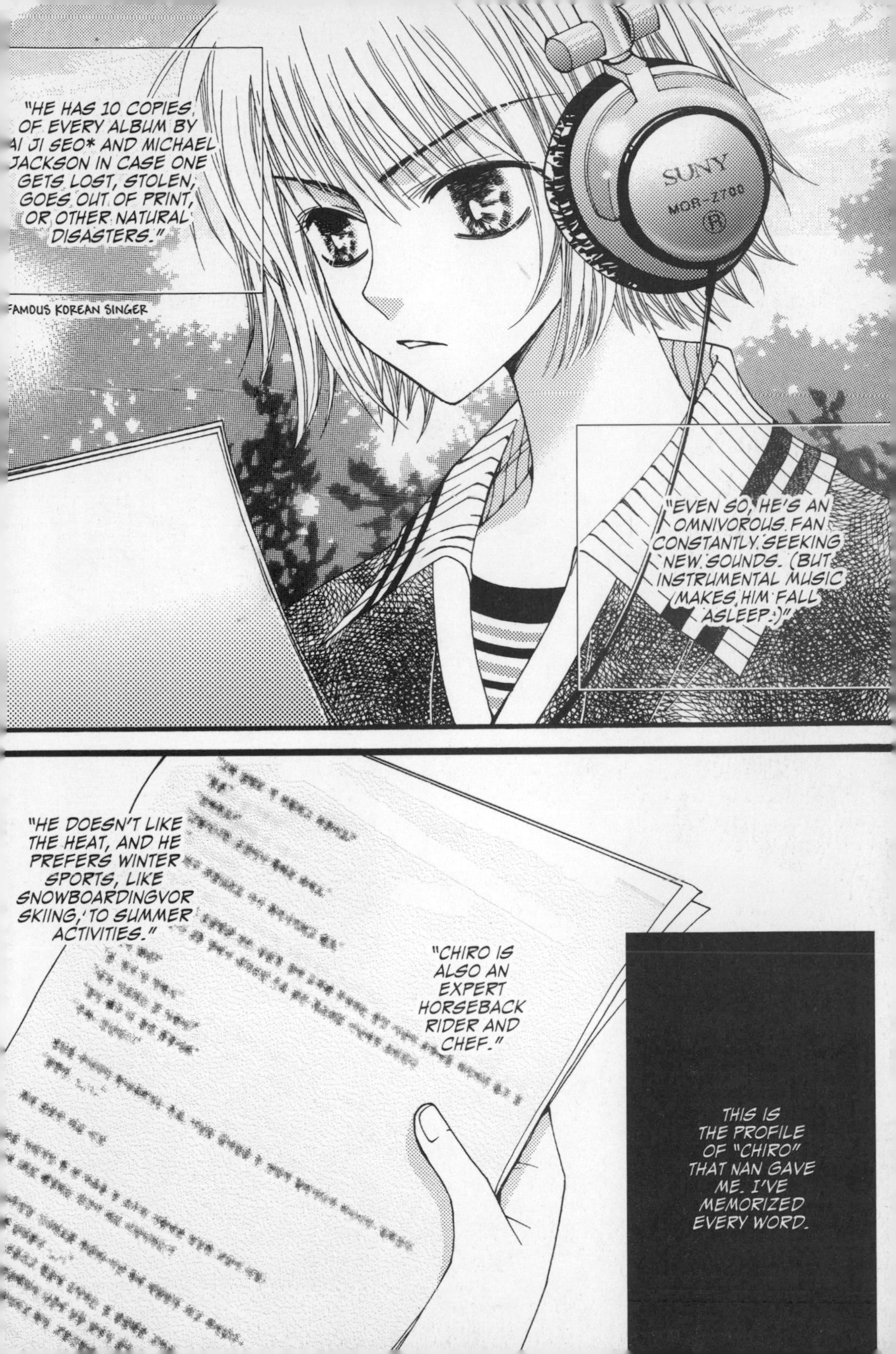
"HE HAS 10 COPIES OF EVERY ALBUM BY AI JI SEO* AND MICHAEL JACKSON IN CASE ONE GETS LOST, STOLEN, GOES OUT OF PRINT, OR OTHER NATURAL DISASTERS."
*FAMOUS KOREAN SINGER
SUNY
"EVEN SO, HE'S AN OMNIVOROUS FAN CONSTANTLY SEEKING NEW SOUNDS. (BUT INSTRUMENTAL MUSIC MAKES HIM FALL ASLEEP.)"
"HE DOESN'T LIKE THE HEAT, AND HE PREFERS WINTER SPORTS, LIKE SNOWBOARDING OR SKIING, TO SUMMER ACTIVITIES."
"CHIRO IS ALSO AN EXPERT HORSEBACK RIDER AND CHEF."
THIS IS THE PROFILE OF "CHIRO" THAT NAN GAVE ME. I'VE MEMORIZED EVERY WORD.

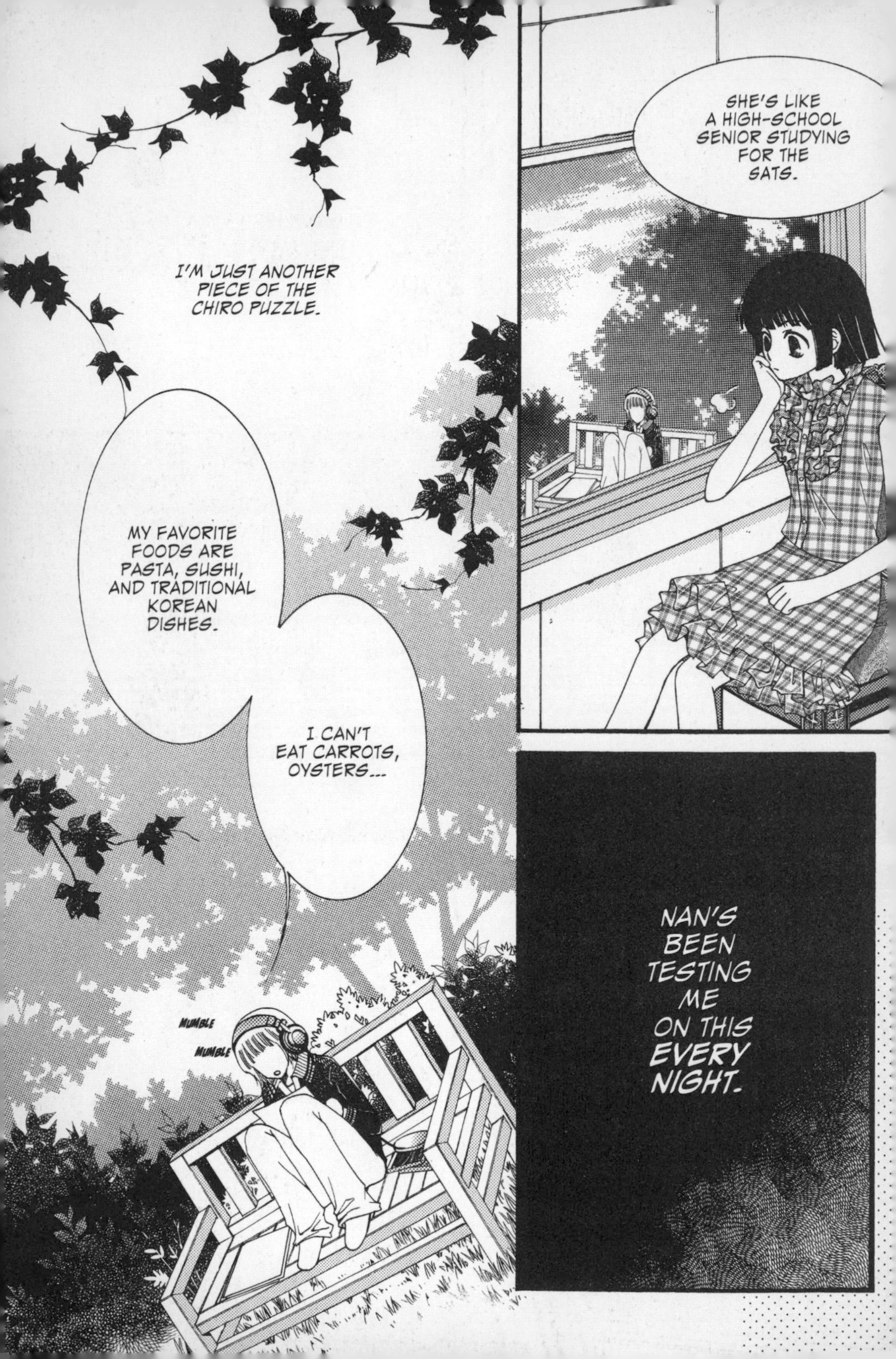

I'M JUST ANOTHER PIECE OF THE CHIRO PUZZLE.
MY FAVORITE FOODS ARE PASTA, SUSHI, AND TRADITIONAL KOREAN DISHES.
I CAN'T EAT CARROTS, OYSTERS...
MUMBLE MUMBLE
SHE'S LIKE A HIGH-SCHOOL SENIOR STUDYING FOR THE SATS.
NAN'S BEEN TESTING ME ON THIS EVERY NIGHT.

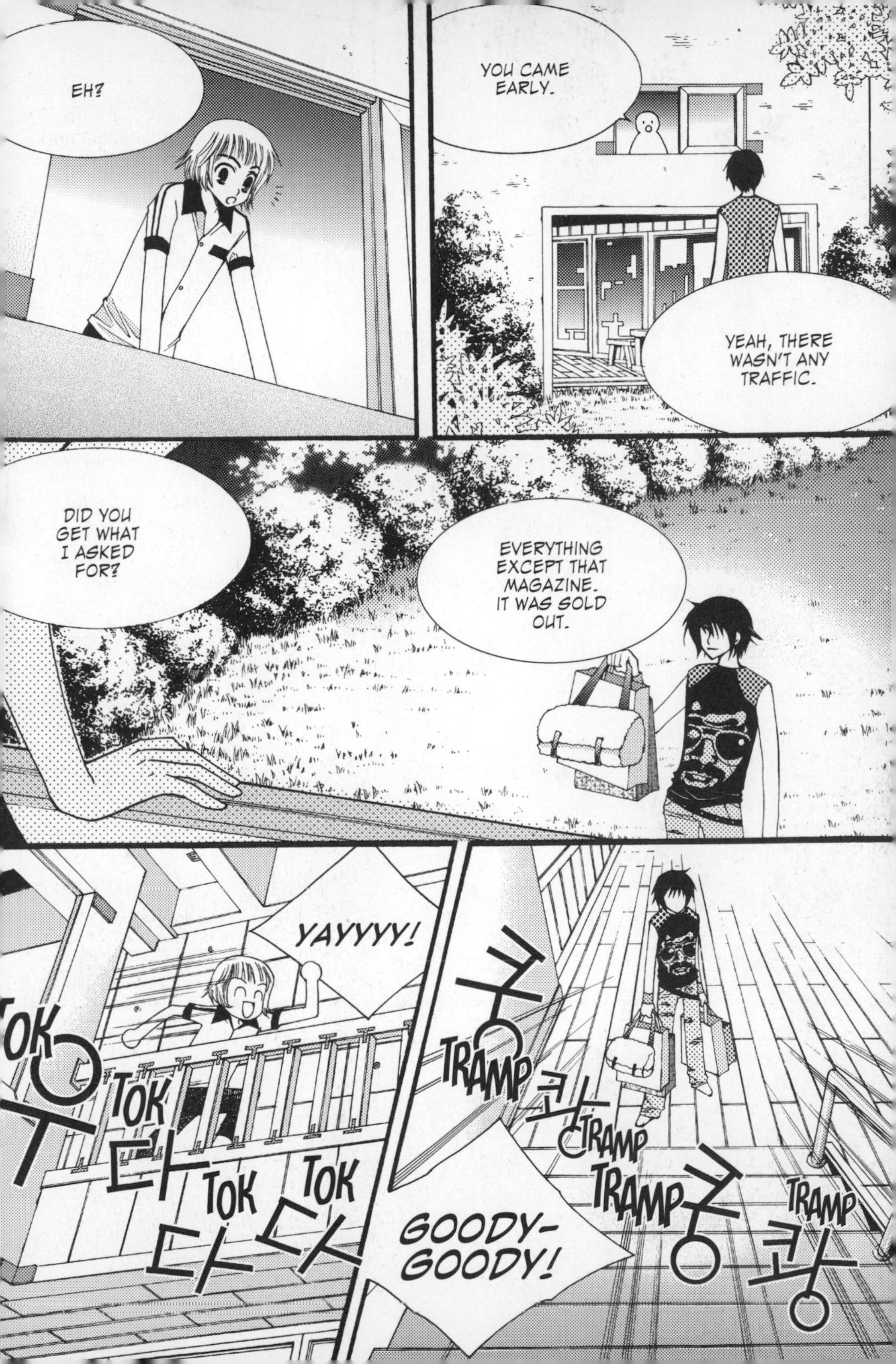
EH?
YOU CAME EARLY.
YEAH, THERE WASN'T ANY TRAFFIC.
DID YOU GET WHAT I ASKED FOR?
EVERYTHING EXCEPT THAT MAGAZINE. IT WAS SOLD OUT.
YAYYYY!
TOK TOK TOK TOK
타다닥
GOODY-GOODY!
TRAMP TRAMP TRAMP TRAMP
쿵쾅쿵쾅

GRINDING

HALT

WAIT.

THIS IS ALWAYS THE HARDEST PART.

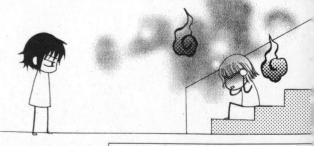

"...FRIENDLY TO EVERYONE... A MINDSET SIMILAR TO THAT OF A CAT'S."

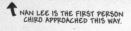 NAN LEE IS THE FIRST PERSON CHIRO APPROACHED THIS WAY.

THE INITIAL ATTEMPT FAILED.

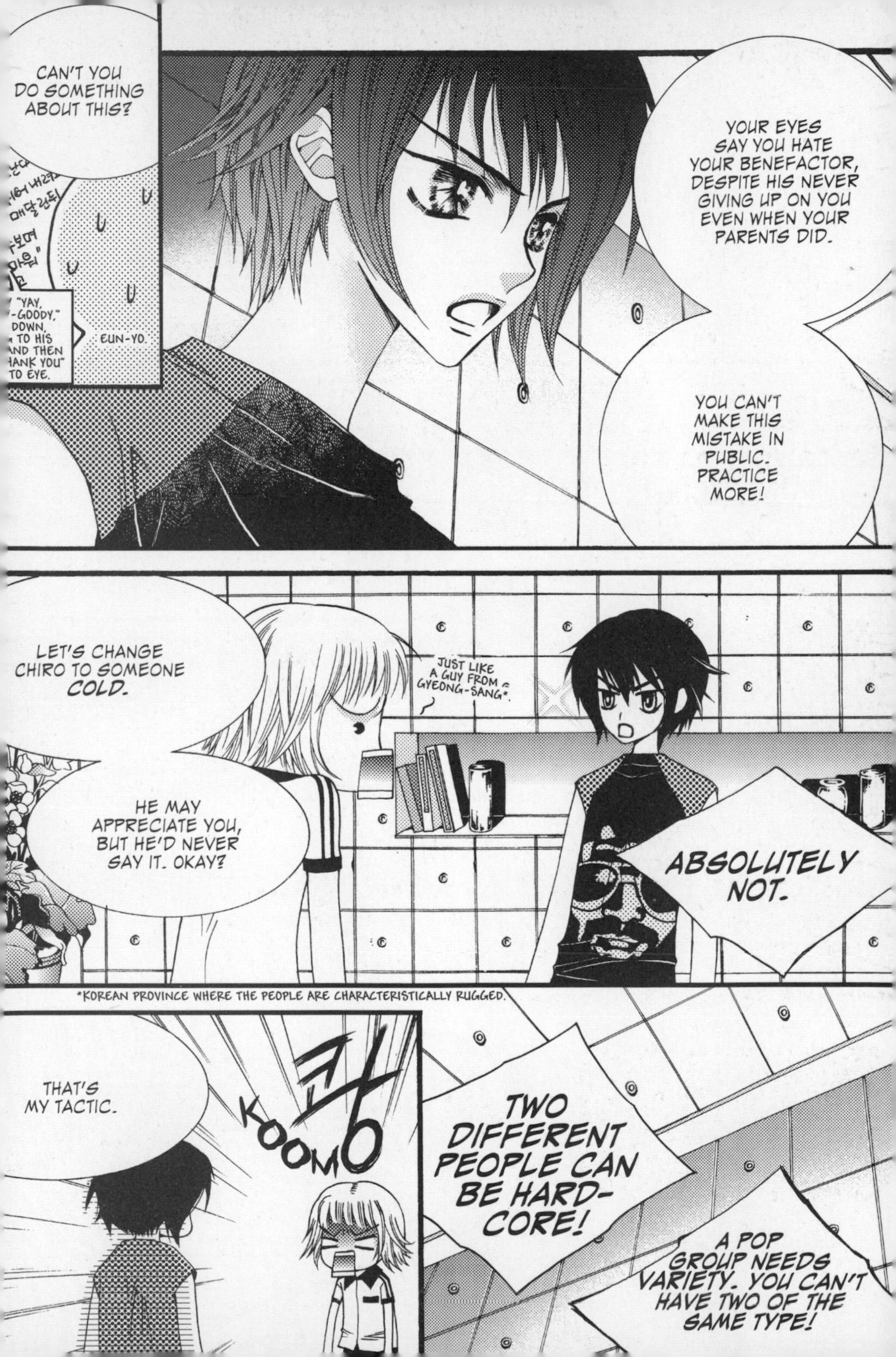
CAN'T YOU DO SOMETHING ABOUT THIS?
EUN-YO.
YOUR EYES SAY YOU HATE YOUR BENEFACTOR, DESPITE HIS NEVER GIVING UP ON YOU EVEN WHEN YOUR PARENTS DID.
YOU CAN'T MAKE THIS MISTAKE IN PUBLIC. PRACTICE MORE!
LET'S CHANGE CHIRO TO SOMEONE COLD.
HE MAY APPRECIATE YOU, BUT HE'D NEVER SAY IT. OKAY?
JUST LIKE A GUY FROM GYEONG-SANG*.
ABSOLUTELY NOT.
*KOREAN PROVINCE WHERE THE PEOPLE ARE CHARACTERISTICALLY RUGGED.
THAT'S MY TACTIC.
KOOM
TWO DIFFERENT PEOPLE CAN BE HARD-CORE!
A POP GROUP NEEDS VARIETY. YOU CAN'T HAVE TWO OF THE SAME TYPE!

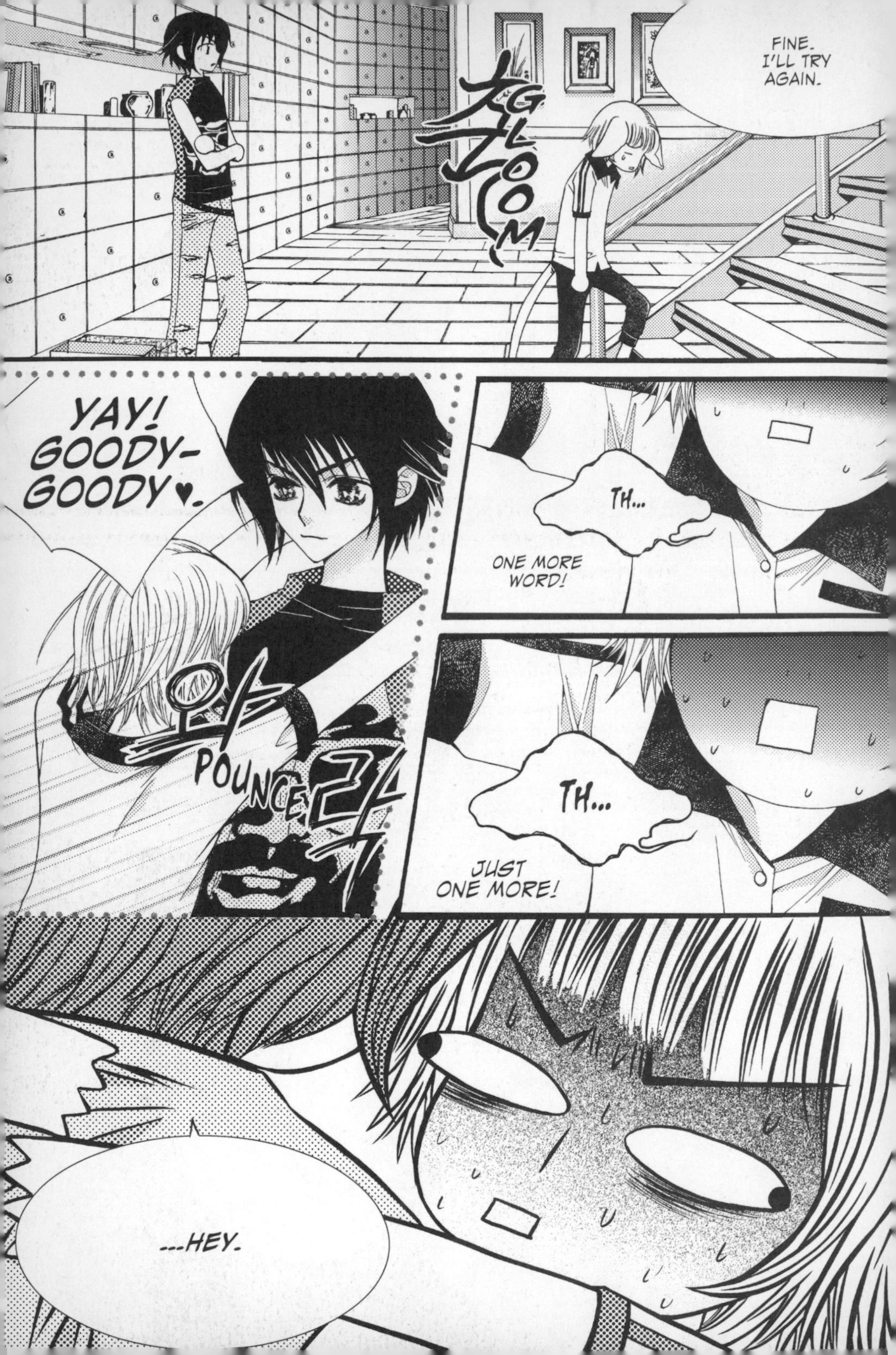
FINE. I'LL TRY AGAIN.
GLOOM
YAY! GOODY-GOODY♥.
POUNCE
TH...
ONE MORE WORD!
TH...
JUST ONE MORE!
---HEY.

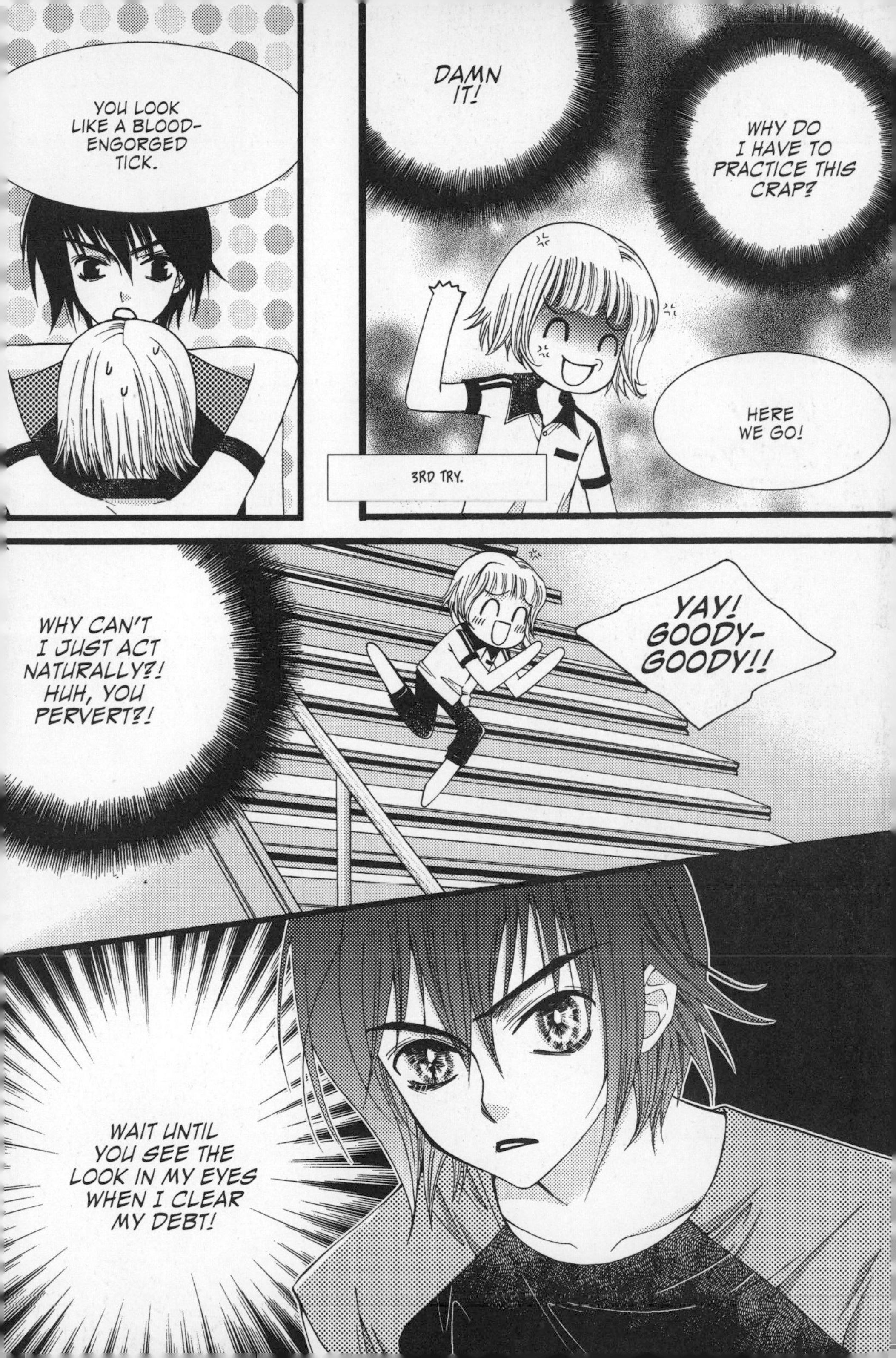
WHY DO I HAVE TO PRACTICE THIS CRAP?
DAMN IT!
3RD TRY.
HERE WE GO!
YOU LOOK LIKE A BLOOD-ENGORGED TICK.
YAY! GOODY-GOODY!!
WHY CAN'T I JUST ACT NATURALLY?! HUH, YOU PERVERT?!
WAIT UNTIL YOU SEE THE LOOK IN MY EYES WHEN I CLEAR MY DEBT!

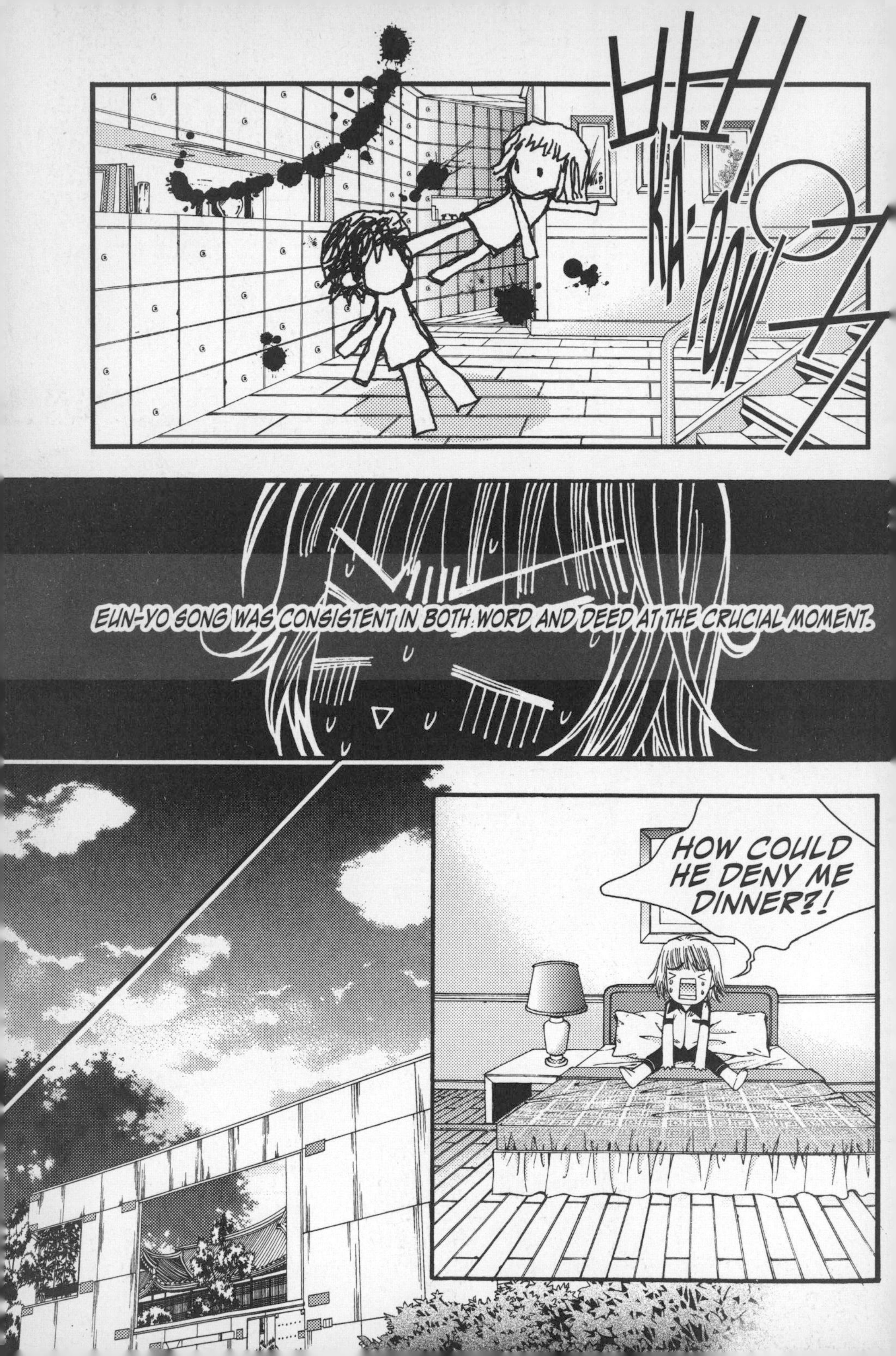
KA-POW!
EUN-YO SONG WAS CONSISTENT IN BOTH WORD AND DEED AT THE CRUCIAL MOMENT.
HOW COULD HE DENY ME DINNER?!

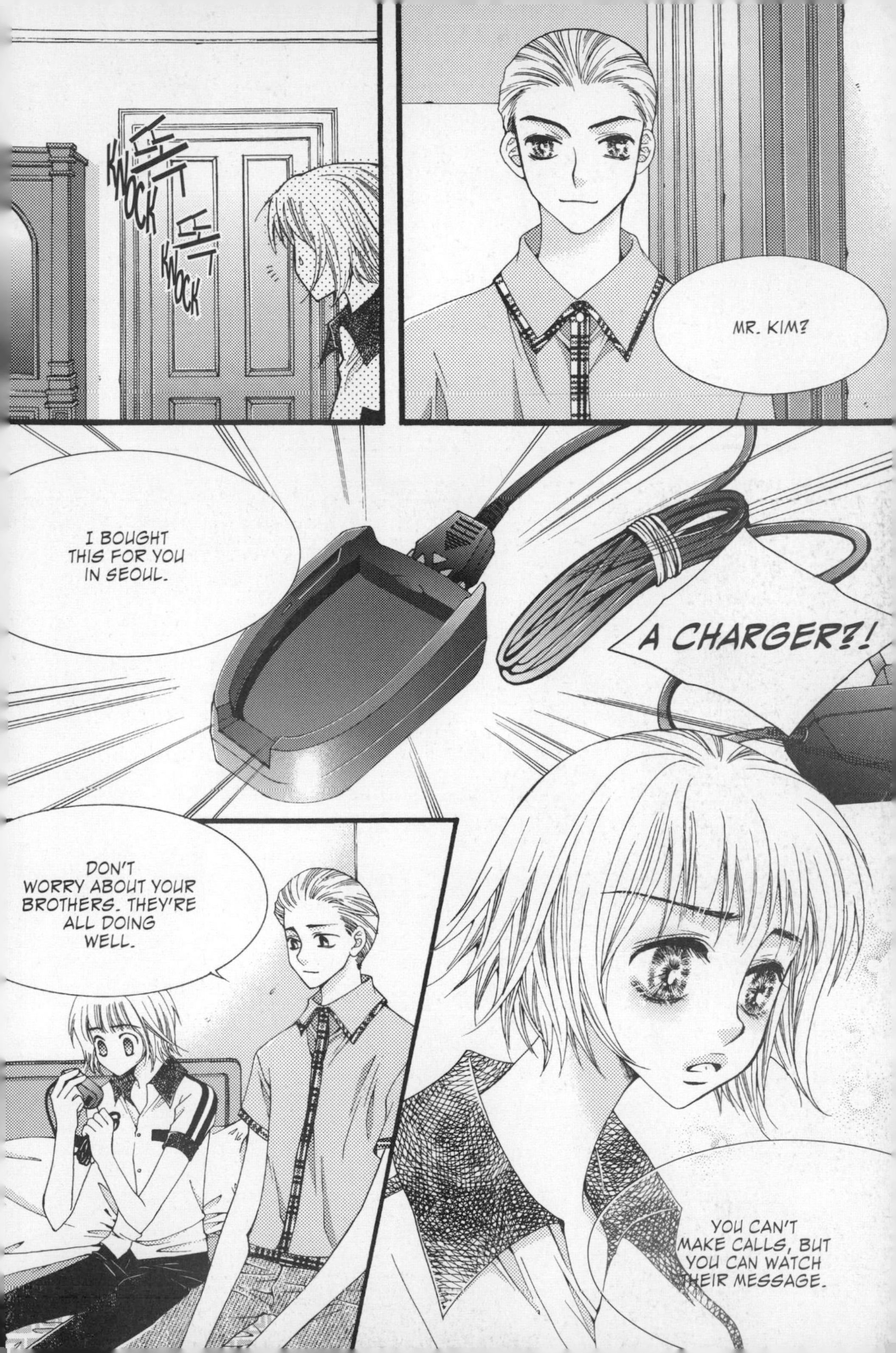
KNOCK
KNOCK
MR. KIM?
I BOUGHT THIS FOR YOU IN SEOUL.
A CHARGER?!
DON'T WORRY ABOUT YOUR BROTHERS. THEY'RE ALL DOING WELL.
YOU CAN'T MAKE CALLS, BUT YOU CAN WATCH THEIR MESSAGE.

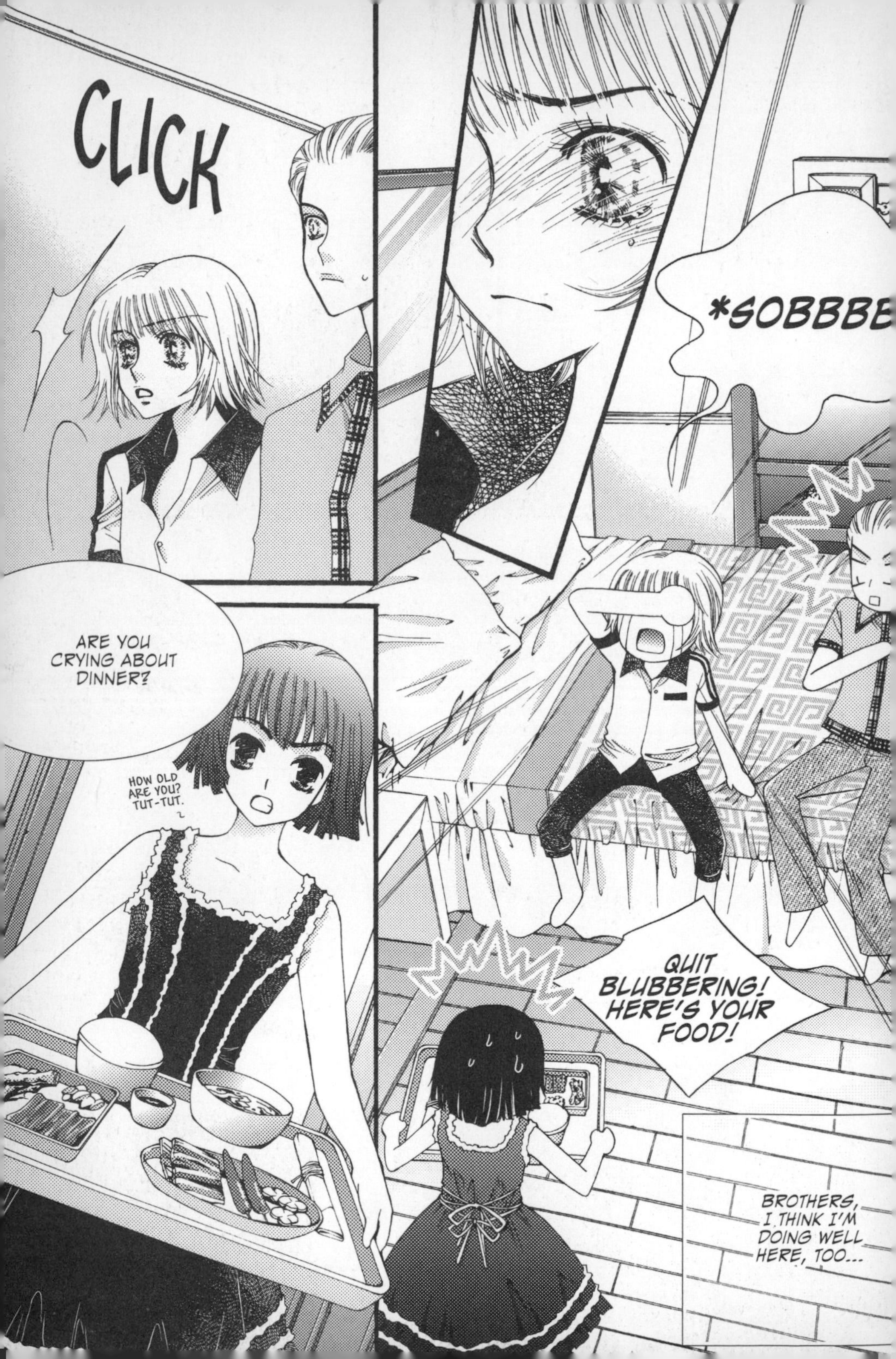
*SOBBBB
CLICK
ARE YOU CRYING ABOUT DINNER?
HOW OLD ARE YOU? TUT-TUT.
QUIT BLUBBERING! HERE'S YOUR FOOD!
BROTHERS, I THINK I'M DOING WELL HERE, TOO...

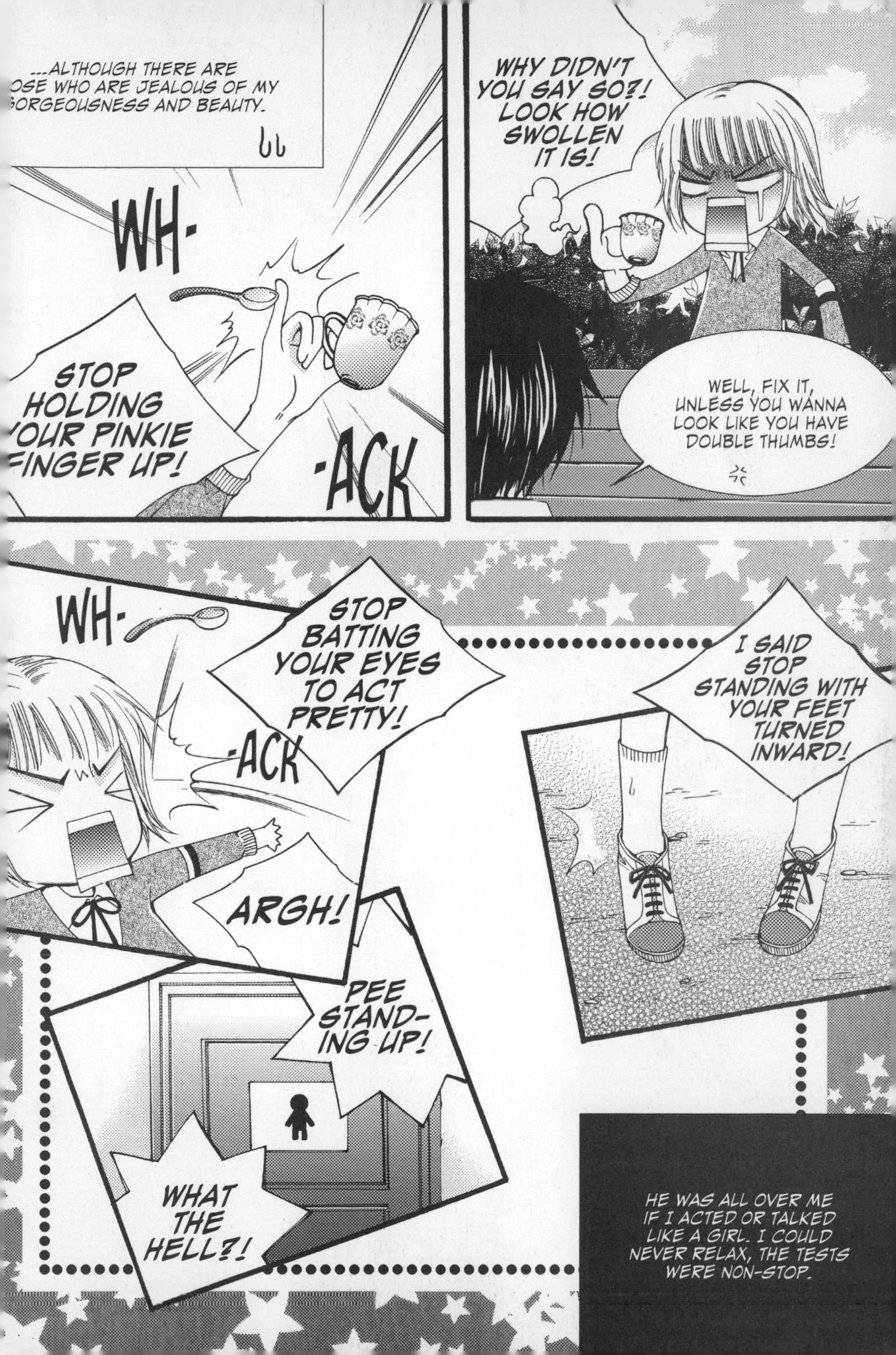
...ALTHOUGH THERE ARE
OSE WHO ARE JEALOUS OF MY
GORGEOUSNESS AND BEAUTY.
WH-
STOP HOLDING YOUR PINKIE FINGER UP!
-ACK
WHY DIDN'T YOU SAY SO?! LOOK HOW SWOLLEN IT IS!
WELL, FIX IT, UNLESS YOU WANNA LOOK LIKE YOU HAVE DOUBLE THUMBS!
WH-
STOP BATTING YOUR EYES TO ACT PRETTY!
-ACK
ARGH!
I SAID STOP STANDING WITH YOUR FEET TURNED INWARD!
PEE STAND-ING UP!
WHAT THE HELL?!
HE WAS ALL OVER ME IF I ACTED OR TALKED LIKE A GIRL. I COULD NEVER RELAX, THE TESTS WERE NON-STOP.

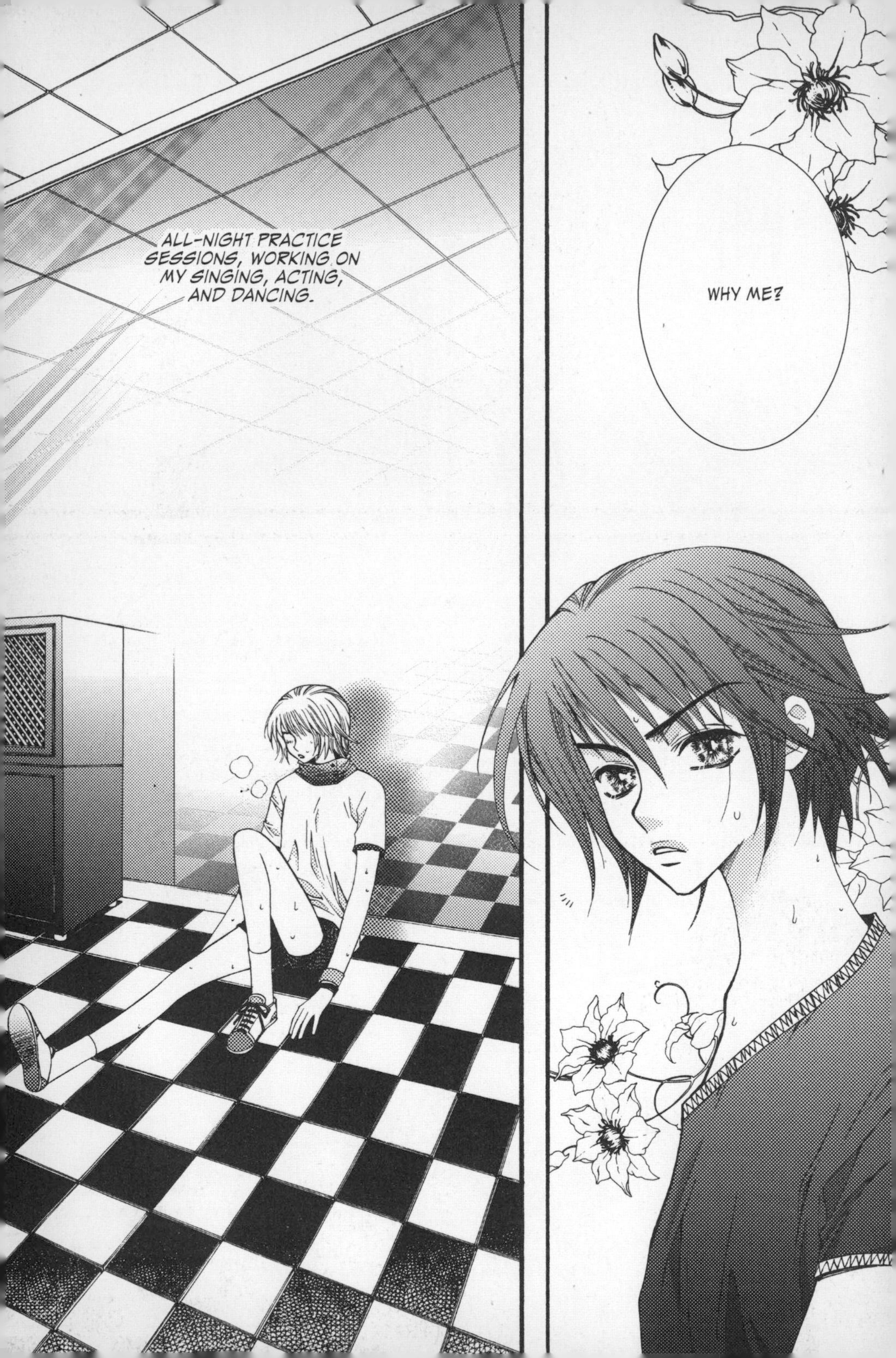
WHY ME?
ALL-NIGHT PRACTICE SESSIONS, WORKING ON MY SINGING, ACTING, AND DANCING.

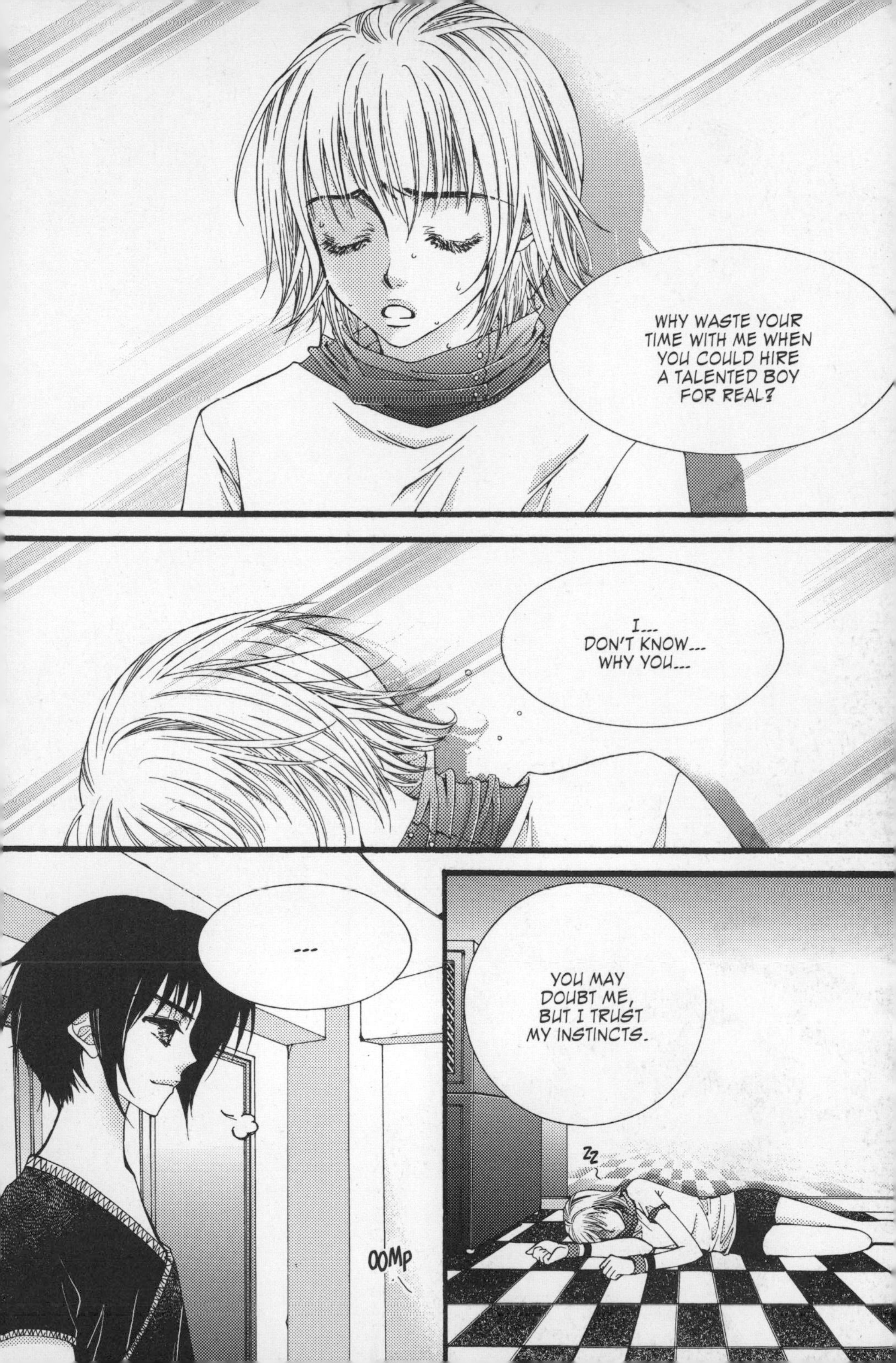
WHY WASTE YOUR TIME WITH ME WHEN YOU COULD HIRE A TALENTED BOY FOR REAL?
I... DON'T KNOW... WHY YOU...
...
YOU MAY DOUBT ME, BUT I TRUST MY INSTINCTS.
ZZ
OOMP

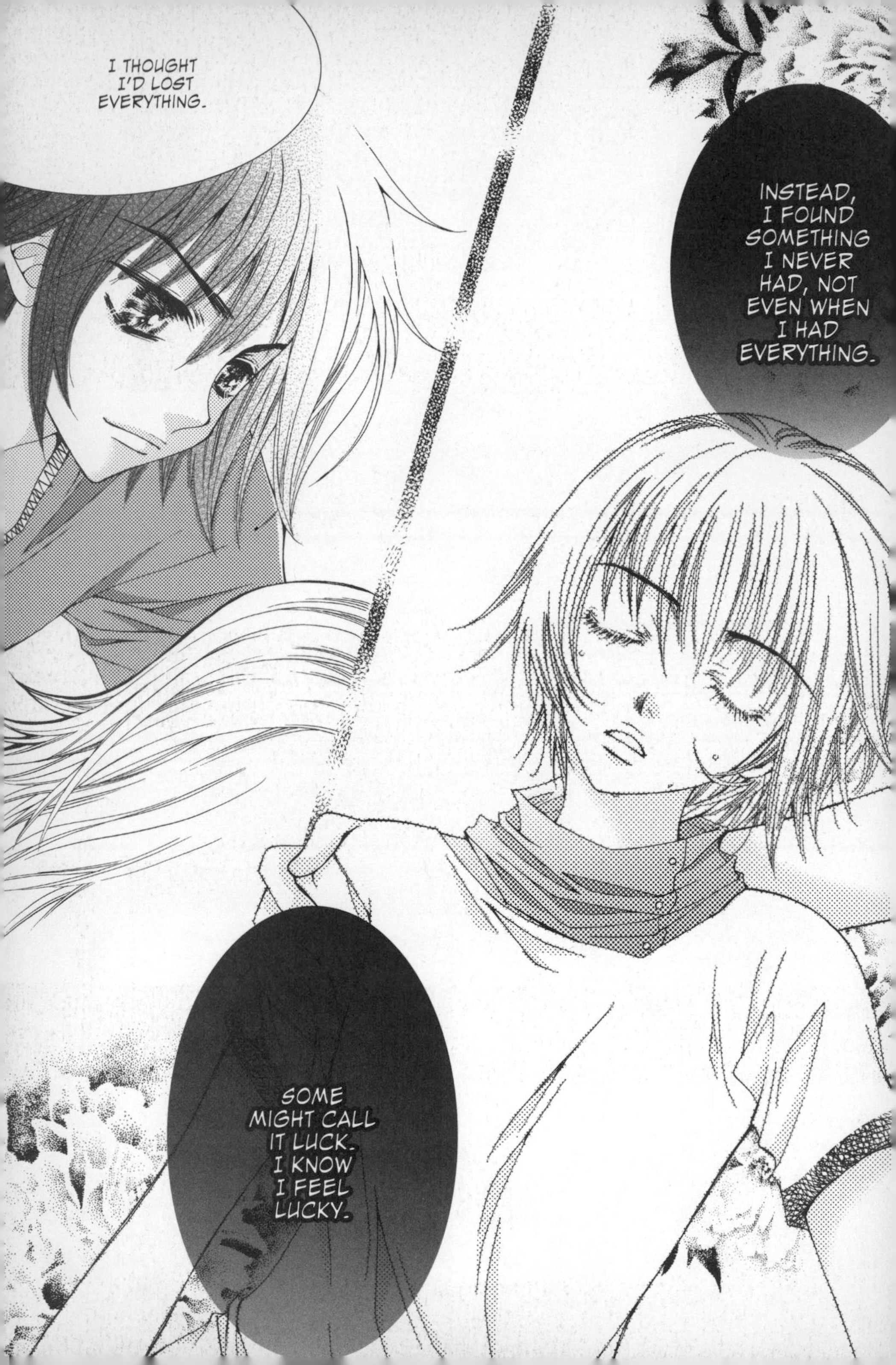
I THOUGHT I'D LOST EVERYTHING.
INSTEAD, I FOUND SOMETHING I NEVER HAD, NOT EVEN WHEN I HAD EVERYTHING.
SOME MIGHT CALL IT LUCK. I KNOW I FEEL LUCKY.

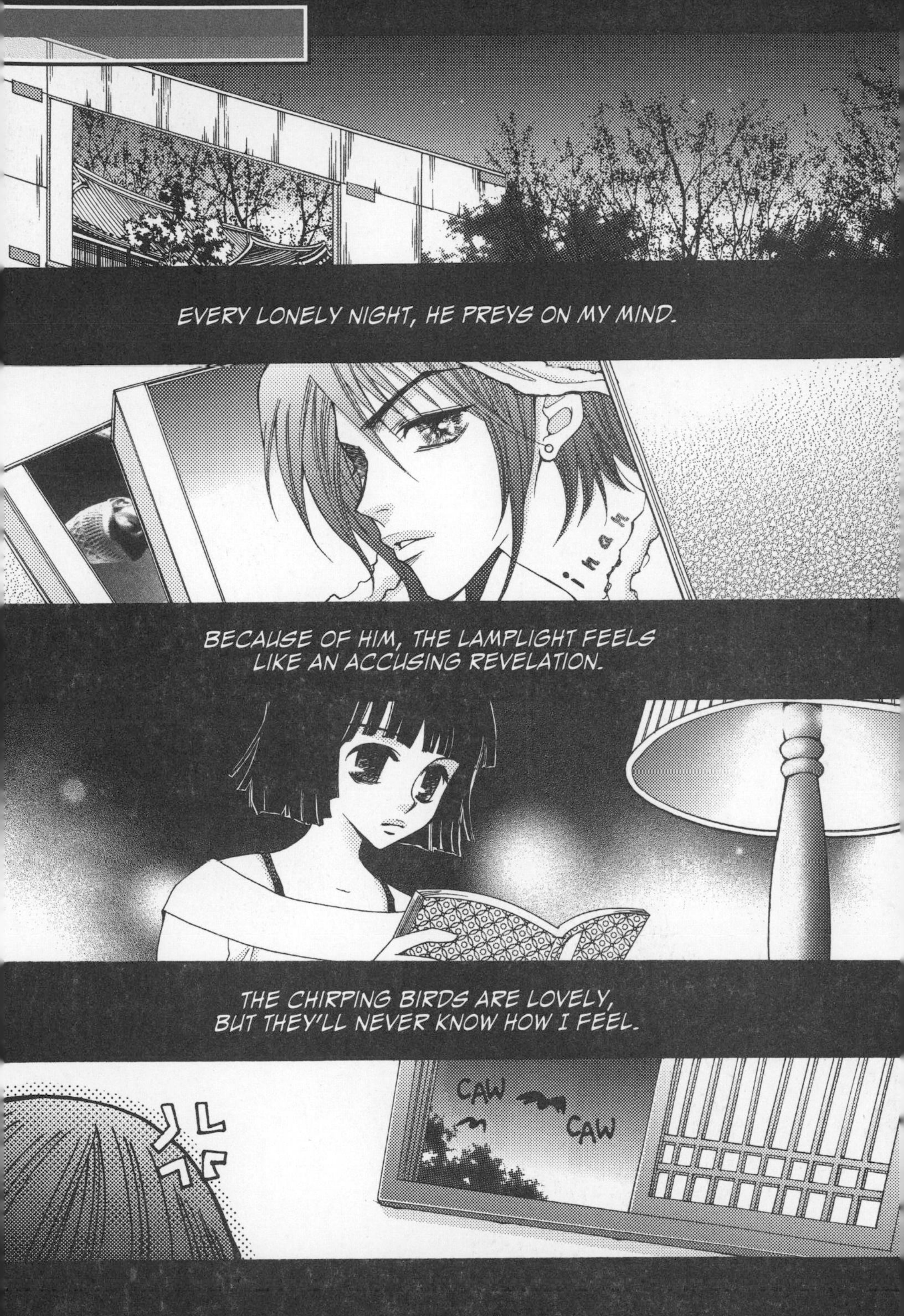
EVERY LONELY NIGHT, HE PREYS ON MY MIND.
BECAUSE OF HIM, THE LAMPLIGHT FEELS LIKE AN ACCUSING REVELATION.
THE CHIRPING BIRDS ARE LOVELY, BUT THEY'LL NEVER KNOW HOW I FEEL.
CAW
CAW

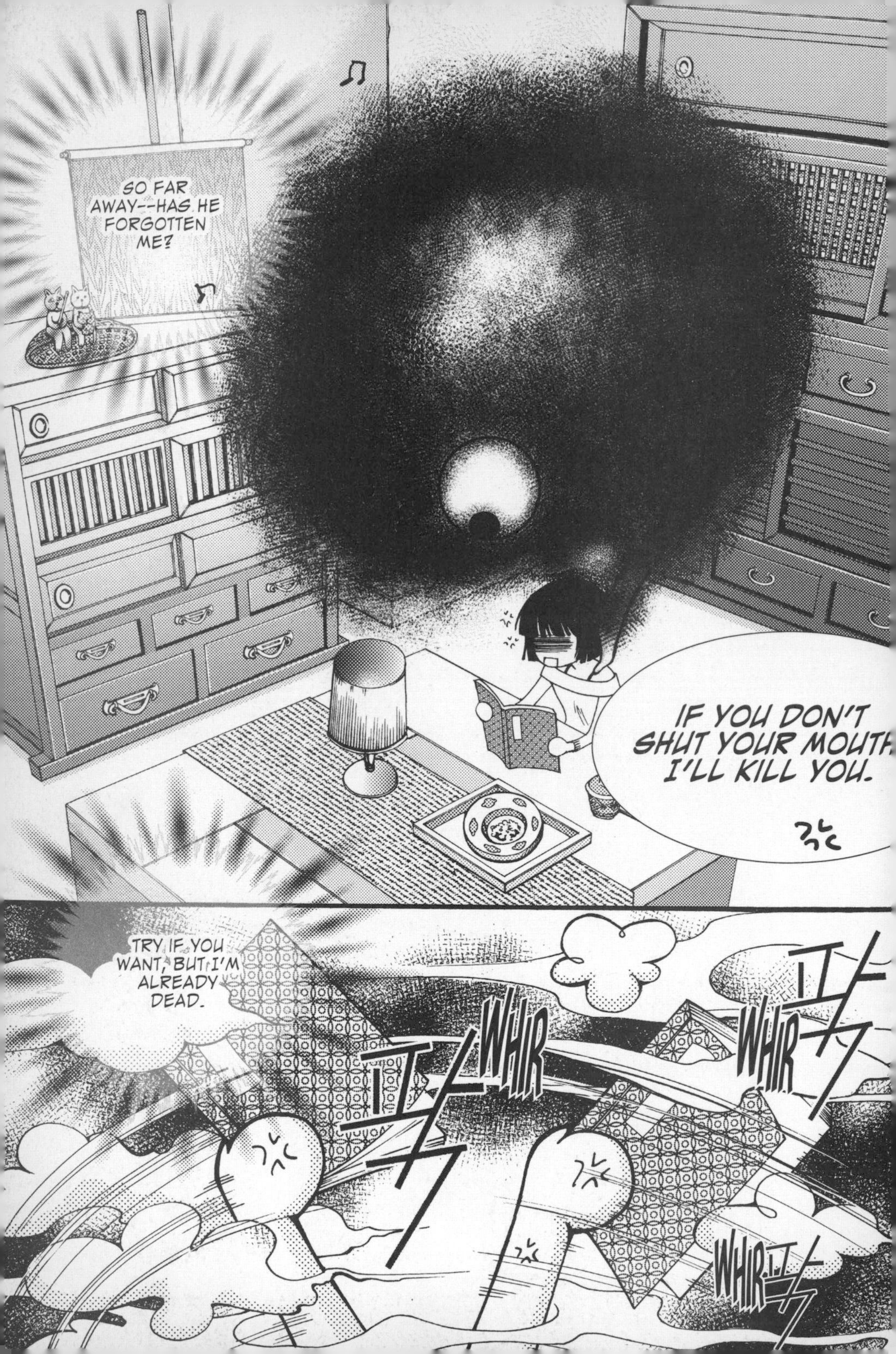
SO FAR AWAY--HAS HE FORGOTTEN ME?
IF YOU DON'T SHUT YOUR MOUTH I'LL KILL YOU.
TRY IF YOU WANT, BUT I'M ALREADY DEAD.
WHIR
WHIR
WHIR

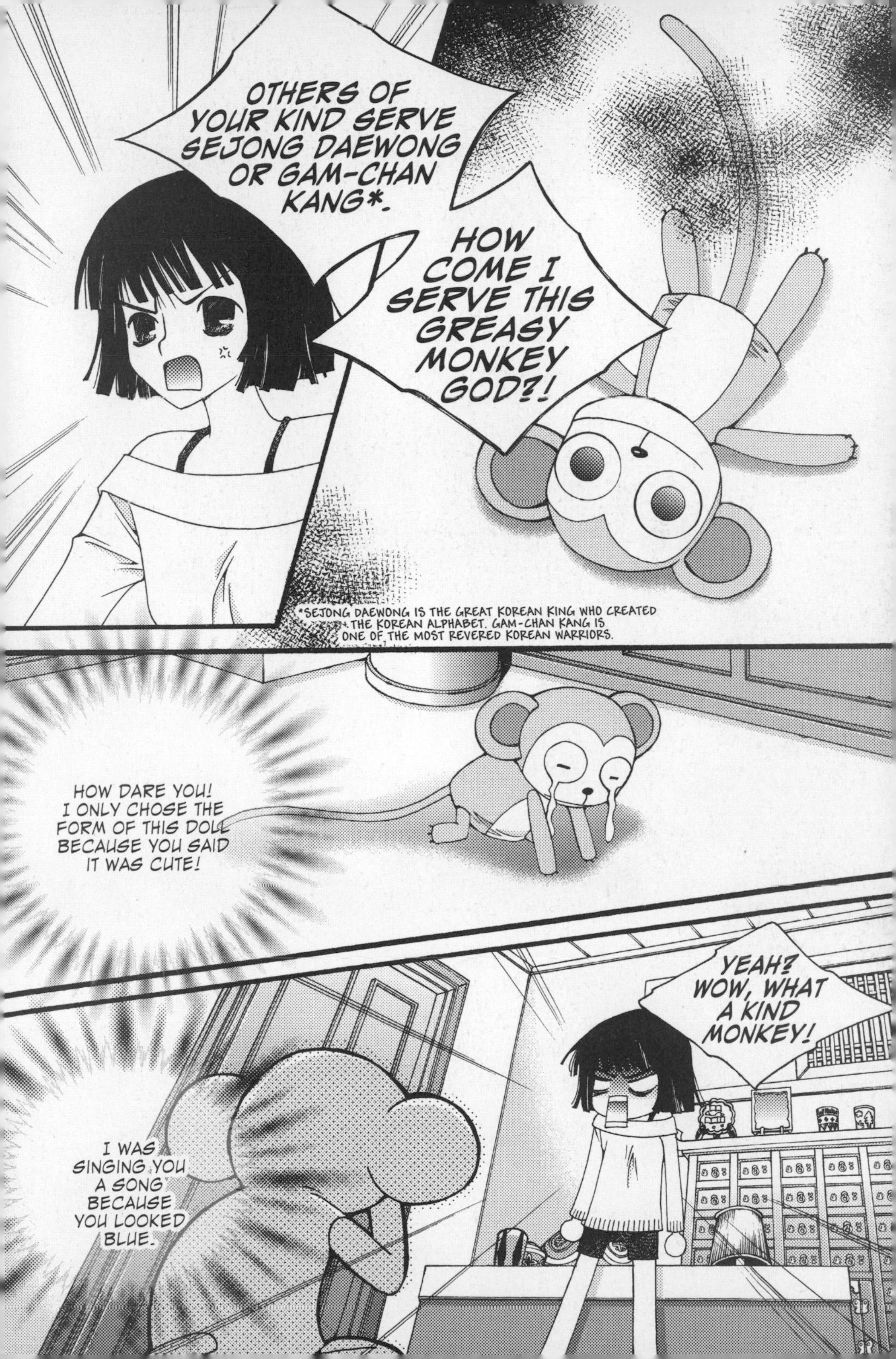
OTHERS OF YOUR KIND SERVE SEJONG DAEWONG OR GAM-CHAN KANG*.
HOW COME I SERVE THIS GREASY MONKEY GOD?!
*SEJONG DAEWONG IS THE GREAT KOREAN KING WHO CREATED THE KOREAN ALPHABET. GAM-CHAN KANG IS ONE OF THE MOST REVERED KOREAN WARRIORS.
HOW DARE YOU! I ONLY CHOSE THE FORM OF THIS DOLL BECAUSE YOU SAID IT WAS CUTE!
I WAS SINGING YOU A SONG BECAUSE YOU LOOKED BLUE.
YEAH? WOW, WHAT A KIND MONKEY!

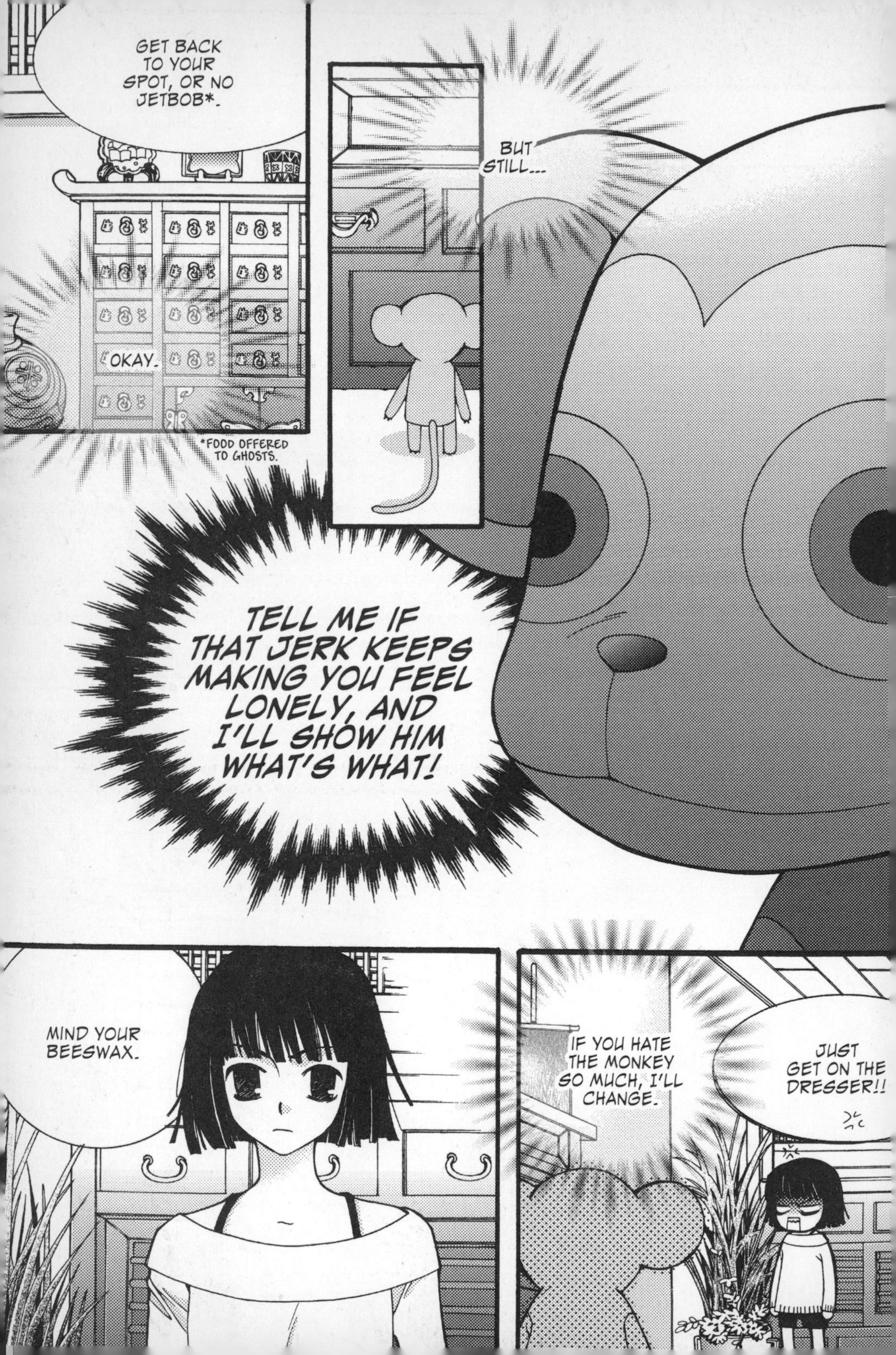
GET BACK TO YOUR SPOT, OR NO JETBOB*.
OKAY.
*FOOD OFFERED TO GHOSTS.
BUT STILL...
TELL ME IF THAT JERK KEEPS MAKING YOU FEEL LONELY, AND I'LL SHOW HIM WHAT'S WHAT!
JUST GET ON THE DRESSER!!
IF YOU HATE THE MONKEY SO MUCH, I'LL CHANGE.
MIND YOUR BEESWAX.

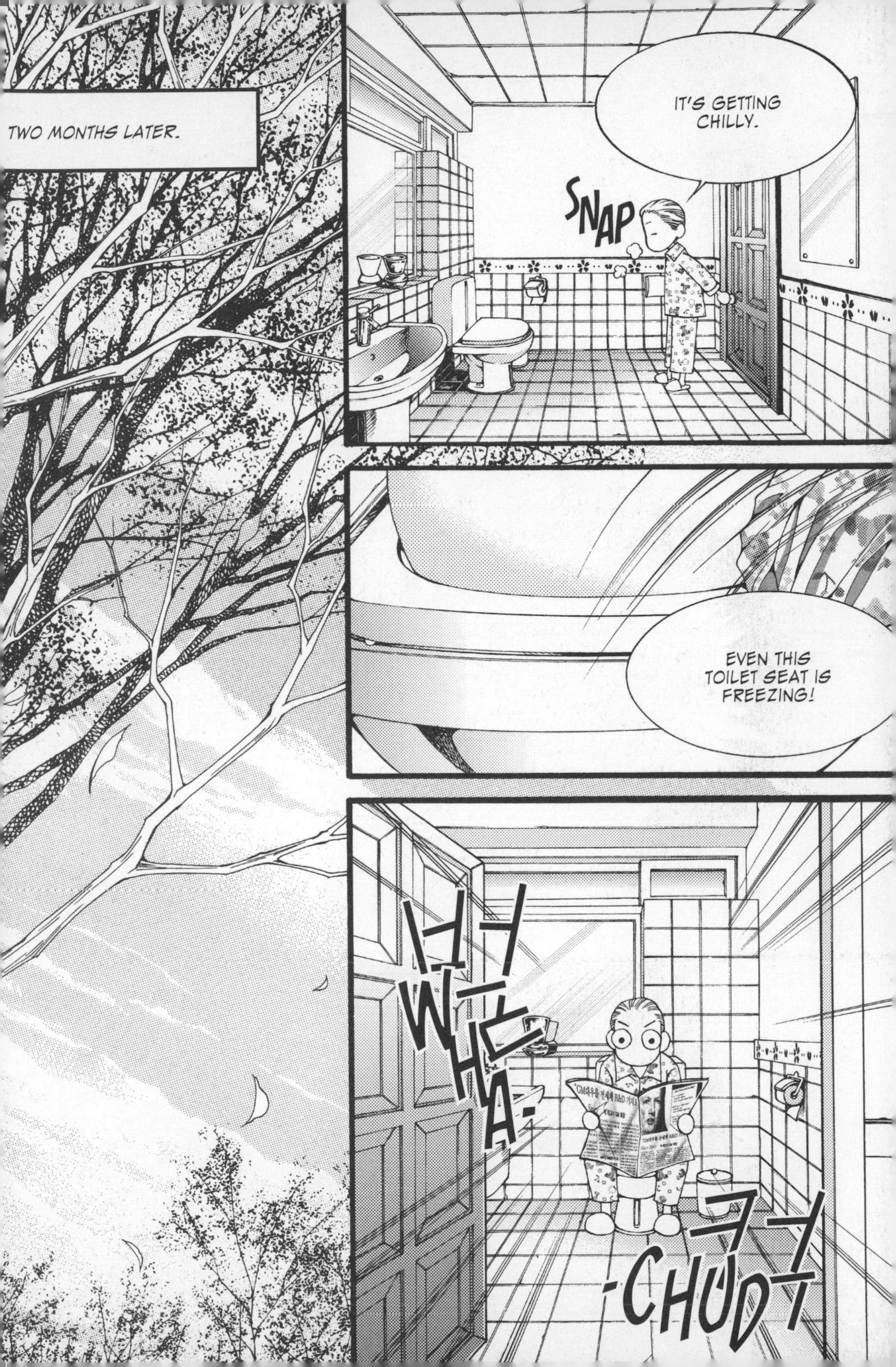
TWO MONTHS LATER.
IT'S GETTING CHILLY.
SNAP
EVEN THIS TOILET SEAT IS FREEZING!
WHA-
-CHOO

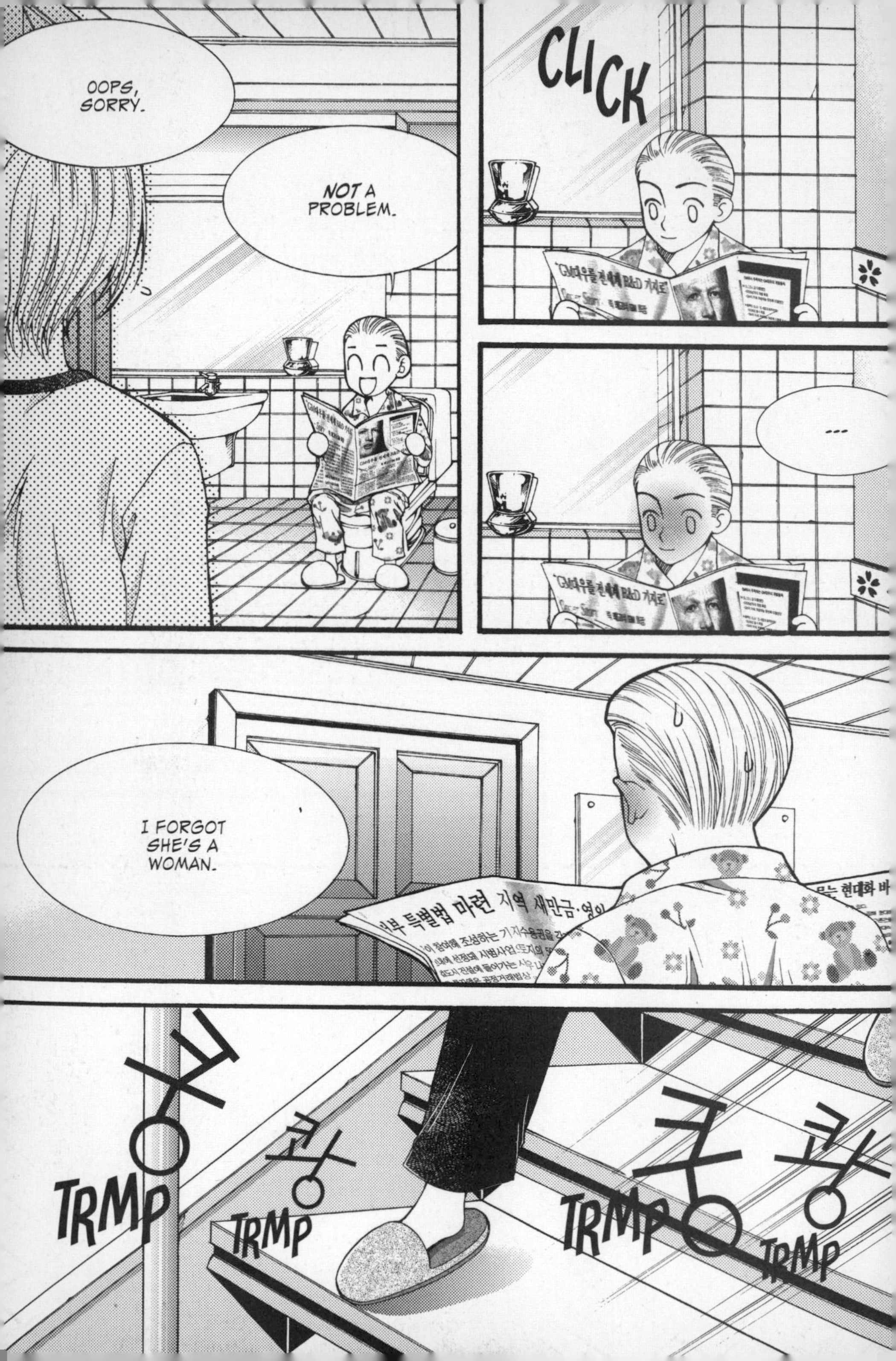
OOPS, SORRY.
NOT A PROBLEM.
CLICK
...
I FORGOT SHE'S A WOMAN.
TRMP
TRMP
TRMP
TRMP

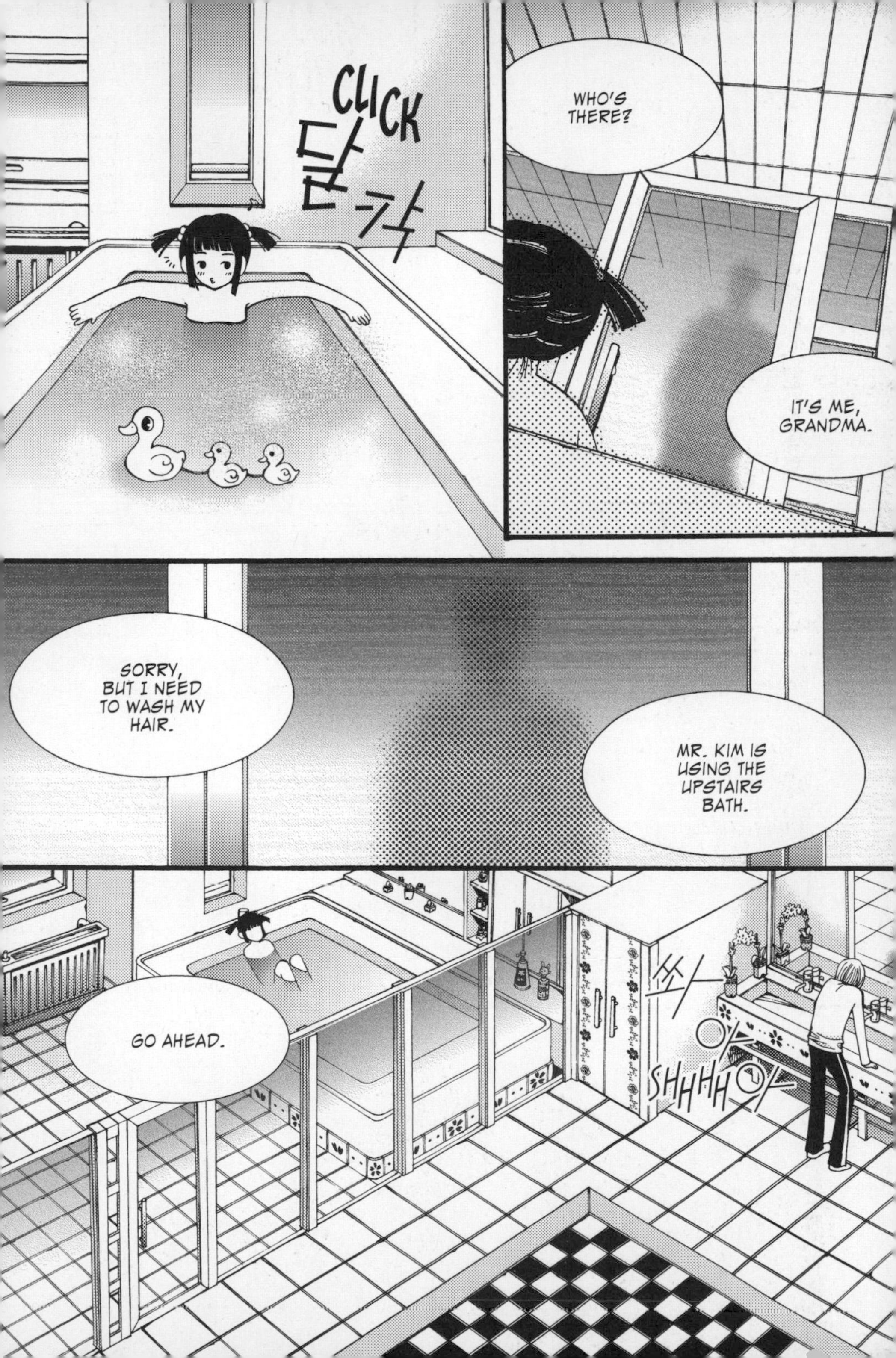
CLICK
WHO'S THERE?
IT'S ME, GRANDMA.
SORRY, BUT I NEED TO WASH MY HAIR.
MR. KIM IS USING THE UPSTAIRS BATH.
GO AHEAD.
SHHHH

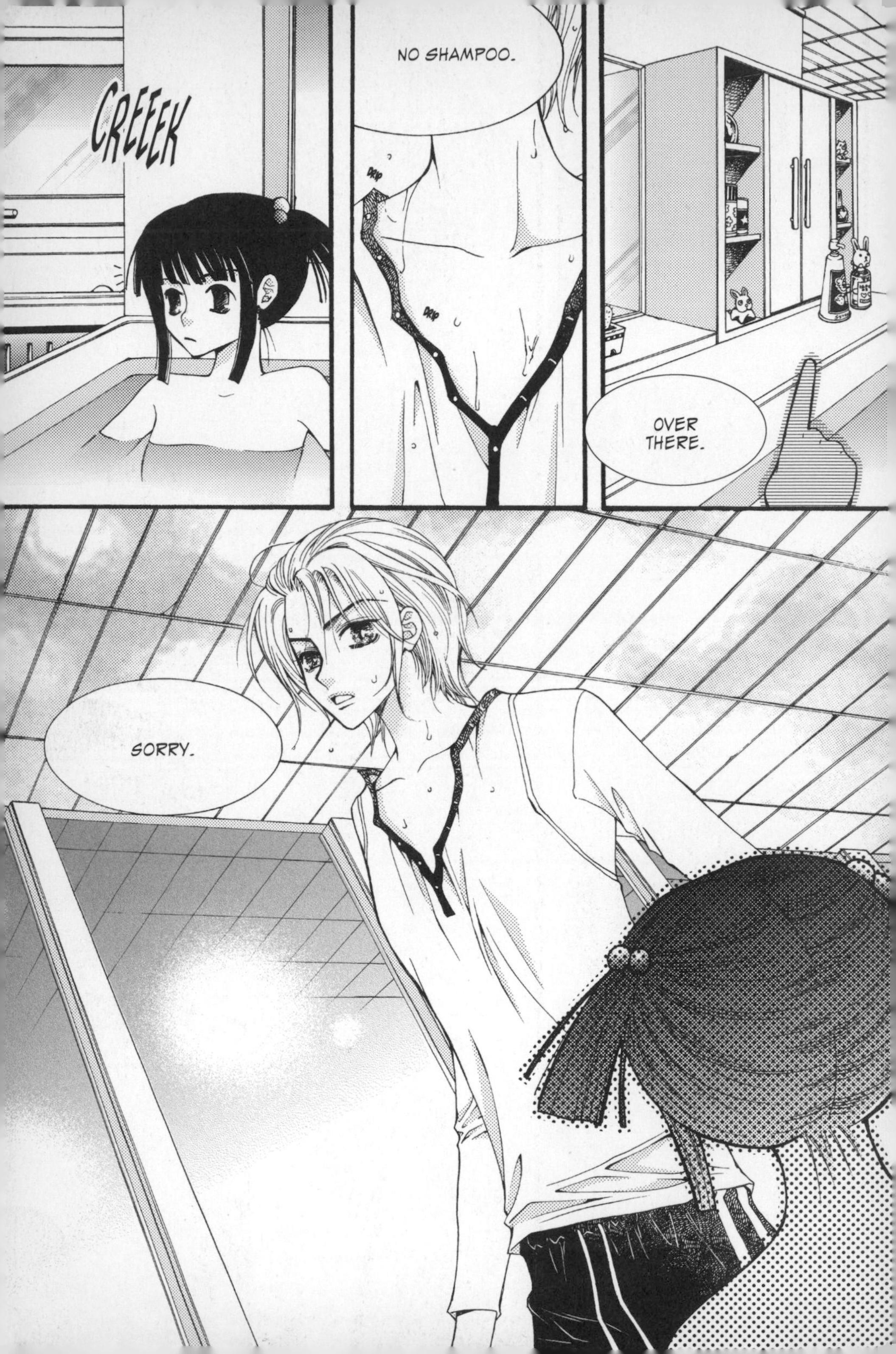

NO SHAMPOO.
CREEEK
OVER THERE.
SORRY.

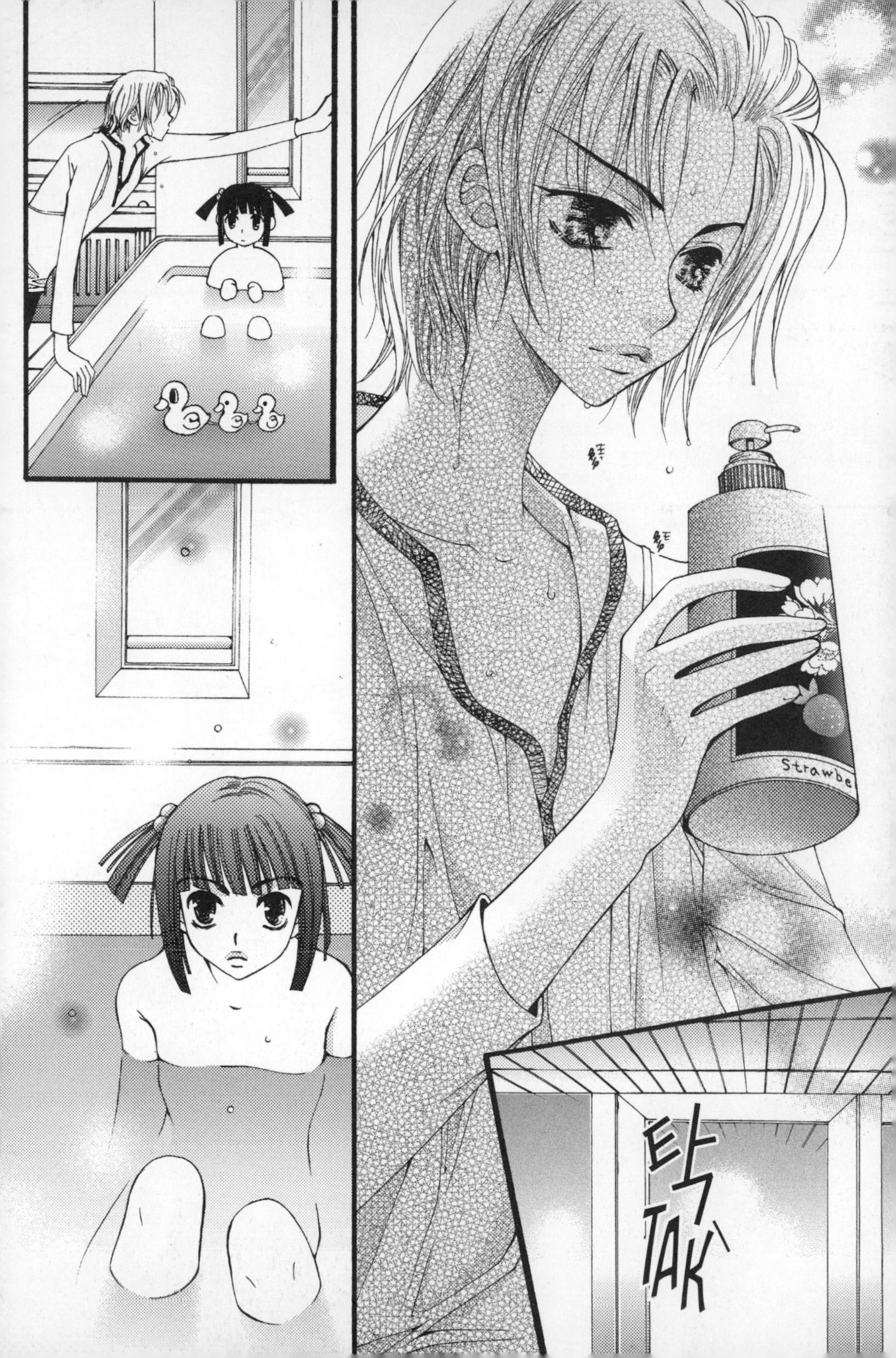
Strawbe
탁
TAK

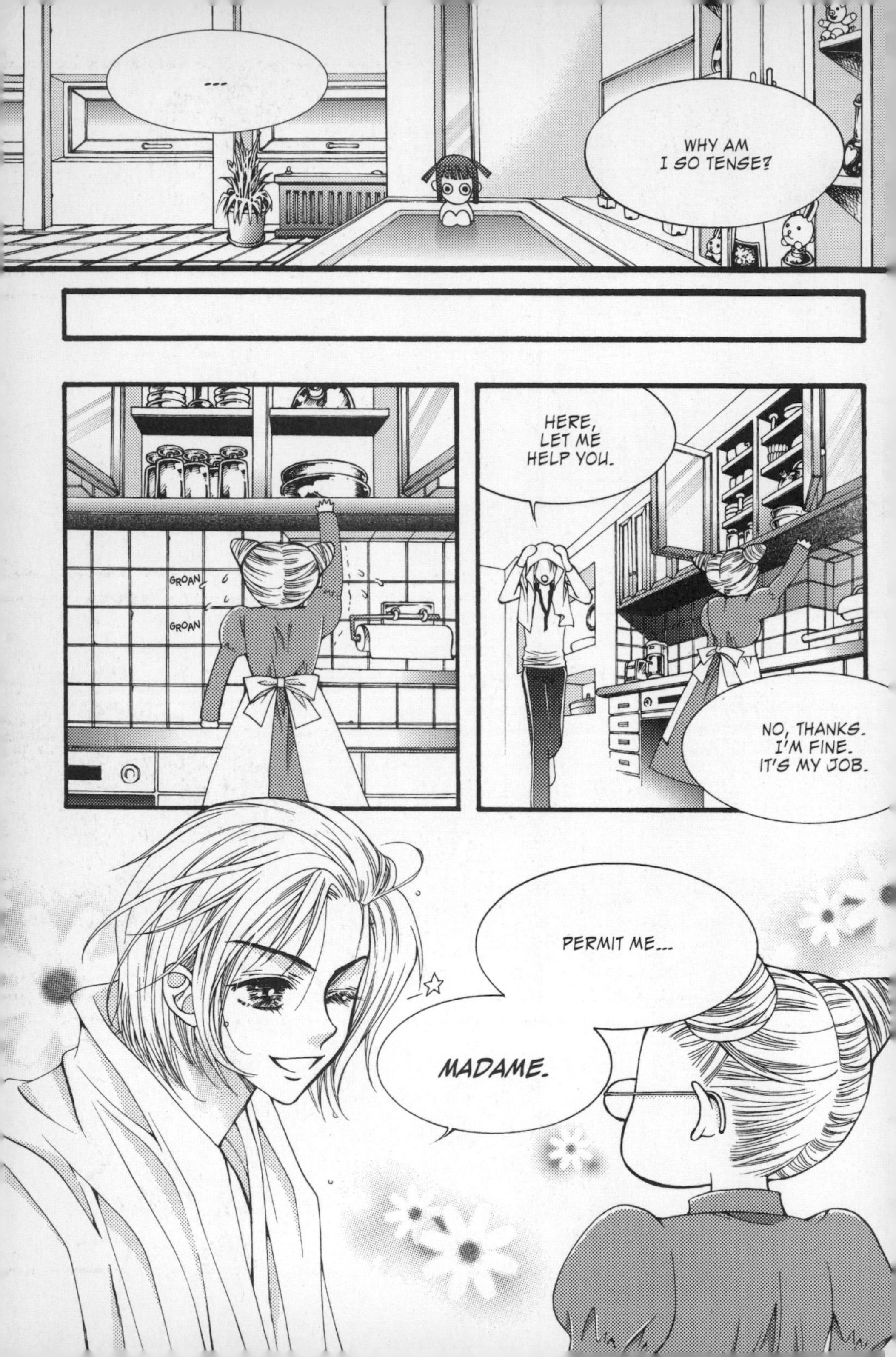
...
WHY AM I SO TENSE?
GROAN
GROAN
HERE, LET ME HELP YOU.
NO, THANKS. I'M FINE. IT'S MY JOB.
PERMIT ME...
MADAME.

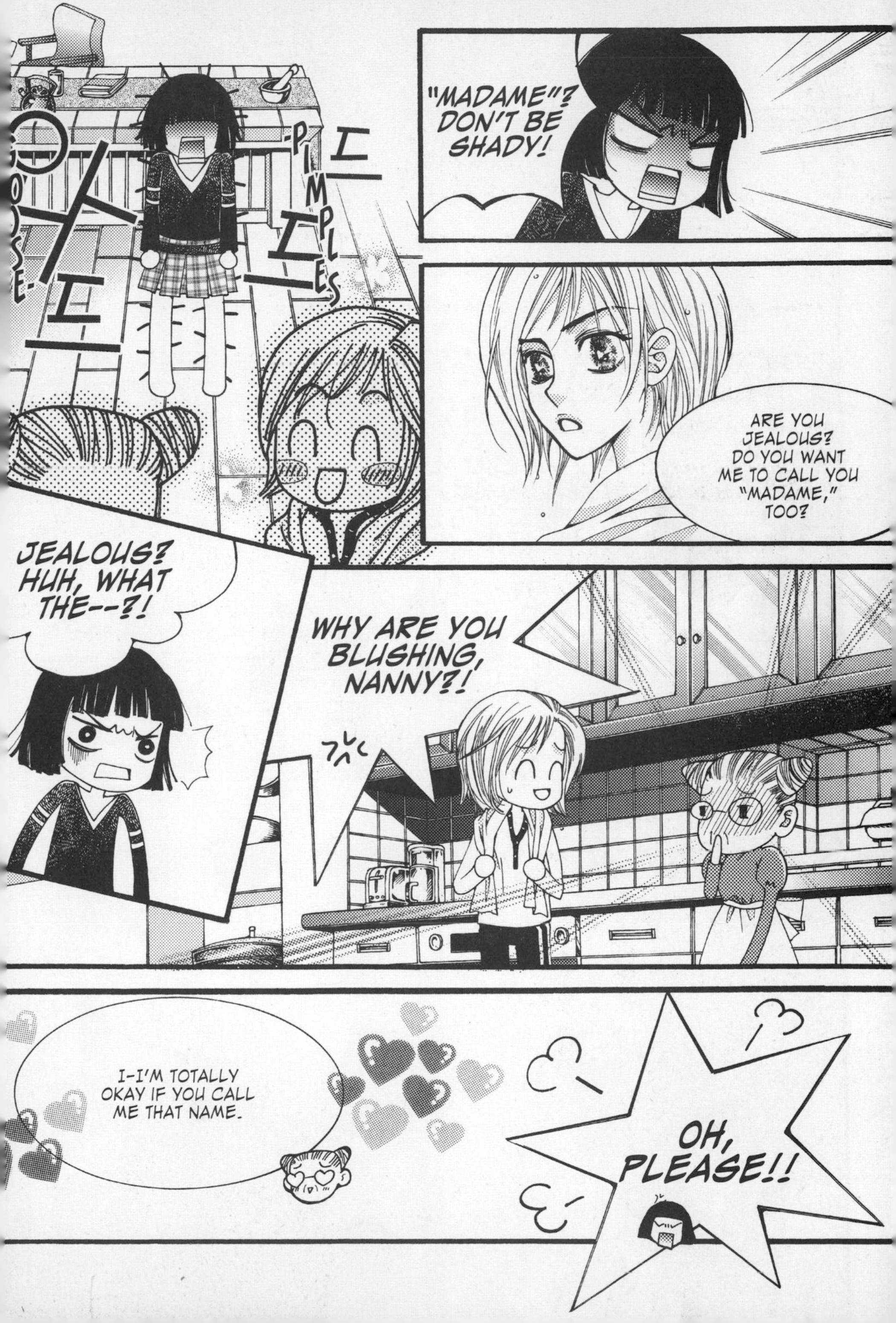
"MADAME"?! DON'T BE SHADY!
ARE YOU JEALOUS? DO YOU WANT ME TO CALL YOU "MADAME," TOO?
PIMPLES
WHY ARE YOU BLUSHING, NANNY?!
JEALOUS? HUH, WHAT THE--?!
I-I'M TOTALLY OKAY IF YOU CALL ME THAT NAME.
OH, PLEASE!!

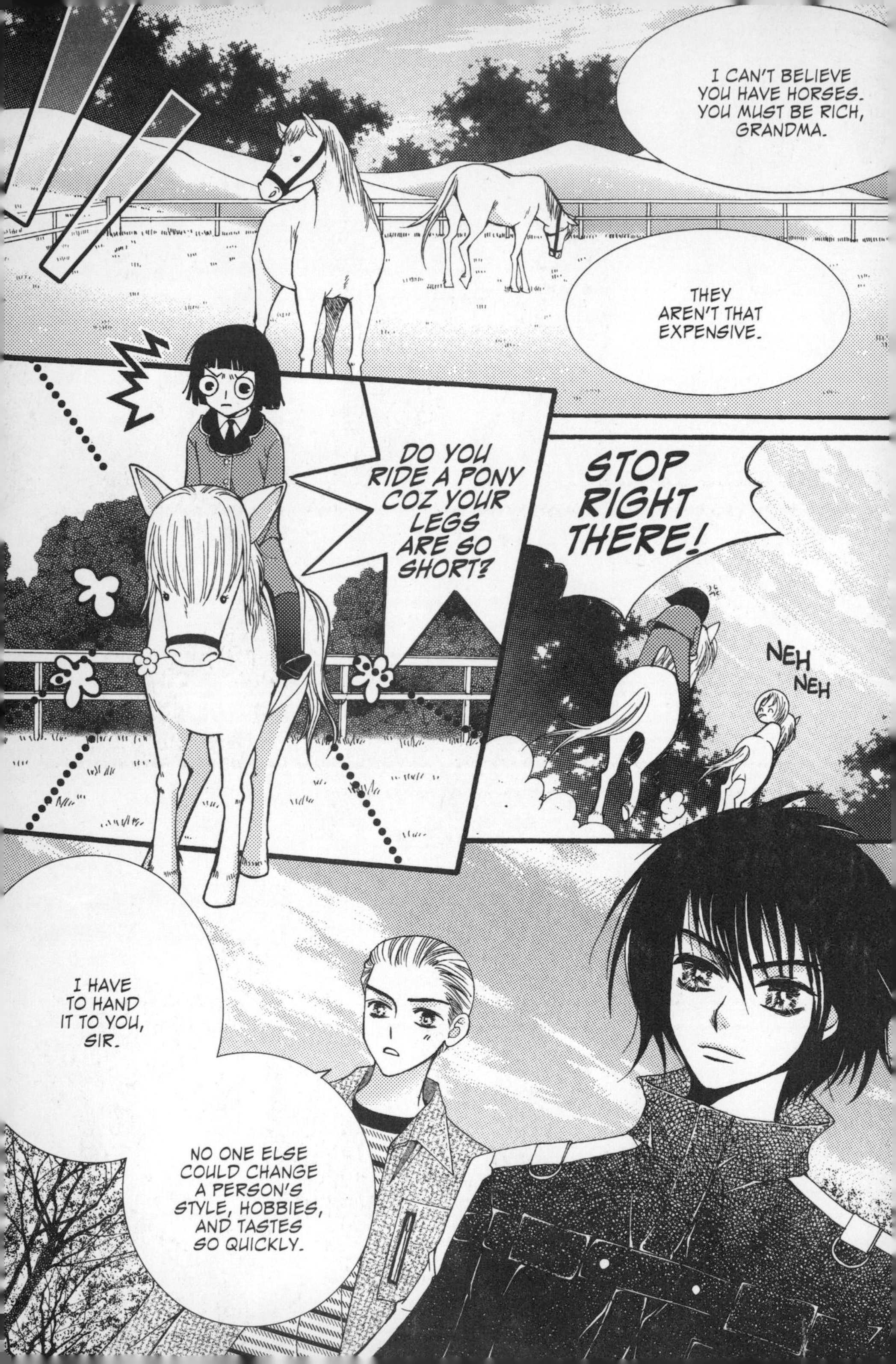
I CAN'T BELIEVE YOU HAVE HORSES. YOU MUST BE RICH, GRANDMA.
THEY AREN'T THAT EXPENSIVE.
DO YOU RIDE A PONY COZ YOUR LEGS ARE SO SHORT?
STOP RIGHT THERE!
NEH NEH
I HAVE TO HAND IT TO YOU, SIR.
NO ONE ELSE COULD CHANGE A PERSON'S STYLE, HOBBIES, AND TASTES SO QUICKLY.

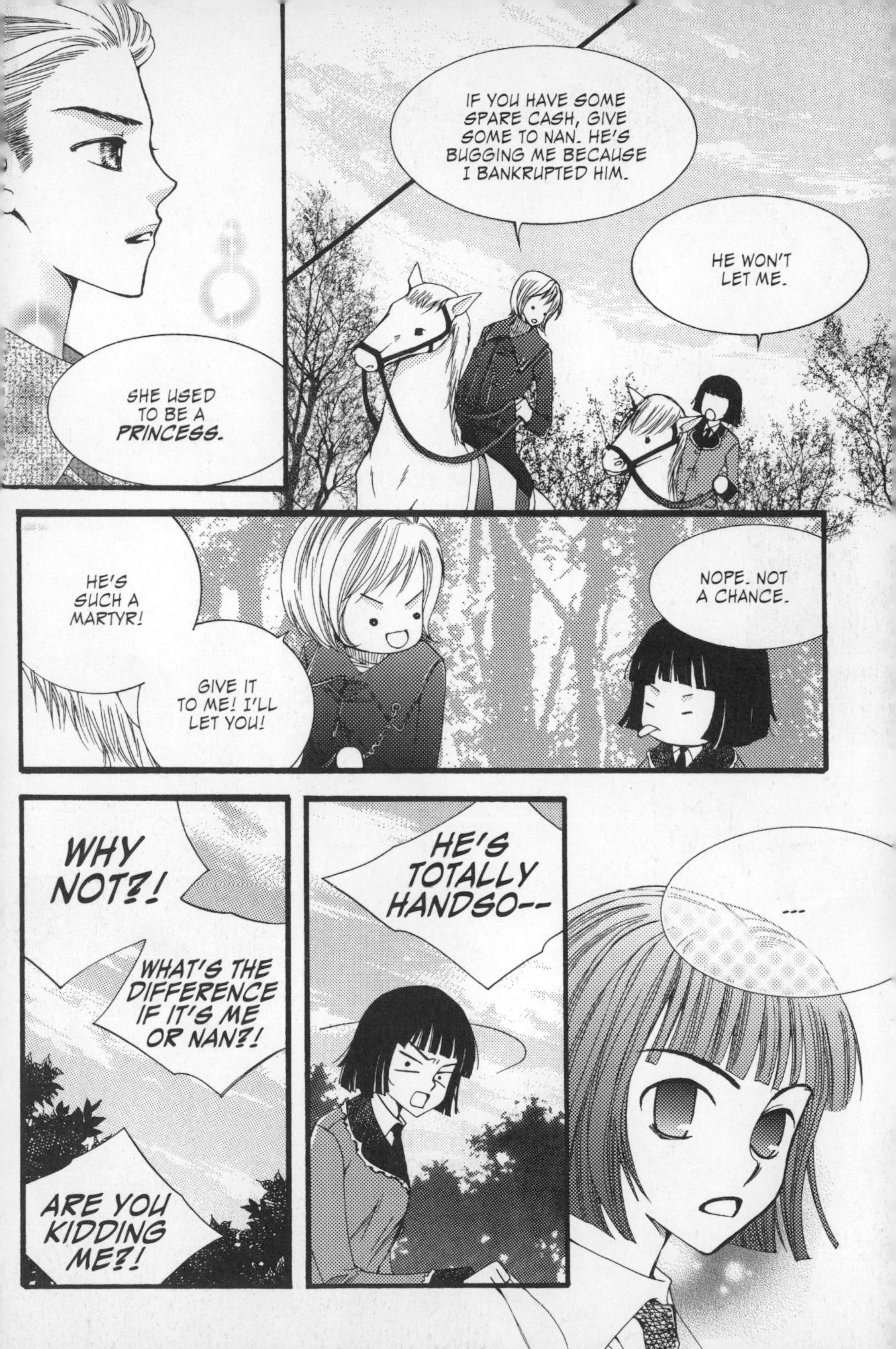
SHE USED TO BE A *PRINCESS*.
IF YOU HAVE SOME SPARE CASH, GIVE SOME TO NAN. HE'S BUGGING ME BECAUSE I BANKRUPTED HIM.
HE WON'T LET ME.
HE'S SUCH A MARTYR!
GIVE IT TO ME! I'LL LET YOU!
NOPE. NOT A CHANCE.
WHY NOT?!
WHAT'S THE DIFFERENCE IF IT'S ME OR NAN?!
ARE YOU KIDDING ME?!
HE'S TOTALLY HANDSO--
...

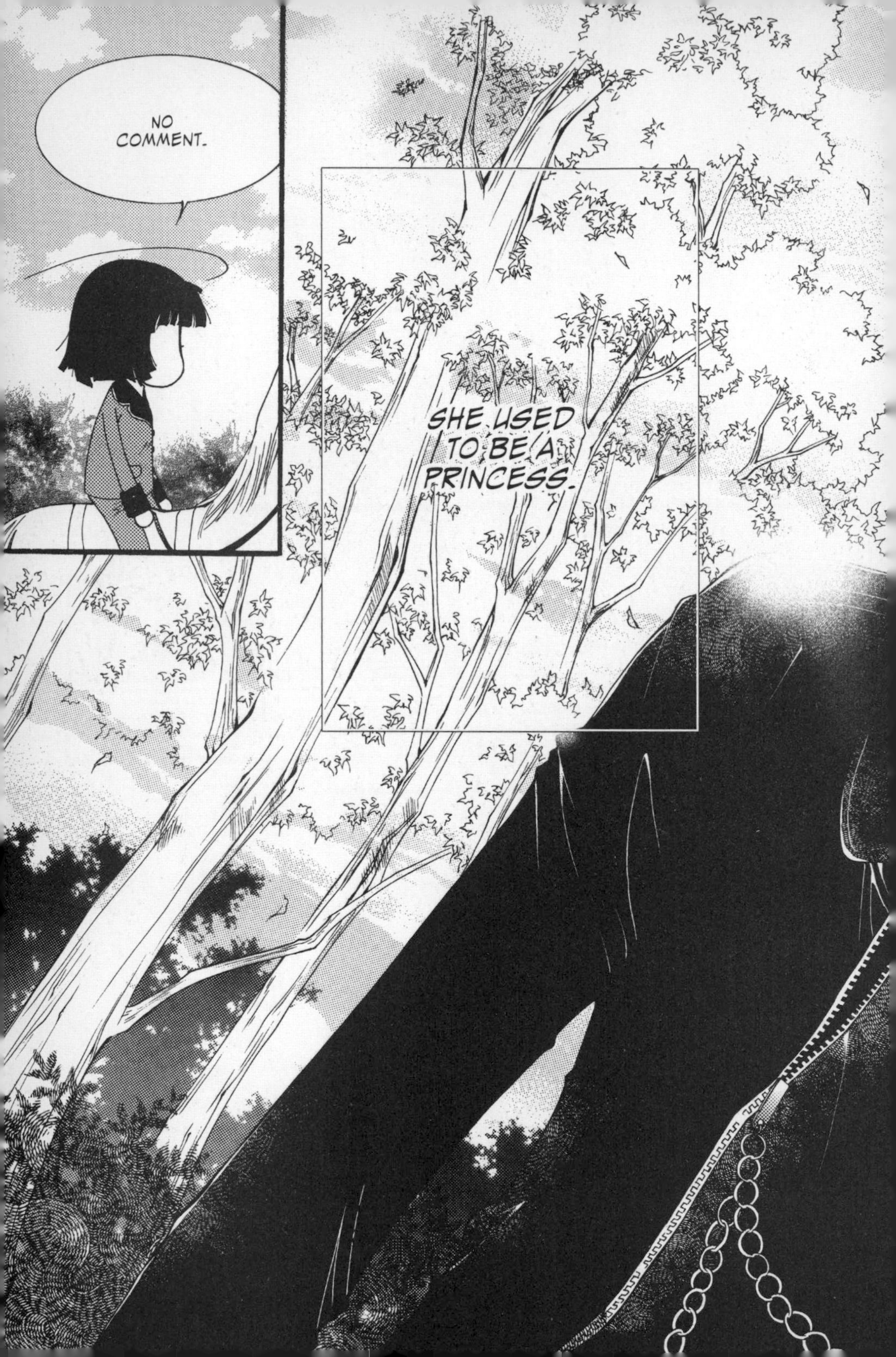
NO COMMENT.
SHE USED TO BE A PRINCESS.

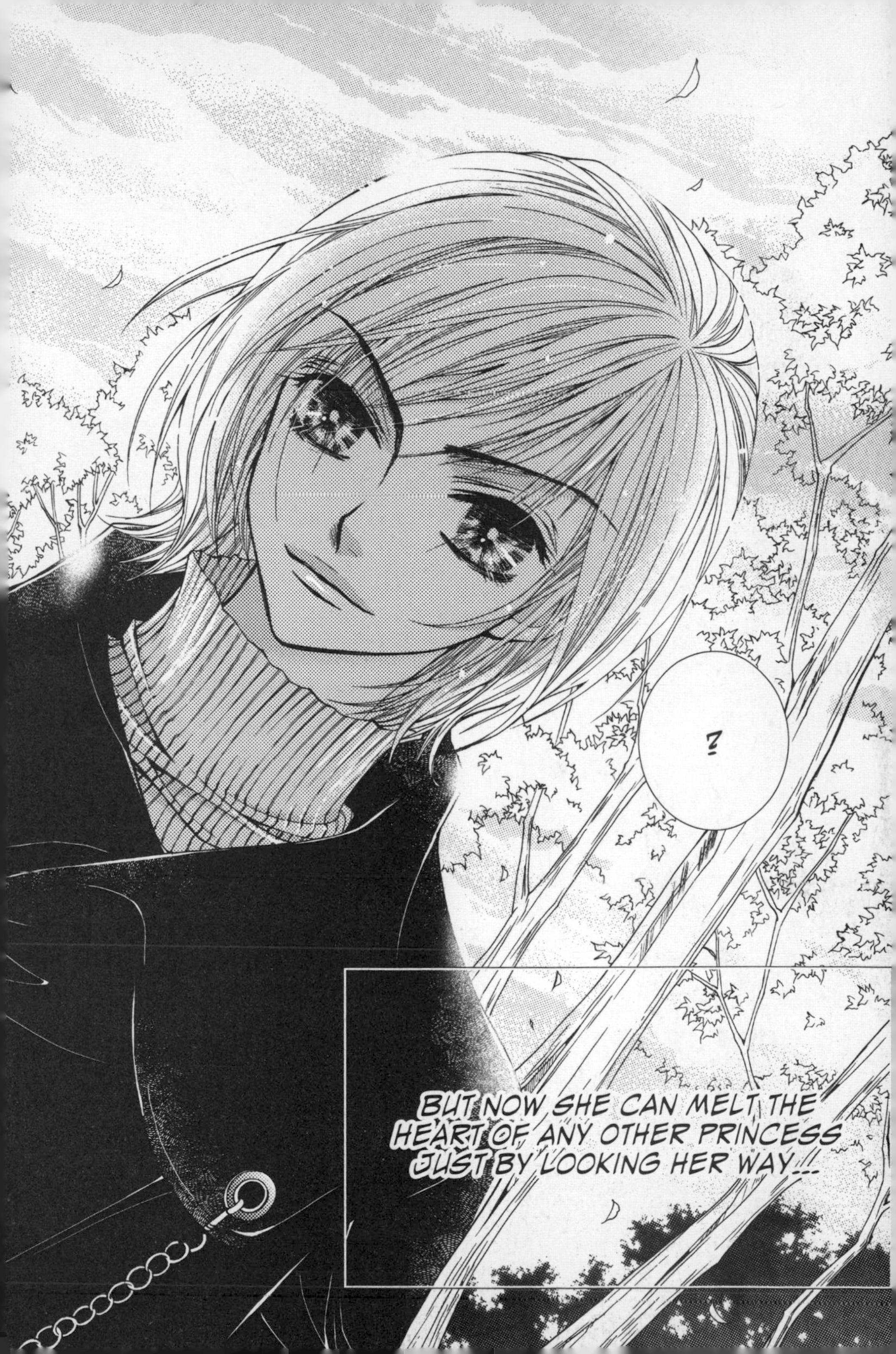
?
BUT NOW SHE CAN MELT THE HEART OF ANY OTHER PRINCESS JUST BY LOOKING HER WAY...

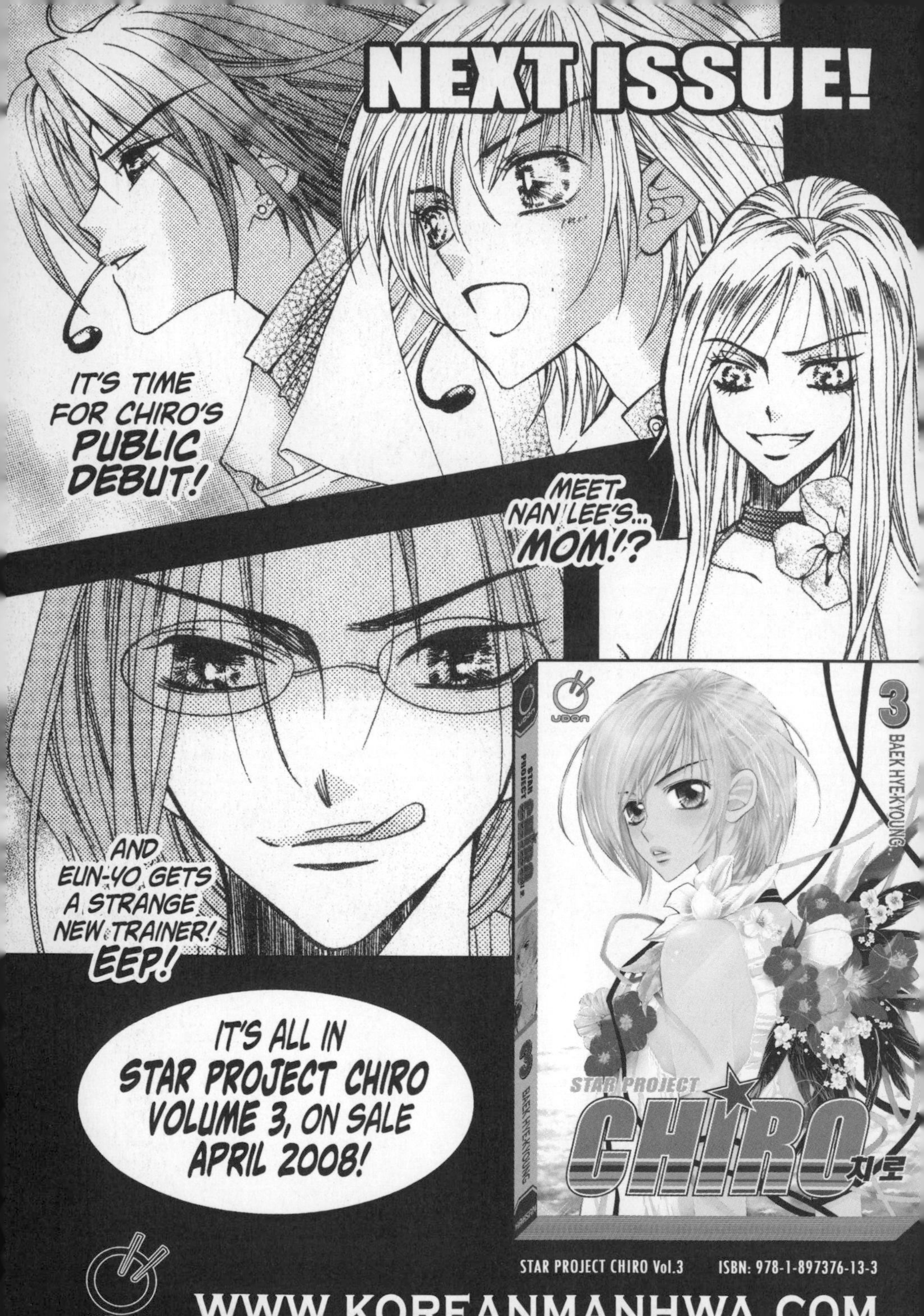

NEXT ISSUE!
IT'S TIME FOR CHIRO'S PUBLIC DEBUT!
MEET NAN LEE'S... MOM!?
AND EUN-YO GETS A STRANGE NEW TRAINER! EEP!
IT'S ALL IN STAR PROJECT CHIRO VOLUME 3, ON SALE APRIL 2008!
UDON
3
BAEK HYE-KYOUNG
STAR PROJECT
CHIRO
치로

STAR PROJECT CHIRO Vol.3 ISBN: 978-1-897376-13-3

CHIRO Gallery

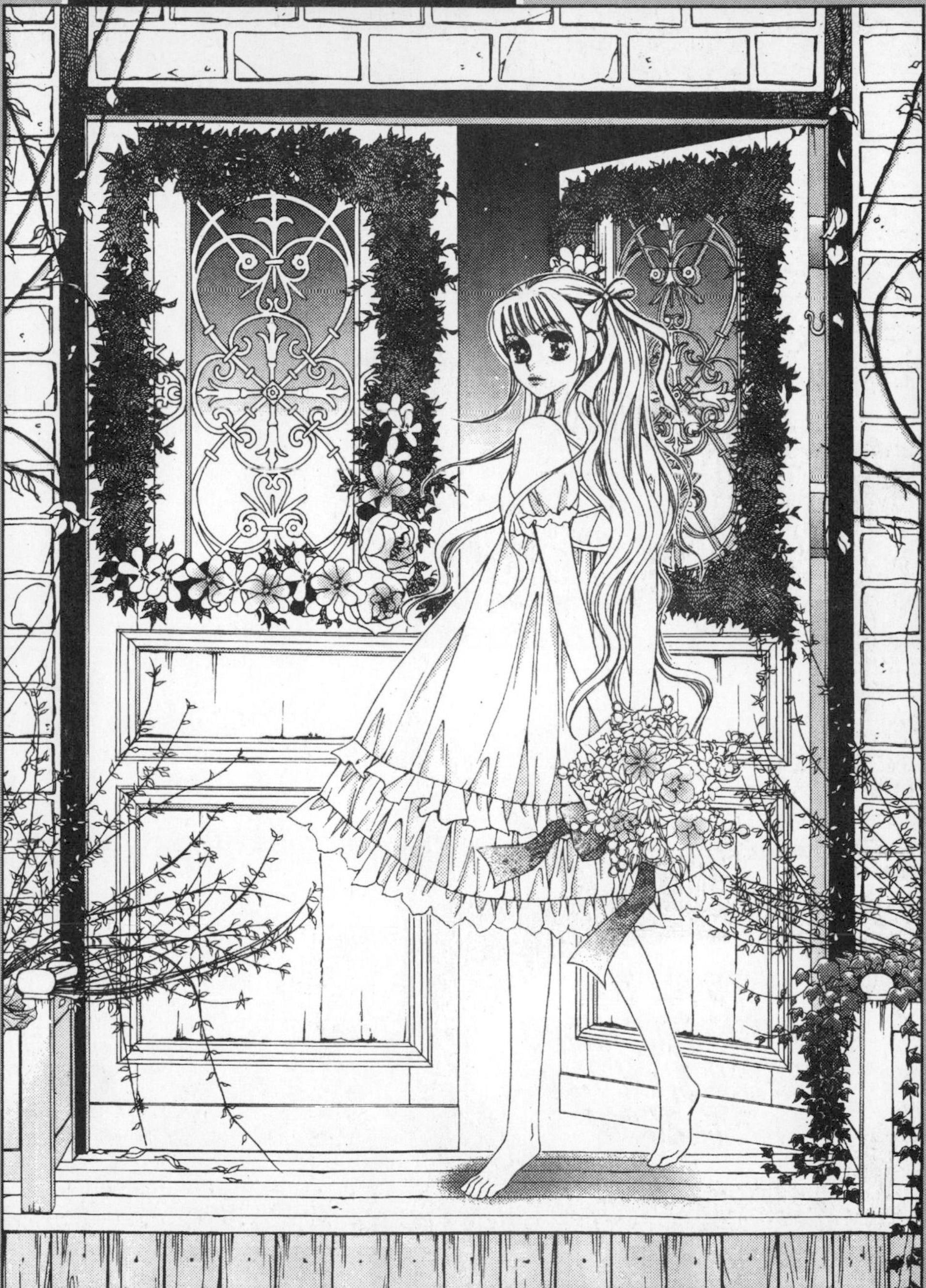

PARTY: October 04

CHIRO Gallery

PARTY: September 04

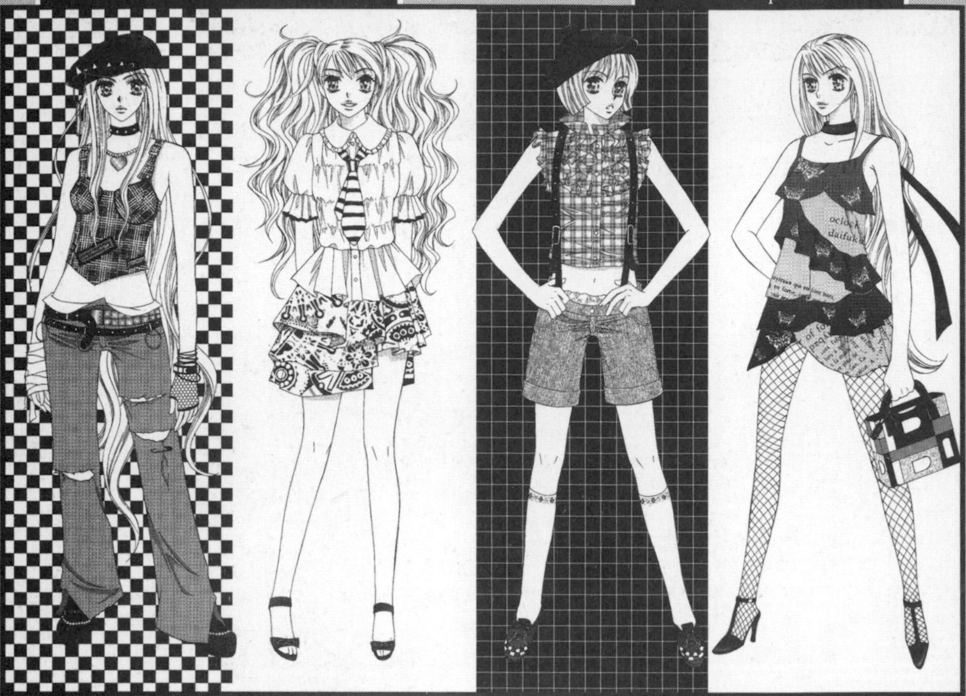

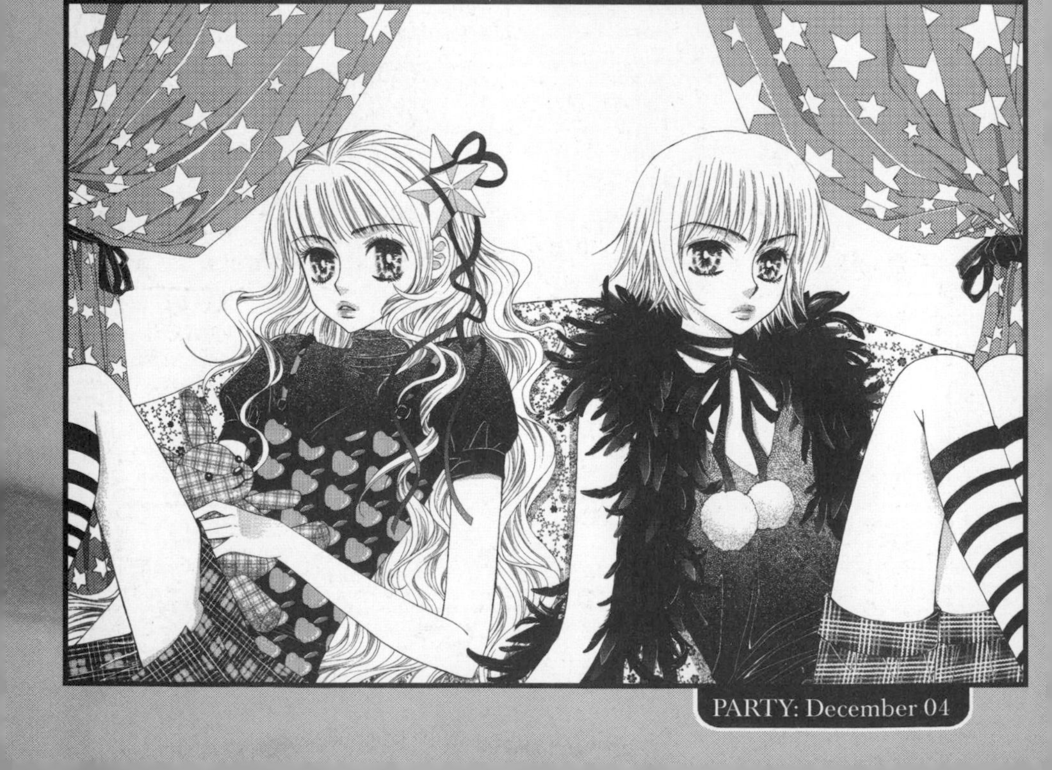

PARTY: December 04

LAUGH & ENJOY

6-PANEL CHIRO COMICS I

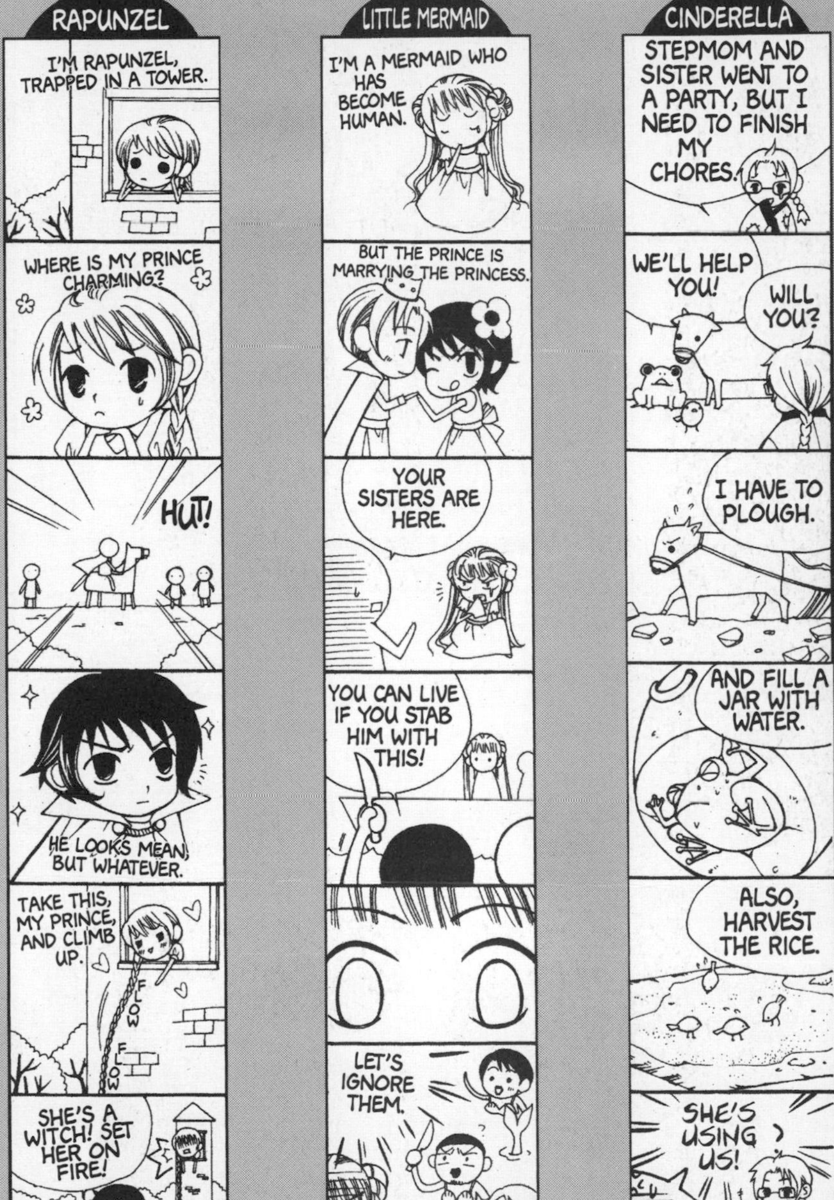
RAPUNZEL
I'M RAPUNZEL, TRAPPED IN A TOWER.
WHERE IS MY PRINCE CHARMING?
HUT!
HE LOOKS MEAN, BUT WHATEVER.
TAKE THIS, MY PRINCE, AND CLIMB UP.
FLOW FLOW
SHE'S A WITCH! SET HER ON FIRE!
LITTLE MERMAID
I'M A MERMAID WHO HAS BECOME HUMAN.
BUT THE PRINCE IS MARRYING THE PRINCESS.
YOUR SISTERS ARE HERE.
YOU CAN LIVE IF YOU STAB HIM WITH THIS!
LET'S IGNORE THEM.
CINDERELLA
STEPMOM AND SISTER WENT TO A PARTY, BUT I NEED TO FINISH MY CHORES.
WE'LL HELP YOU!
WILL YOU?
I HAVE TO PLOUGH.
AND FILL A JAR WITH WATER.
ALSO, HARVEST THE RICE.
SHE'S USING US!
HUFF HUFF

LAUGH & ENJOY

FROG SONG*

ONE TADPOLE IN A STREAM...

...SWIMS IN ZIGZAGS.

POPS OUT HIND LEGS.

POPS OUT FORELEGS.

HOP AND HOP.

IT'S A FROG.

I'M CURSED AND NEED YOUR KISS TO BECOME A PRINCE AGAIN.

CUT THE CRAP! I SAW YOU AS A TADPOLE!!

*FAMOUS KOREAN KID'S SONG.

WILHELM TELL

WILHELM TELL! I HEARD YOU'RE GOOD AT ARCHERY?

SHOOT THE APPLE!

NO, I CAN'T ...!

...UNLESS YOU CHANGE THE APPLE TO A CHERRY... NO, A MILLET. I'LL COVER MY EYES, SPIN, AND DO A HANDSTAND TO MAKE THE SHOT.

JUST KILL ME!!

SNOW WHITE

WHAT'S THE MATTER?

SNOW WHITE ATE A POISONED APPLE.

OH, MY...

SSK

WILL YOU GIVE ME HER BODY?

I'LL DO AN AUTOPSY, FIND THE CAUSE OF DEATH...

BOUNCE

SCHOOL-BOY

LAUGH & ENJOY

6-PANEL CHIRO COMICS III

CINDERELLA 2
HUFF HUFF
THAT WAS CLOSE.
WHAT THE?! A PUMPKIN WAGON FOR THE PUMPKIN.
MEAN BOY.
YOU'RE KIDDING!
I'M BORED.
FEW DAYS LATER:
IT FITS PERFECTLY, YOUR HIGHNESS !!
FINALLY FOUND YOU.
MEAN BOY.
THUD
HOW DARE YOU LEAVE YOUR DIRTY SHOES!!

CINDERELLA 3
TRY IT ON, EVERYONE! IF IT FITS, YOU'LL MARRY A PRINCE!
BLAH
MUR-MUR
BLAH
ALL OF YOU?
SLIP
SHY
HA-HA. WHAT A STUPID WAY TO FIND A WIFE!

WAS IT FUN FOR YOU? GOOD, BECAUSE MORE FASCINATING, EXCITING BONUS STORIES ARE COMING IN

CHIRO VOLUME 3!!

...... CONTINUED FROM THE BACK COVER:

What fun it is to ride and sing...

...a sleighing song tonight...

Jingle Bells!

Jingle Bells!

<X-mas with Muscle Wave Dance>

STAR PROJECT CHIRO Volume 2

Story and Art : Baek Hye-Kyoung

English Translations : Ji-Eun Park
English Adaptations : Jamie S. Rich

Editorial Consultant: J. Torres
Coordinating Editor: Hye-Young Im

Lettering : Marshall Dillon with Terri Delgado

Cover & Graphic Design : Erik Ko with Matt Moylan

English Logo : Alex Chung

STAR PROJECT CHIRO #2
©2007 BAEK HYE-KYOUNG.
All Rights Reserved. First published in Korea by Haksan Publishing Co., Ltd.
This translation rights arranged with Haksan Publishing Co., Ltd. through
Shinwon Agency Co. in Korea.

English launguage version produced and published by UDON Entertainment Corp.
P.O. Box 32662, P.O. Village Gate, Richmond Hill, Ontario, L4X 0A2, Canada.
www.udonentertainment.com
First Printing: January 2008   ISBN-13:978-1-897376-12-6   ISBN-10:1-897376-12-X
Printed in Canada